THE SERMONS AND
DEVOTIONAL WRITINGS OF
GERARD MANLEY
HOPKINS

This volume and *The Journals and Papers of Gerard Manley Hopkins*, edited by Humphry House and completed by Graham Storey, together constitute the second edition, revised and enlarged, of *The Note-books and Papers of Gerard Manley Hopkins*, edited by Humphry House, 1937

Gerard Manley Hopkins
1880

THE SERMONS AND
DEVOTIONAL WRITINGS OF
GERARD MANLEY
HOPKINS

Edited by
CHRISTOPHER DEVLIN, S.J.

LONDON
OXFORD UNIVERSITY PRESS
NEW YORK   TORONTO
1959

Oxford University Press, Amen House, London E.C.4

GLASGOW   NEW YORK   TORONTO   MELBOURNE   WELLINGTON
BOMBAY   CALCUTTA   MADRAS   KARACHI   KUALA LUMPUR
CAPE TOWN   IBADAN   NAIROBI   ACCRA

*Published by leave and with the approval of
the owners of the copyright, the Reverend J. Meskell, S.J.
and the Society of Jesus*

PRINTED IN GREAT BRITAIN

IN AFFECTIONATE MEMORY OF

HUMPHRY HOUSE

Requiescat in Pace

Nihil obstat Carolus Davis, S.T.L., *Censor deputatus*
Imprimatur E. Morrogh Bernard, *Vic. Gen.*
Westmonasterii, die 15a Martii, 1958

FOREWORD

THE sources of Parts I and II of this volume are two distinct manuscript units. Part I, the sermons, is the entire contents of the stout
caheir known as 'Fr Humphrey's book'. Part II is the commentary
written by Fr Hopkins in his interleaved copy of Roothaan's edition
(1865) of the *Exercitia Spiritualia;* to this has been added the contents
of one or two loose sheets which (internal evidence denotes) Fr
Hopkins himself had intended to add before he became weary of
the whole undertaking in 1885. Part III consists of all his other
writings on spiritual matters during his life as a Jesuit; these are
contained in various loose sheets or gathered from odd corners in
a Dublin exercise-book. All the material, except the translation from
Chrysostom in Part III, is autograph.

Any arrangement of such disparate material would probably be
open to criticism; but the present one appears to have three clear
advantages. It is an arrangement strictly according to sources; the
reader is thus enabled to envisage Hopkins's writings as he actually
wrote them. Moreover it maintains a fairly clear division according
to subject matter: public writings in Part I and private writings in
Part II. Part III, it is true, contains extremes of both: his most polished
and impersonal piece, the translation from Chrysostom, and his most
personal and private retreat notes of 1889; but this at least has the
merit of variety.

Finally, there is the incidental advantage of a very rough chronological outline of Fr Hopkins's life as a Jesuit priest. For Part I
covers the years 1879 to 1881, while Part II was mainly written
between 1881 and 1883; and Part III, though it includes a variety of
dates, is perhaps most notable for the hitherto unpublished notes
written during Hopkins's last years, 1885 to 1889.

The need for this volume arose from the decision to reprint *The
Notebooks and Papers of Gerard Manley Hopkins* (O.U.P., 1937) with
all the newly discovered or hitherto unpublished material. The editor,
the late Humphry House, was very anxious that Hopkins's priestly
writings should be handled by a Jesuit as a separate volume. I
pointed out that in my case this would inevitably mean a lowering of
editorial standards. But he answered that the advantage of my being
a Jesuit would outweigh (though of course he did not put it in those
terms) my deficiencies in other respects. We agreed upon a general
editorial policy as laid down by him; but, apart from that, he was
insistent that I should handle the material in my own way and not

in his. This I have done, but I would not have done it without his express encouragement.

House was an editor of genius, combining relentless accuracy with exquisite sensibility; his fine-pointed pen, somewhat after the manner of Hopkins himself, could write the clearest letters in the minutest script. I was relying on a great deal of advice and help from him when his tragic death occurred in 1955. I hope that the dedication of this volume to him will not be too poor a recognition of all that is owed him by the English Province of our Society in the matter of Gerard Manley Hopkins.

As things turned out, being myself posted to a different continent and a different type of work, I had to finish my editing hurriedly in December 1955. The whole burden of correction, arrangement, preparation for the press, &c., has thus fallen upon other shoulders than mine: those of Fr Philip Caraman, who has sponsored this volume on behalf of the Society of Jesus. Without his persistent care it would not have seen the light of day. Those who will profit by it, as containing the total of Hopkins's spiritual writings, will owe him a corresponding debt of gratitude.

I am also most grateful for the help I have received from Fr M. C. D'Arcy, Fr Francis Courtney, Fr James Walsh, and also to Mr Thomas Raworth, who prepared the typescript of the text of Hopkins. It should be noted that I have followed the principles of transcription laid down by Humphry House on pp. xxxiv–xxxv of *The Notebooks and Papers*, and listed again in the Introduction to *The Journals and Papers*. References to the *Poems* are taken from W. H. Gardner's third edition (1948), and to the letters in the third volume from the second enlarged edition of *Further Letters* (1956). The references to Scotus are taken principally from the *Scriptum Primum Oxoniense supra libris Sententiarum Quattuor Petri Lombardi* (Venice, 1515), the edition which Hopkins may well have used. This is designated in the Notes as *Oxoniense*. Where I have been unable to trace Hopkins's exact reference in the Venice edition I have used the Paris edition (1891–5). Scotus's second Commentary on the *Sentences*, the *Quaestiones Reportatae Parisienses* is designated as *Parisiensia*, and his *Quaestiones Quodlibetales* as *Quodlibet*. The English text of the *Spiritual Exercises* of St Ignatius has been adapted from translations of the literal version made by Fr John Morris and Fr Joseph Rickaby.   C. D.

CONTENTS

PART TWO. SPIRITUAL WRITINGS

PART THREE. ISOLATED DISCOURSES AND
PRIVATE NOTES

CONTENTS

INTRODUCTION

ALTHOUGH Gerard Hopkins set small store by poetic fame, he did hope for a career in religion that would liberate his energies and exploit his talents to the best advantage 'for the greater glory of God'. That was something which every Jesuit reaching the priesthood after a decade or more of preparation might reasonably hope for. Hopkins was ordained priest in 1877 at the age of thirty-three. In the years that followed he was wounded three times in his expectation of a full and useful life: first as a scholar, secondly as a preacher, and thirdly as a writer. These are the years that are covered by the sermons and spiritual writings printed in this volume, the years in which he tried hard to direct his literary genius into 'professional' channels.

Of the first of the three wounds not very much is known. He was expecting—as a letter to Bridges of January 1877 shows—to be promoted to a further year of theological studies after his ordination. Success in this could have opened the way to a professorship within his Order—in Sacred Scripture, for example; this would have been a post well suited to his Oxford qualifications, and, as some later writings show, he had a special gift for it as well as a strong attraction. Contrary to his expectation he was not promoted. Guardedly but not altogether accurately the historian of University College, Dublin, wrote of 'the strains of controversy' which had 'marred his earlier years', and added more explicitly: '. . . as a theologian his undoubted brilliance was dimmed by a somewhat obstinate love of Scotist doctrine, in which he traced the influence of Platonist philosophy. His idiosyncrasy got him into difficulties with his Jesuit preceptors who followed Aquinas and Aristotle.'[1]

A glance at the names of Hopkins's 'Jesuit preceptors' makes it hard to imagine anything like acrimonious controversy, nor is there any evidence that he aspired to be a professor. Yet the failure to find an orthodox outlet for his theological ardour was a disappointment at least in the sense of being a maladjustment. In his comments on the *Spiritual Exercises* there is an adverse reference to 'our scholastics' which bears this out. Nothing more is known, though one may contrast his career with that of his contemporary, Fr Joseph Rickaby, who was also a brilliant individualist. Rickaby, by steady application, went on to be an interesting theologian and a useful writer on the *Spiritual Exercises*,[2] while Hopkins turned with apostolic ardour

[1] On the contrary they followed *Suarez*; see note p. 292 (146.2).
[2] It is of interest that two of Rickaby's most original comments in his book on the *Exercises* had been anticipated by Hopkins. See below, pp. 111–12.

to the prospect of being a missioner and a preacher. Of his failure as a missioner the main and decisive cause was ill health; but it was to some extent bound up with his efforts to be a popular preacher.

His success and his failure in these efforts run clearly through the main block of sermons which form the first part of this volume, 1878–81.

There followed his 'tertianship', or third year of noviceship, during which both his soul and his nervous system were refreshed and restored. Intellectually and imaginatively, also, he was flooded with light; there was a new coming-together of his religious ideals and his poetic genius, and he felt the power to produce great works which should be the fruits of both. His writings at this time form the bulk of the second part of this volume, 1881–2.

The last two sections of the third part take up the story in 1883 at a time when his prospects of being a writer were blocked and began to crumble away. The comparison of himself to a eunuch which occurs both in the *Poems* and *Letters* is repeated in his last private notes of 1888. It was not, however, the last word.

Nothing is more striking than the objective enthusiasm which wells up in him unfailingly when some lofty theme or subtle overtone attracts him. The autobiographical element in his sermons and spiritual writings is of very little importance compared with their intrinsic interest. To stress it might well be misleading. But, as long as this caution is borne in mind, it provides a useful way of introducing his sermons and spiritual writings considered as a whole.

PART ONE

THE SERMONS

INTRODUCTION

Hopkins as a Preacher

HOPKINS began at the famous London church known as 'Farm Street' with a series of three Sunday morning sermons in August 1878. His letters to Bridges show that he approached his task keenly and confidently. Farm Street, where his admired Fr Gallwey was Rector, was an auspicious place to begin. But it is unlikely that his stay there was intended to be long. August is the holiday month. In November he was moved to Oxford, to the parish church of St Aloysius, recently erected at the junction of St Giles's with the Woodstock Road.

Oxford is much more likely to have been the place where the Provincial (his old Rector from St Beuno's days) hoped that Hopkins would settle down and find the best outlet for his talents. The parish church was at that time the only Catholic foothold in the City. What was wanted was someone who could cater for the Gown as well as for the Town without giving offence to the University authorities. Hopkins's friendship with the Paravicinis (who held him in deep veneration), not to mention his other acquaintances, might have been an opening for him to become a sort of unofficial chaplain to the Catholic and would-be-Catholic undergraduates. The work that he might have done was actually done in the following year by Fr Joseph Stevenson, the well-known archivist,[1] and by Fr William Humphrey, another gifted convert, who are styled respectively in the Province Catalogue *scriptor* and *concionator* ('writer' and 'conference-giver'), whereas Hopkins was just *operarius*—'worker'.

It was Fr Humphrey, passing through Oxford in June 1879 preparatory to settling there in the new scholastic year, who seems to have impressed on Hopkins the usefulness of having sermons ready to hand when called upon. He gave him the stout *cahier* now known as 'Fr Humphrey's book' which contains almost all the surviving sermons. It begins with the six preached by Hopkins during his last three months at Oxford, 6 July to 21 September 1879. Three of them are alive with poetry; but in general they lack those little sparks or flashes that arise from sympathy between preacher and people. He found it, he said, 'far harder to set the Isis on fire than the Thames'.

His year at Oxford had not been as fruitful for himself as might

[1] See *Letters*, ii. 30.

have been hoped. Neither Stevenson nor Humphrey replaced him in the sense of ousting him, for in the following year the staff was raised from two to four. If this had happened earlier Hopkins would have been spared much labour. As it was he was kept fully occupied with the Infirmary, with the Barracks, and with the auxiliary church in St Clement's, while the more specialist task of dealing with the University remained in the hands of his superior, Fr Parkinson. But whether in any case he would have settled down at Oxford is doubtful. He found 'the Town' uninspiring and he avoided 'the Gown'. According to his letters, he did not 'hit it off' with Fr Parkinson, and he hankered, somewhat perversely, after a more fullblooded type of apostolate.

The superior of St Aloysius's, Fr T. B. (known as 'Truly Benevolent') Parkinson, was, like so many Jesuits of that period, a convert clergyman, but a convert from the Cambridge evangelicalism of Simeon, and he never ceased to prefer Cambridge in a sportive manner to Oxford. His 'manner through life', says his obituary notice, 'still retained much resemblance to that of an Anglican parson, and was particularly suave, serious almost to demureness, and impressive by reason of the judicial gravity and air of conviction with which he in measured terms pronounced his opinions'. Hopkins in a delightful sidelight on 'the Parkinsonian mind' tells how his Superior, in admiration of Bridges's hymn to Nature, '. . . read it murmuringly out over tea, with comments and butter. But as he read it I was struck by a certain failure in the blank verse'.

Fr Parkinson's talents attracted many serious-minded undergraduates to discussions in the Presbytery, but, according to the same obituary notice, he was made painfully conscious that his work outside the strictly parochial sphere aroused disfavour and even opposition from the University authorities. Perhaps that is why Hopkins shrank from becoming similarly involved. On the whole there seems to have been a confusion of motives in his avoidance of the University. He longed for a more robust and responsive type of congregation to preach to, 'for I dearly like calling a spade a spade'. At the same time he had a powerful but not fully-calculated attraction to obscurity and self-effacement. Only once in his Oxford sermons is there a passage—about the experiences of a convert—which seems specially designed to attract inquirers. And that was in his last sermon when he knew he was leaving.

He had received a transfer to the enormously crowded and thriving parish church of St Francis Xavier's, Liverpool. But before Liverpool was ready to receive him he had to put in three months at the small industrial town of Bedford Leigh, near Manchester. It was then and there, during that stop-gap period and in that incongruous place, that he found the greatest happiness in his pastoral life and the most fruitful work. It was an idyllic interlude.

To Bridges and Baillie, who believed (probably rightly) that Oxford was just the place for him and who were evidently distressed by his move, he wrote the most unexpected letters of joy and self-congratulation at the exchange. In this smoke-sodden little town he came up against people who needed him desperately, and their need was what he needed. A man must fall in love with his parish or cure of souls if he is to do well by it. Hopkins fell in love with Leigh as he had never quite been able to do, in spite of *The Bugler Boy* and *The Handsome Heart*, with Oxford. The poems he wrote at Oxford far outstrip those he wrote at Leigh. (At Leigh he wrote *At the Wedding March* and he experienced *Felix Randal*.) But what his poetry lost his sermons gained. There are more *echoes* of his poems at Bedford Leigh than anywhere else. He became a popular preacher in the best sense of the word.

His first Sunday sermon was a lively and simple affair about the man let down through the roof, and he followed it in the evening with a talk on the Rosary full of homely touches and happy piety. November sermons showed him in increasingly close touch with his congregation, and his fourth, on the human qualities of Christ, is perhaps his masterpiece among them all. He was to preach it again at Liverpool, confident of its appeal, and to be sadly disappointed. At Leigh there was the vital link between him and his people. 'It is sweet to be a little flattered', he wrote of them to Baillie, '. . . these Lancashire people of low degree or not of high degree are those who have most seemed to me to welcome me and make much of me'. The December sermons that followed were on the same high level, particularly his last one; and they have all the warmth of assurance that is kindled by the sympathy of an audience. Hopkins was not cut out physically to be an orator; he was small of stature and his voice tended to be shrill. But it seems highly probable that he left Bedford Leigh with an established reputation as a preacher.

At all events on his arrival in Liverpool in January 1880, he was immediately assigned to give a course of four Sunday evening sermons. This in itself was an honour as well as an ordeal. The Sunday pulpit in St Francis Xavier's had a very exacting standard. The historian of the parish writes of the period when Hopkins was there:

Sundays saw a succession of such great preachers as Fr Clare and Fr Harris ascending the pulpit to address immense crowds on the subjects of the day. People were flocking from all over Liverpool so that parishioners had to come early if they would wish for a seat. So great were the crowds, when Fr Tom Burke, O.P., preached the school sermons in October 1880, none of the congregation that heard the 10 o'clock Mass could get out of the church by the ordinary way. They had to leave by the sacristy, the outer tribune and by the back of the High Altar. Even before the congregation was half out, the crowd had forced open the doors, and it was with difficulty that tickets could be collected, and many not having tickets insisted on coming in to pay. Similar events were not infrequent, and soon the locked doors of the church, the queueing crowds and unloading trams on a Sunday were a well known sight until some years after the first World War.

Had Hopkins been destined for a career as a popular preacher he could hardly have had a more signal opportunity than this course of Sunday evening sermons. His first one, on the theme 'Duty is Love', was almost certainly successful. It is an exquisite bit of work with a firm and touching message, sweet and easy to understand. At the least it must have been declared 'promising' by the pundits; the opening sentence of the next one indicates that it was this first sermon that led to his being called on to give the next three.

In the second sermon, improvising a link with his first text (which had been 'taken at random'), he launched into a more ambitious trilogy, not quite on 'subjects of the day', but on 'The Kingdom of God'. The design was: (i) the first kingdom of God; (ii) its glory; and (iii) its melancholy fall. Alas, it was the fall of Hopkins also as a popular preacher in Victorian Liverpool.

Frequently in his other sermons there are reminiscences of that special 'philosophy' of his which is expressed in his poetry and in his private speculations. Usually they would pass unnoticed except as adding a suitable touch of mystery. But in this trilogy he embarked with great dialectical detail on a subject which lay near the heart of his poetic philosophy: the lost kingdom of innocence and original justice.

At the back of it is Scotus's theory of the Incarnation, that in God's original design Christ would have come upon a sinless earth as King and High Priest. In the 'Commentary on the Exercises' Hopkins takes the psychological approach, showing how this original design still plays an indispensable part in our consciousness; for in our consciousness the world of 'possibles' is inseparable from the world of actuality; so it continues, in spite of original sin, to inspire the ideal of human nature and to supply the scope for our free will and for the operations of grace. In his trilogy of sermons he avoided the obscurity inherent in this approach and dealt with the matter in clear-cut terms of political philosophy. But he overran his time and had to omit all mention of the restoration of the kingdom by spiritual warfare. Thus his sermons ended where the ordinary preacher would begin.

In a different century or in a different place—say, in a hypothetically Catholic Jacobean Court—one could imagine solemn and sensitive faces, propped on long delicate fingers, watching him with grave intensity. But under the circumstances one can only wonder at the perverse courage which tried to bridge the three-century-widened gap between theology and poetry.

How far the Rector of the parish, Fr James Clare, appreciated the thread of his discourses is shown by the note at the beginning of the last one ('The Fall of God's First Kingdom'), which should have been the climax: 'I was not allowed to take this title and on the printed bills it was covered by a blank slip pasted over . . .'— and he 'had to leave out or reword all passages speaking of God's kingdom as falling'. (He also found it necessary, two years later, to add a long note to the sermon explaining what he did mean.)

After that there was silence for three months.

But it would be inexact, or at least premature, to speak of Hopkins's 'failure' as a preacher. He was, after all, only a junior curate among five in that large parish; his main work lay in the confessional and in the back-streets of his district; the Sunday pulpit was usually reserved for established preachers, of whom, apart from Fr Clare himself, there were several among the college staff as well as frequent visitors from other churches. The notion of 'failure', therefore, is considerably modified by the fact that on 25 April he was up again —on a Sunday *morning*, this time, when the church was crowded to capacity. Nevertheless, as far as his own feelings are concerned, there are signs of discouragement: '. . . it seems that written sermons do no good. . . . However the Rector wishes me to write.'

Fr Clare was a Lancashireman of noble presence and splendid eloquence. He was warmhearted and magnanimous, with unbounded energy, but with the corresponding fault of forgetfulness. One has the impression that any check he imposed on Hopkins was the result of complaints about which he felt he had to do something, and that for his own part he was impressed by this unusual acquisition to his staff and determined—when he remembered—to use his talents to the best advantage.

Hopkins rose to the occasion with a long and stirring exposition of a text in a Sunday gospel which only a great mind could have grappled with. 'Bend, then, my brethren, your ears and minds to follow and understand . . . it is not for us to stare or sleep . . . to give up at the first hearing of a hard passage. . . .' Even those who found his exegesis too arid and impersonal must have been impressed by the intellectual courage that refused to take the easy way out.

He was billed again next month for another Sunday morning. But this time the Rector may have counselled him to be more condescending to human weakness. For this sermon has a simple and practical lesson, adorned with homely illustrations, and it is full of comfort for the poor. It reads like the sort of sermon that the people would have been helped by. But the stars were against him; it breaks off towards the end with the note: 'This sermon is not to be delivered and therefore will not be finished, as Fr Kavanagh of West Leigh is coming here to preach for his two new missions instead.'

And the sermon after that, for the feast of Saints Peter and Paul, a big occasion, again breaks off with the note: 'This sermon is not to be preached either.'

'Fr Clare', says his obituary notice, 'was generous to his community to a fault, but his impulsiveness and variable moods told hard on some fathers.'

After that Hopkins began to lose heart. In the remaining fifteen months he was to spend in Liverpool he was called upon for only three Sunday sermons, in contrast with the six times he had been billed for Sunday in his first six months. The preacher-elect among the curates was now Fr William Dubberley, who had joined the staff at the same time as Hopkins and was a contemporary of his, from the same class as Rickaby and himself. The historian of the parish recalls Fr Dubberley's sermons in glowing terms, but of Hopkins as a preacher he has no record.

A minor but perhaps crucial discouragement came with a couple of Friday sermons he was told to preach in July, 16th and 23rd, 1880. For the first he had only half an hour's notice, and he took matter from one of his favourites, the one preached at Bedford Leigh, 23 November 1879. He described the result: 'I thought people must be quite touched by this consideration and that I even saw some wiping their tears, but when the same thing happened next week I perceived that it was hot and that it was sweat they were wiping away.'

It is possible and perhaps desirable to take this as a joke; but if so, it must be from the point of view (for which there is a good deal to be said) that all human effort is matter for comedy. But it is also possible to suspect that Hopkins's depression had swamped his judgment; that the people really were moved by the sermon of the 16th, but *not* by that of the 23rd. They had no cause to be moved by that of the 23rd. Its topic was St Mary Magdalen, an appealing one. But Hopkins's treatment of it exemplified a good and a bad quality of his preaching, both of which were quite unsuited to his audience. The good feature was a determination to get the most out of the actual words of the Gospel; but this presupposed a minute familiarity with the text which was probably lacking in the great majority of his hearers. What they wanted, no doubt, was the broad, heart-warming message of the Gospel transposed into modern dress. Hopkins could give them this when he wanted to, as he had done at Bedford Leigh; but at Liverpool, for some reason, he chose not to. The bad feature of his preaching was a frigid, almost 'euphuistic' playing with conceits and a tendency to chop logic.

His next Sunday morning sermon, 12 September, his only one in twelve months, was a defiant masterpiece. The theme, an extremely difficult one, was Christ's dispute with the Pharisees over 'the great commandment'. In this sermon, palpably alive with effort, there is a deliberate forcing of his imaginative power to serve his strictly intellectual purpose. Given the time-limit that he had to observe, it was a triumph. But it is perhaps not unfair to say that he was preaching as much for his own satisfaction as for the audience below him. He ended as follows: 'You see, brethren, I have said nothing by way of exhortation to you to keep those two great commandments of the love of God and the love of your neighbour; I could not do both that and explain the Gospel, and I wanted to explain the Gospel.'

The trouble, which was becoming more and more apparent to himself, was that he did not like the Liverpool people. 'Base and bespotted' he called the crowd at the procession of horses, and, like Swift, he preferred the horses. Even the feckless charm of the 'mere Irish' slum-dwellers, which has endeared them to so many other missioners, encountered a blind spot in his outlook—though only in Liverpool; when he met them again later in Glasgow he made amends.

But his momentary cynicism about the horses was a symptom of two deeper and interrelated causes of depression. His health was particularly bad that autumn. 'I take up a languid pen to write to you,' he wrote to Bridges on 5 September, 'being down with diarrhoea and vomiting, brought on by yesterday's heat and the long hours in the confessional.' And the ill health itself came from something deeper that blighted him spiritually as well as physically: what he saw in the slums and what he heard in the confessional. As early as May he had written a long letter to Baillie about the state of things in Liverpool, but then on reflection had torn it up.[1] It is fairly certain that what was troubling him was the contrast between the loudly flourishing condition of the Church *inside* the church building and the subhuman degradation that swamped some districts outside it. There was lacking that minimum of economic good which St Thomas postulates as necessary for spiritual welfare.

Hopkins was right about this; and it was brought to public notice a few years later when a great simultaneous 'Mission' was conducted by more than ninety priests throughout the whole of Catholic

[1] *Letters*, iii. 244.

Liverpool in 1886. A Jesuit Father who took part in the mission recorded his verdict:

> The success has been astonishing, but the consolation is not unmixed with salutary lessons of fear. . . . Among our poor, habitual irreligion or, which is nearly the same thing, carelessness resulting from warnings neglected and opportunities of grace refused, in process of time hardens down into a feeling of lost hope against which it sometimes seems almost vain to contend. It has for its inevitable ally the demon of drink, and that is another name for a legion of devils. The poor slave of intemperance can no longer call his soul his own. It is at his master's service for every deed of darkness. Many a priest turns sick at heart to see the ravage wrought by this predominant vice of our large towns—but the extent and depth of the injury done are not seen in their appalling magnitude until a simultaneous mission shows that what is true of these streets and of those is a story common to nearly all parts of a mighty city.
>
> These things it is not easy to say in an article in a public newspaper without seeming to imply reproach. Certainly in Liverpool no blame should rest upon the clergy who are hard working and exemplary. . . . May God in His mercy help our ecclesiastical rulers to find some remedy before it is too late!

Here was a sociological swamp which it would take more than the fiery zeal of a junior curate to cleanse. Duty rather than spontaneous zeal sustained Hopkins at this time. 'One is so fagged, so harried and gallied up and down', he wrote on 26 October, and continued: 'And the drunkards go on drinking, the filthy, as the scripture says, are filthy still: human nature is so inveterate. Would that I had seen the last of it.'

From October onwards his preaching virtually ceased. Sermons were a strain which he braced himself to meet but was glad to avoid. This gives a special value to the four or five that remain. A very lovely weekday one, 25 October, on 'Divine Providence and the Guardian Angels', was the occasion of his being censured and 'in a manner suspended' for using the word 'sweetheart', which had passed unscathed at Bedford Leigh. Fr Clare afterwards, typically, 'pooh-poohed the matter'; and it may have been his intention to relieve Hopkins of the strain of preaching rather than to penalize him. Still, it was lamentable that this should have been apparently the only reaction to a sermon in which Hopkins gave of his very best and which is among his tenderest and most beautiful. He gave of his best also in the two or three more allotted to him during his second year at Liverpool, though the last one he was too tired to finish copying out.

Apropos of the 'sweetheart' sermon, it is interesting to compare Hopkins's breach of propriety with the famous device used in the same month and in the same pulpit by the great veteran, Fr Tom Burke, O.P. Says the historian of the parish:

> The story of this sermon is of interest. When Fr Burke ascended the pulpit, he looked around on the vast congregation, and throwing out his right hand he cried three times in crescendo: 'To hell with the Jesuits.' So intense was the effect that the bated breath of the congregation was almost visible. Even his dramatic pause, after his astounding statement, increased anxiety. 'Such', he remarked quietly, 'is the cry of today.'

Clearly Liverpool was not the place for Hopkins. And yet, by attraction of opposites, there was something in the 'Tom Burke' style that he envied and longed to emulate.[1] His Liverpool experiences have left a definite mark on some meditations or 'conferences' which he composed on the First Week of the *Spiritual Exercises* (on 'Death' and 'Hell'). Possibly they were connected with a Lenten Mission which he gave in Cumberland in 1882. 'A Mission', he explained, 'is something like a Revival without the hysteria and the heresy, and it had the effect of bringing me out and making me speak very plainly and strongly (I enjoyed that for I dearly like calling a spade a spade).'

The reader of these is left astounded and almost stunned in places by their blasting vigour and dramatic showmanship: '*I see you, my brethren, a row of corpses.* . . .' But whether they were in fact delivered as written, and whether they were really in a style that suited him, is a matter for doubt. The third address on the *Exercises*—the splendid one on 'The Principle or Foundation'—is in a different category. It makes one regret once more that he could not settle down in the shadow of Oxford where the beauty and precision of his language would have been a help instead of a barrier to his being appreciated.

If it was really his own self-will (Baillie thought it 'an affectation') which exchanged Oxford for the northern slums, he certainly paid for it. Bedford Leigh was a bright interlude where his sermons sprang forth with easy power because he was among people who loved him. But he had not been five months at Liverpool before he realized that he was in for 'a slavery of mind and heart'; it was just at that time that he wrote his long unsent letter to Baillie and that he composed, in nostalgic memory of a Leigh 'child', *Felix Randal*:

> How far from then forethought of, all thy more boisterous years,
> When thou at the random grim forge, powerful amidst peers,
> Didst fettle for the great grey drayhorse his bright and battering sandal!

His protracted stay at Liverpool had withered him spiritually as

---

[1] For GMH's affectionate admiration of Fr Burke see his delightful Latin verses, *Poems*, 137.

well as physically.[1] His charity had been blighted a little; and when charity is blighted ever so little, the greatest virtues are those most liable to pride. He was aware that somehow he had strayed and lost direction—'Sow the wind I would, I sinned'—and he looked forward intensely to the 'tertianship' or third year of probation for which he was now due. 'I feel that I need the noviceship very much and shall be every way better off when I have been made more spiritual minded.' (To Bridges, 16 September 1881.)

The next ten months were to be spent in the still rural solitude of Roehampton, the place where he had made his noviceship, whose trees he loved individually, whose landscape and sky-scapes were part of his religious experience and poetic consciousness.

'We have been having bright and frosty weather,' he wrote on 22 October from Manresa, Roehampton, 'and the look of nature (whose face I had almost forgotten) was very sonsy, as the Glasgow people say. . . . It is besides a great rest to be here, and I am in a very contented frame of mind.'

It seems certain that the First Week of his *noviceship* Long Retreat had contained the profound religious experience which was repro-duced much later in the first part of *The Wreck of the Deutschland*. The only nature note he made at that time at Manresa came at the end of the First Week: 'The clouded sky at dawn was, I noticed, quite purple. There followed a thunderstorm: I saw one flash of lightning rose-colour. Afterwards wind, rain, and graceful changing clouds.'

This may be compared with the last line of the first part of *The Wreck*:

> Thou art lightning and love, I found it, a winter and warm.

The Long Retreat of his *tertianship* in the same place was to be another seed-time of religious and poetic inspiration. He was to lay aside actual composition during the ten months, but he felt the sap of creation full of promise for the future. He had failed as a scholar, he had failed as a preacher; but, in compensation, he felt the power to be a constructive writer, to bring forth some great ode or tragedy, or some deep work of meditation, for the glory of God.

---

[1] He had, however, one close friend, Fr William Hilton, in the Liverpool com-munity. On New Year's Day 1882 he learned that Fr Hilton had died while attending his parishioners stricken with typhoid, and wrote to his mother, 'One of our Fathers, who was for the best part of two years my yokemate on that laborious mission, died there yesterday night after a short sickness, in harness and in his prime. I am saddened by his death, for he was particularly good to me; he used to come up to me and say, "Gerard, you are a good soul" and that I was a comfort to him in his troubles' (*Letters*, iii, 162).

OXFORD SERMONS

FOR SUNDAY JULY 6 1879, FEAST OF THE PRECIOUS BLOOD—TO BE
PREACHED AT ST. CLEMENT'S, OXFORD[1]

(1) Why it is called Precious;
(2) Why it is so precious, so dear, to the Eternal Father;
(3) Why it should be so to us

(1) (A) Preciousness of blood in general,
     (B) of Christ's in particular

(A) The Scripture says *the blood is the life. It is,* that is to say, *the stream which carries life* round the whole body; when its circulation weakens life flags, when it stops life ceases. Life is precious, it is in this world our being; therefore the blood. *Any considerable loss of it lowers vitality,* the sense of life; often it is never recovered; the memory sometimes greatly weakened by a great loss of blood. A greater loss is death. Again *it marks the motions of life* in mind and body—anger, shame, fear, interest, suspense etc, which all tell that something we prize, something important to us is at stake, something with which our life is in some way bound up; it sympathises with life, which is so precious, and so is precious itself

We naturally take it as precious. When children see a drop of it spilt, even without pain, they turn pale or shed tears or faint. Many people faint at the sight of much of it. It shews they see in it some great loss, something approaching the loss of life

Men bring it into their oaths, quite senselessly. But it makes the things they talk of seem important, more worth your listening about than if they did not call them by its name. It is because they feel it is important, precious, and its very name seems to communicate importance to other things

Men sign in their own blood to give importance to what is written

And if the blood thus drawn from a living man, which leaves him in life and itself dies, is deemed precious | *much more so the blood shed in death,* with which the precious life rushes forth and passes away, is precious in our eyes. Hence people prize handkerchiefs dipped in the blood of heroes, martyrs, innocent political victims, and so on

(B) If all blood precious *much more Christ's.* His life the most precious, therefore his blood. *In the natural order* Christ's the most precious body and soul, life, blood. This blood traced from Adam's veins through Abraham's, royal David's, to Mary's; from her blood he took it with all his human frame: it had the *noblest lineage in the world. Beauty and perfection of his body*, its health untouched by any sickness or ache; hence the peerless healthfulness of his blood's beating

It beat and sympathised with the feelings of his heart, performing nobler offices than any other blood can ever do

Moreover it was shed, first in small quantity and with comparatively slight pain in the Circumcision; then by dreadful and unnatural channels in the Agony; then cruelly in the scourging, crowning, and crucifixion; then so completely after death as to empty the veins. If generous shedding can make blood precious none could be more generously than Christ's

[This consideration belongs logically rather to the 2nd or 3rd point, for anything valuable, as money, is not more valuable for being paid. However its value, seen by what it fetches, may be ascertained in spending it. Or thus: the generous shedding or payment is like a blessing, an addition to, an interest given on the sum paid]

But *supernaturally* it is far more precious. It is *united to the Word of God*, who was made flesh and therefore blood, for flesh is not without blood. It is, every drop of it is, as holy as God himself. No wonder then it is called precious

[Here ought to be added that it was precious, that is / that it must be precious, because of what it purchased, the whole world]

(2) It is so especially precious and *dear to the Eternal Father because it is the blood of the great sacrifice*, not only his divine son's blood but that shed in his honour, shed as an act of perfect devotion, of the utmost piety towards him

Religion is the highest of the moral virtues and sacrifice the highest act of religion. Also self sacrifice is the purest charity. Christ was the most religious of men, to offer sacrifice was the chief purpose of his life and that the sacrifice of himself.

Reigning in heaven he could not worship the Father,[1] but when he became man and entered upon his new nature the first thing he did in it was to adore God in it. As entering church we bless ourselves, as waking in the morning we are told to lift our hearts to God, so Christ no sooner found himself in human nature than he blessed and hallowed it by saluting his heavenly Father, raising his new heart to him, and offering all his new being to his honour. That offering was accepted, but he was told that the sacrifice must be accomplished on the cross of shame, and so from the first his sorrow was always in his sight. Every moment of his life he was unflinchingly renewing or keeping up his first offer, offering his body to crucifixion, his blood to be shed. This was Christ's sacrifice and how unspeakably dear to the Eternal Father was this devotion of his only begotten son! This then is why Christ's blood is so precious in the Eternal Father's eyes

(3) Christ's blood should be *precious in our eyes* because though it was shed for *his Father's honour it was shed for our advantage*, namely to redeem us, to save us. He was thinking of us every moment of his life, of each of us separately; first meaning to die for us and then dying. He hoped we should hear of his devotion to us, of his history, that we should be grateful, love him for it; he hoped and meant that we should do so and therefore took means to this by providing us with witnesses to the facts by word of mouth and also with a written account in the Gospels. And knowing the facts now it is wonderful we are not more touched by the goodness and selfsacrifice of our noble lover, our prince, our champion. And yet we are not: we forget him, we do not want to hear of him; we go further, we set his blood at nought, dishonour and outrage him by crying sins of robbery, drunkenness, cruelty, impurity, and the rest—things which he forbids, things which he lived to teach us to shun, which he died to get us forgiven

Some words may be added on the Sunday catechism to get parents to send their children, shewing that this is for the children to know Christ and the not doing it for them to forget him

[I preached this in the main again July 1 1883 at Stonyhurst.[1] I had only one day to prepare. I did draw up another sermon to satisfy my conscience, but thought it safer to preach the above in the end]

FOR SUNDAY AUG. 10, 10TH AFTER PENTECOST, AT ST. CLEMENT'S —*Parable of the Pharisee and Publican* (Luke xviii 9–14). These notes are got mainly from the sermon preached last year at Farm Street on the same gospel

(1) Persons, (2) words, (3) actions

(1) *Pharisees*: strictest sect of the Jews. Sects of the Jews not distinct religions, like our sects, with distinct places of worship but schools or ways of thinking. As they kept the Law strictly they were tempted to pride and being tempted to it fell into it

Publicans: not publichouse keepers but taxgatherers, excisemen. Roman taxes got in on a bad system, which exposed the persons employed to temptation of avarice. Being tempted to it they fell into it —theft, falsehood, slander, extortion.

Publicans in our Lord's judgment *better than the Pharisees*. Why? for the love of money the root of all evil; *avaro nihil est scelestius: quid super-bit terra et cinis?* (Ecclus. x 9.) and leads even to *pride*. Moreover good and bad come to men from their employments and ways of life: he who touches pitch etc and in like manner he who handles flour will be whitened. But the explanation is the Pharisees were esteemed, the Publicans despised; hence the first were, the latter were not, proud[1]

(2) *The Pharisee's words* not in themselves sinful. *Lord, I thank thee*: we should often thank God for his mercies and in particular for keeping us from sin. *Extortioners, unjust, adulterers*—sins under the 3 heads of pride of life, desire of the eyes, desire of the flesh. Explain this. *As also is this publican*: he seems to have known the man personally. Here he passes from what he does not do to what he does. *I fast twice in the week, I give tithes* etc—that is keeps the law in the most burdensome detail and adds to it burdens of his own! He implies too that he who gives tithes to God of all that is his will never be extortionate or unjust to another nor he who tames his flesh by fasting commit sins of the flesh. We may suppose he was guiltless of outward sins of the kinds named; for he was speaking to God, whom he could not deceive nor mean to deceive.

His words were then *not in themselves sinful*, yet they were very displeasing to God, the reason of which we shall presently see.

The Publican: *O God, be merciful to me a sinner*. This is true repentance: to acknowledge yourself with sorrow a sinner and ask God to forgive your sin. He was forgiven and went down justified to his house.

(3) *Their deeds* were the going up to the temple, praying there, and going down again. Force of *going up, going down*. We are to understand that what we are told they said was mainly all they wanted to say, it was their whole mind. The Pharisee said nothing of his sins or sorrow for them, he only spoke of the sins of others, and for them he did not ask God's pardon. He shewed he was presumptuous towards God, uncharitable and contemptuous towards men. Charity or love towards God is love towards a sovereign, which lies in humble obedience.[2] In this man was no humility though he said he was obedient to God's commandments. He was ready however to break them: the Pharisees crucified our Lord. Still less had he charity towards men, though he said he did them no injury. He wronged the Publican, who was then penitent, whereas he spoke of him as if he would always be an extortioner. His harsh, rash, and wrong judgment injured the man in his honour, a greater injury in itself than injury in goods. So too he robbed God of his honour, and after that what does God care for tithes of potherbs? In all this we are not told that the man committed a mortal sin, we are only told the Publican was justified *rather than* he; but the proud and pitiless man will sin

mortally when the occasion comes. The Publican on the other hand threw his whole self, body, voice, and soul, into his acknowledgment of his sins and such humility was pleasing to God and he was justified.

Dangers of rash judgment—as we see of the Pharisee upon Publican. Still worse of Publican on Pharisee. Our Lord had both in his eyes. —St Matthew and St Paul.

Goodness of contrition—Greatest sins forgiven in a moment, as here. Promise of confession, because appointed by God: so here Publican went up to the Temple.

[Much this preached again[1] at Clitheroe July 22 1883]

FOR SUNDAY AUG. 17, 11TH AFTER PENTECOST, AT ST. CLEMENT'S— —*Cure of the Deaf and Dumb Man*; *Ephphetha* (Mark vii. 31–37.)

If we learn no more from a Gospel or a sermon on the Gospel than to know our Lord Jesus Christ better, to be prouder of him, and to love him more we learn enough and we learn a precious lesson. He is the king to whom we are to be loyal and he is the general we are to obey. The man that says to himself as he walks: Christ is my king, Christ is my hero, I am at Christ's orders, I am his to command/, that man is a child of light—*qui sequitur me non ambulat in tenebris, sed habebit lumen vitae*, who follows etc. So that it would be a good practice if you are walking alone sometimes to say over many times to yourselves: Christ is my master; then after a time: Lord, what wilt thou have me do? then to answer yourselves: My daily duties, just the duties of my station / and: I wish to do my daily duties to thy glory, my God / and in particular you may name one or more. This is mental prayer

After saying this need only point out how our Lord behaved in the case before us. *He behaved with gentleness and secrecy* according to his wisdom; at other times according to the same wisdom with sternness and open vehemence, but here with gentleness and secrecy.

They bring him *a deaf and dumb man to be cured*. We learn from St. Matthew that *he had a devil*. That is / his deafness and etc were not natural nor due to faults of the organs, an evil spirit had possessed himself of them; a sullen stubborn spirit, hiding both himself and his victim's reason. Therefore not generally known that he was possessed, this dreadful circumstance could be concealed and the evangelist conceals it because Christ did so. It is true we learn it from St Matthew, but after a time all reason for concealment passed away, the people could no longer be identified. To conceal then this painful circumstance our Lord took the sufferer aside. Here you see his considerateness for his creatures' feelings.

He puts his fingers into the man's ears—as if to break down the hindrance which barred up his hearing and deafened him; but gently, with the fingertips, as if it were some delicate operation the heavenly physician had in hand, not a work of mighty power. Those things which are said to be done by the Lord's arm are God's works of power, those by his finger are the subtle workings of his wisdom. Here we may understand how men through sin had become deaf to God's calls, when his son, coming in flesh, by his gentle dealings with them once more opened their hearts.

He touched his tongue with spittle from his mouth. When the mouth is parched and dry it is hard to speak, moistening it gives it the power of speech again. Here we may understand how men had ceased to pray, or to pray as they should (for the Greek says μογιλάλον, that spoke with an impediment, could hardly speak) when Christ by the sweetness of the lessons of his mouth made their tongues free and lissome again

Then having made the organs ready to hear and speak *he looked up to heaven and groaned*—It was an appeal, a prayer to his heavenly Father, full of pity for this poor possessed man and for all mankind. *And said*: *Ephphetha, Be opened*—The evangelist tells us the very word which had this magical or rather miraculous effect. He spoke to the man and not rebuked the devil, but the devil nevertheless fled away. *And immediately etc*

Then our Lord told the cured patient and his friends *not to speak of it*, but the ears he had opened did not heed him nor the tongue he had loosened obey. Nevertheless little harm, as I suppose, was done by this: for their own interest he had kept the matter quiet and bidden them do so; but, if they chose to speak, their interests and their good name were now in their own keeping to do as they liked with. Besides he would not punish them for preferring his honour to their own

He hath done all things well etc—that is / the whole thing. They admired the completeness and delicacy of the cure. Much more should we admire what Christ has done for us—made us deaf hear, if we will hear, not with a touch of his fingertips but with his hands hardnailed out and appealingly stretched on the cross; made us dumb speak in praise and prayer to God not by a moistening of spittle but by the shedding of all his precious blood

FOR SUNDAY AUG. 31, 13TH AFTER PENTECOST, AT WORCESTER[1]—
the Ten Lepers (Luke xvii 11–19.)

Ten lepers had a faith in the Prophet of Nazareth, in our Lord Jesus Christ; they heard he was on his way to their part of the world; they thought here was recovery and health coming at last; they agreed all to meet him and call upon his mercy for a cure; a three-fold cord, the Scripture says, is hard to break, much more the faithful prayer of ten; they call him not lord but ἐπιστάτα, *praeceptor*, teacher, a word not common in the Gospel, as much as to say / Heavenly physician, give us a prescription for our leprosy; learned doctor in the Law, tell us of something that will do us good; he gave them such a prescription, it was seemingly nothing but what had always been in the Law laid down for the recovered leper, but in his mouth it had the power of a miracle. The Law of Moses ordered that a recovered leper should shew himself to the priest, who, if he were satisfied of the cure, should take him outside the camp or town; there the man should make offerings and the priest touch him with the victim's blood and with oil; after some days he might go into the world and mingle with men. Christ told these ten lepers to go and do all this: he wanted, no doubt, to shew the respect that was due to the divine Law. They went, and it shews their faith; they started with their leprosy all upon them, which if it lasted till they reached the priests, would make them seem more loathsome and more forlorn than before: but however there was no fear; before they reached the place it was gone, they were as clean as consecrated priests could be.

Their faith then, brethren, saved these men, it *saved them in the body*; from sick and afflicted they became sound and hale, from unclean in the eye of the Law they became clean, from being unfit to live with men they entered once more into the life of the world. But were they in the long run better for the change? They were better in the body, were they better in the soul? That does not appear. Rather they were worse: they thought no more of their benefactor, they gave no glory to God, they found themselves better off and there they rested, their hearts carried them no further. I mean, my brethren, according to what the Gospel tells us: in time perhaps and with the Samaritan's good example they came to a better mind, but we must speak according to our text, and so far they were the worse for their cure, being ungrateful to God who wrought it; besides that sickness and contempt—for lepers were sick and despised and put aside and shunned—sickness and contempt drive a man to God, health and to be had in honour send him to the world: now he that forgets God even in his recovery, how much more will he forget him in the ordinary and even run of health!—which leads me to say, brethren, by the way, the man or woman, the boy or girl, that in their bloom and heyday,[1] in their strength and health give themselves to God and with the fresh body and joyously beating blood give him glory, how near he will be to them in age and sickness and wall their weakness round in the hour of death!

But now to return, *there was to this ingratitude one* exception found. There was one that when the white and hideous leprosy dropped away and rosy health and nature's tints returned along his skin, not the skin only and the outer man looked handsomely, but the heart and spirit in God's eyes flushed and with that far fresher and lovelier colours. His first thought was Christ's kindness, God's goodness; his first act was to return to thank Christ, to let all the word know and those especially before whom he had asked the grace know how the grace had been granted, publicly to give glory to God. He was a Samaritan and he cast himself down on his face at the feet of this prophet of the Jews; he acknowledged that salvation was of the Jews, not of the Samaritans; he humbled himself and his own belongings to glorify Christ and God; therefore he touched the sacred heart of Christ, he drew words of honour and encouragement from divine lips, he saved his soul, and his praise is in the Gospel for ever.

Here then our Lord let the feelings of his heart be seen. He felt as we might feel. Were there not etc. Then he said / Arise, go thy way, for thy faith hath saved thee. The faith of the others had saved them too, but only in the body, as I have said; *this man was saved in the soul.* He was not a leper any longer, he was not a sinner any longer, he was not a Samaritan any longer; he was a Christian, he was a disciple of Christ. But where were the nine? They were no longer lepers but they might still be sinners; they had never been Samaritans but they were still Jews, not Christians, gone to their priests indeed but not returned to Christ the Messias foreshadowed in the Law.

Ingratitude—to God and man. Always hateful. *Hear our great poet,* he says it is bitterer than the wind and frosts of winter: 'Blow, blow, thou winter wind' etc

We are all guilty of it, we may be sure. *Classes of people especially subject to it—children* and the young: love and pains and thought without end lavished on them and they take little notice. *The infirm*: cease to think of those who nurse them, are exacting and discontented. *The destitute*: think after a time you are bound to do what you do freely; grasp, having one thing at once ask for another; think what they get little, whereas *nobilis amator non tam* etc[1]

Dreadful to say *people even hate their benefactors.* Story of Johnson's and Reynolds' first meeting.[2] The observation true but should not have been made

Gratitude to God harder than to man. Nothing reminds us of it. If children go away without a Thank you someone says to them / Come, what do you say? or a look shews us our duty, but with God etc. We must force ourselves, we must form a habit. *Nobilis amator* etc: dwell on that; once think how great God is, how kind, and his least gift will seem priceless. Besides what pleasure has he in giving if we shew no acknowledgment?

Besides *he has died for us*; always remember that. Think of his becoming man, of his choice of means and circumstances to attract us, his sweet mother, his own beauty, wisdom, kindness; his laborious life, thinking of every one of us every moment—will this please him or her? will he be won to goodness by this?—his bitter Passion and death. Let men make him their hero, women the spouse of their souls

In the evening I preached on the *Guardian Angels*, it being the feast, but have not kept the notes

FOR SUNDAY SEPT. 7, 14TH AFTER PENTECOST—GOSPEL FROM THE SERMON ON THE MOUNT (*No man can serve two masters* etc, Matt. vi 24—end), AT ST. ALOYSIUS', OXFORD

The Gospel from the Sermon on the Mount, that river of divine wisdom, which rising on Christ's lips flows from that mountain down all time to the sweetest refreshment of those who will come to taste it and live by it. In the piece which makes today's Gospel Christ speaks of prudence and of providence, of prudence in man and providence in God, how they go together, man's best prudence to trust God's providence, his least wisdom his own worldly wisdom, and all this to comfort us, to save us trouble and care, so thoughtful and compassionate is our Master's heart. The burden of it is *nolite solliciti esse* / Do not be anxious, words within a short space repeated thrice, therefore strongly pressed by Christ upon us and by us well to be taken to heart and dwelt on deeply.

No man can serve two masters. See how plainly and downright he speaks, cutting a knot there is no untying. Give up the task, no man can do it. But why not?—If they employed him at different times or in an order and rotation like guests at table or at an inn or as when a servant has both master and mistress or the young master and the old master it may be done; but this is not to serve two or many masters: there is but one real master in the house and all is in the end ruled by him or else the servant's whole time and services are not claimed by each but only a turn of them; but no, he says two masters, each claiming all, the whole time, the whole service, and then it is plain why not: they will clash, give contrary commands, neither yield to the other, and he must choose which to obey.

Either he will love . . . one of two things, he will follow his likings or his interests. If his likings then he will serve the one he loves and not serve but disobey the one he hates—and not serve two masters;

if his interests, then the one he fears or has expectations of he will attach himself to and hold by, though he should be a hard and hated master, and serve *him*, and the one he has not much to fear nor to hope from, though gentle and good, he will leave unattended to, neglect, despise, that is, and disobey—and that way too he will not serve two masters.

You cannot serve God and Mammon—Who is this Mammon that is God's rival? Mammon means Treasure or Riches: some say he was the god of riches among the Syrians, as Plutus among the Greeks. But no mention of him is made by ancient writers. Why then are Riches spoken of as if some person? Why say Mammon as if it were someone's name?—To answer this watch some man who 'hastens to be rich', goes to work early, works hard, returns late, spares his purse, scants his pleasures, and ask for whose sake he lives thus, *slaves* thus?—Not for God's, he does not pretend it; nor for his own, for he seeks his peace neither in the world to come nor yet in this; then surely for some hard master, behind the scenes; but no, we know there is no such personage, money is his master and money is no person; therefore our Lord gives it a name as if it were some person, some idol, some god, being only money all the while

We cannot then serve God and do what he asks of us if our first thought is of money or other worldly goods. But yet we must take some thought of them and the question is how much. For no one is to be idle and shelter his sluggishness behind this text, since St. Paul plainly says / If a man will not work neither shall he eat. Then how much? This is an important question and must be answered with heed and care.

First of all then the Sermon on the Mount teaches the way of perfection, it teaches the Counsels, what we had best do, not what we must do to be saved: the Commandments were given from a mountain too in thunder and lightning, by angelic voices, the Counsels by God's own lips but these the common-seeming lips of man. The Counsels are higher than etc, for he who keeps the Counsels keeps the . . . whereas . . . need not keep the Commandments.

To the question then / How much care we may take of money and worldly goods / we have Christ's answer / Seek first etc. That is where God's service and the world's clash. God is the master, not the world, God must be obeyed, the world neglected. In other words he who would keep God's commandments but aims at nothing higher may take as much care of money as will not make him break the commandments and fall into mortal sin. But for one who wishes to keep Christ's counsels the answer is / Provide for necessities and leave the rest to God, and to such a man this Gospel comes most home.

Do not be anxious, he says, and he gives a reason full of wisdom. Is

not the life more etc. This might seem a reason for being anxious, for
the life must be kept up by food, the body protected by clothing.
Only the food is for the life, not the life for the food; the clothing
for etc. When therefore we have necessary food and clothing we have
enough: Having food and clothing, the Apostle says, let us be content.
The life is more than the food; it is against reason, it is the cart before the horse to wear out life in toiling for food; to waste and weary
the body in labouring for clothing. By food and clothing understand
all things that support and furnish us in our way of life

    I wrote out no more notes

    The next Sunday Sept. 14 at St. Clement's *on the duty of hearing
Mass*, of which I have not found time to enter here the notes[1]

FOR SUNDAY SEPT. 21, ST. MATTHEW'S DAY, FOR ST. CLEMENT'S AND
ST. GILES'S BOTH[1]—ON ST. MATTHEW'S CALLING (Matt. ix 9
sqq., Marc. ii 14 sqq., Luc. v 27 sqq.)

    Suddenness of the call; a casual-seeming thing, 'as Jesus passed
thence'; not while St. Matthew was at his leisure mending nets, like
James and John, nor even casting them for a livelihood, like Peter
and Andrew, but while serving others, whose needs seemed to de-
mand his presence, 'in the custom-house'.[2] Hence also its difficulty:
he was, besides everything else, under a contract, a government em-
ployee; yet he knew that Christ knew best. Hence its reward: he
became one of the Twelve Apostles

    St. Jerome against Julian and Porphyry on the *prudence of the
obedience.* He was not prepared to be called but he was prepared to
obey the caller, of whose miracles he had heard. Moreover Christ
exerted a magnetic spell, as the saint says. What was this spell?—
The grace of vocation. And what is that grace?—It is God's will
making itself felt not everywhere, not towards all duty and right-
doing, but from one particular quarter and to one particular end.
And to hear God's voice and obey his will in such particular channels conveyed and conveying is spiritual and saving prudence

    On Vocation—Obedience of brute nature to God's voice. *Fiat lux et*
etc; *ecce adsumus* etc (Baruch iii 33 sqq.) etc. So too he calls our souls
into being and we come. Many things are called into being, but
few are chosen to be rational men

    They are brought up some by heathen, some by Christian parents.
Many called to be men, but few chosen to be Christians: being
misled from childhood men do not know God's will. And so of
Protestants and Catholics: many called to be Christians, but few
chosen to be Catholics—that is *fewer than all*, this is the meaning.

Yet God goes further, he calls the infidel, heathen, heretic to his Catholic faith. He draws all more or less on, but some much more than others; of these only we will speak; and of those who are thus strongly drawn are all obedient, all converted?—No, many are so called to the faith, but few are chosen to accept it. Why not chosen, by whom not chosen?—By themselves; not chosen, not self-chosen, not *choosing*, for God offers them the grace to take or leave. Or again, some take it and then leave it, become Catholics and apostatise: many are called into the church, but few, that is fewer than all, are chosen to persevere—are chosen, that is / themselves choose

This calling then of many and choosing of few, whether few in proportion to the others, the many, or few only because *fewer* than those others, is *the mystery of God's particular will*

God is goodness itself. All who know of God know of him as something most good, most holy. It is impressed on men that when they do right they obey God, when they do wrong they sin against, offend, displease him; that he favours good, is against evil. This comes from his nature and is his general will.

Right is God's law, wrong is offence against him, breach of his law. One might suppose he had none but this general will. Some people do suppose so: story of Mun the Water bailiff.

Yet every absolute ruler has a particular will. He must wish this rather than that in the state from time to time and enact his wishes. A limited monarch can only ask to be obeyed within the bounds once laid down, the law expresses his general will and enforcing that he 'reigns without governing'. But God not only reigns, he governs, and that by new and particular ordinances. He has a particular will

All sacred history shews this. Even in the Ten Commandments, which express and reenact the law of nature, God's general will, one, the 3rd, is a positive enactment and expresses a particular will: why not 8th or 6th day? Enoch may have pleased God by keeping the natural law, but Noe had to build an ark, of such and such measurements too. Abraham's forefathers may have sacrificed according to inclination or custom, but Abraham was commanded to offer Isaac. The law of Moses expressed God's particular will. And the whole of sacred history shews the working of God's particular will down to Christ's coming and the preaching of the Gospel of Grace and founding of the church.

God's particular will now is for all men to come to the knowledge of him the only true God and Jesus Christ, whom he has sent, in the church which Christ founded. It is true this may be reduced to God's general law of truth and right, because on an examination of all religions reason would shew that the Christian was the only one that could successfully claim to be completely free from error or fault. But most men would be unable to follow up such an enquiry, therefore they are led to the Church by God's particular will becoming known to them

How does it become known?—In a thousand ways, as many ways as there are men. Books, example, miracle etc. But all converts agree in feeling that they are led by God's particular will. They are bound to go, it will be sin to stay, God calls them, bids them etc: 'I hear a voice you cannot hear' etc. We who are converts[1] have all heard that voice which others cannot or say they cannot hear, have seen that beckoning finger which others etc

Some words on *religious vocation*

BEDFORD LEIGH SERMONS

FOR SUNDAY OCT. 5, 18TH AFTER PENTECOST AT ST. JOSEPH'S,
BEDFORD LEIGH[1]—on the *Cure of the Sick of the Palsy* (Gospel
Matt. ix 1–8.: see also Mark ii 3 sqq., Luke v 18 sqq.)

They brought to him one sick of the palsy—let us consider the affliction
of this man and of all sufferers from palsy or paralysis. Palsy is the
most thorough of all cripplings, it is a living death. The poor and
wretched, the hungry, the unhappy can stir abroad; prisoners can
move in their cells though small and help themselves; the sick can
hope for recovery and then to go about; the bedridden even can stir
their limbs and feel some power in them; but to the palsied not only
their bedroom is their tomb, their bed their coffin, their linen their
shroud, but their very body is their corpse, and yet they live. Despair
of relief, helplessness, shame at being thrown on others, all afflict the
palsied man
    Nevertheless all is not lost, they might well be worse—for *they
have power of the mind*, that is not palsied, that works and has its play.
That has neither the feebleness of childhood nor the dotage of age
nor the ravings of fever nor the foul mouth of drunkenness, nor the
drivelling of idiotcy nor the frenzy of madness. They can help themselves by speech or, if that too is gone, still by some sign and get
others to do for them what they cannot do themselves. See what
spirits and energy this man had. He did not call our Lord to him or
meet him in the way or come to him in quiet or even push his way
where he was through the crowd; nothing would do but if he could
be got at no way else he would break an entrance through a roof and
be swung down in his bed. For so we read in the two other accounts.
The place described. Imagine then the surprise of those assembled
there, the sound of feet scrambling on the tiles, the light of heaven
breaking in, a mattress coming through swung by four ends of rope,
and a man that had for many years perhaps been confined to one
room now dangling between heaven and earth over the heads of a
crowd of strangers
    Thy sins are forgiven thee—All were wondering what Christ would
say and do. He began by forgiving sin. Now this had not been asked.
The sick man perhaps felt a pang of disappointment. It is so hard to
set the soul above the body, our spiritual good and interests above
our temporal. And the scribes blasphemed. But let us consider the
wisdom of our Lord's behaviour

This sick man and his bearers had come to him to get from him some good, and a crowd had followed and was round him. A crowd had followed him: they followed him in the wilderness heedless of food; they so came and went that we read the disciples had not time to get a meal; here they so crowded him that the bearers had not been able to come through. And the more the crowd made it hard to come at him the more they were bent on doing it, for the harder the work the more it seemed worth doing. But what does a crowd prove? Any quack or false prophet, any conjuror or showman can draw a crowd. Now mark these two classes of people. The quack and false prophet offer something worth having—the health of the body or the knowledge of God; but they are impostors and lie, and what they offer they cannot give. On the other hand the conjuror and showman are honest, they can display something out of the common and that others cannot do, but then the things they show are little worth. Now the crowd might go to our Lord as to a show out of curiosity, which is no virtuous motive; or for their soul's good, as to a prophet, which is a virtuous motive; or as to a physician, for their body's good, which is betwixt and between. As to a show, for he worked miracles, which are more worth witnessing than any conjuring: the one is the sleight of hand of man, the other is the finger of God. And we know they did come to our Lord not to hear him but to have their fill of bread brought to them by a miracle. Christ could not then be satisfied that men should come to him as to one who could shew them a sight of miracles, as though he were no more than a divine conjuror come down from heaven for their idle wonder. This was what Herod wanted him to be. Nor could he be satisfied if they came to him as a physician, for so they might to any physician that could cure them, not come from heaven, and their souls be no better after the cure. Or they might come to him as a prophet: but then there are false prophets and no more could he be satisfied that they should come to him with the same disposition as and with no better proof that he came from God than if it were an impostor in God's name that they went to. He had then to do two things—to set their dispositions right, making them look to what was holy and spiritual, not what was low and temporal, and again to guide their faith, that it might rest on God's word and not on man's. There were the scribes also to be set right. When they heard him say / Thy sins etc they had said he blasphemed. They meant that being man he took to himself power that belonged only to God. And they blasphemed themselves. Consider how rash and wrong these bad men were. For either Christ was God as well as man or he was man only and neither way would he blaspheme. If God etc he could forgive sins. If man only, still God could give him power to forgive sins as he gives it to priests now.

But they blasphemed both God's person and his power—his person, the second person of the Trinity there before them, and his power denying that he could give power to man. He had then to lift up the thoughts of those who came to him to the things of God and, that done, to rebuke the unfaith of some and confirm the faith of others by a mark that God had sent him. With this, brethren, now mark the wisdom and subtlety of what he did.

He begins by raising their minds to the true and best good, the soul's good: thy sins, he said to the man, are forgiven thee. Then he leads them to the faith of God. *Whether is easier?* he asks. Mark this: he does not say / which is easier to *do*? for we know it is easier to heal the body than the soul. But his question is / which is easier to *say*?[1] which costs the speaker most? For / Thy sins are forgiven thee, any impostor can say that. Who will know? The soul is not seen; sick or sound, disfigured with sin or lovely with grace, it does not come before men's eyes; and if you profess to heal it and do not who is the wiser? But say to a cripple / Arise and walk, and the next minute shews whether you have power from God or no. If then Christ could in the power of God say the harder / Arise and walk / and what he said be done: so in the power of God he could say the less hard / Thy sins are forgiven thee / and what he said be done there too. *Then said he to the sick of the palsy* etc. Fancy the shudder of fear and the leap of joy that passed through them when they saw that man that could not lift of himself one trembling limb rise hale and strong, shoulder the mattress that had so long carried him, and thrust his way through them home.

The multitude feared and glorified God, that he had given such power to men—So should we. This is the purpose of the world, the end of our being: when we have once said from our hearts / Glory be to God / we have answered the end of our being, we have born fruit to our maker, we have made it worth his while to create us, we have not lived in vain. At good news, the conversion of a sinner, a recovery from sickness, whatever it may be, we should glorify God

Some words on faith—Faith / to believe without doubting all that God reveals, hear him whenever he speaks to you. But it is not enough to be ready to believe anything God may reveal, who will not do that? we have not the faith unless we believe he has spoken and can say what (in some however general way) and believe that. Now only the Catholic can truly tell you what and where God has spoken, viz. in the Catholic Church and all the Catholic Church teaches. In this case the Pharisees believed in God, but when God was there before them working miracles they denied and blasphemed him. The sick man and his bearers had found out where God spoke and where his finger worked in power (not that they knew Christ was

God yet, that could not be expected and our Lord did not ask that of men, but to own that he was a true prophet, was *sent* by God for their good and had business with them, a mission to them) and they made their way to him. And our Lord attested the truth of his mission by a miracle; he confirmed their faith. So if enquirers feel themselves drawn to the Catholic Church let them take notice whether it does them good, whether it is God that leads them and drives them on, whether he does not give by miracles and other marks a confirmation of their hope and first opinion, and so listen to the calling voice and follow the beckoning finger

In the evening, it being Rosary Sunday, on *the Rosary*, with text 'S. Maria, succurre miseris' etc from the office

(1) History of Feast. St Dominic. Use of beads by monks of the Desert and even by heathens. But that not the Rosary any more than wheels, straps, and bearings tell you what a machine is: you must know all the parts and how geared; so here

Lepanto (1571) and other victories

(2) How best to say the Rosary. One way to dwell on the persons of the Mystery: examples. Another by giving a special meaning to the words of the Hail Mary, as *Full of grace*, according to the mystery in hand: examples

Though a devotion in honour of B. V., all the Mysteries but two to do with our Lord and the sorrowful Mysteries exclusively so. It is dwelling on Christ's life in Mary his mother's company, calling her to witness how good he is, how merciful, how afflicted, how glorified by God, and so forth

(3) See text: number of *classes* of men recommended to the B. V.'s protection. cf. titles of her litany. She is in fact *the universal mother*; however unlike her children loves them all. No wonder she can, for in her met things that are thought to be and even are opposite and incompatible, viz. maidenhood and motherhood; then courage and meekness, height and lowliness, wisdom and silence, retirement and renown

St Bernard's saying, All grace given through Mary: this a mystery. Like blue sky,[1] which for all its richness of colour does not stain the sunlight, though smoke and red clouds do, so God's graces come to us unchanged but all through her. Moreover she gladdens the Catholic's heaven and when she is brightest so is the sun her son: he that sees no blue sees no sun either, so with Protestants.

God is holiness, loves only holiness, cares only for it, created the world for it (which, without man, if churned or pressed would yield God none). The B. V. like God in this, loves and cares for this only. Now holiness God promotes by giving grace; the grace he gives not direct but as if stooping and drawing it from her vessel, taking it down from her storehouse and cupboard. It is in some way laid up in her. She sympathises for all of us as though she and not we were in the circumstance, a sinner doing penance, though so innocent; a soldier in battle, though herself a woman. But when all is said heart cannot think her greatness, tongue cannot tell her praise

On Sunday Oct. 12 being the eve of *St. Edward* I preached on him and on the blessings of the Catholic faith, which England has lost though this congregation has kept it; but I do not put down notes

On Friday Oct. 24 *an address to the Confraternity of the Sacred Heart*, of which the notes are here on loose pieces[1]

FOR SUNDAY NOV. 9 1879, ST. JOSEPH'S, BEDFORD LEIGH—*on the Healing of Jairus' Daughter and the Woman with the Issue of Blood* (Gospel Matt. ix 18–26.: see Mark v 22 sqq., Luke viii 41 sqq.)

In this Gospel *two miracles, not one after the other, but* first the beginning of one, then the other, then the end of the first; as when you drive a quill or straw or knitting needle *through an egg*, it pierces first the white, then the yolk, then the white again. And in the two other accounts the same, though commonly the Evangelists change the order of things freely according to the purpose they have in hand; but here they all agree to follow the order of the events. There must be a reason for this and there is.

We read of many miracles our Lord worked. There were no doubt many more we do not read of, but whatever the number of the whole *there might of course have been more,* many more; all the sick in the world were not cured, nor all in the Holy Land nor all even in Jerusalem. He cured then many but he might have cured far more. And then there are all those that lived before his coming and that have lived since. *Miseratio hominis circa proximum suum, misericordia autem Domini super omnia opera sua /* a man shews mercy upon his neighbour, but the Lord's mercy is over all his works: our Lord came as man; as God he pitied all, but as man he cured only his neighbours in place and time, and not all of them, but some he cured and some he did not. He acted according to providence and prudence, he acted on a plan, and his plan took in some and left out others. He looked first to the soul to cure that, the cure of the body was always to help towards the cure of the soul, and where it would not help no doubt the miracle was not wrought; again he looked to the general good, the good of the one was to help towards the good of the many, and where it would not help the miracle was either not wrought or was not wrought in public. And in general you will find that what Christ aimed at in his miracles was to breed faith in him or it being bred to nurse it; to breed it and to nurse it, I say, both in the receiver of the miracle and in all who should witness it or hear of it. You will please, brethren, take notice of this with me in the two miracles of today's Gospel. Not only so but in these two miracles he was teaching lessons, besides faith, of hope and of brotherly charity.

There came to him then *a ruler* and, as we read elsewhere, a ruler of the synagogue. Such men were not, we know, friendly to him, they were his bitterest enemies. And this man, Jaïrus himself, he perhaps, had things gone prosperously with him, for prosperity feeds pride, might never have come to Christ; but love will drive men to shifts, *sorrow bows the proud head*; his daughter, his only child, in her first-bloom had drooped, lay dying; she had been given over, hope was out, and yet it was not the father saw one hope, the prophet of Nazareth, to him he made his way. He did his pride down to the ground, he sent no messengers, he made no measured and reserved advances, upon his knees he fell, he ended low, and with earnest and humble entreaties from a broken heart he besought help for his dying daughter

My daughter, we read he said, *is even now dead.* Another account tells us he said she was *dying.* How is this? You may say, if you like, that he *meant* she was dying but to shew how near to death she was, how extreme her need, how great his own anguish he called her dead; so that one way of telling the story would shew us what his meaning was, the other what his very words were. This may be, *this is a good explanation, but there is a better*, which will come in its place presently. Meantime I shall suppose / what he really said was that his daughter was dying.

But come, lay thy hand upon her and she shall live. Here you see what *his faith was, true but shortsighted.* Christ must come, must touch the child; if he but touched her he was sure she would live, but his power, he seemed to think, did not reach beyond his fingertips; eager, in all haste as the man was / it did not occur to him to shorten the road and make a way through the crowd by a miracle worked there and then; no but Christ must rise and come; accordingly Christ, as his manner was, took him at his word, arose, and went.

We read in St. Mark that *a great crowd followed and thronged him.* Take notice of this. If there ever was a time when a man could have wished the road clear and no bar or hindrance in the way it was then. And the crowds must needs follow and throng him! Fancy, my brethren, fancy that father: the crowd was between Christ and his daughter's life. They, those lusty men and women, for no doubt they seemed strong and hale enough, with all their sound limbs thrusting and thronging were crushing out the last spark of life from one poor girl's spent and wasted body. They were, for they would not make way fast enough for Christ to come at her. Alas, and this was not enough. At this most unhappy, most unseasonable, most agonising moment, comes in that woman with the issue of blood, she that could have come and better come at any time but that, and there must be a delay and a search for her made and an opening cleared and questions asked and a discourse delivered and his daughter every precious moment dying or perhaps dead. Indeed he was right; what he feared we know, the worst had come, she *was* dead, and the messengers were at that moment on their way to tell him.

Now as this afflicted father had to wait while Christ healed the woman and as the Evangelists make his story wait, turning to the woman's, so let us leave him awhile and turn to her. She had been sick, we read, twelve years. Now the sick girl was twelve years old. So many years as that child had had of life so many had this woman had of sickness, to the girl they had been years of growth and gain, to the woman they had been of loss and wasting, grievous loss in purse and person. But now the girl's case was worse than hers, for her fresh life was that hour passing away and the woman's wasted one might spend and be spent for some wretched years longer. However these two were to glorify God by their cures on one and the same day.

She said within herself etc—The event shewed she was right. True, she might have been cured at a distance, but God may have inspired the thought nevertheless. Her disease might suggest it: that stained and defiled her garments and made unclean those she touched, Christ her saviour to his very garments conveyed a healing and a cleansing virtue. There need then be no want of faith in this nor selfishness in wanting to be cured first then, for she may not have known of Jairus' need or thought her cure would hinder his daughter's. But her faith came short in this, that she thought Christ would not know, and she was selfish in this, that she meant the cure to benefit none but herself and left out of sight God's glory and her neighbour's advantage: She said *within herself*.

Christ's wisdom: the same act should build up both her faith and the father's, correct both her self love and that father's.

FOR SUNDAY NOV. 16, 24TH AFTER PENTECOST—GOSPEL FROM 6TH AFTER EPIPHANY: *the Mustard Seed* and *the Leaven** (BEDFORD LEIGH)

Christ compares the Kingdom of Heaven, that is his Church, to this and to that; the Kingdom of Heaven, he says, is like . . .; but *it cannot be said he compares it to what is all good*. He clearly shews, and he

* Matt. xiii. 31–35.; cf. Mark iv. 30 sqq., Luke xiii. 18 sqq.

takes pains to shew, it will be mingled, that is in this world it will, of many sorts, of good, bad, and indifferent. (Here quote the Ten Virgins and the Net.) And yet men are scandalised when they find it not all perfect: here there is one bad, there a bad family, somewhere else, a bad town or country, and one whole age of the Church may be not so good as another. There will be black sheep among the white; there will be even bad shepherds, I mean priests, the pastors of Christ's flock. Scandals must come, only woe to him etc.

In the place this Gospel is taken from Christ speaks of the Kingdom of Heaven in four or five parables (see St. Mark for one, iv 26.), there may have been more. The first is that of the Sower: this brings out that the good seed may fail for want of good ground. Another is that of the Cockle: this shews that it may be mingled with evil seed when there is an evil sower. But to shew the fault is not in what God gives but in the way it is dealt with he tells three other parables, one how the corn grows though the farmer takes no notice of it (Mark); the second of the mustard seed; the third of the Leaven. The Mustard Seed shews the Kingdom of Heaven has in it a prodigious life and power of growing; the Leaven shews its power to act upon the world.

To compare God's kingdom to a mustard plant seems quaint and odd. We read that our Lord said / What is the Kingdom of Heaven like and to what shall I liken it? as though he himself were astonished at it and could in all his world find nothing that could be its match. Then he found the mustard plant. He meant not our mustard plant, which does not grow high, but the tall mustard of the East: it grows so high that it is not a herb at all nor even a bush but a tree outright. What he says of the seed must be taken roughly, that it is very small; for no doubt there are others smaller, even that cannot be seen with the naked eye.

But why is the Kingdom of Heaven like this plant?—Because its beginnings are very small and it grows to be very great. Consider this in the Church; (2) divinity, theology, divine wisdom, the knowledge of God; (3) the soul of each man

(1) Once the Kingdom of Heaven (for I put aside the Blessed Virgin / the tree in which the seed had grown) was all in one little infant frame in her womb. The Twelve Apostles, the early Church, the Church now 200,000,000 of men. It will be greater, is to cover the earth *like a sea*, the mass to be offered *in every place*

The branches are national churches, as those of Spain, France, Ireland, England (part withered); dioceses, as that of Liverpool, Shrewsbury, Westminster; parishes, as this; families; single men, as every one of you. Here speak a few words of the Branch Church doctrine. The Church of Rome at the root

The birds of the air / angels that wait upon the Church and dwell on God's wisdom in it; guardian angels sitting one on every spray also the wandering minds of men that here find rest

(2) From the Person of Christ gathered the doctrine of the Trinity, of the Incarnation, of the Blessed Sacrament. A few words dropped by him spread into theology, which is yet growing

FOR SUNDAY EVENING NOV. 23 1879 AT BEDFORD LEIGH—Luke ii 33. *Et erat pater ejus et mater mirantes super his quae dicebantur de illo* (text taken at random)

St. Joseph though he often carried our Lord Jesus Christ in his arms and the Blessed Virgin though she gave him birth and suckled him at her breast, though they seldom either of them had the holy child out of their sight and knew more of him far than all others, yet when they heard what Holy Simeon a stranger had to say of him the Scripture says they wondered. Not indeed that they were surprised and had thought to hear something different but that they gave their minds up to admiration and dwelt with reverent wonder on all God's doings about the child their sacred charge. Brethren, see what a thing it is to hear about our Lord Jesus Christ, to think of him and dwell upon him; it did good to these two holiest people, the Blessed Virgin and St. Joseph, even with him in the house God thought fit to give them lights by the mouth of strangers. It cannot but do good to us, who have more need of holiness, who easily forget Christ, who have not got him before our eyes to look at. And though we do have him before our eyes, masked in the Sacred Host, at mass and Benediction and within our lips receive him at communion, yet to hear of him and dwell on the thought of him will do us good.

Our Lord Jesus Christ, my brethren, is our hero, a hero all the world wants. You know how books of tales are written, that put one man before the reader and shew him off handsome for the most part and brave and call him My Hero or Our Hero. Often mothers make a hero of a son; girls of a sweetheart and good wives of a husband. Soldiers make a hero of a great general, a party of its leader, a nation of any great man that brings it glory, whether king, warrior, statesman, thinker, poet, or whatever it shall be. But Christ, he is the hero.[1] He too is the hero of a book or books, of the divine Gospels. He is a warrior and a conqueror; of whom it is written he went forth conquering and to conquer. He is a king, Jesus of Nazareth king of the Jews, though when he came to his own kingdom his own did not receive him, and now, his people having cast him off,

we Gentiles are his inheritance. He is a statesman, that drew up the
New Testament in his blood and founded the Roman Catholic
Church that cannot fail. He is a thinker, that taught us divine
mysteries. He is an orator and poet, as in his eloquent words and
parables appears. He is all the world's hero, the desire of nations.
But besides he is the hero of single souls; his mother's hero, not out of
motherly foolish fondness but because he was, as the angel told her,
great and the son of the Most High and all that he did and said and
was done and said about him she laid up in her heart. He is the true-
love and the bridegroom of men's souls: the virgins follow him
whithersoever he goes; the martyrs follow him through a sea of
blood, through great tribulation; all his servants take up their cross
and follow him. And those even that do not follow him, yet they look
wistfully after him, own him a hero, and wish they dared answer to
his call. Children as soon as they can understand ought to be told
about him, that they may make him the hero of their young hearts.
But there are Catholic parents that shamefully neglect their duty:
the grown children of Catholics are found that scarcely know or do
not know his name. Will such parents say they left instruction to the
priest or the schoolmaster? Why, if they sent them very early to the
school they might make that excuse, but when they do not what will
they say then? It is at the father's or the mother's mouth first the
little one should learn. But the parents may be gossiping or drinking
and the children have not heard of their lord and saviour. Those of
you, my brethren, who are young and yet unmarried resolve that
when you marry, if God should bless you with children, this shall not
be but that you will have more pity, will have pity upon your own.

There met in Jesus Christ all things that can make man lovely and
loveable. In his body he was most beautiful. This is known first by
the tradition in the Church that it was so and by holy writers agree-
ing to suit those words to him / Thou art beautiful in mould above
the sons of men:[1] we have even accounts of him written in early
times.[2] They tell us that he was moderately tall, well built and tender
in frame, his features straight and beautiful, his hair inclining to
auburn, parted in the midst, curling and clustering about the ears
and neck as the leaves of a filbert, so they speak, upon the nut. He
wore also a forked beard and this as well as the locks upon his head
were never touched by razor or shears; neither, his health being
perfect, could a hair ever fall to the ground. The account I have
been quoting (it is from memory, for I cannot now lay my hand
upon it) we do not indeed for certain know to be correct, but it has
been current in the Church and many generations have drawn our
Lord accordingly either in their own minds or in his images. Another
proof of his beauty may be drawn from the words *proficiebat sapientia*

et aetate et gratia apud Deum et homines (Luc. ii 52) / he went forward in wisdom and bodily frame and favour with God and men; that is / he pleased both God and men daily more and more by his growth of mind and body. But he could not have pleased by growth of body unless the body was strong, healthy, and beautiful that grew. But the best proof of all is this, that his body was the special work of the Holy Ghost. He was not born in nature's course, no man was his father; had he been born as others are he must have inherited some defect of figure or of constitution, from which no man born as fallen men are born is wholly free unless God interfere to keep him so. But his body was framed directly from heaven by the power of the Holy Ghost, of whom it would be unworthy to leave any the least botch or failing in his work. So the first Adam was moulded by God himself and Eve built up by God too out of Adam's rib and they could not but be pieces, both, of faultless workmanship: the same then and much more must Christ have been. His constitution too was tempered perfectly, he had neither disease nor the seeds of any: weariness he felt when he was wearied, hunger when he fasted, thirst when he had long gone without drink, but to the touch of sickness he was a stranger. I leave it to you, brethren, then to picture him, in whom the fulness of the godhead dwelt bodily, in his bearing how majestic, how strong and yet how lovely and lissome in his limbs, in his look how earnest, grave but kind. In his Passion all this strength was spent, this lissomness crippled, this beauty wrecked, this majesty beaten down. But now it is more than all restored, and for myself I make no secret I look forward with eager desire to seeing the matchless beauty of Christ's body in the heavenly light.

I come to his mind. He was the greatest genius that ever lived. You know what genius is, brethren—beauty and perfection in the mind. For perfection in the bodily frame distinguishes a man among other men his fellows: so may the mind be distinguished for its beauty above other minds and that is genius. Then when this genius is duly taught and trained, that is wisdom; for without training genius is imperfect and again wisdom is imperfect without genius. But Christ, we read, advanced in wisdom and in favour with God and men: now this wisdom, in which he excelled all men, had to be founded on an unrivalled genius. Christ then was the greatest genius that ever lived. You must not say, Christ needed no such thing as genius; his wisdom came from heaven, for he was God. To say so is to speak like the heretic Apollinaris,[1] who said that Christ had indeed a human body but no soul, he needed no mind and soul, for his godhead, the Word of God, that stood for mind and soul in him. No, but Christ was perfect man and must have mind as well as body and that mind was, no question, of the rarest excellence and beauty; it was genius. As Christ lived and breathed and moved in a true and not a phantom human body and in that laboured, suffered, was crucified, died, and was buried; as he merited by acts of his human will; so he reasoned and planned and invented by acts of his own human genius,[1] genius made perfect by wisdom of its own, not the divine wisdom only.

A witness to his genius we have in those men who being sent to arrest him came back empty handed, spellbound by his eloquence, saying / Never man spoke like this man.

A better proof we have in his own words, his sermon on the mount, his parables, and all his sayings recorded in the Gospel. My brethren, we are so accustomed to them that they do not strike us as they do a stranger that hears them first, else we too should say / Never man etc. No stories or parables are like Christ's, so bright, so pithy, so touching; no proverbs or sayings are such jewellery: they stand off from other men's thoughts like stars, like lilies in the sun; nowhere in literature is there anything to match the Sermon on the Mount: if there is let men bring it forward. Time does not allow me to call your minds to proofs or instances. Besides Christ's sayings in the Gospels a dozen or so more have been kept by tradition and are to be found in the works of the Fathers and early writers and one even in the Scripture itself: It is more blessed etc.[2] When these sayings are gathered together, though one cannot feel sure of every one, yet reading all in one view they make me say / These must be Christ's, never man etc. One is: Never rejoice but when you look upon your brother in love. Another is: My mystery is for me and for the children of my house.

And if you wish for another still greater proof of his genius and wisdom look at this Catholic Church that he founded, its ranks and constitution, its rites and sacraments.

Now in the third place, far higher than beauty of the body, higher than genius and wisdom the beauty of the mind, comes the beauty of his character, his character as man. For the most part his very enemies, those that do not believe in him, allow that a character so noble was never seen in human mould. Plato the heathen, the greatest of the Greek philosophers, foretold of him:[3] he drew by his wisdom a picture of the just man in his justice crucified and it was fulfilled in Christ. Poor was his station, laborious his life, bitter his ending: through poverty, through labour, through crucifixion his majesty of nature more shines. No heart as his was ever so tender, but tenderness was not all: this heart so tender was as brave, it could be stern. He found the thought of his Passion past bearing, yet he went through with it. He was feared when he chose: he took a whip and singlehanded cleared the temple. The thought of his gentleness towards children, towards the afflicted, towards sinners, is often dwelt on; that of his courage less. But for my part I like to feel that I should have feared him. We hear also of his love, as for John and Lazarus; and even love at first sight, as of the young man that had kept all the commandments from his childhood. But he warned or rebuked his best friends when need was, as Peter, Martha, and even his mother. For, as St. John says, he was full both of grace and of truth.

But, brethren, from all that might be said of his character I single out one point and beg you to notice that. He loved to praise, he loved to reward.[1] He knew what was in man, he best knew men's faults and yet he was the warmest in their praise. When he worked a miracle he would grace it with / Thy faith hath saved thee, that it might almost seem the receiver's work, not his. He said of Nathanael that he was an Israelite without guile; he that searches hearts said this, and yet what praise that was to give! He called the two sons of Zebedee Sons of Thunder, kind and stately and honourable name! We read of nothing thunderlike that they did except, what was sinful, to wish fire down from heaven on some sinners, but they deserved the name or he would not have given it, and he has given it them for all time. Of John the Baptist he said that his greater was not born of women. He said to Peter / Thou art Rock / and rewarded a moment's acknowledgement of him with the lasting headship of his Church. He defended Magdalen and took means that the story of her generosity should be told for ever. And though he bids *us* say we are unprofitable servants, yet he himself will say to each of us / Good and faithful servant, well done.

And this man whose picture I have tried to draw for you, brethren, is your God. He was your maker in time past; hereafter he will be your judge. Make him your hero now. Take some time to think of him; praise him in your hearts. You can over your work or on your road praise him, saying over and over again / Glory be to Christ's body; Glory to the body of the Word made flesh; Glory to the body suckled at the Blessed Virgin's breasts; Glory to Christ's body in its beauty; Glory to Christ's body in its weariness; Glory to Christ's body in its Passion, death and burial; Glory to Christ's body risen; Glory to Christ's body in the Blessed Sacrament; Glory to Christ's soul; Glory to his genius and wisdom; Glory to his unsearchable thoughts; Glory to his saving words; Glory to his sacred heart; Glory to its courage and manliness; Glory to its meekness and mercy; Glory to its every heartbeat, to its joys and sorrows, wishes, fears; Glory in all things to Jesus Christ God and man. If you try this when you can you will find your heart kindle and while you praise him he will praise you—a blessing etc

FOR SUNDAY MORNING NOV. 30 1879, FIRST OF ADVENT, AT ST. JOSEPH'S, BEDFORD—on the Ep. (Rom. xiii 11–14.) and particularly *'Sicut in die honeste ambulemus,* non in commessationibus et ebrietatibus, non in cubilibus et impudicitiis, non in contentione et aemulatione'

You hear, my brethren, how the apostle speaks: this life is night, it is night and not day; we are like sleepers in the nighttime, we are like men that walk in the dark. For though our translation says 'the night is past,' this is not to be understood as if it said the night were wholly past and day come, but rather, as we see by looking at the original language, that the night has got on and day is approaching. Life then is night, although he bids us walk in it as if it were day. And our Lord speaks in the same way when he says we do not know at what hour of the night he our master will come, whether in the first watch or at midnight or at cockcrow or at morning, that is / when the night is all but over. The time then that is passing between Christ's first coming and his second is night and his second coming will be the day. And yet in another place our Lord called this life day and the other life or death night, saying: work while it is day, for the night is coming when no man can work, that is / work while life lasts, for death is coming, when it will be too late. So then the Scripture in one place calls life night and in another calls it day. But these do not disagree. In respect of truth and the clearness we see it with / life is night and what comes after life is day; in respect of doing work in God's service and earning a reward hereafter life is day and what comes after is night. But you yourselves, brethren, are some of you well aware of this: to most men the daylight is the place to work in but those that work in the pit go where all is darker than night and work by candlelight and when they see the light of day again their work is over, as if day were night to them and night day, so then this life is dark, a pit, but we work in it; death will shew us daylight, but all our work will then be done.

To return then to where I began, this life is night, it is a night, it is a dark time. It is so because the truth of things is either dimly seen or not seen at all. The thoughts in men's hearts are dark, they are not seen, because this life is night. One man is in God's grace, another is in sin, but they look alike, for life is night and all things are alike in the dark. Good is done but is unspoken of and unrewarded, because this life is night; evil is done but is unsuspected and unpunished, because this life is night. Or else things are seen, but not seen well. We see that wrong is bad, but we do it, yet we sin, because life is dark: if it were daylight sin would be too nakedly hideous, we should be ashamed of it. We see that right is good, but we do not do it, because life is dark: if it were daylight virtue would look so lovely and noble we could not but follow it.

Well then, brethren, this night, this night of life, is far gone; day is at hand, St. Paul says. What is the sun that makes that day?—It is no other than our Lord Jesus Christ. 'In him was life and the light was the light of men and the light shone in darkness and the darkness did not take it in'. This sun has risen and set once already, but in such a way that men did not know of it. Some could not, others would not. 'The light shone in darkness and the darkness did not take it in'. 'He came to what was his own and his own did not receive him', they shut their eyes, their barred up doors and shutters against the daylight of the soul. The Wise Men came from the East to say that this sun was risen, that Christ the king was born, and the Jews themselves knew where, at Bethlehem; but there they would not go. Time passed and miracles were done, thousands were fed on a few loaves, the blind saw, the dead rose to life, these bright and shining miracles bore witness to the sun being high, to Christ being in his height of power, but his enemies that could not deny them would not be converted by them. Then the clouds gathered, the hour of storm, the power of darkness came, the sun got bloody red, Christ was crucified; and his enemies that loved darkness better than light triumphed that he was gone. On Easter day this same sun had another rising, Christ rose from the dead, and soon on Ascension Day one may say another set, for Christ was seen no more.

So then the world is again dark without him, because Christ the light of the world is gone. The Catholic Church, which he set up, rehearses and tells over his teaching and shines by his light as the moon by the sun's. Otherwise it is dark: it is night and night is dark at best. And this night is not of so many hours, a number known beforehand; it is of quite uncertain length; and there is no dawn, no dayspring, to tell of the day coming, no morning twilight, the sunrise will be sudden, will be lightning, we are told, will overtake us without warning, will entrap us, will come as a snare upon all that are on the face of the earth. There are indeed to be signs, but none but believers will heed them, and these signs will still leave the time uncertain though they will shew that it is near. So when Christ comes his coming will still surprise, men will be unaware and will be overtaken.

It may not be in our time, none of us may live to see it. But if our judge does not come to us we shall go to him: we shall die and after death is the judgment. For every man is judged at death though at the Last Day all men are to be judged together: those that are judged already, their judgment will not be set aside; it will be confirmed with all the world to hear it. And when we see our judge, whether he come upon us or we go to him, that is whether at our death or at his second coming, then the night of this life will be over, the day of the next world will have come; we shall see things as they are, our judge as he is, the world as it is, ourselves as we are, our good works and our sins as they are.

Now, brethren, as the time of Christ's second coming is uncertain so is the time of our death. Both are certain to come, both are uncertain when. But one thing may be said of both and the apostle says it: The night has got on, the day is nearer. This is, my brethren, always true and always getting truer. Mark these two things: every minute true, for it is at any minute true to say our life has got some way on, our death made some approach, or again that the world has gone on some time since Christ's first coming and made some approach to his second; and also every minute truer for every minute we and the world are older, every minute our death and the world's end are nearer than before. For life and time are always losing, always spending, always running down and running out, therefore every hour that strikes is a warning of our end and the world's end, for both these things are an hour nearer than before. But there is a difference between our death and the world's end: the world's end though every generation, one after another, is warned of it, yet one only will be overtaken by it, the rest will have passed away before; but death comes to every one and none escapes. Therefore God has given us more warnings of death: age is a warning, sickness is a warning, and the deaths of others that go before us are a great warning. For the last day none have seen, but almost all men have seen death.

However, whether for the world's end or death, the apostle's warning is the same, to walk honestly, that is honourably, becomingly, wellbehavedly, as in the day, not etc. And Christ's warning is like it (Luke xxi 34.): But take heed to yourselves that your hearts be not loaded with overeating and drunkenness and cares of this life, and that day come upon you unawares. And these things that they warn us of, they abound; who needs the warning more than we? for the evils abound. Now more than ever is there riotous company, drunkenness, lewdness, strife, brawling, even bloodshed. To speak against all these things is too much. But look, brethren, at the order of them. First comes rioting or revelry, unruly company: here is the beginning of evil, bad company. Bad company seem hearty friends, goodnatured companions and such as a man should have: must not a man have his friend, his companion, unbend from his work at times, see company and life? Must he sit mum? must he mope at home? But, brethren, look at these things nearer. A friend is a friend, he loves you, he thinks of you and not only of his own pleasure.

A rout of drinking companions do not love one another, they are selfish, they do not love their own, how can you think they care for strangers? Their own children may be hungry, their mothers or their wives in tears, their homes desolate and they are so good as to spend their time, their money, and their health with you. One of two things: you treat them or they you. If you treat them you like a fool spend your money on the worthless; if they treat you often you are eating their children's bread, you are draining the blood of their little ones. There is no friendship here, no love; there is no love, I say, where nothing comes in but selfishness.

And unruly company leads to drunkenness. Though many and many a tongue is now telling of it what tongue *can* tell the evils of drunkenness?—Drunkenness is shameful, it makes the man a beast; it drowns noble reason, their eyes swim, they hiccup in their talk, they gabble and blur their words, they stagger and fall and deal themselves dishonourable wounds, their faces grow blotched and bloated, scorpions are in their mind, they see devils and frightful sights. A little drunkenness is sad, a thing pitiful to see, and drunkenness confirmed and incurable is a world of woe. It defiles and dishonours the fresh blooming roses of youth, the strength of manhood, the grey hairs of age. It corrupts the children yet unborn, it gives convulsions to the poor sucking child. It is ugly in man, but in woman it is hideous beyond what words can say. And the world is laid waste with it.

It lays waste a home. There is no peace, there is no reverence or honour. The children are scandalised and taught to sin. Nay, it breaks home quite up, breaks the bond that God fastens, what he has joined it puts asunder, wife runs from drunken husband or husband from drunken wife.

It wastes, it spends, it brings on poverty. Times may be good, wages may abound, and yet in the house is seen want and slovenly disorder, for gold and silver and clothes and furniture and all are gone one way, down the belly. Or times may be bad and then surely there is nothing to spend on drink. But there is: feet may go bare and hearth be cold but the fire in the throat must be quenched with liquor or rather with liquor fanned to flame. And not only must the body want but the soul too is to fast and lose its food: the family cannot go to mass, obey the Church's commandment, worship God on his holy day in his holy place and be present at the great sacrifice; though it should cost not a penny they cannot do it, because the clothes are pawned.

And lastly drunkenness leads to worse sin than itself, leads to crimes —to cursing, blasphemy, abuse, the foul mouth; to all incontinence and impurity; to brawls and blows and bloodshed.

What then is the remedy?—I am not now, brethren, to speak of rioting and drunkenness in particular, their cause and cure, but on the epistle of the day. The cure the Apostle gives is / to put on Jesus Christ, that is the white robe of justice and God's grace or, as he says above, the armour of light. This is a robe, this is armour, that all of you either have never lost or at least can easily put on: You can go to the sacrament of penance. And though temptation is here, because it everywhere abounds, yet this is a place, brethren, where those who will be good can be. Here the young woman can grow up, live, and die in maidenly or in motherly innocence; here the young man can make and keep his strength and manhood sacred to God. And if you have fallen, if you have fouled your white robe and stained your lightsome armour, you can with ease recover all again. God's grace either always to have kept or having lost to recover is a blessing I wish you all, in the name etc

[The first 6 paragraphs of this I delivered confusedly and the last I added in preaching and have written since]

FOR FRIDAY EVENING DEC. 5 AT ST. JOSEPH'S, BEDFORD, *on the Immaculate Conception*, to open a triduum to be kept in honour of the 25th anniversary of the Definition

On the 8th of Dec. 1854, 25 years ago, Pius IX the last Pope before the now reigning Pope Leo XIII, defined the Immaculate Conception, that is to say he taught the whole Catholic world what we were to believe and hold about this doctrine. The occasion was solemn, the bishops in large numbers had been assembled, and the holy Pope himself was so deeply affected as he read the decree that, it is said, his handkerchief was wet through with his tears.

The doctrine of the Immaculate Conception is this—that the Blessed Virgin Mary was never in original sin; that, unlike all other men and women, children of Adam, she never, even for one moment of her being, was by God held guilty of the Fall; and this great grace was granted her beforehand for the merits of her son our Lord Jesus Christ, that was then not for 14 or 15 years to be born. So that the Blessed Virgin was saved and redeemed by Christ her son not less than others but more, for she was saved from even falling but they were let fall and then recovered (that is / redeemed): now, as the proverb says, prevention is better than cure. Well then may she say in her Magnificat that her spirit rejoices in God / her saviour. All others but Mary, even the holiest, have fallen at least in Adam, St. Joseph and St. John the Baptist so fell: her privilege has been granted to none but her. This then is the meaning of the Immaculate

Conception, that the Blessed Virgin Mary was for Christ her son's sake never in original sin.

I must also add that she was not only not guilty of it but that God kept her also from the worst effect of it, which effect of original sin always accompanies the guilt of original sin. This worst effect is concupiscence, that is to say / a readiness to commit sin, fresh sin of their own, which all men have in them. Everybody feels at least *some* inclination to heat of temper, to gluttony or drunkenness, to impurity, to love of money, and so on, one or all of these things, and more or less they fall into them, some more, some less. But if God by a special grace were ever to have kept anyone, as perhaps he may have kept St. John Baptist, fromf alling into any the least sin, still such a man would have the inclination to sin left though he did not yield to that inclination: a watch wound up but kept from going has the spring always on the strain though no motion comes of it.[1] Such a mainspring of evil in us is the concupiscence that comes in with original sin and lasts even when original sin has been taken away by baptism. Now our Lady had none of this. She had neither the guilt nor yet concupiscence, the worst effect, of original sin. Eve too before she fell was free from concupiscence within and yet she sinned. But then Eve was tempted from without, but the Blessed Virgin, for a further privilege, it is believed was never even tempted.[2] If she had been tempted she would not have fallen, any more than Christ her son fell when he was tempted. Yet this does not make her merit the less, for goodness lies not only in not doing evil but, much more, in doing good. She did all the good she possibly could, acted up to all the countless graces God gave her; whereas if God were to keep *us* from all temptation, perhaps instead of being better we should turn into mere nondescripts and rest at a standstill doing neither good nor evil. Such then was the Blessed Virgin's Immaculate Conception: she was from the first conceived without original sin and also without concupiscence, the leaning towards evil which goes along with it, and this for the sake of Christ her son.

And here I will mention before I have done dealing with the doctrine of the Immaculate Conception that original sin has another great and terrible consequence and punishment besides concupiscence; I mean death. Now since the Blessed Virgin was saved from the guilt of original sin and even from its first great consequence one might have thought that God would have saved her also from so great an evil as death, being a consequence of the same sin: she had done nothing to deserve it and was not under the sentence that had been passed on other men. And perhaps he would have kept her from it if she had so wished, but her son had undergone it, Jesus Christ her Lord had died, and she could but wish to be like him. So she died, but not by violence, sickness, or even age, but as, it is said, of vehement love and longing for God. From sickness indeed she was, like her son, always free, her bodily frame perfect in beauty and health.

This is all I shall need to say of the *doctrine* of the Immaculate Conception, which Pius IX a quarter of a century ago published to all the world to be held as of faith and under pain of sin. It was known and believed by almost all Catholics long before; it was told by our Lord to his apostles, it is to be found in the Scriptures, in the works of the Holy Fathers and of great divines; still there were some who denied it and a small number were left even in 1854 still disputing against it. But when the Pope spoke they obediently bowed their heads, gave in their submission, and made an act of belief like other Catholics. It is a comfort to think that the greatest of the divines and doctors of the Church who have spoken and written in favour of this truth came from England:[1] between 500 and 600 years ago he was sent for to go to Paris to dispute in its favour. The disputation or debate was held in public and someone who was there says that this wise and happy man by his answers broke the objections brought against him as Samson broke the thongs and withies with which his enemies tried to bind him.

And now I must speak of how we should pay honour to the Immaculate Conception. We cannot copy our Blessed Lady in being conceived immaculate, but we can copy her in the virtues by which she became her privilege and her privilege became her. She did not indeed merit this privilege of God nor could claim it as a right; it was God's favour and free grace granted her before she was conceived or could know or do good or evil; nevertheless God could foresee that she and she alone among men would, if it were granted her, not dishonour it, would honour it and do it justice. A king looking among his subjects for a bride to share his throne might say of many a young woman: I could indeed raise so-and-so to be my queen; but she is unworthy, her lowbred manners would soon break out and disgrace the lofty station she was never born to: at last he might find one of whom he could say: Here is a maiden that now thinks of no such honour, but if I raise her to it she will make it seem that she was born to nothing else, so well will it become her: here is the maiden for me, she and no other shall share my royalty. It was thus God foresaw of the Virgin Mary and predestined her first to be conceived without spot and then to be the mother of his son.

What then were the great virtues he saw in her and so pleased him, which we too may see in her and please him by copying?—I suppose the two virtues she is most famous for are her purity and her humility.

How beautiful is purity! All admire it, at least in others. The most wicked profligate man would wish his mother to have been pure, his wife, sisters, daughters to be pure. And in men it is honoured as in women: the man that this same profligate knows he can trust where he could not himself be trusted he cannot but deeply honour. When purity is lost comes shame and a stain within the mind which, even after God has long forgiven us, it seems our own tears would never wash away. And for this virtue the Blessed Virgin became the mother of God and St. John the bosom friend of the Sacred Heart.

(Some words on humility, which I had not time to write)

A. M. D. G. FOR SUNDAY EVENING Dec. 14 1879, 3RD IN ADVENT, AT ST. JOSEPH'S BEDFORD—on *St. John Baptist* (Gospel John i 19–28.)
Et hoc est testimonium Joannis . . . et confessus est et non negavit et confessus est: Quia non sum ego Christus

St. John Baptist, brethren, if I praise St. John the Baptist to you tonight I shall be praising him whom Christ himself praised before a great crowd of men, if I make much of the Baptist I shall be making much of him that the Holy Ghost makes much of in the sacred Gospels.

To begin then. St. John the Baptist was asked the question: Art thou the Christ? Never before, I suppose, was man asked that. But who asked him?—The learned Pharisees, the proud Pharisees, the would-be-thought-holy Pharisees: 'Those that were sent', says the Scripture, 'were of the Pharisees'—learned, they would not ask a foolish question; proud and jealous, they would not willingly find the Christ in a stranger from the wilderness; seeming-holy, they had no wish for a master who should tell them they must repent. Gladly, no doubt, they would have passed the matter by, would have seemed to take no notice of the man; but they could not; things had come to too great a pass, there was a man come to whom all men were flocking, ask him they must, and they did, that awful and honourable question: Art thou the Christ?

THE FOLLOWING TO BE PREACHED INSTEAD, on *Gaudete in Domino semper: iterum dico, gaudete. Modestia vestra nota sit omnibus hominibus. Dominus prope est*—Phil. iv 4, 5. (from the Epistle)

Since *we have a procession tonight* I wish, brethren, to be but short. 'Rejoice in the Lord always', says the Apostle; 'again I say, rejoice':

we do rejoice, we have a procession, which is a joyous and festival thing, and in the Lord, for it is in his honour and his Blessed Mother's. However the procession will not last long, tonight is not always, and we are always, he says, to rejoice in the Lord. I will speak then of this always rejoicing in the Lord.

If we are *to rejoice in the Lord we must be in his grace*, we must be out of mortal sin. How can a mortal sinner rejoice in the Lord? He has offended the Lord, the Lord is his judge, the Lord condemns him, what joy can he have to think of him? Nay what joy at all? since he is under sentence, is threatened with hell, everlasting fire is his portion; how can he forget that dreadful thought? how can he have any joy at all?—but he can; I will not deny they do; they drown thought in drink and passing pleasure; it is not happiness, but enjoyment of a sort it is, and yet life is full of deaths and dangers, many above ground and underground more still. But if the man has faith and fears, though he does not serve, God, what is this joy worth? He hears of a sudden death and he is touched with fear, fear poisons pleasure, it embitters his sweet cup and stings him in his easy bed. And far better it should, since it may bring him to repentance, than that he should live at ease and dying wake in hell. There is a crowd of you, brethren, and amidst that crowd some must be in this road[1]—I mean are out of your duty, out of God's grace, and in mortal sin. You are cowardly, you are slothful, and with that you are insolent: you are bold to break God's law and yet you are not bold enough to help your own souls. [Here add a few words.]

Rejoice in the Lord is said to those who love God, whose sins are forgiven, for whom a crown is laid up in heaven. This is a joy which nothing, which no man, as our Lord said to his Apostles, can take from you. Otherwise there are many who could not rejoice. One might say: I am in such want that I am not sure of my next meal: how can I have any joy? Another says: I have just lost a child, a wife or a husband: how can I rejoice? Another is in sickness or pain or ill-used or slandered by unkind tongues. The things I have named are afflictions, they are sorrows so great that for a time they may take from the world all comfort, but they leave you your heavenly hope; of that comfort they cannot rob you. If you are poor, why then you are blessed because yours is the kingdom of heaven; if meek, that is patiently bearing illtreatment, you are blessed because you are to inherit the earth; if a mourner you are blessed because you are to be comforted; and so forth. If you say that when all is said you feel your sorrows still; why yes, for comfort is not to undo what is done and yet it is comfort, yet it comforts. If we feel the comfort little, there, my brethren, is our fault and want of faith; we must put a stress on ourselves and make ourselves find comfort where we know the comfort is to be found. It *is* a comfort that in spite of all, God loves us; it *is* a comfort that the sufferings of this present world (St . Paul says) are not worthy to be compared with the glory that is to be revealed in us; such thoughts *are* comfort, we have only to force ourselves to see it, to dwell on it, and at last to feel that it is so. Cheerfulness has ever been a mark of saints and good people. The Apostles went rejoicing we read, after their scourging from the sight of the Council, because they were found worthy for the name of Jesus to suffer insult; the martyrs were cheerful: when at one time the Christians were led to execution mingled, through their persecutors' malice, with common convicts / all would not do, the martyrs by their joyous looks could easily be told from those who were to suffer the just reward of their crimes; Margaret Clitheroe[1] as she went through York streets, to be pressed to death on Ouse Bridge, all along the road as best she could with her pinioned hands dealing out alms to the poor, looked, it is said, so marvellously cheerful and happy that her murderers, like those Pharisees who of Christ her master said that he cast out devils by Beelzebub, had nothing for it but to pretend she was possessed by 'a merry devil'. Goodness then, my brethren, is cheerful and no wonder, and if there are, as to be sure there are, some good people whose looks are commonly downcast and sad, that is a fault in them and they are not to be copied in it.

I have been speaking of a holy joy which those who are in God's grace may have even in the midst of their sorrows and misfortunes, but most people at most times are not, most of you now are not, in sorrow and misfortune: henceforward I am going to speak for the most part of people, for the most part of you, how you should rejoice in the Lord—always understood that you are in God's grace and free from sin. 'Rejoice in the Lord always; again I say, rejoice'—and how?—The secret is soon out: *by dearly loving the Lord himself, our Lord Jesus Christ.* If this world is going fairly well with you you have no such need, just for the time, to long for another, better one: you should of course always hope for it, but you are not forced to do so as a relief and comfort against the trials of this. But to rejoice in the thought of our Lord Jesus Christ, that we should always do, not only to sweeten our sorrows but also to sanctify our joys.

(The rest shorter)—Love of God means the preferring his will to ours: it is the love of a subject for his ruler. By this we shall be saved, but this is but a cold sort of love. Love for Christ is enthusiasm for a leader, a hero, love for a bosom friend, love for a lover. Now when we love God he first loved us, first loved us as a ruler his subjects before we loved him as subjects their ruler; so when we love Christ with a fonder love than that / he with a fonder love[2] than that first loved us. It has been said that God prays to men more than men to

God: Christ called to us from his cross more than we call to him there. We call to him for comfort, but long ago he said: Come unto me. Long before John or Edward, Margaret or Elisabeth ever said / I love our Lord Jesus Christ / he said / I love John, I love Edward, I love Margaret, I love Elisabeth. His servants rejoice in him, at least St. Paul says they should, but much more does Christ rejoice in them. Are they handsome, healthy, strong, ableminded, witty, successful, brave, truthful, pure, just? He admires them more than they can, more than they *justly* can, themselves, for he made all these things, beauty, health, strength, and the rest. But we admire ourselves and pride ourselves: we should leave that to him, he is proud enough of us. If we do well he smiles, he claps his hands over us;[1] he is interested in our undertakings, he does not always grant them success, but he is more interested in them than we are. The wife wants her master a good husband, Christ wants it more; the child wishes him a good father, Christ etc; the employer wants him a faithful workman, he is satisfied with moderately good work, Christ is not, he looks at it with a keener artist's eye; and so on. We must then take an interest in Christ, because he first took an interest in us; *rejoice in him because he has first rejoiced in us.*

LIVERPOOL SERMONS

I

A. M. D. G.

FOR ST. FRANCIS XAVIER'S, LIVERPOOL, SUNDAY EVENING JAN. 4
1880—*Thy will be done on earth as it is in heaven* (taken at random)

We are all of us bound to love God, so bound that if we do not it will be
a mortal sin and we shall be lost. For this is God's first and great
commandment: *Thou shalt love the Lord thy God with thy whole heart
and with thy whole soul and with thy whole mind and with thy whole strength:
this is the first commandment* (Mark xii 30.). And in that hymn which
is called St. Francis Xavier's it is said: 'O Deus, ego amo te: Non
amo te ut salves me Aut quia non amantes te Aeterno punis igne' |
'O God, I love thee,' I love thée—Not out of hope of heaven for me
Nor fearing nót to love and be In the everlasting burning'. He speaks
| not of hating God but, short of that, of not loving him; he says those
who *do not love* God are punished with everlasting burning. We are
then in duty deeply bound to love God, and this is God's first commandment.

*Here, then, brethren, may rise in any one of our hearts the searching and
painful question*: Do I love God? Do I love him enough? Do I feel for
God love enough to be saved?—even in the hearts of those who are
serving God to the best of their power; whose sins have been by
penance forgiven; who do their daily, weekly, and yearly duties; who
thought, and with reason, that they were in God's grace—in the
hearts of such persons the fear may nevertheless stir, that after all
there is a commandment they are not keeping and that the first of all,
that they have been thinking about and doing small duties and over-
looked and left undone the great one, that they do not *love God* and
for want of love will be lost at the last. Cruel and comfortless thought
in the hearts of God's servants! and like that other one which torments many: I have searched my conscience, I have with whatever
shame told all my sins, I have heard my absolution at the priest's
lips spoken, I have done the penance enjoined, and I have no peace,
I fear all has gone for worse than nothing, that my repentance is
hypocrisy and my sacrament sacrilege, because I was not in my heart
sorry for my sins. I shall try, brethren, with the divine assistance tonight
to answer the first of these questions so as to set both it and you at

rest. What I shall say will be to most of you familiar and well known, but there may be some to whom it is new, to whom it will be comforting and serve to put an end to their distressing thoughts.

The love of God or *divine charity is to wish God's will done* and when God's will is against ours to wish his will done rather than ours because God is God and we are only men: this is divine charity, this is to love God, this is to keep the great commandment and all the commandments, this is to be in the way of salvation. He that says, and means, 'Thy will be done on earth as it is in heaven' will in that state of mind be saved, he cannot be lost. I do not care how cold his love may be, he loves God; he may never have shed a tear over Christ's passion, heaved a sigh for his own sins, felt his heart kindle at anything holy, he loves God: he may seem to obey unwillingly, but if he can say / God is God and I am only a man and therefore his will ought to be done in this matter and I will do it /, that man loves God and loves God more than himself, that man has divine charity.

Some will perhaps say: That is not what I should call love of God at all; it is duty towards God, it is obedience, but it is not love, and the Scripture expressly says we are to *love* God.—I answer that it is love.

In what does love consist? in what is love seen? by what is love tried? —By doing the beloved's will. Therefore requests are made: If you love me do this; if you have any love for me grant me that. For indeed what is happiness? since in some way or other for happiness our friend must wish.—It is to have our will, to wish and to have, to wish and not be disappointed. Our best, our true happiness is to have our best wish granted; the wish for our best good; that longing which is always in every, even the wickedest, heart. Our lower happiness is to have our lower wishes, our wishes of the moment, granted. All love higher or lower, true or false, deep or shallow, lies, just so far as it deserves that name of love, in granting, in forwarding the beloved's will: if it is the beloved's best and highest will, his wish for his own undying and eternal good, then it is the truest love, it is holy charity; if it is his lower and passing will it is a lower and a passing love, but for the time love. Why look even at selflove, for charity begins at home: true and just selflove lies in wishing and in promoting our own best good and happiness, this is charity towards ourselves; short-sighted selfish love of ourselves, which is selfishness and not true selflove even, lies in the consenting to and gratifying the wishes of our lower, our worst, selves, our selves of flesh, our selves of this world and of time. But take it how you will, high or low, true and lasting or selfish and short-sighted, all love is seen in the doing the beloved's will; to oblige people, to befriend them, to be their friends, to shew them love, to love them, is to do their will. So then it is with God: to love him is to do his will. And so he says himself: If you love me *keep my commandments*.

For, my brethren, *what kind of love should we give God?* what kind of love should he, or reasonably can he, ask of us? who is God that he wishes our love?—There is the root of the matter. A sovereign, a lord and master, a king, a sovereign; he a sovereign, we his subjects. A sovereign asks his subjects for love, not, mark you, his courtiers, his family, his friends, those who are about him and see him daily, but those who know him least, know him only as their lawful and their just sovereign, the last and least of all these he asks for love; and he must mean that sort of love which only / subjects as such can give and so which only / sovereigns as such can ask—*the doing his sovereign will*, willing obedience. Willing obedience is a subject's love to his sovereign. Earthly sovereigns, there are many things no doubt they will or wish and their subjects do not know of or cannot give them, some to be had, some not to be had, as long life, children, success, health, peace of mind; but we do not call these the sovereign's will: by the will of the sovereign we mean one thing only, his claim on our obedience. So God as our sovereign has only one will and that will we ought to do and to do it is to love him; it is / willingly to obey him, and this *willing obedience is divine charity*.

I say willing obedience, for if *the obedience falls short of willing, then it falls short of charity*. For God, that almighty sovereign, enforces his will by what is called a sanction, he offers us heaven as our reward if we do it, hell as our chastisement if we disobey it. To obey and do God's will from hope or fear is good, is right, but it is not charity: it is holy hope but not holy charity. We *should* act from hope and fear but not only nor first; first is to act from charity. And to act from charity is both easy and common. For, brethren, I put aside the words love and charity and infinite perfections and all we find set down in acts of contrition: ask any simple man or woman or child why he does this or that duty which you see him doing. Sometimes no doubt he will answer / Because I shall go to hell if I do not; Because I mean to go to heaven and this is the way; but how often, oftener I am sure, the answer will be: Because it is right, Because it is my duty, Because I ought, Because God has commanded it, Because it is God's will—and if you press him / God's will! but why not do your own will? will he not be shocked and say / God is God, God's will ought to be done first—? My brethren, I will be bound when you yourselves are tempted the first good thought most of you have is not / I shall be damned if I do / but I must not, God is against it, God is God and he says No and there is an end of it. If so, you prefer God's will to yours and God to yourselves and act from divine charity, and if you do so in all cases of grievous sin and not only in some of them, then you are *in* divine charity. If therefore you wish to make an act of charity say / I will do God's will and not my own, because God is God and I am only man and it is right that man should obey God. And the same of an act of contrition. For this state of mind is love of God and divine charity.

Nay, my brethren, *this is not only love but it is as high as the highest.* There is a sweeter, tenderer love, a love more working and effectual, which may be added to it and grow out of it, of that I shall not speak tonight, but the love I have spoken of comes first and none can be higher. For the love a sovereign first of all and above all claims is the love of him as sovereign: he will be glad of a dearer love than that but he will not insist on it, the doing his sovereign will he will insist on. Say he is popular because he is young and handsome, accomplished, renowned in arms, gracious in his manners, but so may his nobles be or any of his subjects; but there is one love none but he can claim and without that all other love is worthless— obedience. And so with God; gifts will not do nor sacrifices, sighs and tears will not do nor cries of enthusiasm unless his sovereign will is done: obedience is better than sacrifice; seas of tears and sighs to fill the firmament are waste of water and loss of breath where duty is not done. *Duty is love.* What a shame to set duty off against love and bloat ourselves because we act from love and so-and-so, our dull neighbour, can but plod his round of duty! *There is nothing higher than duty* in creatures or in God: God the Son's love for God the Father is duty. Only when I speak thus highly of duty I mean duty done because it *is* duty and not mainly from either hope or fear.

Such then, my brethren, is love of God, to wish his will done on earth as it is in heaven, their duties done by men as their duties are done by angels, and not wish it done only, but do it; for wishing without doing, where we can do, is not true wishing even. May God's will be done on earth as it is in heaven, a blessing I wish the earth and you in the name etc

L. D. S.

FOR SUNDAY EVENING JAN. 11 1880, THE 1ST AFTER EPIPHANY, AT ST. FRANCIS XAVIER'S, LIVERPOOL—on *God's Kingdom*: 'Thy Kingdom come' (last Sunday's being on 'Thy will be done')

The Sunday evening sermons given in this church for the most part follow a course; I shall try therefore, my brethren, to link mine together and since last Sunday I took for my text 'Thy will be done' tonight I take the petition next before that in the Lord's prayer, 'Thy kingdom come'. This is to go backwards, but for my purposes this order will serve well enough. Those of you who were here last Sunday evening may remember that I spoke on the love of God and shewed you that the love which all men are bound to bear towards God was nothing else than a willing obedience to his sovereign will, for God is a sovereign and the love of subjects towards their sovereigns lies first and foremost in willing obedience to their declared will. I did not need to shew you that God is a sovereign, for you would none of you doubt it. But now I wish to speak of God's sovereignty or kingdom, what it is like; tonight therefore let our thoughts be turned to God's kingdom as it was first founded upon earth and next Sunday we shall, I hope, see its history, its glory and its fall.

God is our king. *The Lord is a great king*, says the Scripture, and it tells us of what, of sea and land, the heights of the mountains and all the bounds of the earth; it calls them his and says / *But we are his people and the sheep of his pasture: come let us adore him.* So then God is a king and men are his people, his subjects, the nation he rules over. But how does God come to be our king? is it because he created us? —The same Psalm seems to say so, for it says: The sea is his *and he made it* and *his hands founded the dry land* / and again: Let us bewail before *the Lord who made us*, for he is the Lord our God (Ps. xciv.), as if to have created anything were to be king over it.

But no. God is our king, but creating us did not make him so. God is our owner and master, but creating us did not make him so. God is our father, but creating us did not make him so. This may sound surprising, yet I must repeat it. We are God's subjects; and again we are God's things, his goods and chattels, his property, his slaves; and lastly we are God's children; but yet his creating us did not of itself make us any of these three things. Most certainly it gave him a title to them all: there was a crown for him if he chose to wear it; there was an estate for him if he chose to own it; there were children for him if he chose to adopt them. But it did not follow that he would. The crowns of the earth sometimes go begging among men and do not always find a wearer; there are pieces of property which are no man's and may be owned, *or disowned*, by the first finder; and as for children, who would dream that men are either bound to adopt or always do adopt children they have never begotten: now God created us by nature, he did not beget us; by nature then we are his creatures, not his sons, nor yet his property nor yet his subjects. Nay God has not only created us but every moment preserves us, giving us ever fresh and fresh being, whereas an earthly father begets but once upon a time: yet this does not make God a father; again God holds us and all things with a faster hold not only than man can hold his goods, for how can the wealthy landowner grasp his acres in the palm of his hand? even than the miser grips his gold: yet this does not make God an owner; once more, whereas it is sometimes said of constitutional sovereigns, that the king or queen reigns but does not govern, meaning that he of his dignity gives a name and marks a period but does not manage the state by his own mastery, God on the contrary must govern, must direct and master the world, or it would fly to pieces: yet this governing is not reigning, as reigning is not governing, and does not make God a king. A fresh act of his will is needed: to make us sons he must adopt us; to make us of his property he must own us; to make us his subjects he must ascend our throne. He has the right and title but he must employ it, he must make the claim; if he should not then *we* cannot claim *him*: *we* cannot father ourselves on God to be his children; *we* cannot bestow ourselves on God to be his property; *we* cannot force a crown on God to be his subjects. For certainly we have not the power, and we have not the right either.

Nevertheless *now* we *are* God's subjects and he our king; we are his property and he our master and owner; we are his sons and he our father. Was this always so?—No. Was it so in the beginning?—Yes. It was so at the beginning, then it must have ceased to be, and now it is again: here there is a world of things to be known; but this evening I wish to speak of what was in the beginning and after what manner it was that God was then man's king and master and father. Now, my brethren, what I am going to say may be dark, it may be dry; yet I shall make it as clear as I can, and men's thoughts may well be spent in taking pains to master the things of God.

Wherever there is a sovereign power, a king, an emperor, any kind of prince, ruler, governor, one such or more of them, or even a whole people selfgoverning and selfgoverned, there must always some understanding have gone before about the governing and the being governed—I mean those who are governed must have agreed to be governed and those who govern, they too must have accepted the task of government. Whether this understanding is well-known and a matter of history, as suppose the people have chosen a king and offered him the crown, or whether it is lost in the darkness of the past how it came about, nevertheless at any particular time when orderly government is going on there *is* such an agreement, there exists such an understanding: the subjects obey, at least they are not in rebellion; the rulers govern, at least they have not thrown up the reigns of power. For if the governed had never, neither at first nor after, submitted to be ruled / all would be riot, order could never have come about; if the ruling power had never, neither at first nor after, accepted the task of government how could he or his house or heirs or representatives be now upon the throne? The agreement, the understanding, the contract, must have somehow *come about*, and it will always have been brought about for the good of both parties, governor and governed, for their common good, their *common weal*; and this is what we call a commonwealth. For men are met in towns and assembled into states for their common wellbeing, to buy and sell, to marry and be given in marriage, for mutual defence, for learning's sake and company's sake, for a thousand reasons all gathered up in the words common weal or commonwealth. A leader and lawgiver for them there must be and they may choose one, but for the most part there is no need to enquire who was chosen or when, for people are born to things and rest content with them much as they are: look at ourselves, we have no two thoughts about the matter; we find the queen on her throne, houses of parliament, judges sitting or going, the army, the police, the postoffice at work; the common good is being provided for, we share it more or less, we share the common weal, we are part of the commonwealth; we may dislike this or that ministry or measure, move and agitate to get it changed, but as for refusing to be ruled at all and putting ourselves out of the commonwealth, to most people the very thought would never occur; they are born to share its advantages and therefore they suppose themselves born to share in its duties and be in its allegiance. I do not wish to speak of an oppressed country, where the burdens and not the blessings of government are felt, that sighs under a heavy yoke, but of a fairly well-governed one, and in such I say that those who find themselves born to the blessings and avail themselves of those blessings know they must be born to bear the burdens and that it is their duty to bear them.

Remark these two words, wellbeing or advantage and duty, for on them the commonwealth turns. The aim of every commonwealth is the wellbeing, the welfare of all and this welfare of all is secured by a duty binding all. For, as we have said, there is an understanding, there is a contract, which once made, once allowed, is in justice binding: he that undertook to govern bound himself to look to the common good and for that he makes his laws; they that undertook to be governed bound themselves to obey his laws and perform what should be by them commanded. Hold fast this thought, I say it once more: a commonwealth is the meeting of many for their common good, for which good all are solemnly agreed to strive and being so agreed are then in duty bound to strive, the ruler by planning, the ruled by performing, the sovereign by the weight of his authority, the subject by the stress of his obedience.[1]

Now what follows from this?—Something very beautiful and noble and honourable. A covenant, a contract, an agreement, I mean of course a lawful one, once made binds in justice and as it cannot be broken without injustice and wrong, so it cannot be kept without justice and right: therefore two that make and carry out a contract are both just, both in the right. And mark this too, both *equally* just, equally in their right. For this is the wonderful property of justice to equalise those who share it: if I buy the baker's bread I cannot be juster, righter, for paying my silver than he for delivering his bread, nor yet he juster and righter for his bread than for my silver, but the fair price having been asked and paid, we are both in our duty, both in our rights,[1] both equally in the right of it. So in the commonwealth: the prince may have more prudence in planning the campaign, the soldier more fortitude in storming the breach, but justice, justice is halved between them or, if you like, whole in each of them, the sovereign on his throne cannot be juster for claiming obedience than the subject for yielding it. How bright a thing then is good government and loyal submission, how bright a thing a wellordered commonwealth, where all the citizens, every least member of the state, is glorified by one equal justice! every man a just man, an honest man, an honourable man! for just means honest and honest means deserving honour.

And now, brethren, one more thought and that a surprising one far higher, far more glorious, than any I have hitherto entertained, and this thought will bring tonight's discourse to an end. What if God were to come to terms with man; make a covenant, a contract with him; share with him a common good, a common weal, undertaking a task and binding himself to duties; were, I say, to make one commonwealth with man, himself the sovereign, the king, man the subject; then in this divine commonwealth, in this kingdom of God, while man did his duty, for God could not fail in his, both sides would be just, equally just—unspeakable stately dignity of man! man as just as God, just with God's own justice? What if this were to be?—It was. When there was but one man Adam, not only *a* man but man, for Adam was the whole of humanity, he was mankind in one person, God entered with man, with that one man and then presently with him and his wife the one woman, into a noble commonwealth, which was God's kingdom, and it was held together by justice, that famous *original justice* of which you have all heard, which is passed away, except for Christ and Mary, for ever. *O the depth of the wealth of the wisdom and knowledge of God! How incomprehensible are his decisions and unsearchable his ways! Who ever knew the Lord's mind or who was ever his adviser? or who gave to him first and is to have it repaid him? No, from him and through him and in him are all things* (Rom. xi 33 sqq.). He brings together things thought opposite and incompatible, strict justice and mere mercy, free grace and binding duty. For this very justice, original justice, that was in Adam, who but God freely bestowed it? since if he had chosen to enter into no contract with man, make with man no commonwealth, wear the crown of no human kingdom, where would man's justice have been? And yet he did and man was as just as God. This was the first kingdom of God and his justice, and to it every other boon and blessing was added. And all fell, all is gone: it was divided against itself, the subject against the sovereign, man against God, and every kingdom, said the Son of God, even God's kingdom divided against itself must come to desolation, no commonwealth or household, not even God's commonwealth, God's household, divided against itself, can stand. Next week, my brethren, with the divine assistance we will look at God's first kingdom in detail, first in its early glory, then in its melancholy fall.

L. D. S.

FOR SUNDAY EVENING JAN. 18 1880, 2ND AFTER EPIPHANY, AT ST. FRANCIS XAVIER'S, LIVERPOOL—God's Kingdom in the Earthly Paradise (text: 'Thy kingdom come,' as last Sunday)

Let me recall to your minds, my brethren, *what I said in this place last Sunday*. I spoke of God's kingdom, of what is meant by the words, so common in the Gospel, *the Kingdom of God*, that is a sacred commonwealth to which both God belongs and man, God being the sovereign there and men the subjects. For of every commonwealth this is the essence and the nature: it is the meeting of many for their joint and common good, for which good all are solemnly engaged to strive and being so engaged are then in duty bound to strive, the ruler by planning, the ruled by performing, the sovereign by the weight of his authority, the subject by the stress of his obedience. This, I say, is what a commonwealth means and God's first kingdom upon earth was such: God had a place in it and man, God was to gain by it and man, God bound himself by duty in it and man, God was justified in it and man. For this, you remember, was that wisdom and merciful gracious condescension I pointed out to you of God's when first he dealt with Adam, that he, being by nature just, would raise man, being then by nature neither just nor unjust but a thing indifferent, earthy like the earth he was made from, infinitely above manself to the divine justice and would consent himself to be tried by his behaviour, as a man is tried in the events of life, whether he, God, were faithful and honest or no. For everyone that enters into a contract must therefore undergo this trial of his honesty in performing or dishonesty in failing, and God entered into such a contract and bound himself by justice so. Now then what are the terms of that contract between God and man, in other words what was

the constitution of that commonwealth? what was the good it
aimed at? what the duties to be done in it? what its laws? and what
its forfeits?

There are then, as you know, in commonwealths ranks or (as they
say) *estates*; for instance in our own are three, the crown, the peers,
the commons. In this divine commonwealth, *in this kingdom of God
were two* estates—God and man. Man was at first but one man, Adam,
who was mankind, he was all man in one person; then there were
two; and there *were to have been* more, Adam and Eve's children; and
when these were born they would have entered at once into the
compact with God, would have stepped into their places in the
commonwealth, without any fresh agreement or act of mercy on
God's part but of right and justice. These were the estates of the
realm, these were the persons of whom the kingdom of God consisted. Neither was the king invisible only and his throne hidden in
heaven: he let himself be seen, he played his part, as we may say, in
the show and pageantry of the country, he was indeed on familiar
terms with his subjects. For we read of God talking with Adam; we
hear of his walking in Paradise 'ad auram post meridiem', to take the
afternoon air—we should never have guessed it, but so the Scripture
speaks. As her Majesty is seen at the opening of Parliament, as she
drives in her Parks in the sight of her subjects / so God in those days
took his delight in some bodily shape to be with man.

Now *what was the common weal?* what was the joint and common
good of that kingdom?—it was that God should be glorified in man
and man glorified in God. Man was created to praise, honour, and
serve God, thus fulfilling God's desire in bringing him into being,
and by so doing to save his soul, thus fulfilling his own desire, the
desire of everything that has being. He was created to give God
glory and by so doing to win himself glory. This was the good that
first commonwealth aimed at, this was its common weal; and surely
it was the good of all persons, parties, and estates in the commonwealth, all bound up together, in a way and to a degree truly
worthy of the divine wisdom that planned it.

But *the common good is to be realised*, it is to be brought about, *by all*
the citizens or members and estates of the commonwealth *doing their
duty*: so we said. A commonwealth, we said, was bound together
by duty; the sovereign was bound by duty as the subject. Here then
what was the duty God undertook?—Providence. That was the
part, function, office, and duty in that commonwealth God took
upon himself, first to foresee both his and man's joint and common
good, then by his policy and legislation to bring it to pass; to make
the laws, allot the posts and duties, find ways and means, lend
sanction and authority. And man's duty was to obey the laws the

sovereign made, fill the posts, use the means, and put the policy in execution. These were the duties.

Now *to duty answers reward or recompense*. What was to be God's fruit or recompense for doing his duty of providence?—What but to live in the praise and glory which come to successful wisdom? eternal praise and glory from his subjects, men and also angels. And what was to be man's reward and wages for his work done?—Eternal life, glorious peace and power and praise and satisfaction from his king and his angel companions and his own conscience, peace and the sense of life everlastingly in mind and body for the efforts made, the pains taken, the strength spent. For the natural reward of duty, as St. Paul tells us, is life—life in some shape or other, the continuance or the lengthening or the heightening of life, life here or life hereafter or the life of fame in others' minds or life in one's line and offspring or wages, food or money, which are the means of life—every way, for man or God, life is what answers to duty done. But what more particularly the praises and rewards of that kingdom were, how far earthly besides heavenly, how they were to be won and by doing what duties, I think it is needless, perhaps presumptuous, to enquire, for the great machine of that commonwealth and constitution had but made a few strokes when it was shattered and what was after to have been we cannot clearly see. Only these two things we read, that man was put into Paradise to dress and keep it and that he was bidden to increase and multiply and fill the earth and subdue it: he was to keep Paradise, no doubt, against the Devil, for what other creature could have harmed it?—it would have been no Paradise if it were liable to drought and storm, plague, blight, or locust—and next as men multiplied man was to spread over the earth, then as now outside Paradise full of thorns and thistles, and reclaim it piece by piece to the condition of Paradise itself. But alas! he did *not* keep it and so far from turning the waste wilderness of the outside earth into a Paradise he was cast from Paradise out into the waste wilderness.

Next *what were the laws of this kingdom?*—Some laws, you know, command and tell the subject what to do: such were those two that I have just named, of keeping Paradise and of subduing the earth; and others forbid and tell the subject what not to do: there was in God's first kingdom one such law, the famous prohibition to eat of the Tree of Knowledge. Were there, you will ask, no other laws forbidding; none forbidding murder, theft, adultery?—None published in set terms, though murder, adultery, theft, lying were sinful and forbidden then as now; but there it lies, the bliss of that Paradise, the native virtue of that green garden, the easy constitution of that first commonwealth of God, just there it lies, that no frown of God's, no stern and threatening law was needed then; for the still and

private voice of conscience, reason sovereign within the heart, spoke
at the right time the Yes or No and applied God's few laws to the
multitude of circumstances, forbidding murder because how could
man multiply if one man killed another? forbidding adultery because
it was against God's institution of marriage, forbidding theft because
it was against property (if in that Paradise all things were not to be
common, as perhaps they were to be) and so of the rest: they were
against reason, against the good of the commonwealth; that was
enough, they were forbidden, they must not be. *Afterwards* the same
laws were published in thunder from Mount Sinai. There were then,
so far as we know, in that commonwealth but three set and spoken
laws, two commanding and one forbidding, and the two first were so
much in man's own nature that we might almost say there was but
one, the law of the Forbidden Tree. And this law only we need consider.

What was *the forfeit for the breach of it*?—*Death*. Death in the full
sense or in some sense, the ending or the shortening or stinting of life,
is the own necessary punishment of offences against the commonwealth. For, as St. Paul says, in all Law, in every constitution he
means, in every case where laws are made and are in force, *he that
does them shall live by them*;[1] life, as we have heard, is the reward of
law kept, of duty done. And it follows, death is the reward of law
broken. For death is the utmost penalty that can be inflicted by
man: it may not always be the most dreaded, but in itself it is the
greatest and worst, for it ends all. Death takes a man's all, it takes
his being; death ends all. And the other penalties inflicted by the
state and by the laws have the shadow of death in them and that
makes them terrible, they are deaths in miniature: banishment is a
civil death, a being departed, dead and gone, to all the blessings
of the commonweal, home and country, friends and neighbours,
power, the franchise, all; disfranchisement is a civil death *within*
the commonwealth; infamy is a death to fame; imprisonment is a
death to freedom, an abridgment of life's play; fines an abridgment
of life's means and support. All these penalties may be in their
nature suitable and just and death itself most plainly so and answerable to crime. For he that would by high treason break up the
commonwealth or cut off its sovereign head, he that would cut his
brother citizen off from its advantages or make life within the commonwealth a curse instead of a blessing, he shall be cursed and
broken off and cut away from the commonwealth. So that this is the
general rule of commonwealths and the laws in them—the man
that keeps them shall live in them and enjoy their blessings, he that
breaks them utterly shall lose them utterly and die. Therefore death
was the forfeit in the divine commonwealth, in God's first kingdom,

for the breach of the one law; for God the sovereign had staked his honour and authority on that one law and to break it was to revolt, throw off allegiance, dethrone the sovereign, break the contract, and undo the commonwealth.

But, brethren, that I may not be too long and weary you, *here against my first purpose I have resolved to give over for tonight*. And next week we shall have leisure to consider the fall of God's first kingdom and commonwealth, the famous and fatal Fall of Man, in all our history the greatest event after that which came after it and undid it, the crucifixion and man's redemption. For indeed I had at first hoped to speak of God's second kingdom, of that kingdom of God which Christ brought in, of the new City of God and commonwealth of the Catholic Church, but it is too much, the heavenly Jerusalem will not be huddled in a corner, and so I leave this mighty theme altogether untouched. *Next Sunday* then, with God's assistance, *of the Fall.*

L. D. S.

A. M. D. G.

FOR SUNDAY EVENING JAN. 25 1880, SEPTUAGESIMA SUNDAY, AT ST. FRANCIS XAVIER'S, LIVERPOOL—on *the Fall of God's First Kingdom*—'Every kingdom divided against itself shall be made desolate and every city (commonwealth) or house divided against itself shall not stand (Matt. xii 25.)'

[I was not allowed to take this title and on the printed bills it was covered by a blank slip pasted over. The text too I changed to last week's, and had to leave out or reword all passages speaking of God's kingdom as falling]

I am to speak tonight of the fall of God's first kingdom, of the Fall of Man. Those of you who have heard this month's evening sermons will understand how this comes now in due course. God entered in the beginning into a contract with man that they two should make one commonwealth for their common good, which was that God might be glorified in man and man in God; God was the sovereign in this commonwealth and kingdom and man the subject; God by his providence, his laws and appointments and man by his obedience and execution of them undertook to bring this good about; both parties were bound by justice and in justice lived, which in man was called original justice, but lasted / not long. It ended with the Fall, of which I am now to speak.

Before God was king of man he was king of angels and before man fell angels had fallen. Then man was made that he might fill the place of angels. But Satan, who had fallen through pride and selflove, resolved that through pride and selflove man should be brought to fall and that, whereas a breach had been made in God's kingdom in heaven, God's kingdom on earth should be broken utterly to pieces. And as he could not do it by force he would do it by fraud. Now the wise assailant attacks the weakest spot, therefore Satan tempted Eve the woman.

He chose his disguise, he spoke by the serpent's mouth; he watched his time, he found Eve alone. And here some say she should have been warned when she heard a dumb beast speaking reason. But of this we cannot be sure: St. Basil[1] says that all the birds and beasts spoke in Paradise: not of course that they were not dumb and irrational creatures by nature then as now, but if a black spirit could speak by them so could a white and it may be that the angels made use of them as instruments to sing God's praises and to entertain man. Neither would Satan needlessly alarm the woman, rather than that he would invisibly have uttered voices in the air. But when she heard what the serpent said, *then* she should have taken alarm. So then to listen to a serpent speaking might be no blame; but how came Eve to be alone? for God had said of Adam / *It is not good for man to be alone: let us make him a helpmate like himself* /; and Eve was without the helpmate not like only but stronger than herself. She was deceived and Adam, as St. Paul[2] tell us, was not nor would have been. Then why was Eve alone?

Now, I know, my brethren, that the Scripture does not tell us this and we cannot with certainty answer the question, but yet it is useful to ask it because it throws a great light on what God's first kingdom was and how it came to fall. Take notice then that, besides those things which we must do whether we like or no, which we cannot help doing, such as breathe, eat, and sleep, there are three sorts of things that we may lawfully do, that are right in us, that we are within our rights in doing. The first are *our bounden duties*, as to hear mass on Sunday: these God commands. The second are *what God sanctions* but does not command nor in any special way approve, as to amuse ourselves. The third are what God does not command but specially approves when done, as to hear mass on a week-day: these are called *works of supererogation.*[3] All these are good, not only the things God commands and the things he specially approves and accepts but also the things he only sanctions, for he sanctions nothing but what is good, that is to say / nothing but what is in itself harmless and which his sanction then makes positively good, and when a man says / *I do this because I like it and God allows me* / he submits himself to God as truly as if it were a duty and he said / *I do this because God wills it and commands me.* But though all are good they are not equally good; far from that. In the things God sanctions and we do for our own pleasure the whole good, the only good, comes from God's sanction and our submission to his sovereign will; for that he may reward us, but not for anything else: for the rest, we are doing our own pleasure and our own pleasure is our work's reward. But when we do what God commands or what God specially approves, then he is ready to reward us not only for our submission of ourselves to his sovereign will but also for the work done, for the pains taken; for we were doing *his* pleasure, not our own. Now you will easily understand, indeed you know, that it is the mark of a truly good will to do the good God approves of but does not bind us to, to do, in other words, works of supererogation. it shews that good is loved of itself and freely. And it is the mark of a cold heart, of a poor will, I will not say a bad one, to do nothing that God especially approves, only what he commands or else sanctions: it shews that there is little love of good for good's sake. And though no one can be lost but for sin, yet those who do the least good they lawfully can are very likely indeed to fall into doing *less than that least* and so to sin. Now if this applies to us now / very strongly does it apply to man unfallen. For Adam and Eve though they were in God's kingdom not sovereign but subject, yet they were king and queen of all this earth, they were like vassal princes to a sovereign prince, God's honour was more in their hands than it is in any one of ours; we are but ourselves, they represented mankind, they represented the commons in God's commonwealth; if I dishonour God today one of you may make up by honouring him, but if they left him unhonoured who was to honour him? the beasts and birds and fishes? When Adam obeyed God / mankind was obeying its sovereign; when Adam offered God of his own free will unbidden sacrifice / mankind was all engrossed in a work of supererogation, in giving God fresh glory; when Adam was doing his own pleasure / mankind was in its duty indeed but God's honour was not growing, the commonwealth was idle. Now, brethren, with this thought turn to Eve's temptation and look for what shall appear there.

Eve was alone. It was no sin to be alone, she was in her duty, God had given her freedom and she was wandering free, God had made her independent of her husband and she need not be at his side. Only God had made her for Adam's companion; it was her office, her work, the reason of her being to companion him and she was not doing it. There is no sin, but there is no delicacy of duty, no zeal for the sovereign's honour, no generosity, no supererogation. And Adam, he too was alone. He had been commanded to dress and keep Paradise. What flower, what fruitful tree, what living thing was there in Paradise so lovely as Eve, so fruitful as the mother of all flesh, that needed or could repay his tendance and his keeping as she? There was no sin; yet at the one fatal moment when of all the world care was wanted care was not forthcoming, the thing best worth keeping was unkept. And Eve stood by the forbidden tree, which God had bidden them not to eat of, which *she* said God had bidden them not even touch; she neither sinned nor was tempted to sin by standing near it, yet she would go to the very bounds and utmost border of her duty. To do so was not dangerous of itself, as it would be to us. When some child, one of Eve's poor daughters, stands by a peachtree, eyeing the blush of colour on the fruit, fingering the velvet bloom upon it, breathing the rich smell, and in imagination tasting the sweet juice, the nearness, the mere neighbourhood is enough to undo her, she looks and is tempted, she touches and is tempted more, she takes and tastes. But in Eve there was nothing of this; she was not mastered by concupiscence, *she* mastered *it*. There she stood, beautiful, innocent, with her original justice *and with nothing else*, nothing to stain it, but nothing to heighten and brighten it: she felt no cravings, for she was mistress of herself and would not let them rise; she felt no generous promptings, no liftings of the heart to give God glory, for she was mistress of herself and gave them no encouragement. Such was Eve before her fall.

Now, brethren, fancy, as you may, that rich tree all laden with its shining fragrant fruit and swaying down from one of its boughs, as the pythons and great snakes of the East do now, waiting for their prey to pass and then to crush it, swaying like a long spray of vine or the bine of a great creeper, not terrible but beauteous, lissome, marked with quaint streaks and eyes or flushed with rainbow colours, the Old Serpent. We must suppose he offered her the fruit, as though it were the homage and the tribute of the brute to man, of the subject to his queen, presented it with his mouth or swept it from the boughs down before her feet; and she declined it. Then came those studied words of double meaning the Scripture tells us of: *What! and has God forbidden you to eat of the fruit of Paradise?*—Now mark her answer: you would expect her to reply: No, but of this one fruit only: he has given us free leave for all the trees in Paradise excepting one—but hear her: *Of the fruit of the trees in Paradise we do eat*—no mention of God's bounty here, it is all their freedom, what they do: 'we do eat'—*but the fruit of the tree in the midst of Paradise*—as though she would say / of the best fruit of all—*God has commanded us not to eat of, nor so much as touch it, or we shall die:* then she remembers God when it is question of a stern and threatening law. She gave her tempter the clew to his temptation—that God her sovereign was a tyrant, a sullen lawgiver; that God her lord and landlord was envious and grudging, a rackrent; that God her father, the author of her being, was a shadow of death. The serpent took the hint and bettered it. Well was he called subtle: he does not put her suggestion into words and make it blacker; she would have been shocked, she would have recoiled; he gives the thing another turn, as much as to say: Why yes, God would be all this if you took his law according to the letter. No no; what does 'death' mean? you will not *die*: you will die to ignorance, if you will, and wake to wisdom: *God knows, on the day you eat of it your eyes will be opened and you will be as gods, knowing good and evil.* And with these words he dealt three blows at once against God's kingdom—at God as a lawgiver and judge, at God as an owner or proprietor, at God as a father; at God as a lawgiver and judge, for the Serpent said / God has made this the tree of the knowledge of good and evil, that is / which shall decide for him whether to call you good or evil, good if you keep from it, evil if you touch it: be your own lawgivers and judges of good and evil; be as God yourselves, be divinely independent, why not? make it *good* to try the tree, *evil* to leave it untasted; at God as a proprietor, for as owner of man and the earth and all therein and sovereign of the commonwealth God had given the other trees of Paradise to his subjects but reserved this one to the crown: the Serpent advised them to trespass boldly on these rights and seize crown-property; and at God as a father, for God like a fatherly providence found them food and forbad them poison: the Serpent told them the deadly poison was life-giving food. It was enough: Eve would judge for herself. She *saw that the tree was good to eat*, that it was *not* poison, it was the food of life—and here was the pride of life; *that it was beautiful to the eyes*, a becoming object to covet and possess—and here was the desire of the eyes; *and that it was delightful to behold*, that is / sweet and enjoyable in imagination even and forecast, how much more in the eating and the reality!—and here was the desire of the flesh; she freely yielded herself to the three concupiscences; *she took and eat* of this devil's-sacrament; she rebelled, she sinned, she fell.

She fell, but still God's kingdom was not fallen yet, because it turned upon the man's obedience, not the woman's. Then came the meeting between the husband and the wife and she learnt that she was deceived and undone. Then her husband must share her lot for better and worse; this selfish and fallen woman would drag her husband in her fall, as she had had no thought of God's honour in her innocence, so in her sin she had no charity for her husband: she had so little love for him that she said, if he loved her he must share her lot. Most dearly he loved her, and she stood before him now lovely and her beauty heightened by distress, a thing never seen before in Paradise, herself a Tree of Knowledge of Good and Evil and offering him its fruit; herself a Tree of Life, the mother of all flesh to be. For he thought his hope of offspring would go with her. He was wrong: God, who gave back to Abraham for his obedience his all but sacrificed son, would have given back to Adam for his obedience his fallen wife; but he did not pause to make an act of hope. He listened to her voice. He left his heavenly father and clave to his wife and they two were in one fallen flesh; for her he took the stolen goods and harboured the forfeit person of the thief, rebelling against God, the world's great landlord, owner of earth and man, who had bestowed upon him Paradise, who had bestowed upon him the body of his wife; for her he eat the fatal fruit, making a new contract, a new commonwealth with Eve alone, and rebelling against God his lawgiver and judge. With that the contract with God was broken, the commonwealth undone, the kingdom divided and brought to desolation. God was left upon his throne but his subject had deserted to the enemy, God was left with his rights but the tenant had refused him payment, God was left a father but his children were turned to children of wrath. Then followed the disinheriting of the disobedient son; then followed the first and most terrible of evictions, when Cherubim swayed the fiery sword and man was turned from Paradise; then followed the judgment of death and the execution of the sentence which we feel yet. *Wretched men that we are, who shall deliver us from this body of death?—The grace of God through Jesus Christ our Lord* (Rom. vii 24, 25.). *For the wages of sin are death, but the grace of God is eternal life in Christ Jesus our Lord* (ib. vi 23.), a blessing etc.

L. D. S.

[Notes—The first contract and the only one that bound posterity was made with Adam, not Eve, and he broke it as freely as he made it, for he was not deceived. On his sin also the penalties of death, and of the loss of integrity depended; therefore Eve did not feel concupiscence at her own fall (some try to answer this, but the purport of the Scripture is clear).* The punishment to be inflicted on her would have had to be determined by Adam had he stood: he would have been her judge, that is / whether to banish her from the commonwealth or no. Moreover we may conclude that she would have been forgiven and restored for his sake. And some even say she fell by her sin from sanctifying grace only but not from original justice. Perhaps we should distinguish personal justice, of which by such a mortal offence she must have lost the habit, and (so to say) political justice, of which she might have the status still until her trial and sentence. The precept about the Tree is given in the singular, Eve

* But he cannot have known or have thought of this at the time.

repeats it in the plural. The Serpent always puts his temptation in the plural, as though it were a joint act that he was aiming at and to this the Scripture agrees, making Adam's sin the consummation of Eve's, something as though her's were the consent of the lower nature in one man, which is not culpable, or not decidedly and mortally, till the higher consents too.

Man, like the angels, was created in sanctifying grace; then invited to enter into a free contract, covenant, commonwealth / with God, which was original justice.[1] And the remark above seems true too, that we must distinguish there too personal and political justice. The distinction then of sanctifying grace and original justice is almost complete, for the former was before the latter and the latter was, in part at all events, after the former. It is answerable to this that now sanctifying grace is given in baptism and the political justice of belonging to the Catholic Church, to which with the age of reason there either must accede that personal or free justice which depends on free contract or personal and actual sin and injustice and with it the loss of sanctifying grace, but not, in a Catholic, the loss of the political justice of communion with the Church.[2] Eve too was created in political justice. Jan. 11 1882]

FOR SUNDAY APRIL 25TH, THE 4TH AFTER EASTER, AT ST. FRANCIS XAVIER'S, LIVERPOOL, on the Gospel John xvi 5–14. and in particular 8–11 ('*arguet mundum de peccato et de justitia et de judicio*' etc)

[Skip to next leaf]

Notes (for it seems that written sermons do no good)—This Gospel and those for the other Sundays after Easter taken from Christ's discourses *before* Easter, before his Passion, and in particular from the discourse delivered at the Last Supper. They are out of their season and why. Cannot give them the proper attention when engrossed with the Passion. But when he should be gone, Christ said, the Holy Ghost would remind them of what he had said: that time is now and, very suitably, at the earliest opportunity after Easter.

(However the Rector wishes me to write)

Brethren, you see that this Gospel I have just read is taken from that discourse which Christ our Lord made to his disciples the night before he suffered. So is the Gospel for last Sunday, so is the Gospel for next Sunday. The words we read in these Gospels were spoken *before* Easter, on the night before the Passion, and we read them *after* Easter. They come then out of their season. But this cannot be helped; it is reasonable, it is wise and right. During Lent, during Passiontide, it is the Church's wish that the minds of Christians should be full of the Passion, should be engrossed with Christ's sufferings: the mind cannot pay full and proper heed to two thoughts at once, cannot be in two moods at once, and so it cannot, if it is fixed on Christ's sorrows and what he underwent, be free to dwell on Christ's wisdom and the words he said. That must be put off, it has been wisely put off till after Easter and yet not long after, but at the first suitable opportunity to Christ's words the Church returns and so you hear them in last Sunday's and today's and next Sunday's Gospels. But indeed Christ's own words on that same occasion explain all: This, he says (xiv 26.), I have said to you while with you, but when the Holy Ghost is come, *he* shall teach you all my meaning and remind you of all I have said. That time is now come: Christ is gone to heaven, the Holy Ghost has been sent and is, and has long been, at his work of teaching the Church Christ's meaning and reminding it of Christ's words. Therefore it comes about that with the assistance of the same Holy Ghost I must this morning endeavour to bring out Christ's meaning in that Gospel which is this day appointed to be read.

[Begin thus—] In the Gospel which you have just heard, brethren, are words reckoned etc

And that, brethren, is no easy task; for in this same Gospel of today are found words reckoned by writers on Holy Scripture to be among the very darkest and most mysterious that the sacred page contains. But since many enlightened minds and many learned pens have in the course of Catholic ages been busied upon them, it is now to be supposed that this darkness and mystery is in part cleared up and that with their help we need not go far astray. Bend then, my brethren, your ears and minds to follow and understand, for it is the Church that has appointed the words to be read and not for nothing, not for us to stare or sleep over them but to heed them and take their meaning; besides that it seems to me a contemptible and unmanly thing, for men whose minds are naturally clear, to give up at the first hearing of a hard passage in the Scripture and in the holiest of all kinds of learning to care to know no more than children know.

Here then are the mysterious words which we are to consider: *And when he*, that is the Holy Ghost, whom our Lord in this place calls the Paraclete, *has come he will convince the world of sin and of justice and of judgment*, and he adds a reason to each: *of sin*, he says, *because* so and so, *of justice because* so and so, *and of judgment because* so and so. This is what needs explanation and in explaining it / by these steps I shall go: first I shall say what a Paraclete is and how both Christ and the Holy Ghost are Paracletes; then I shall shew what a Paraclete has to do with those three things, sin and justice and judgment; lastly I shall shew why Christ as a Paraclete would not do alone, why it was better for him to go and another Paraclete to come, why Christ's struggle with the world taken by itself looked like a failure when the Holy Ghost's struggling with the world is a success. And in so speaking the meaning of the text will, I hope, have by degrees grown plain.

The first is to say what a Paraclete means. As when the Holy Ghost came on Whitsunday upon the Apostles there was heard a rush of air before the tongues of fire were seen / so when we hear this name of Paraclete our ears and minds are filled with a confused murmuring of some mystery which we know to have to do with the Holy Ghost. For God the Holy Ghost is the Paraclete, but what is a Paraclete? often it is translated Comforter, but a Paraclete does more than comfort. The word is Greek; there is no one English word for it and no one Latin word, *Comforter* is not enough. A Paraclete is one who comforts, who cheers, who encourages, who persuades, who exhorts, who stirs up, who urges forward, who calls on; what the spur and word of command is to a horse, what clapping of hands is to a speaker, what a trumpet is to the soldier, that a Paraclete is to the soul: *one who calls us on,* that is what it means, a Paraclete is one who calls us on to good. One sight is before my mind, it is homely but it comes home: you have seen at cricket how when one of the batsmen at the wicket has made a hit and wants to score a run, the other doubts, hangs back, or is ready to run in again, how eagerly the first will cry / Come on, come on!—a Paraclete is just that, something that cheers the spirit of man, with signals and with cries, all zealous that he should do something and full of assurance that if he will he can, calling him on, springing to meet him half way, crying to his ears or to his heart: This way to do God's will, this way to save your soul, come on, come on!

If this is to be a Paraclete, one who cries to the heart / Come on, no wonder Christ is a Paraclete. For he was one, he said so himself; though the Holy Ghost bears the name, yet Christ is a Paraclete too: *I will send you,* he says, *another Paraclete,* meaning that he himself was a Paraclete, the first Paraclete, the Holy Ghost the second. And did he not cry men on? Not only by words, as by his marvellous teaching and preaching; not only by standards and signals, as by his splendid miracles; but best of all by deeds, by his own example: he led the way, went before his troops, was himself the vanguard, was the forlorn hope, bore the brunt of battle alone, died upon the field, on Calvary hill, and bought the victory by his blood. He cried men on; he said to his disciples, Peter and Andrew, James and John, Matthew at the custom-house, and the rest: Follow me; they did so; he warned all: He that would come after me let him deny himself and take up his cross and follow me; but when they would not follow he let them go and took all the war upon himself. *I have told you,* he said to those who came to arrest him, *that I am Jesus of Nazareth: if therefore you seek me let these go their way.* For though Christ cheered them on they feared to follow, though the Captain led the way the soldiers fell back; he was not for that time a successful Paraclete: *all,* it says, *they all forsook him and fled.* Not that they wanted will; *the spirit was willing:* *Let us go too,* said Thomas, *that we may die with him;* Peter was ready to follow him to prison and to death; *but the flesh was weak:* Peter denied him in his Passion, Thomas in his resurrection, and all of them, *all forsook him and fled.* I say these things, brethren, to shew you that God himself may be the Paraclete, God himself may cheer men on and they too be willing to follow and yet *not* follow, not come on; something may still be wanting; and therefore Christ said: *It is for your own good that I should go; for if I do not go away the Paraclete will not come to you, whereas if I go I shall send him to you.* The second Paraclete was to do what the first did not, he was to cheer men on *and they to follow;* therefore he is called, and Christ is not called, *the* Paraclete.

(2) I have said, brethren, what a Paraclete is and shewn that God the Son as well as God the Holy Ghost is a Paraclete. Next I am to say *what a Paraclete has to do with those three things—sin and justice and judgment.*

If a Paraclete is one who cheers us on to good it must be good that is hard, good that left to ourselves we should hardly reach or not reach at all; it must be in the face of hardships, difficulties, resistance, enemies, that he cheers us on. For now, after the Fall, good in this world is hard, it is surrounded by difficulties, the way to it lies through thorns, the flesh is against it, the world is against it, the Devil is against it: therefore if a Paraclete cheers men on it will be to good that is hard. Now one way or another all that makes good hard is / or comes from / sin. So that a Paraclete must cheer us on to good *in the face of sin.* And one question out of three is soon answered: we see well enough what a Paraclete has to do with sin.

But a Paraclete has also to do with justice. And how?—Why, justice is that very good to which the Paraclete cheers men on. Justice in the Scripture means goodness. If a Paraclete cheers men on to goodness / that is to say he cheers them on to justice. ['And yet' etc—omit all down to the end of the paragraph] And yet, mark you, cheering men on against sin is not the same as cheering men on to justice, though now the two things go together. For if there were no sin in the world and yet man as dull in mind and heart as he is now / a Paraclete might well be needed still to stir him up and set him on, to shew him what justice was and how great its beauty, before man would rouse himself to pursue it. And again if there were no true goodness in the world, nothing, I mean, that would make men just before God, yet if his law still bound them, forbidding sin, they would need a Paraclete to cheer them in resisting sin. However now the Paraclete does both at once, cheers us on to follow justice and to stand against sin. So much then of what a Paraclete has to do with sin and with justice.

There remains what a Paraclete has to do with judgment. Though the Paraclete's voice cry to men to come on to justice and cry to them to stand firm against sin, this will not do alone; the bare word will not do, nay the bare example will not do; there must be some bait before them and some spur or sting behind. This bait and this spur are the thought of God's judgments. There is the bait or prize of hope, the crown in heaven for the just, and there is the spur of fear, the fire of hell for the sinner. And the Paraclete waves before them that golden prize and plies their hearts with that smarting spur. And thus, brethren, it is clearly brought out that a Paraclete has to do, has everything to do, with sin, with justice, and with judgment.

(3) And now lastly we are to hear why it was good that Christ the first Paraclete should go and the Holy Ghost the second Paraclete, *the* Paraclete, should come and why this second Paraclete was to accomplish that task in the world which the first had not, *in his lifetime*, succeeded in accomplishing. This task was to convince the world of sin, of justice, and of judgment. The reason why Christ did not and the Holy Ghost does is not certainly that God the Son is less powerful than God the Holy Ghost: *the Father*, says the Athanasian Creed, *is almighty, the Son almighty, and the Holy Ghost almighty, and they are not three almighties, but one almighty*; their almightiness, their might, their power is one and the same thing. Neither is the reason that though Christ as God is almighty as man he is weak. No, *for the Father*, we read, *had put all things into his hands*. To understand it let us look at what this convincing the world of sin, justice, and judgment means.

When then it is said that the Paraclete *will convince the world* of three things it is meant that he will convict the world of its being wrong about these things, will convince it of himself being right about them, will take it to task about them, reprove it, and so bring the force and truth of his reproof home to it as to leave it no answer to make. He will take it to task upon three heads and leave it no answer. Now did Christ do this, did he leave the world no answer?—Certainly not. To all that Christ taught and did the world's answer was to put him to death and when he rose from the dead the world's

answer for a time was that his disciples had stolen his corpse away—
for a time; that is to say / till the Holy Ghost came.

The world to which Christ spoke was, you know, not the world at
large, not the Roman empire, much less the other kingdoms of the
earth; he spoke only, as he said himself, to the House of Israel. And
he did not convince the world he spoke to, he did not convince
Israel. Neither indeed has the Holy Ghost convinced them yet, but
then they are not the world he speaks to; they are but a very little
part of it. To Christ they were the only world he spoke to and he did
not convince them of his being in the right, did not convict them of
their being in the wrong, on sin or on justice or on judgment. He
spoke to them first of sin: he sent the Baptist before him to preach
the baptism of repentance, then he came himself saying, as we read
(Matt. iv 17.): *Repent, for the kingdom of heaven is at hand.* Did they
repent? remember that when we say the world we mean most
people, not a few: did most of the Jews, did the world of them
repent?—They added to their sins by unbelief, they crowned their
unbelief by crucifying him, the very prophet and Paraclete that
thus reproved them.

Again he spoke to them of justice. He preached the Sermon on
the Mount; he set before the world of them a new standard of goodness and of holiness; a justice higher than that, he said, of their
Scribes and Pharisees; a justice indeed without which he said they
could not enter into the kingdom of heaven, could not be saved.
And not by words only but by his own example; he *did* and taught,
he went about doing good, he challenged them himself to prove a
fault against him: *Which of you*, he asked, *convinces* or *convicts me of
sin?* They could not prove but they could accuse, they could not
convict and yet they would condemn: they called him glutton and
winebibber, sabbathbreaker, false prophet, blasphemer, deserving
of death, no matter by what name, *a malefactor* any road, crying
without shame to the Roman governor when he asked for a particular charge: *If he were not A MALEFACTOR we would not have brought him
to thee.* And they prevailed: as a malefactor he was judged, between
thieves he was crucified, *cum iniquis reputatus est* / he was counted
among evildoers, Jesus Christ the just. So they were not convicted
about sin nor about justice, they were not left without an answer,
Crucify him / was their answer, and they crucified him.

Of judgment it is the same. He warned them of God's judgments:
unless they repented, he said, they should all perish; unless they
believed in him they should die in their sins; the fallen angel was
their father, his desires they would do and of course would share his
fall; Depart, they would hear said of them, cursed, into everlasting
fire, prepared for the Devil and his angels. Their answer was still

the same: *he* was the sinner, the blasphemer, and cursed by God; it was *he* that was on the Devil's side and cast out devils by Beelzebub prince of the devils; it was *he* that by God's own law deserved to die —and should die too, by stoning or somehow: they failed to stone him, get him crucified they did. The world was not convinced about judgment nor put to silence; *he* was put to silence, put to trial, put to death, got rid of. And, mark you, brethren, it was not like a martyrdom now: the tyrant when he has done his worst upon the martyr knows that he has but cut off one Christian or ten or a thousand, there are others yet that he cannot reach; he may wreak his rage on Christians, he cannot rid the world of Christianity. But when Christ the shepherd was struck down the sheep were scattered and without him would not have reunited; when the head was off the body would go to pieces; when Christ died all his words and works came to the ground, all seemed over for ever and the world his enemy's triumph looked that day complete.

But they did not know that their seeming triumph was total defeat, that his seeming defeat was glorious victory. For it was not the world Christ had come to fight but the ruler of this world the Devil.[1] The world he came not to condemn but to save: *God did not send his son into the world*, Christ said, *to judge* (or *condemn*) *the world but that by him the world might be saved*. Only while he preached to them, trying to save them, they were judged by their way of receiving him; therefore he said *Now it is the trial of the world, now the ruler of the world is to be cast out; and I, though taken off the earth, got rid of from the earth, shall draw all things to me*. This then had happened: the rulers of this world, the devils, had crucified the Lord of Glory and at the instant of his death they saw themselves defeated, condemned, cast out, their empire of sin over the souls of men undone and the reins of power on all things drawn into the hand of the crucified victim. They felt it with unutterable dismay and despair but the world did not at that time feel it; the hellish head was crushed but the earthly members were not aware of a wound. They were therefore not convinced or convicted of their sin, of Christ's justice, or of God's judgments.

Christ was gone and in 50 days the Holy Ghost the new Paraclete came. He lost no time, but from nine o'clock in the morning of the first Whitsunday began his untiring age-long ever conquering task of convincing the world about sin and justice and judgment. But first he would play the Paraclete among the disciples before he went out to convince and convert the world. First he cheered *them*, but he cheered them on not like Christ by his example from without but by his presence, his power, his breath and fire and inspiration from within; not by drawing but by driving; not by shewing them what to do but by himself within them doing it. His mighty breath ran

with roaring in their ears, his fire flamed in tongues upon their fore-
heads, and their hearts and lips were filled with himself, with the
Holy Ghost. And they went forth and he went forth in them to convince the world. Hear a sample of how he convinces it. St. Peter spoke
to the multitude, a crowd well representing the world, for there were
men there, it is said, from every nation under heaven. At the end of
his speaking 3000 souls were added to the Church. Three thousand
were at one stroke convinced: here was a beginning of the world's
being convinced and converted indeed. Hear too how it was done.
First he told them that Jesus of Nazareth, a man marked by miracles
with the stamp of God's approval, they had put to death: here then
they were convinced of *their sin* because they had not believed in
Christ. Then he said that this same Jesus God had raised again, that
he had gone up to heaven, and that it was he who had that very day
poured out the Holy Ghost: here then they were convinced of *Christ's
justice*, because he had gone to the Father and could be seen no more.
Lastly he bid them save themselves from that wicked generation,
and they obeyed: they were then convinced that the world they had
belonged to was doing the Devil's work and condemned like him;
they were convinced what God's judgment on the world was, because
its prince was Satan, and he was already judged.

And now, brethren, time fails me. Else I should shew you how the
Holy Ghost has followed and will follow up this first beginning,
convincing and converting nation after nation and age after age till
the whole earth is hereafter to be covered, if only for a time, still to
be covered with the knowledge of the Lord. I should shew too the
manner of his convincing the world, the thousand thousand tongues
he speaks by and his countless ways of working, drawing much more
than I have drawn from my mysterious text, but I must forbear: yet
by silence or by speech to him be glory who with the Father and the
Son lives and reigns for ever and ever. Amen.[1]

FOR SUNDAY MAY 30, THE 2ND AFTER PENTECOST, AT ST. FRANCIS
XAVIER'S, LIVERPOOL—on the Gospel Luke xiv 16–24. (*the
parable of the Supper and the Guests that would not come*)

[This is not, I think, the same as that in Matt. xxii 1–14.,
though they are variants and the same in general bearing]

This parable, brethren, that we read today is like one to be found
in the xxii. chapter of St. Matthew, the parable of the Marriage
Feast and the Wedding Garment. In most points they are alike, in
some they are different, so that some writers say they are the same,

others that they are not; but they were, as it seems, spoken at different times and if so it is not surprising that our Lord varied the story to suit the circumstances and his own purpose. In the same way if one of you had to tell a story to country children and afterwards to town children you might well put in some things and leave out others to suit your little hearers, speaking to the country children of fields and daisies, to the town's children of streets and shops.[1] So then here.

The parable itself is not a hard one, it needs no very long explanation. However I shall speak of one or two points or difficulties in it; next I shall give its meaning and application to the world and history; lastly I shall speak of how it applies to ourselves.

The first of the difficulties or strange points to be found in the parable is that many were asked to the supper, we are told, and *all* of these refused to come—which seems a thing incredible, for one man might make one excuse, another another, out of many, and not come, that might happen, but that all should refuse, that out of those many not one should do his duty; shew common civility; nay if it were no more than care for a handsome entertainment, not even care for that, how do we account for this?—how, brethren, but by remarking those words *with one accord*? 'With one accord', we read more clearly in the Greek, 'they began to excuse themselves'—at one signal, as it were. For so it was, it was a conspiracy, a thing got up among them to pass a joint and public slight on the most eminent of their fellow citizens, a slight much more grievous than individual neglect and more shamefully thankless, graceless, heartless, and malignant. How else could they have refused with one accord? This then is how that came to pass. They meant him with his empty hall and untasted banquet to be the laughingstock of the whole town: it turned out otherwise. He laughs best that laughs last, he laughs best that has the most to laugh with him; and so it happened with their host and them.

So then instead of the well-to-do guests who were above coming were called the poor that had never thought to be asked and for those the men of business, the men of action, the men of pleasure that went off after their own enterprises, their newbought farms and oxen, or stayed at home with their brides, were brought in the feeble and the blind and the lame, those that could scarcely come if they wished, that must be carried, led, or helped to the banquet hall, and after these again for townsfolk and neighbours the farm hands and outlying country people, that had not so much as seen from out of doors the splendour of a city feast, all these were led, carried, drawn, or driven in till the house was filled.

This must have taken time. For suppose the supper or dinner, as we should rather call it, had first been fixed for, say, two in the afternoon, then when each of the invited guests had made his excuse and the servant had returned with these to his master and gone forth again with orders to bring the poor, feeble, blind, and lame and had brought them or got them brought, which could scarcely be over before evening, after this, I say, when he was gone the third time forth and further, into the open country, had scoured the country, the lanes and hedges, and with his fellowservants and men under him brought the throng of country people in, it must have been nightfall and dark before the house was full and the supper served to all of them. The hall would be lit up, the town alive with the guests flocking thither, no supper would be so famous as that one.

The parable ends with the words 'But I say unto you that none of those men that were invited shall taste of my supper' and in these there is something that may seem surprising. For why, one might ask, what need of saying that? Of course they will not taste of it; it is what they do not care to do, do not want to do, have expressly refused to do, have gone out of town not to do: why then does the host lay such a stress on his not giving the thing they will not take? Is it that the first bidden guests repented and would gladly have come when it was too late and every place was filled? And why should they repent?—Because the tables were turned; because—no other word puts it so clearly—the tables had been turned on them. They had meant to leave their host's house empty and it was filled, his supper untasted and all the world, so to say, tasted it but themselves; they had meant him to be left by himself a laughingstock to the town, and town and country had gathered to him; they only were left out; they were the laughingstock; they had meant to give the chief citizen a slight which should lower him below the least of themselves and they found themselves replaced by strangers, put below beggars and cripples. This then is what those words mean, 'But I say unto you that none of those men that were invited shall taste of my supper', that is / They say they will not taste of it, they shall not; they shall find the tables turned on them; it shall not be they that refuse me, I tell you I refuse them; my feast shall go forward with lights and wine and music into the night, I have my guests in plenty, but they—no, not one of *them* shall taste my supper.

We come now to the interpretation of the parable. And the purport of it is that the Jews were first called and when they would not come in their place the Gentiles, the rich and learned were first addressed and when they would not hear the poor had the Gospel preached to them. For we read that the parable was spoken at the dinnertable of a Pharisee; there something our Lord had said gave occasion to one of the guests to say 'Blessed is he that shall eat bread in the kingdom of God', and on this Christ in return spoke our parable. For this man, the guest of a Pharisee, himself, it is likely, a Pharisee, said what was true enough—it *is* blessed to eat bread, that is go to communion, in God's kingdom here and feast on the open vision of God in his kingdom hereafter—but did not see that if he believed in Christ, who was beside him at the table, he would himself then and there be eating bread in the kingdom of God. And this hint Christ gave him in the parable.

For the man that gave the supper means God and the supper is the kingdom of God, which Christ had come to set up on earth, namely the Catholic Church and the true and divine religion. He had appointed the time of this supper by the mouth of his prophets beforehand and in particular by his prophet Daniel and lastly St John Baptist and the place, namely that Christ should be born in Bethlehem of Juda, that he should teach in Galilee, and be a king in Jerusalem. These prophecies were known to the learned, to the educated classes: these were therefore the guests first invited to the feast. Then when the time was come God sent his servant, by which is meant not so much John the Baptist as Christ our Lord himself; for Christ, who as God is equal to the Father, as man is his servant. He told them that the kingdom of heaven was at hand. But they did not heed him and went away some in pursuit of wealth and power, like that man who went to see his new farm; some in love with learning or name and fame and honour, like that other that went to try his ploughing oxen, for as the oxen are taught to bear the yoke, draw the plough, and tread straight the furrow, so the Doctors in the Law taught each generation of the young Israelites the tradition of their fathers and took a pride to lay the stress of their own minds and influence on the minds of the younger men; and lastly some for love of pleasure, like the man that said he had married a wife and could not come. And this they did with one accord, for when they agreed not to believe in John the Baptist then they gave a general sign that they would not come to Christ nor enter the kingdom he was setting up.

But whereas the learned and wealthy, who knew the Law and the Prophets, that is / who had been invited long beforehand, would not come to Christ, those who little knew them came, the shepherds and fishermen, the publicans and sinners, the poor and feeble and blind and lame of the parable, and of these for the most part the Church at first was made up and it was but small, they were but a few thousand Jews, there was room for many many more.

So the Gentiles were called and before them St. Paul Apostle of the Gentiles, who was treated with violence and, as the parable puts it, compelled to come in. And as we may suppose the great man's servant as he caught one countryman took him with him and turned him to call others, so St. Paul and thousands of others heretofore, now, and hereafter have been and are and will be engaged in converting souls and bringing them to the Catholic Church, to the holy altar, and to the supper of God's kingdom. When all the elect are brought in, then it will be nighttime, the night of the world, the world's end; then those who have refused to come, not only the proud among the Jews but all unbelieving heathens, misbelieving heretics, and disobedient Catholics, will be shut out in the outer darkness and will have it said over them: Not one of them shall taste of my supper.

And this, brethren, concerns us; of this lastly I shall speak. It is not a question of Jews or heathens, of things far off or long ago: where is God's supper spread?—Where but in every town that has a Catholic Church, where but here at this altar? The supper, the feast is the Holy Mass; to be at the feast is to assist at mass, to hear mass, to share the feast is to go to communion. The guests are ourselves, you and me; we are the invited guests; yes you are the guests that were first asked, for since your childhood you have known your duties, you have heard the invitation to mass and communion. Then when the time comes we are warned again, when Lent begins we are reminded of our Easter duties and as for our weekly duties the very coming of Sunday, the sound of the bells are a warning and a reminder to us that God's supper is ready and we must go.

[This sermon is not to be delivered and therefore will not be finished, as Fr. Kavanagh of West Leigh is coming here to preach for his two new missions instead. May 22 1880]

LIVERPOOL SERMONS

II

A. M. D. G.

FOR THE FEAST OF ST. PETER AND ST. PAUL JUNE 29 1880—AT
ST. FRANCIS XAVIER'S, LIVERPOOL

On this day, my brethren, is kept the feast of the two great
Apostles Peter and Paul, in dignity the greatest of the Apostles; the
one of them the rock on which the Church is built, the doorkeeper
to whom are given the keys of the kingdom, the Prince of the
Apostles, Christ's first viceroy, the Church's first head, after Christ
ascended, upon earth; the other the Apostle of the Gentiles, the
great vessel of election, the twice-sevenfold mouthpiece of the Holy
Ghost. They died on one day, today, by the cross and by the sword;
they sealed the Gospel they preached by their blood; lovely and
loveable in their lives in death they were not divided; their sacred
bodies make holy the city of Rome.[1] Out of their lives and deaths
this is the thought that tonight I shall gather: God's strength is made
perfect in weakness, God that did such great things for these his two
Apostles can do great things for the weakest and the worst of us here.

St. Peter was a fisherman, a poor man, a man of low degree. He
could have had but little schooling even in the Law and the learning
of the Jews and none at all in that of the Gentiles. He was therefore
very unfit to have to dispute, as he afterwards had, out of the Law
and the Prophets with men who were deeply read in them and still
more was he unfit to reason with the philosophers of the Greeks,
with whose philosophy and manner of reasoning he could have no
acquaintance whatever. But you will say that he had at least zeal
and energy, which might go far to make up for the want of learning,
and that he had the priceless blessing of more than 3 years' constant
training by Christ himself. He had, but he could not be depended
on; he trusted in all this himself and fell; in the moment of trial he
was found wanting, he denied his master; he said that he would die
for him, but at a word from a woman he denied him and fell. His
master had called him by a name that meant Rock, yet when something was to be built upon his firmness, lo, he turned to sand, the
building fell and to this day, so to speak, we hear ringing the crash
of it: *I tell you, I do not know the man.*

[This sermon is not to be preached either]

FOR FRIDAY EVENING JULY 23 1880 AT ST. FRANCIS XAVIER'S, LIVERPOOL—*on St. Mary Magdalen* (whose feast is July 22) and the love of the Sacred Heart shewn towards her (these Friday evening sermons are supposed to have to do with the Sacred Heart) as gathered chiefly from the Gospel for the feast Luke vii 36–50.

[I preached also the Friday before, but at half an hour's notice and have no notes. The sermon was made out of an old one in this book and was on our Lord's fondness for praising and rewarding people. I thought people must be quite touched by this consideration and that I even saw some wiping their tears, but when the same thing happened next week I perceived that it was hot and that it was sweat they were wiping away]

Notes—St. Mary Magdalen's feast yesterday: her history is of all things we read the great encouragement for sinners and a bright picture of the mercy of the Sacred Heart. This also will shew what I spoke of last Friday, how Christ loves to praise and to reward

She had heard of Christ, knew he was a prophet, a man come from God, a lover of men, bringing a message of forgiveness for sinners; now *she hears he is in the very town*, a chance has offered itself, mercy is at her doors, she will not let the good day, the golden opportunity slip. Christ was her good and she would make her way to it. He was dining at a Pharisee's, to that house she went

Here see *her faith*—she knows where God is. Bad as she was she would not be blinded. She did not love darkness rather than light though her works were evil; rather she came to the light though she was to be made manifest, to be shewn a sinner, by it. But how many a heretic loves his heresy, how many a bad Catholic loves his impurity or his fraud better than the light of truth and virtue! keeps from the church, the mass, the priest, wants to live in peace, that is in sin, even sometimes to die in peace, that is in calm despair and damnation.

Her humility: she exposes herself to the contempt of the company, to the severe judgment of Christ, to rebuff and refusal—

Her boldness: Unasked she thrusts in and while she humbles herself at Christ's feet faces the scene and the company. This humility mixed with courage or itself courage. She did what others would not have stooped to, would not have dared—

Her generosity: the rich ointment, the vessel of costly and translucent alabaster—[1]

Her devotion, the dedication of herself to her work: her wealth first, then the hair of her own head and the kisses of her endearments of a person the beauty of which had hitherto been given over to self and to sin and to Satan

The scene: imagine the silence, the conversation dropping off, all eyes gradually drawn to the strange spectacle, all waiting what is to follow. How will he take it? The thoughts of one we know, the host: Simon was saying to himself, 'If this man were a prophet' etc: he thinks Christ is detected

At last Christ speaks: the Creditor with the Two Debtors, Simon's answer, Christ's application

Wisdom of this answer: There is no wisdom, there is no prudence, there is no counsel against the Lord (Prov. xxi 30.); Simon had dug a pit and fell himself into it; the wise man was caught in his own shrewdness (1 Cor. III 19, Job v 13.). He had thought to detect Christ and prove him no prophet, but Christ detected *him* and proved himself a prophet and more than a prophet. For he not only knew the woman was a sinner but he read Simon's secret thoughts. Though indeed his attempt to catch Christ was not a wise one, it was a piece of folly and not of wisdom; for a man may be a true prophet and yet not know everything: Balaam the prophet was a bad man and would gladly have had king Balac's gold, but he acknowledged he could say nothing but what God told him and know nothing but what God shewed him. If then Christ had been a prophet and no more than a prophet, why was God bound to shew him whether each man and woman was just or a sinner? But Christ's answer did shew that he was a prophet and more than a prophet, a searcher of hearts

Kindness of the answer all round: he defends Magdalen, he does not reproach Simon his host. Her he acknowledges to have been a sinner, but he makes her just; and Simon he supposes to have little sin to answer for. He does not undervalue Simon's service, for the things Simon had not done he was not expected to do; only he fully values Magdalen's and seems to say / After all you did not go so far as this

Her reward: the forgiveness of her sins. *Remittuntur ei* etc. Here a difficulty. Was she forgiven because she loved or did she love because she was forgiven? The words are that she was forgiven because she loved, but surely it should be the other way; for the two debtors first were forgiven and then loved. But the meaning is / Where you see in a sinner much love, as you see it in this woman, you may suppose there has been much sin, again where you know there has been much sin, as there has been in this woman, there you may expect to find much love, as here you find it; and on the other hand where there is little love shewn, as you have shewn little compared with hers, there we may hope there has been little sin to forgive, and where we suppose there has been little sin, as we suppose of you, there we must not be surprised to find little love. It is then a kind of compliment to both and a warning to both; a compliment to her for her generosity, to him for his good life; a warning to her to do penance, to him to have more charity

But more may be said. She not only loved because she was forgiven, she was also forgiven because she loved: both things are true. When she came she came as a sinner, she had heard no forgiveness spoken, she came to get it, and to get it she shewed all that love: in this way then she was forgiven because she loved. On the other hand she knew of Christ's love, she knew he *offered* mercy to the sinner, to the great sinner great mercy, this love of his was first, mercy, forgiveness, *offered* forgiveness, on Christ's part came first and because he forgave her, that is offered to forgive her she loved: So then she loved because she was forgiven

[And a little more. After this sermon one of my penitents told me, with great simplicity, that I was not to be named in the same week with Fr. Clare. 'Well' I said 'and I will not be named in the same week. But did you hear it all?' He said he did, only that he was sleeping for parts of it]

FOR SUNDAY SEPT. 12 1880, 17TH AFTER PENT., AT ST. FRANCIS XAVIER'S, LIVERPOOL, on the Gospel Matt. xxii 35—end (the Answer to the Pharisees about *the Great Commandment* and the Qn. to them about *Christ the Son of David*)

When Christ our Lord, brethren, near his life's end was at the height of his renown as a prophet at Jerusalem and taught in public in the Temple / his jealous enemies, who were in the end to kill him, tried by fairer means first to put him down and overthrow his reputation. They put to him questions in public which if he did not satisfactorily answer he would be publicly discredited. And first, we read, the Pharisees sent to him their disciples with the Herodians. They did not go, the leading men among them, themselves, they would manage things if they could by a catspaw; so they send their *disciples*, as if in dispute with the Herodians, worldly men Herod's partisans; the Pharisees' disciples holding in that dispute that it was not lawful to give tribute to Caesar the Roman emperor and the others, supporters of Herod the king, who was himself supported by the favour of the emperor, maintaining that it was. To Christ they referred the question, meaning if he decided against Caesar to get him into trouble with the Roman governor and if in Caesar's favour to make him unpopular with the people. But he made such an answer as was bound to satisfy all except those whose bad purposes were baffled by it. After this came, openly and in their own persons, the Sadducees, that sect that denied the Resurrection; *they* had a question to catch Christ by, the question about the woman with the seven husbands, but by the answer he made they were themselves caught and put to silence. And the Pharisees, for they were the other great sect among the Jews, more right-thinking than the Sadducees but fuller of spiritual pride, they, you may be sure, were very glad that their rivals should have had this public encounter with Christ before themselves; for whichever way it turned out, they had said to themselves, it would be to their advantage. *They* were friends neither to the Sadducees nor to Christ: if Christ could not answer the Sadducees, there was an end of Jesus the prophet, false-prophet they called him, of Nazareth; or if Christ got the better of it, there was a blow at the Sadducees. Either way they would be the gainers. Therefore when Christ put the Sadducees to silence they were not sorry: now, they thought to themselves, he has put them down; we will put him down, and we shall have all the glory, we shall be left masters of the field.

Therefore they skilfully chose a question to put and they skilfully chose the person to put it. This was a man learned in the Law, one of themselves indeed, a Pharisee, but well inclined towards Christ and, what was much to their purpose, who could ask a question of him not captiously as if to entangle him but with a friendly and respectful manner and indeed with the sincere wish to hear Christ's judgment; for Christ, we read in St. Mark, told him that he was not far from the kingdom of God. The question therefore which he put may have been of his own choosing; the Pharisees his friends may have heard it first, approved of it, and as good as said to him: Hear what the man you admire makes of this and judge him accordingly. For they thought it was one that Christ would not find it easy to answer.

The question then was, as we read in today's Gospel, what was the great commandment in the Law. The Law, my brethren, is long; it contains first the Ten Commandments, then a multitude of other, more detailed commandments about right and wrong, sin and justice; about tithes, offerings, and sacrifices; about feasts and holidays; of how to make war and treat enemies; of how to treat animals; of how to make the tabernacle and all its parts and furniture; of what the priests and of what lay men should and should not wear; of how the tribes should march; of where they should settle, with the names of all their boundaries; and all this mingled with threats and promises and words of exhortation. Now it has always been considered the mark of a wise and philosophical mind to be able to reduce a great deal to a little compass, to draw from things their pith and kernel, and to speak volumes in a proverb or an epigram, something as Christ was asked to do here. But there was more than this; for he needed to say not what was the purport, the meaning, and the main drift and duty of the Law, which he might have done in his own words, but to find his answer, if that were possible, in the words of the Law itself. For that clearly would lay him much less open to denial and dispute, quibbling and quarreling. However the Pharisees knew well enough that this task, delicate as it was, might very likely successfully be accomplished by such a mind as they felt Christ's to be, and that would not have done for them; no, they hoped that under the circumstances Christ was in the trap whatever his answer should be; they thought that their question might be answered, but never by Christ—*he* was the one man who could not be served by *any* answer to it.

Why so?—Because, my brethren, they said to themselves / This upstart of Galilee, this would-be prophet, this man sent from God, as he pretends, and his way prepared by the Baptist, another pretender, is not satisfied with the Law,—he aims at overthrowing, at superseding it; he is always talking of, of late especially he has been telling parable after parable about, a certain Kingdom of God and Kingdom of Heaven, which men must enter, which we the Pharisees and lovers of the Law have not entered; as though Israel were not God's kingdom and the Law, mark this, as though the holy law given by God himself on Sinai did not tell the way to heaven plain enough for all the true prophets and holy men of old, our fathers for generations and generations before us. And that Law we study, we know, we practise ourselves, as all the world sees we do, and teach to others; while he both breaks it and approves of breaches in it: he forbids divorce, which the Law allows, and allows Sabbath-breaking, which the Law forbids; he dares to despise it, makes it a worn-out gone-by cast-away thing, an 'old wineskin' and spoken 'to men of old time'[1] and not for our days. Now then at last let him speak in public and to us, not on mountains of Galilee and in corners to his partisans, but to readers of the Law in the Temple of Jerusalem: is he for God's Law or is he against it—one or the other? If he is *for* the Law let him only tell us what is the great commandment in it; that by his own shewing will be the main thing to do and teach; *we* practise and we teach it, whatever it is, for so we do all the Law; then let him say why he does not spend his pains in preaching *that*, if he is a prophet, and further let him say why he does not fall into the ranks of our disciples, the Law's recognised interpreters, and submit to our guidance. But if he is against the Law let him dare to say so in the hearing of all this people in this most holy place and we shall soon see what men will say of him; his ambition is dashed to the ground for ever. Or perhaps, since he will scarcely venture to speak against it, he will put himself above it and say plainly he is the Messias, as John Baptist said he was, of whom the Law prophesies: ah, let him say where the Law prophesies of *him*, a Galilean Messias, born who knows where?[1] It will be strange if we who know the Law cannot tell the marks of the true Messias when he stands before us, and certainly we find them not in him: we hold him and with reason an impostor, we are against him and we are right to be. Now at last it will be clear who is right and who is wrong in this struggle and this rivalry and it is his own mouth that shall condemn him.

Thus, brethren, they thought, but there is no wisdom, there is no prudence, there is no counsel against the Lord. It was their last question. After this they could only use violence and when the High Priest bid our Lord tell him if he were the Christ he forced the answer from him by calling on him in the name of the Most High God.

Let us then hear Christ's answer. And fully to understand this and the scene that was taking place we must look not only at the account St. Matthew gives in today's Gospel nor at St. Mark's either but also at what St. Luke has in quite another place,[2] where however I cannot doubt he is writing about the same event, though it suits him to change its order. Christ had to say what was the great commandment of the Law, not what *he* thought was such but to shew what it was that the Law itself put forward as its great commandment. He did so: he answered the question about the Law from the Law, in the words of the Law, nay he was wiser, he went further, he got it read out from the roll of the Law by the very man that had put the question. For it would seem from St. Luke that Christ called for one of the volumes or rolls of the Law, which the Jews kept in Temple and synagogue as we keep missals in churches, unrolled it, found the place he wanted—it was the 6th chapter of the Book of Deuteronomy, the 4th and 5th verses—handed it to his questioner, and bid him read, *What is written in the Law?* he asks; *how readest thou?* that is to say / Thou shalt have the very words of the Law, here they are, read them out thyself. And here St. Mark's Gospel[3] gives us not the sense of the passage but the very words then read: *Hear, O Israel, the Lord thy God is one God, and thou shalt love the Lord thy God with thy whole heart and with thy whole soul and with thy whole mind and with thy whole strength.* These words the lawyer read; then said Christ: *Thou hast answered rightly,* that is to say / That is the right answer and that is the first and great commandment; for the answer, you understand, was Christ's answer, *he* had found the passage, but he had made it in the Law's words and from the lawyer's lips; therefore he says, in St. Luke's account, '*Thou* hast answered rightly.'

And here, brethren, you can fancy the feeling of the assembly and how at this all the hearers drew breath. There, they said to themselves, at least is an answer. And the plot, as we say, thickened, the interest and excitement heightened; for, thought they, as far as words go, as far as question and answer go, our question is answered and very clever and adroit it was of the Galilean too in the manner of its making. Only now comes the pinch, now his foot is in the trap and his own wisdom has betrayed him; *now* he has got to tell us, if this is the one great commandment, what more it is he has come to teach Israel than Israel has in the Law already. If this is the way to the Kingdom of Heaven what need have we of him to shew us the way and what right has he to tell us, as he does, that we are not already in it? What breath is there, besides, of his being the Messias in words like these? Let him leave us our great commandment and we can do without both John the Baptist and Jesus of Nazareth.

And perhaps they were coming forward again, but Christ did not allow it. He was master of the situation now. They had expected that he would add something to the great commandment, something on his own behalf: he did add something, but not what should give them fresh handles on him but what should silence them the more entirely. He had told them the first commandment, he now spoke of a second. *This*, he said, *is the first and great commandment, and the second is like it*, that is / is in keeping with it, is what you would expect from it, and follows from it. And here we may suppose he found the other place—it was from the Book of Leviticus, the 19th chapter and the 18th verse—and made the lawyer read that too: it was *Thou shalt love thy neighbour as thyself*. There was, he said, no other commandment to be compared with these two: the one was the first, the other the last, they took all duty in and on them hung all that was written in Law and Prophets.

Now the wisdom of this answer all present felt, but it acted on them in opposite ways. For as the sun, we know, melts wax and bakes clay and as one man's meat is another's poison, so Christ's answer both angered and silenced his enemies and they dared ask no more, but the lawyer whom they had put forward to question Christ and who, as I have said, was not his enemy but well disposed, he was pleased and his tongue loosened and he did ask another question even. Struck with admiration, he said that surely what Christ had taught was true and that so to love God and so to love one's neighbour was more than all holocausts and sacrifices. For, at that moment, he had an insight of the truth which when he had read the Law among his Pharisee instructors perhaps he had never seen, namely that all we do is nothing and cannot help us unless we do it for God's sake and that religion outwardly is barren unless there is charity within. And because of his wise insight Christ told him that he was not far from the Kingdom of God, giving him and all present to understand that they *did* stand in need of Christ, that they *had* something new to learn of him, nothing indeed that was not included in those two commandments, for so Christ himself allowed—*Keep these*, he said, *and live*—but nevertheless something they did not truly know, *how* to keep them. The lawyer therefore spoke again, wishing, we are told, to justify himself, that is / to become just before God and save his soul: *And who*, he asked, *is my neighbour?* Christ in answer told the story of the Good Samaritan, which however is not read in the Gospel of today.

So much for the best among the Pharisees, the wellmeaning one, but now for the others, for Christ's enemies. They were silenced, they were beaten, for they felt that Christ had put himself in the right and them in the wrong; he had made it appear that he kept the great commandments and they did not. For it was known, they could not deny, that he went about, seemingly at least, doing good to all men, comforting the afflicted, forgiving sinners, healing the sick, raising the dead, in all things loving his neighbour and willing to help him, including themselves the Pharisees, though himself a stranger, a Galilean, something like a Samaritan; and all this under the shew, they could not deny that it was the shew, of love and zeal for God. Whereas they, that also professed a zeal for God, they, priests and levites, were not famous for their charity to men and towards Christ in particular their enmity no longer was disguised. So that he might after all be the Messias sent by God and they to blame for not receiving him. And while they stood thus sullen in their confusion, Christ, not to insult or triumph over them, but that being defeated they might never rally, to make his victory secure, and fasten the minds of his hearers weak in their faith and doubting, asked *them* a question in his turn, a question about the Messias. This question we will not now discuss, time does not allow, but the force of asking it was this: the Pharisees would not hear of Christ's being the promised Messias; did they then know who the Messias was to be, what he would be like, what were the marks to know him by when he should come? did they, students of the Law and the Prophets, know what the Law and the Prophets said of him and could they explain it? Christ tried them with a passage and they could not. And all who witnessed understood that there was about Messias some great mystery and that Christ who asked this question knew the secret of it, but that that was hidden from the Pharisees, according to that saying attributed to Christ: *My mystery is for me and for the children of my house.*

[In preaching I then added] You see, brethren, I have said nothing by way of exhortation to you to keep those two great commandments of the love of God and the love of your neighbour; I could not both do that and explain the Gospel, and I wanted to explain the Gospel. After all every sermon we hear, every pious book we read, everything in religion is always bidding us to keep these two commandments, on which hang the Law and the Prophets, the Old Testament and the New. My endeavour was to put before you another sample of Christ our Lord's wisdom, of the divine wisdom which dwelt in him, of the human wisdom and genius which were his as man; which think of them and study as we may we shall never reach to the bottom of, but yet by thinking of often we may come to make more of and love more every day; a blessing etc.

L. D. S.

FOR MONDAY EVENING OCT. 25 1880 *on Divine Providence and the Guardian Angels,* THE 24TH BEING THE FEAST OF ST. RAPHAEL (I have preached on Monday the 4th and the 11th also, but could put down no notes)

Notes—God knows infinite things, all things, and heeds them all in particular. We cannot 'do two things at once', that is cannot give our full heed and attention to two things at once. God heeds all things at once. He takes more interest in a merchant's business than the merchant, in a vessel's steering than the pilot, in a lover's sweetheart than the

[In consequence of this word *sweetheart* I was in a manner suspended and at all events was forbidden (it was some time after) to preach without having my sermon revised. However when I was going to take the next sermon I had to give after this regulation came into force to Fr. Clare for revision he poohpoohed the matter and would not look at it]

lover, in a sick man's pain than the sufferer, in our salvation than we ourselves.[1] The hairs of our heads are numbered before him. He heeds all things and cares about all things, but not alike; he does not care for nor love nor provide for all alike, not for little things so much as great, brutes as men, the bad as the good, the reprobate who will not come to him as the elect who will. It was his law that the ox should not be muzzled that trod out the corn, but this provision was made for an example to men, not for the sake of the beast; for: Does God care for oxen? asks St. Paul; that is to say, compared with his care for men he does not care for them. Yet he does care for them and for every bird and beast and finds them their food. Not a sparrow, our Lord says, falls to the ground without your Father, that is / without his noticing and allowing and meaning it. But we men, he added, are worth many, that is / any number of, sparrows. So then God heeds all things and cares and provides for all things but for us men he cares most and provides best.

Therefore all the things we see are made and provided for us, the sun, moon, and other heavenly bodies to light us, warm us, and be measures to us of time; coal and rockoil for artificial light and heat; animals and vegetables for our food and clothing; rain, wind, and snow again to make these bear and yield their tribute to us; water and the juices of plants for our drink; air for our breathing; stone and timber for our lodging; metals for our tools and traffic; the songs of birds, flowers and their smells and colours, fruits and their taste for our enjoyment. And so on: search the whole world and you will find it a million-million fold contrivance of providence planned for our use and patterned for our admiration.

But yet this providence is imperfect, plainly imperfect. The sun shines too long and withers the harvest, the rain is too heavy and rots it or in floods spreading washes it away; the air and water carry in their currents the poison of disease; there are poison plants, venomous snakes and scorpions; the beasts our subjects rebel, not only the bloodthirsty tiger that slaughters yearly its thousands, but even the bull will gore and the stallion bite or strike; at night the moon sometimes has no light to give, at others the clouds darken her; she measures time most strangely and gives us reckonings most difficult to make and never exact enough; the coalpits and oilwells are full of explosions, fires, and outbreaks of sudden death, the sea of storms and wrecks, the snow has avalanches, the earth landslips; we contend with cold, want, weakness, hunger, disease, death, and often we fight a losing battle, never a triumphant one; everything is full of fault, flaw, imperfection, shortcoming; as many marks as there are of God's wisdom in providing for us so many marks there may be set against them of more being needed still, of something having made of this very providence a shattered frame and a broken web.

Let us not now enquire, brethren, why this should be; we most sadly feel and know that so it is. But there is good in it; for if we were not forced from time to time to feel our need of God and our dependance on him, we should most of us cease to pray to him and to thank him. If he did everything we should treat him as though he did nothing, whereas now that he does not do all we are brought to remember how much he does and to ask for more. And God desires nothing so much as that his creatures should have recourse to him.

But there is one great means he has provided for every one of us to make up for the shortcomings of his general and common providence. This great and special providence is the giving each of us his guardian angel. *He has given,* the Scripture says, *his angels commands about thee, to keep thee in all thy ways.* And we learn from what our Lord said to his disciples that every child, that every human being, however low and of little account, is given in charge to a blessed and heavenly spirit, a guardian angel: *Beware,* said he, *of despising one of these little ones* (which means not only children but all who are in any other way little or of little account): *I tell you their angels always see the face of my Father in heaven* (Matt. xviii 10.).

Consider, brethren, what a wonderful honour this is. We men are cared for by angels, fallen men by blissful spirits; we who are so full of the miseries of the flesh that we cannot bear at times to be in each other's presence are watched without ceasing by these glorious beings, and while they have us poor wretches in their sight they are at the same time gazing on the face of God. How much does God make of us when he will have his very courtiers, those who are about his throne, to look after us men, even the lowest amongst us! It may fill us with shame to be so honoured; it may also fill us with shame to think how we are watched and seen, for there is nothing we do but comes under the eye not of God only but of another witness besides, our guardian angel. He counts all our steps, he knows every hair of our heads, he is witness of all our good deeds and all our evil; he sees all and remembers all. Even our hearts he searches, for he sees them in the light of God's knowledge and God reveals to him all that can be of service to him in his charge and duty of leading the human being entrusted to him to the kingdom of heaven. But though he knows and remembers all the harm we have done he will not be our accuser; where he cannot help us he will be silent; he will speak but of our right deeds and plead in our defence all the good he has observed in us. His whole duty is to help us to be saved, to help us both in body and soul. We shall do well therefore to be ashamed of ourselves before our guardian angel, but not to have no other feelings than shame and dread towards him; for he is our good faithful and charitable friend, who never did and never could sleep one moment at his post, neglect the least thing that could be of service to us, or leave a stone unturned to help us all the days that we have been in his keeping. We should deeply trust him, we should reverence and love him, and often ask his aid.

Here, brethren, I must meet an objection which may be working on your minds. If everyone has so watchful and so strong a keeper at his side why is there such a thing as sudden death, as catching fever, as taking poison by mistake, as being shot or any way injured, even as a stumble or a fall, a scald or a sprain? What are the guardian angels doing that they let such things be?—To begin with, many mischiefs that might befall us our guardian angels do ward off from us: that is the first answer to be made. Next their power over us depends in part on the power we give them and by willingly putting ourselves into their hands, by expressly asking them to help us, we enable them to do so; for always God's special providences are for his special servants. They are not to save us from all the consequences of our own wickedness or folly or even from the wickedness and folly of other men; for we are our own masters, are free to act and then must take the consequences; moreover man is his brother's keeper and may be well or ill kept, as Abel was by wicked Cain not kept but killed. But the fullest answer is this—that in appointing us guardian angels God never meant they should make us proof against all the ills that flesh is heir to, that would have been to put us in some sort back into the state of Paradise which we have lost; but he meant them, accompanying us through this world of evil and mischance, sometimes warding off its blows and buffets, sometimes leaving them to fall, always to be leading us to a better; which better world, my brethren, when you have reached and with your own eyes opened look back on this you will see a work of wonderful wisdom in the guidance of your guardian angel. In the meantime God's providence is dark and we cannot hope to know the why and wherefore of all that is allowed to befall us.

However, my brethren, to confirm men's faith in God's providence through the guardian angels a record has been left in writing for us, the Book of Tobias. The Book of Job shews us the power of the fallen angel, of Satan, the Book of Tobias that of the holy angel St. Raphael; and both alike justify God's providence over his servants. We learn from one passage of this book what are the principal services which our guardian angels render us: *He has led me*, says young Tobias (xii 3.), *both going and coming, safe; it was he that received the money from Gabelus; it was he that procured me my wife and restrained the evil spirit from its power over her; he gave joy to her parents; me he delivered from being devoured by the fish, thee too he has made to see the light of heaven; and with all good we have been filled by him.* The guardian angels then (1) lead us in the way of salvation, conversing with us on the way, not that our ears hear them, but that many a good inspiration by which we are guided the right way or kept from the wrong comes from them. (2) They help us in our worldly business, even in money matters. (3) They bring about happy marriages. (4) They control the power of the Devil over us. (5) They give spiritual joy. (6) They save us from death and heal us in disease. And (7) we learn from the words of St. Raphael himself (ib. 12.) that they offer our prayers to God.

Some words on devotion to our guardian angels.

L. D. S.

ON FRIDAY THE 10TH OF DECEMBER, FALLING WITHIN THE OCTAVE OF *the Immaculate Conception,* a sermon on that mystery, mainly taken from one in this book (Dec. 5 1879)
Tomorrow Friday the 17th I must preach and have taken a text at random, John iv 34. *Dicit eis Jesus: Meus cibus est ut faciam voluntatem ejus qui misit me, ut perficiam opus ejus*

The event in the Gospel of which I wish to speak to-night took place about this time of the year. The harvest in the Holy Land, where the air is so warm and balmy, is in the middle of the Spring: it was 4 months before the harvest; therefore in this month. Our Lord was on a journey from Jerusalem back to Galilee; he was passing thro' Samaria, which lies between; and he sat down wearied on the brim of a well there, while his disciples went on to the nearest village to fetch food. If they had been as wearied as he was he would not have sent them and spared himself, but we may suppose that he had been teaching and preaching long or that he had been praying while they slept. There came to that well a woman of the town to draw water; he asked her for a drink. She was surprised, for the Jews were not on terms with the Samaritans her countrymen, and she did not give it, but it led to a conversation in the course of which she was converted, repented of her bad life, believed in Christ, and then ran off to the village to bring other converts. In the meanwhile the disciples came with food; were surprised to find their master talking to the woman, but said nothing; and when she was gone pressed him to take his meal, saying: *Rabbi, eat. But he said to them: I have meat to eat that you do not know of. They said one to another: Has anyone brought him anything to eat?* Now this was so far from being the case that the woman had not given him even a drink of water. He did not tell them that, but to clear his meaning he said: *My food is to do the will of him that sent me, it is to finish his work.* And it would seem that he would then take nothing.

My brethren, I wish to consider with you these holy words. Why was it that our Lord, spent and thirsty, would then not eat? I suppose we should think that the disciples ought to have answered: Yes, Lord, eat now, and strengthen thyself to do thy work: the more thy work the more thy need of food. They no doubt did not venture to say more, but only wondered at him, not knowing what he aimed at. But their wonder ceased and ours will cease on seeing what was then coming, and shortly after came, to pass. The converted woman had told her tale in the town, many had listened and believed her, and a company of them were on their way to our Lord at the well. He would not wait, he would not keep them waiting; before he would open his lips to eat he would open them to teach these good and willing people, hungry for the truth, eager for salvation; before he would taste water he would have them watered in baptism. That was, no doubt, what the well and pitcher served for, the well which our Lord would not stir from, the pitcher which the zealous woman in her eagerness for her people's good had set down and left behind her. And the disciples were back in time to baptise them, for, as St. John tells us a few verses before (ib. 2), Jesus himself did not baptise but his disciples. So then, my brethren, Christ our Lord was weary, but he would not rest till he had done his Father's work; he was hungry and thirsty, but he would not taste bread or water till he had his fill of duty and quenched his thirst for men's salvation.

Before however these people came he had more to say to his disciples. *Do not you say*, he said, *it is four months' time to the harvest: I tell you, lift up your eyes and see how the country is already white to harvest.* You see, my brethren, he was speaking a parable and playing upon words: it *was* four months to the harvest of common corn, but there was a spiritual harvest of men's souls to be made in that place, as if they lifted up their mind's eye they would see, and indeed with their bodily eyes they might perhaps then have seen those Samaritans upon their road to where they stood; the spiritual wheatfield was ready for the reaping now, that is to say, the men were ready for baptism, and yet the seed had been but an hour or so sown. Christ was the first sower of that seed in the woman's heart, she in her turn sowed it in others; now she and they alike did but want baptising, which was the reaping and gathering of them into Christ's kingdom. Christ goes on: *And the reaper gets his wages and gathers fruit into life everlasting, so that both sower and reaper may rejoice together.* This means: Be ready to baptise and do your duty, which is the bringing men into my church and kingdom: you will have the joy of knowing everlasting wages are for your good service due to you and I shall have the joy of seeing the seed I sowed come so soon to harvest. *For in this*, he went on, *the saying is true, that it is one that sows and another that reaps.* This was a proverb, meaning that a man may begin what he will not live to finish or may have the pains where another than he will have the profit, but Christ gives the saying a happier turn, for in this case sower and reaper both would gain and both rejoice together.

I have sent you out, he says, *to reap that in which you have not laboured: others have laboured and you have entered on their labours.* For Christ had converted the woman all in weariness, she had converted others all in haste and heat; the disciples there in their place had but to baptise them. And then the Samaritans came up and when all was done asked him to stay with them: *then* no doubt and not before, with them and not alone by themselves, he and disciples took their meal. He stayed with them two days and many more were converted.

The moral of this is, brethren, that God's work is first to be done, then ours; first the soul's good looked to, then the body's. This rule our Lord laid down in the Sermon on the Mount. *Seek first the kingdom of God and his justice, and the rest*—such as food and clothing and our other needs of this life—*shall be added to you.* Now Christ our Lord both did and taught; he practised beforehand what he preached afterwards; and in this place we see, brethren, most touchingly how he put God's work before his own comfort, the good of souls before the good of bodies. He was hungry, but he made it his meat, his food, to do the will of God who sent him and finish that work.

SERMON FOR SUNDAY MAY 15 THE FOURTH SUNDAY AFTER EASTER AT ST. FRANCIS XAVIER'S, LIVERPOOL—on the Gospel John xvi 5–14. (I preached on this last year here)

The words read in today's Gospel are taken from our Lord's last sermon, his last discourse, the last conversation he held with his apostles all before he suffered. It was at the Paschal Supper. After they had eaten the Paschal Lamb, after they had partaken of the Agape or Lovefeast, after he had washed their feet, after he had set on foot the Sacrament of the Holy Eucharist, offered in a bloodless shape the Sacrifice of his Body and Blood which the next day he was to offer in blood upon the cross, and given them their first communion, after all these he delivered a long, solemn, and mysterious discourse, which, abridged as no doubt it is, fills four chapters of St. John. It is not to be supposed that they then understood all he was saying, but one thing in particular struck them in it and took a deep and saddening hold on their minds: they gathered from it that he was soon to leave them. He was going, he said, to him that sent him and, because he had told them so, sorrow filled their hearts.

Had they then never heard this before?—They had, but they had not believed it, as when St. Peter told his Master that the dreadful death he had foretold would not really befall him, or they had thought, that it was yet a long while off or they had imagined that his kingdom upon earth and triumph over all his enemies would begin at his resurrection only three days after his death, as when the two sons of Zebedee asked that they might sit the one at his right hand, the other at his left, in his kingdom; at any rate they had not understood Christ's warnings nor much had heeded them. Now at last they felt that Christ's departure was a truth, that it was near at hand, and that it was to be for them a lifelong parting, and as this more and more broke upon them with everything Christ said the sadder they grew and sorrow filled their hearts to overflowing.

How good, brethren, faithful, and loving were these Apostles! though they failed for a time in the time of trial and terror, yet how good were they at heart! Christ had called them from their comforts, he had made them poor and homeless, he had led them a hard life and taught them doctrines high and hard for flesh and blood, they knew that he had an eye to all their failings and sometimes had with sternness rebuked them, his presence was a great restraint upon them and in its way a heavy burden, but what of all this? they so loved him that when they really learnt he was to leave them it overwhelmed them and the sorrow of it filled their hearts. Tho' they were yet imperfect yet they had set foot firmly on the way of perfection, they had with violence made their entrance into the kingdom of heaven, turned their back on this world and placed their thoughts and hopes upon the other. They lived by faith, hope, and charity; they believed in Christ, from him and not from the world they hoped whatever good was to befall them, and they loved him dearly and could not bear the thought of parting. For where their treasure was there their hearts were also: Christ was their treasure and when they heard that they were to lose him they lost all heart and were sunk in sorrow.

My brethren, in all this sorrowful love of theirs there was mingled something imperfect, unspiritual, earthly, and mistaken: so Christ consoled them, but in giving comfort he also gave correction. The Apostles believed in him; under his human nature, the flesh and blood they saw, they had faith in his godhead unseen; but yet it seems that unless they could *see* him, unless they had him before their eyes, they could not believe this: he foretold to them that he should rise again, the holy women told them he *had* risen again, but till they saw him they would not, or scarcely would, believe it; Peter and John at least needed to see the linen cloths; as for Thomas, he went further: Unless I put my finger into the print of the nails—you know the words—*I will not believe*. They were blessed then in believing, but they had not at that time the blessing of those who do not see and yet believe. Again they hoped in him, but hoped what?—such things as to sit on his right hand and his left, to be greatest in the kingdom of heaven: see how the dross is mixed with the gold and the gold with the dross—they wanted to be with Christ and in the kingdom of heaven, but to have earthly honours in it; they wanted to have earthly honours, but those in the kingdom of heaven and Christ to give them. They were wise then in hoping, but unwise, unspiritual in the things they hoped for. And they loved him; but their love made them look to their own good, rather than his; for as he told them, if they loved him they should be glad, not sorry, he was going to the Father, because the Father was greater than he, that is to say, in so far as Christ our Lord is man he is infinitely below God; if therefore he was going to be raised to God's throne he was going to an infinite honour, boon, blessing, and felicity. But they wanted to keep him down on earth below, that he might be always with them. So then they loved Christ, but their love was not wholly unselfish, it was not pure well-ordered charity.

Now since it must always happen that when we look first to our own interest and well being and to God's afterwards we miss what we want, defeat our own purpose, and are the worse off and the less happy for it in reality, so here Christ showed his loving Apostles it was even for their own good that he should leave them and would be to their disadvantage if he were not. For in that other world he was soon to set out for he was going, he said, to prepare a place for them: unless he went he could not prepare it; and into this world he was going to send the Paraclete to be with them: unless he went that Paraclete could not come. The Paraclete is the Holy Ghost, he came and is with us now; it was for the Apostles' gain and it is for our gain that Christ should be gone and the Holy Ghost be here instead. Let us, my brethren, see how this is.

Christ our Lord and the Holy Ghost are two Paracletes, both God the Son and God the Holy Ghost are Paracletes and not the Holy Ghost only, for Christ said '*another* Paraclete', meaning that he was the first. But from the nature of things the Holy Ghost can as a Paraclete do more than Christ could do or rather chose to do.

What then is a Paraclete?—A comforter or consoler, but it is much more than that. A Paraclete is one who encourages men, stirs them up, or calls them on to do good. It is plain that Christ our Lord was a great Paraclete: he comforted the sick by healing sickness, the widow by raising her son to life, the sinner by forgiving his sins and giving him peace with God, and all in general that laboured and were burdened, if they would but come to him, he gave them rest. And not this only, but he encouraged men, stirred them up, and led them on to good in every way by his words and works, by sermons, by miracles, and most of all by his example. But in all he did there was one shortcoming, it is this: Christ lived but a short time and in one place. He came as mortal man, in some seventy years therefore he must at any rate have died and in fact his enemies made an end of him long before that time. What was this to those millions that were to be born after? And he came to the Jews, to the house of Israel, a very small part of the whole world: what was this to the millions of gentiles? Comparatively few could benefit by his miracles, comparatively few could hear his preaching, and even his example, if there had been no other Paraclete to set it every day before men's eyes, that too would have died away. Happy then were those that knew Christ in the flesh, but it was for the good of mankind at large, nay it was even for their good, that he should go away and another Paraclete should come.

Christ our Lord, as has been said, is one, he lived but one life and at one time and place. Now the Holy Ghost, he too is but one person, indeed, but it is his will and answerable to his name and the manner of his being to shew himself as if he were many. He delights in multitude. When he takes up his dwelling in man it is in the shape of seven gifts, seven spirits they are called by the prophet, he being but one spirit all the while. When he came upon the disciples at Pentecost it was in the shape of parted or divided fiery tongues, a fire parted and distributed out to many, and *it*—so says the Scripture—sat on every one of them. When they spoke it was in many languages to a host hearing them each in his own. And St. Paul is careful to tell us that there are all sorts and varieties of spiritual gifts, each of them the working and the manifestation of the one spirit. Therefore he is called the finger of the Father's right hand, that is all the fingers, for the fingers are to the hand or arm as many things are to one. This, I say, is answerable to his name and the manner of his being—to his name, which is Spirit or Breath, for as the breath is drawn from the boundless air into the lungs and from the lungs again is breathed out and melts into the boundless air so the Spirit of God was poured out from the infinite God upon Christ's human nature and by Christ, who said: Receive the Holy Ghost: as my Father sent me so I send you/, was breathed into his Apostles and by degrees into the millions of his Church, till the new heavens and new earth will at last be filled with it. And it is answerable to the manner of his being; for the Spirit, we read, searches all things, even the depths of God: if the Holy Spirit searches the infinite riches of the godhead it is but little for his subtlety to search every corner of the world. The Holy Ghost then is, as I may say, a spirit of multitude and can spread and scatter his being and breath and be where Christ, being but one and like but one, cannot.

You will ask, was not the Holy Ghost like this and did he not work like this before Christ left the world, nay before Christ came into it? did he not then search hearts? did he not then live in the hearts of the just? did he not then inspire good thoughts, encourage and stir up and draw men on to good? did he not at all times play the Paraclete? What difference then so far has Christ's coming or his going made?

The Holy Ghost, I answer, did all these things before Christ came and at all times, but only as all three persons of the Trinity do and have always done them. God is in every place, therefore God the Holy Ghost was then in every place. God searches hearts, therefore the Holy Ghost was then searching hearts. God inspires good thoughts, therefore God the Holy Ghost did then inspire them. And if the Scripture says the Holy Spirit or the Spirit of the Lord did this or that, why God is a spirit and holy and the Spirit of the Lord is the Lord himself: the things done were not in reality the special work of God the Holy Ghost. But when the dove descended upon Christ at his baptism, when the fiery tongues fell upon the disciples at Pentecost, it was not the Father, it was not the Son, it was the Holy Ghost himself who came. When Christ breathed on his disciples, saying / Receive the Holy Ghost, when the Bishop says the same over the priest he is ordaining, or smears the oil in confirmation it is not the Father, it is not the Son, it is the Holy Ghost that is then given. When the Apostles wrote: It has seemed good to the Holy Ghost and to us, it was not the Father, it was not the Son, it was the Holy Ghost himself who had passed that judgment. To be sure, the Father and the Son are always with the Holy Ghost; but so are the Father and the Holy Ghost always with the Son; yet when we go to communion we say only that we receive Christ's body, though we receive with it his blood, his soul, his godhead, and God the Father and God the Holy Ghost. As it was Christ that with the words / Lazarus, come forth / raised Lazarus to life, though he himself said that the words he spoke he spoke not of himself, but it was the Father abiding with him who did the work; as it was Christ that suffered, though he said that in his Passion he was not alone, for the Father was with him; as it was Christ who rose again and that of his own power, though we read that God raised his son to life, so the Holy Ghost has his work now to do, which is his own work and not the Son's and not the Father's. This work he could not do till Christ was gone: the Spirit was not given, says the Scripture (John vii 39.), because Jesus was not yet glorified.

And in this Gospel, brethren, we read what is the work the Holy Ghost has come to do: it is to glorify God the Son. Christ came into this world to glorify God his Father; the Holy Ghost came to glorify Christ. Christ made God known by appearing in human shape, the Word took flesh and dwelt amongst us; the Holy Ghost makes Christ known by living in his Church, he makes his temple in

Christian hearts and dwells within us. Christ glorified the Father by his death and resurrection, the Holy Ghost glorifies Christ by the persecutions and the triumphs of the Catholic Church. Christ was himself but one and lived and died but once; but the Holy Ghost makes of every Christian another Christ, an AfterChrist; lives a million lives in every age; is the courage of the martyrs, the wisdom of the doctors, the purity of the virgins; is breathed into each at baptism, may be quenched by sin in one soul, but then is kindled in another; passes like a restless breath from heart to heart and is the spirit and the life of all the Church: what the soul is to the human body that, St. Austin says, the Holy Ghost is to the Church Catholic, Christ's body mystical.[1] If the Holy Ghost is our spirit and our life, if he is our universal soul, no wonder, my brethren, no wonder he is our Paraclete, to lead us and to lift us and to fire us to all holiness and good, a Paraclete in a way too that Christ alone could never be. On this great mystery no time is left to dwell: I leave it for your thoughts to ponder. In the name of the Father etc.

L. D. S.

FOR SUNDAY JUNE 26 1881 BEING THE SUNDAY AFTER THE OCTAVE OF CORPUS CHRISTI AND NEAREST THE FEAST OF THE SACRED HEART (WHICH THIS YEAR IS TO BE KEPT ON MONDAY THE 27TH); AT ST. FRANCIS XAVIER'S LIVERPOOL—on *the Sacred Heart*[2]

Our Lord said that a scribe learned in the kingdom of heaven would be like a householder who brought out of his store things new and old—that is not only brought some new things and some old things but things that were both new and old, things kept so long that they were old and kept so well that they were as good as new. This is what the Church does or the Holy Ghost who rules the Church: out of the store which Christ left behind him he brings from time to time as need requires some doctrine or some devotion which was indeed known to the Apostles and is old, but is unknown or little known at the time and comes upon the world as new. Such was the case with the worship of the Sacred Heart: we find it in St. Gertrude's prayers[3] and in St. Bernard's sermons,[4] but little notice was in their days taken of it, and when the Bd. Margaret Mary[5] said that our Lord himself had revealed it to her it struck people as a new thing and many called it a dangerous or a foolish one and spoke and wrote against it and opposed it with all their power; nevertheless good Catholics the more they knew it the more they loved it and it grew to be, what now we see it, one of the dearest devotions of the Church.

There are some perhaps among those who hear me, Protestants or others, to whom the name of the Sacred Heart has a strange sound, an unmeaning sound, or even an unpleasing and repulsive sound. For the sake of such persons I shall on this day, the Sunday nearest to the festival of the Sacred Heart, say what it is exactly that the Sacred Heart means, and to you also, my Catholic brethren, this explanation of what you know will not, I hope, be wearisome. My purpose then is to instruct and not to exhort, nor is there any need of exhortation, for Christ has only to be known in order to be loved and if the Sacred Heart is but understood devotion of itself will follow.

By the Sacred Heart we mean the heart of our Lord Jesus Christ: no other heart of man deserves in comparison with that the name of sacred, since this heart and this alone is united with the godhead. For in Christ there is nothing that is not either godhead or united with the godhead. Christ is god and man; there are in him these two things, godhead and manhood. His manhood again is two things, body and soul. And again his body is two things, flesh and blood; so we are in the habit of speaking, and this at least is exact, that the body consists of solid parts which are permanent or changed slowly and of liquid parts which move to and fro, and are fast renewed. The heart is one of these solid parts, of these pieces of flesh, and is a vessel of the liquid blood; it is an essential, a necessary part of the body, as no one will deny; it is found in Christ, was born with him, beat for 33 years in his breast, ceased beating at his death, was pierced by a lance after death upon the cross, and rose again with him at his resurrection with all other parts and members belonging to the perfection of the human body; it is therefore now in Christ's breast in heaven. And since, as I have said, everything in Christ is either godhead or united with the godhead, the heart, like all Christ's flesh, like Christ's whole body, like all Christ's human nature, is united with the godhead and deserves, requires, and must have paid to it, divine worship, that worship which is called in Greek λατρεία and is due to God alone.

This matter, brethren, once explained cannot be disputed and I take it for granted that no man, Catholic or Protestant, would be so bold, nay so impious, as to deny that if we *are* to concern ourselves with Christ's heart we cannot help paying it divine honours and worship. But I can fancy some people, sincere and reverent-minded persons too, saying that they do not wish the thing to be put before them in that light, that there is no need, that it is better not, that it is repulsive to them to have one piece of Christ's flesh thus nakedly thrust upon their mind's eye, that even out of reverence for Christ they would rather worship in him the whole man, the whole being and person, and not, however sacred, every separate and dissected detail. My brethren, this is an objection in its principle sound and deserving of all respect; instead therefore of denouncing it I shall go on to shew only that in this particular case it is unfounded, that to the Sacred Heart it has no application.

I draw your attention therefore to these two points: first that the heart is by common consent one of the noble or honourable members of man's body; next that when we worship Christ's heart it is a great deal more than the heart that we mean, it is after all Christ himself that we worship. The heart, I say, is agreed to be one of the noble or honourable members of the body. There would no doubt be something revolting in seeing the heart alone, all naked and bleeding, torn from the breast; but that is not in question here: Christ's heart is lodged within his sacred frame and there alone is worshipped. And considered as within the breast, who is there however truly and delicately, who is there however even falsely and affectedly, modest that ever thought it shame to speak of the human *heart*? Is not all language, is not common talk, is not eloquence, is not poetry, all full of mention of the heart? Nay I have remarked it, so honourable, so interesting to us is the heart, that there are people who whatever in head or throat or lung or back or breast or bowel ails them will always have you believe it is the heart that is affected, that their complaint is of the heart. Want of reverence then there cannot be in the worship of the Sacred Heart.

The next point, brethren, was that when we worship Christ's heart it is a great deal more than the heart of flesh we mean, it is after all Christ himself that we worship. For, my brethren, this is how we speak in many things. We say that in a town there are so many thousand souls: we mean so many thousand that have souls, so many thousand men, women, and children and not their souls only. We speak of a kind body, a busybody: we mean some man or woman that is kind or that is busy and not his or her body only. We call sailors or labourers hands, we say 'all hands', 'a new hand', and so on: it is men we mean, not their hands only. We call Plato and Shakspere great minds: it is Plato and Shakspere themselves we mean, not their minds only. Nay we call a man a warm heart, the very word, a large heart and the like: it is the man we mean and not his heart only. So then when we say the Sacred Heart it is of Christ himself we are thinking and not of his heart only. Not but that there is a good reason for so speaking in all these cases: if living men are called souls it is because the soul is the source of life in man, if they are called bodies it is because the body strikes the eye, if sailors and labourers are called hands it is because their hands are what they work with, if great thinkers are called minds it is because by their minds they have become famous, if kind people are called large hearts it is because the qualities of the heart make them more remarkable than others.

And here is the place to say what you will have forestalled me in thinking, that when we speak so often of the heart, a great heart,[1] a narrow heart, a warm heart, a cold heart, a tender heart, a hard heart, a heart of stone, a lion heart, a craven heart, a poor heart, a sad heart, a heavy heart, a broken heart, a willing heart, a full heart, of heart's ease, heartache, heartscald, of thinking in one's heart, of loving from one's heart, of the heart sinking, of taking heart, of losing heart, of giving the heart away, of being heartwhole—it would be endless to name all the ways we bring the heart in—, in all these expressions what we call heart is not the piece of flesh so called, not the great bloodvessel only but the thoughts of the mind that vessel seems to harbour and the feelings of the soul to which it beats. For the heart is of all the members of the body the one which most strongly and most of its own accord sympathises with and expresses in itself what goes on within the soul. Tears are sometimes forced, smiles may be put on, but the beating of the heart is the truth of nature. And as in others so in Christ: the Sacred Heart is that heart which swelled when Christ rejoiced in spirit and sank when he was sad, which played its dark and sacred part in all Christ's life, in all he did and suffered, which in his Agony with frightful and un-natural straining forced its blood out on him in the shape of teeming sweat, and after it had ceased to beat was pierced and spent its contents by the opening in his side. The Sacred Heart is all Christ did for us; the Sacred Heart is all Christ's joys, griefs, hopes, fears, love unto death, heroic courage, tender pity; the Sacred Heart is Christ's most perfect character. Once see the matter in this light and surely there is no Christian that will blame, none that will not admire, there should be none that would not practise, the devotion to the Sacred Heart.

No, my brethren, the wonder now is why the worship of the Sacred Heart was not earlier practised, was not always practised, and not why it is practised now. In substance indeed, as you see for yourselves, it always was: Christ's human nature, his virtues, his love and goodness, his holy life and passion and death were always in the minds and mouths of Christians, for this is Christianity; but the Sacred Heart by name was not, the worship of Christ's heart of flesh by name and in itself was a thing scarcely known a little over two centuries ago. Now why is this? why did the Church so long hide, why did God not reveal a treasure so precious before? God's counsel, brethren, I do not fathom, but since the divine wisdom may have for what it does many reasons, at once some of them within our comprehension, others not, it is lawful for me to say what one of them may have been, and this I proceed to do.

If then you compare the times before the Sacred Heart was commonly known and worshipped with our times, in other words what are called the Middle Ages with the age we live in, and consider the difference between them and the change that has in the meantime passed upon the world, this difference and this change will be by general agreement very great, though all will not agree in what it lies. And now I wish to put aside the *events* of these centuries, their wars and struggles and revolutions, for all history is full of these and, as our Lord said, 'These things must needs be'; nay more, I put aside the great religious changes that have been, the Protestant Reformation and the spread of infidelity; in a word I put out of sight all those things in which men take opposite sides and are divided and I wish to look only at things in which all, roughly speaking, have a common interest, in which all men share alike. Now within the space of time of which I speak the New World has been discovered and peopled from Europe; the means of travelling and the speed of it have increased prodigiously; communication between men, by print, by letter, by telegraph, and by other ways, has been made easy in a still more extraordinary degree; the realm of nature has been laid bare and our knowledge of it widened beyond measure. And these are things shared in by Catholic and Protestant, believer and unbeliever alike. Yet after all these are not the things that make much difference to human nature. *Caelum, non animum mutant qui trans mare currunt*, the Latin proverb says; men may travel, but do not change their minds with change of latitude. We write to one another a hundred times as fast and often as our forefathers could, but we do but say fast and often what we should still have said seldom and slowly. And learning, the knowing more or knowing less, leaves us with our characters, our passions, and our appetites much what they were. It is not then in these things that the great change is.

In what then does it lie, that great and profound change which has within the time of which. . . . [1]

PART TWO

SPIRITUAL WRITINGS

INTRODUCTION

THE bulk of Hopkins's spiritual writing was done during his year of tertianship, especially during the Long Retreat of November–December 1881. There are earlier entries and there are important later entries; but the creative year was 1881–2. All his ideas stem from the making of the Spiritual Exercises; he has several valuable comments on the text of the Exercises; and it seems that parts of his work were meant as raw material for a treatise on the Exercises. Nevertheless, his writings as they stand cannot be considered as a *Commentary* on the Exercises; they contain too many gaps and too many digressions. Nor does their main interest lie in their being a partial commentary. Their main interest is in their personal reliving of the Christian and Catholic revelation in the light of the Exercises.

Their central inspiration was, in his own phrase, 'the great sacrifice'. It was remarked a little earlier that the original inspiration of *The Wreck of the Deutschland* can be traced back to the experience of a certain exercise in the First Week of his noviceship Long Retreat. It was this same exercise, made in the same place thirteen years later, during his second Long Retreat, that provided the inspiration of 'the great sacrifice'.

The exercise was a meditation on 'Three Sins'—the sin of Lucifer, the original sin of our first parents, and the actual sin of some unnamed hypothetical person today. With startling clarity the exercitant is made aware that in his own heart there is the same flicker of ill will as in Lucifer's, the hidden deviation from the Creator's will, the switching of the points which sends all our lives to destruction unless it is corrected. But, in the 'colloquy' that concludes the meditation, shame and abasement are swallowed up in a cry of wonder and adoration. For in the colloquy the Son of God is presented bleeding on the Cross, having come down from the radiance of eternity into the dark prison of material suffering to redeem his own.

The fall of Lucifer and the secret workings of free will were to be the subjects of some of Hopkins's longest discourses; but it was the colloquy that gave him the inspiration of 'the great sacrifice'. He saw it suddenly in the light of St Paul's famous passage to the Philippians (ii. 5–11); and he saw it at once as the divine history of the universe and as the private ideal of his own life, his own special insight into the mind and heart of God:

Christ's life and character are such as appeal to all the world's admiration, but there is one insight St Paul gives us of it which is very secret and seems to me more touching and constraining than everything else is. This mind he says, was in Christ Jesus—he means as man: being in the form of God—that is, finding, as in the first instant of his incarnation he did, his human nature informed by the godhead[1]—he thought it nevertheless no snatching-matter for him to be equal with God, but annihilated himself, taking the form of a servant; that is, he could not but see what he was, God, but he would see it as if he did not see it, and be as if he were not and instead of snatching at once at what all the time was his, or was himself, he emptied or exhausted himself so far as that was possible, of godhead and behaved only as God's slave, as his creature, as man, which also he was, and then being in the guise of man humbled himself to death, the death of the cross. It is this holding of himself back, and not snatching at the truest and highest good, the good that was his right, nay his possession from a past eternity in his other nature, his own being and self, which seems to me the root of all his holiness and the imitation of this the root of all moral good in other men.

He was writing in this letter with an eye to moral conduct only, but at the back of his mind were three stages of Christ's descent into creation; he saw Christ's sacrifice as repairing a triple breach made in the order of creation; by the free will of Lucifer, the free will of our first parents, and the individual free wills of fallen men. One might compare his vision to the upward gaze of a worshipper in some great and lovely baroque cathedral. At the summit of the cupola, seeming to stretch into infinity, is the painted halo of the Blessed Trinity; then, seeming a long way farther down, is the ring of angels with their trumpets; then, round the base of the cupola, but still very high up, are the stone figures of holy men sculpted larger than life-size; finally, on the ground before the altar, is the sweating mass of humanity in the flesh. Through those stages—through the angelic world and through the earthly paradise—he saw God the Son descending to the altar from his place by his Father's side and reascending again. He wrote of it in another letter, in June 1882, trying to describe to Bridges the significance of a Corpus Christi procession:

But the procession has more meaning and mystery than this: it represents the process of the Incarnation and the world's redemption. As Christ went forth from the bosom of the Father as the Lamb of God and eucharistic victim to die upon the altar of the cross for the world's ransom; then rising returned leading the procession of the flock redeemed / so in this ceremony his body *in statu victimali* is carried to the Altar of Repose as it is called and back to the tabernacle at the high altar, which will represent the bosom of the godhead. The procession out may represent the cooperation of the

---

[1] The word 'informed' is not used by GMH in its technical and scholastic sense, but simply refers to the hypostatic union.

angels . . . the return the Church Catholic from Christ's death to the end of time.[1]

But he did not see God the Son's descent into creation merely or primarily as the reparation for sin. He saw it as an act of love which would have taken place in one form or another whether or not there had been any sin. Since He was God himself He could not perform the act of an inferior nature; so from all eternity He willed to become a creature so as to express that aspect of his love which was impossible to him as God alone. This is 'the great sacrifice': a sacrifice of joy and adoration, which only incidentally, as it were, became one also of sorrow and reparation.

At this point the teaching of Duns Scotus had once more a decisive effect on Hopkins's thought. Scotus rejected the theory of certain theologians that only the death of a God-Man could satisfy an offended God;[2] he refused to believe that God the Son's assumption of a created nature was contingent upon the sins either of angels or of men: 'I say then that the Fall was not the reason for Christ's predestination. Even if no angel had fallen, nor any man, Christ would still have been predestined—yes, even if no others were to have been created save only Christ.'

Hopkins had held this theory ever since he began reading Scotus. He saw creation as dependent upon the decree of the Incarnation, and not the other way round. The worlds of angels and of men were created as fields for Christ in which to exercise his adoration of the Father, fields for him to sow and work and harvest. Hence, perhaps, the imagery of grain and barn that ran through Hopkins's poetry, 1876–8, from *The Wreck of the Deutschland* (stanza 31) to *Poems 32* and *38*.

But after his ordination to the priesthood his interest shifted increasingly from the presence of God's design or inscape (that is, Christ) in inanimate nature to the working-out of that design—by stress and instress—in the minds and wills of men. In 1878 he had come across in the writings of Marie Lataste (see Appendix I) the passage about the two 'strains' or intentions by which God moves the world. There is the creative strain which moves things according to their natures; and there is the redemptive or sacrificial strain which depends on the personal choice of free agents. Hopkins joined

---

[1] *Letters*, i. 149. Cf. the Church's eucharistic hymn:

> Verbum supernum prodiens
> Nec linquens Patris dexteram,
> Ad opus suum exiens,
> Venit ad vitae vesperam.

[2] See ch. 5, n. 4: 'Et ideo ad alliciendum nos ad amorem suum, ut credo, hoc praecipue fecit.' 'And so it was to entice us to his love, as I believe, that chiefly he did this. . . .'

this to Scotus's theory of Christ's predestination apart from sin; he joined it also to Scotus's distinction between nature and personality. His mind leaped to the conclusion that redemption or sacrifice of some sort, so as to give an opportunity for love by free choice, would have been necessary even had there been no sin; but there has been sin in fact; so the 'Three Sins' of the meditation are the actual circumstances in which Christ performs his adoration of the Father —as it were in three descending rings or circles. Four rings, really: one *ad intra*, and three *ad extra*. The inner ring is the mystery of the Blessed Trinity.[1] But of this 'mystery from which sacrifice takes its rise', Hopkins never found time or ability to write, except in one or two very beautiful but obscure passages:

Why did the Son of God go thus forth from the Father not only in the eternal and intrinsic procession of the Trinity but also by an extrinsic and less than eternal, let us say an aeonian one?—To give God glory and that by sacrifice. . . . This sacrifice and this outward procession is a consequence and shadow of the procession of the Trinity, from which mystery sacrifice takes its rise; but of this I do not mean to write here. It is as if the blissful agony or stress of selving in God had forced out drops of sweat or blood, which drops were the world, or as if the lights lit at the festival of that 'peaceful Trinity' through some little cranny striking out lit up into being one 'cleave' out of the world of possible creatures. The sacrifice would be the Eucharist. . . .

What he did write about at considerable length was Christ's descent into the first outer ring of creation: the world of 'aeonian' or angelic time (the scholastic *aevum*). The centre of his picture (for it is a picture rather than a theory) is the revolt of Lucifer and the ensuing 'battle in heaven' described shadowily in the Apocalypse, chapter xii.

In so far as it is a theological opinion, it is derived from an hypothesis of Suarez—in book viii, chapter 13, of his *De Angelis*: that Lucifer revolted when he understood that to Christ's created nature had been granted that ineffable union with the godhead which he desired for himself; being himself most like to God *in nature*, he could not admit that a creature apparently lower than himself was one by grace and favour with the only perfect image of the Father.[2]

Suarez's opinion is based on hints in earlier writers that the angels

---

[1] Cf. *Poems, 107*, p. 162:

> She caught the crying of those Three,
> The Immortals of the eternal ring,
> The Utterer, Uttered, Uttering,
> And witness in her place would she.

[2] 'Whether the sin of Lucifer concerned the excellence of the Hypostatic Union, by inordinately desiring it for his own nature.' *Opera Omnia* (Paris, 1856), ii. 880–90.

had to pass through some sort of test, and on Scotus's theory that the
decree of the Incarnation was prior to that of the creation of angels
and men. In this sense he interprets the *iterum*[1] in the verse of
Hebrews i. 6: '. . . that the first entrance of Christ was by faith,
especially into the angelic minds; the second in actual fact at his
conception'.

Rickaby, Hopkins's contemporary, adopted the same theory,
though he did not mention Suarez:

In the *Revue Thomiste*, Janvier–Fevrier, 1908, an article *Le Preternaturel* by
Père Alexandre Mercier, O.P., throws a flood of light on the Sin of the Angels,
and thereby on the Spiritual Exercises. What follows is based on that article,
eked out by the theological opinion of Scotus and St Francis of Sales, and
(so it seems to me) by the teaching of St Paul (Colossians i), that all creation
from the first was in view of the Incarnation, and that even antecedently to
the sin of Adam the Word Incarnate is the principle of the elevation of
angels and men to the supernatural order and to the dignity of children
of God. The theory then proceeds thus. Lucifer was by nature the highest of
the angels and chief of God's creation, administering the world as a sort of
prime minister under God. In some way God let him know, through him let
the rest of the angels know, that hereafter His own Divine Son would assume
a nature inferior to theirs, and would be their chief, their eldest Brother,
they being sons of God only inasmuch as they were His brethren, they
having by grace what was His by nature, namely the Divine sonship and
with it the right to see God face to face, which is the consummation of the
supernatural order. The Word Incarnate was shown forth as King of the
supernatural, and all created nature was declared subject to Him. The
angels were bidden to adore Him as their King and their God. Then Lucifer
cried out, as Herod in the Epiphany hymn,—

Successor instat, pellimur:

'There is a successor coming on, we are driven from our throne.' . . . Thus,
ages before the Incarnation, Lucifer had registered himself as the enemy of
the Word Incarnate, and of the Kingdom of the Word Incarnate, which is
the Kingdom of grace, a supernatural Kingdom, the Church.[2]

Between this pictorial representation of Suarez's theory and Hopkins's pictorial representations (cf. chs. 2, 5, 6, and 8) there are
obvious similarities. But there are several important differences.
Rickaby thinks that the war in heaven happened 'ages before the
Incarnation', and that what the angels had was an intellectual
foreknowledge of the Incarnation, not actual knowledge of Christ in
the flesh. But Hopkins is quite definite—and here he is more in
harmony with the patristic tradition—that Lucifer had no full

[1] 'Et cum iterum introducit primogenitum in orbem terrae, dicit: et adorent
eum omnes Angeli eius.'
[2] Joseph Rickaby, *The Spiritual Exercises of St Ignatius Loyola* (London, 1915),
pp. 29–30.

understanding of the mystery of the Hypostatic Union; what Lucifer saw was Christ in the flesh—'flesh', adds Hopkins, rather vaguely, 'being the name for a condition of matter'. Christ, he thinks, was *materially* present in the same sort of way that he is present in the Eucharist:[1] a material substance, but without actual extension.

Clearly there are two great difficulties here, one of time and the other of place; and there is a third, a doctrinal difficulty: that Hopkins's position would make Christ's Incarnation a different event from his conception and birth in historic time at Bethlehem in the reign of the emperor Augustus.

Hopkins seems to be trying to answer the difficulty about time at the outset of Chapter 8, where he distinguishes between the order of time and the order of intention. This is a question touched on in the notes and in an appendix. Briefly, the order of intention is the rational order in which events are planned: the end first, and then the means to the end; whereas in the temporal order the means come first and the end afterwards. 'Primum in intentione', as Scotus says, 'est ultimum in exsecutione.' So much is obvious; but the point is that Scotus appears to attach *reality* to the intentional order, a created reality outside God's Mind and apart from the temporal order in which it is, so to speak, embodied. In ordinary parlance, then, one could think that God's purpose at present working in the world has already (though the word 'already' is confusing) been worked out on a higher plane in a different order of reality.

But even if this is allowed, it is difficult to see how it helps. It is scarcely possible to identify the order of intention with the angelic *aevum*; yet it is in the angelic *aevum* that Hopkins definitely places Christ's first appearance as a created nature. The angelic *aevum* is an obscure subject. One might suggest, using a well-worn image, that it stands to our time as a three-dimensional space would to a two-dimensional surface; but in this way: that every movement in the space can touch the whole or any part of the surface, while preserving an intensity of depth outside the surface's receptivity— though not altogether (reverting from the image) outside the power of our spiritual consciousness to experience. Thus a single event in angelic duration could be coincident with the whole of our time, and a series of events (in depth) in angelic duration could be coincident with a single instant of our time.

Scotus appears to suggest this. The passage in which he does so is possibly obscure.[2] But it is important to note that it is a

---

[1] GMH appears to mean that Christ was present to the angels in the same sort of way as He is present in the Eucharist. Such substantial presence is impossible to ordinary human or angelic knowledge. But to God in His eternity all things are present in their actual substance. According to the thought of GMH God communicated this kind of presence to the angels.   [2] See note p. 300 (177. 2).

passage which Hopkins had almost certainly read. It comes next to
the passage on the fall of Lucifer which Hopkins actually cites; and
both he and Scotus use chapter xii of the Apocalypse to recreate the
order of events in the battle in heaven.[1] The occasional coincidence
of angelic duration with human time before and after the fall of
Satan was evidently in Hopkins's mind when he wrote that 'spirit
and flesh started together'; and that:

. . . the attack on the woman which the dragon makes was, though I
cannot yet clearly grasp how, the actual attack which he made, is making,
and will go on making on the human race.

and that:

. . . his birth and the Gloria in excelsis, the persecution by Herod, the
flight into Egypt, the massacre of the innocents, the return to Nazareth and
life of toil there, all symbolise the manifestation of the eucharistic victim to
the angels, Satan's attack on it, its disappearance from his eyes in the world
of matter, the ruin of man—which reminds one again of that river that after
all did not drown the woman in the vision. . . .

Following this line of thought one might argue that Christ's
manifestation to the angels and his life on earth were *parallel* execu-
tions of the same order of intention. And this seems to be the most
likely interpretation of Hopkins's meaning.

The difficulty about place, closely related to the foregoing, is no
less formidable; but it can be dismissed more shortly. It is simply
a question of accepting or not accepting Scotus's treatise on the
Blessed Sacrament; this is plain from Hopkins's use of the word
'adduction' which is an exclusively Scotist term signifying bodily
presence brought about, not by local motion, but by the removal
of distance.

In order to prove the rational possibility of Christ's physical
presence under the appearance of bread, Scotus sets about a radical
revision of the Aristotelean categories of quantity, place, and position. It is enough to say here that he proves to his own satisfaction
how the apparent laws of nature could be modified without violating
the laws of the mind that made the laws of nature. Quantity, for
example, is not primarily, but only secondarily, the extension of
parts outside parts; primarily it is the formula of the interrelation
fo parts in a substance, its harmony or bodily form. His final conclusion is that it is within God's power to make the Body of Christ
really present *universaliter*, anywhere or everywhere in the universe.
This leads him to a corollary which is highly relevant to Hopkins's
speculations:

I say then, but without insisting on it, that before the Incarnation and

---

[1] See notes, p. 286 (132. 1[1]) and p. 300 (179. 2).

'before Abraham was', in the beginning of the world, Christ could have had a true temporal existence in a sacramental manner. And if this is true, it follows that before the conception and formation of the Body of Christ from the most pure blood of the Glorious Virgin there could have been the Eucharist (*Oxoniense*, iv, dist. 10, qu. 4).

There can be little doubt that this passage was in Hopkins's mind when he wrote of 'the manifestation of the eucharistic victim to the Angels'.

There remains the third difficulty, the doctrinal one already mentioned. But for Hopkins this is no difficulty. It is a conclusion which he wholly accepts. He distinguishes quite definitely between Christ's real entry as a creature into the angelic world and his conception on our earth in historic time; and he conjures up two Greek terms to emphasize the distinction. *Ensarkosis*, 'the taking of flesh', was the former. *Enanthropesis*, 'the becoming man', was the latter. It is like distinguishing two events in the great sentence of St John: 'The Word was made flesh—and came to dwell among us.'

This is Hopkins's most startling and original theological innovation. It must be left to the theologians to judge it.[1]

Two things, however, may perhaps usefully be said. In the first place, supposing that one rejected the distinction just mentioned, supposing also that one rejected all the paraphernalia of the battle in heaven, Hopkins's devotional insight would still be a valid and most fruitful one. True devotion, to be born, requires close union with a personal saviour; but to be nourished it must be able to move at ease on the great heights of revelation. Any experience which puts one *inside* the doctrines of the Church is of the utmost value. Such an experience, for Hopkins, was the perception of Christ adoring the Father. It took him as nearly as possible to the heart of theology and, one might say, to the heart of God. It made him friends at once not only with the central mysteries of the Trinity and the Incarnation, but with those aspects of revelation which more recent times have stressed and amplified: the Mass and the Mystical Body, the Sacred Heart and the Immaculate Conception. Indeed it might be said that the whole tendency of modern devotion —the integration of the liturgy with one's personal life, 'per ipsum et cum ipso et in ipso',—the institution of new feasts such as the Kingship of Christ and the Coronation of Mary—is moving in a direction which Hopkins seems to have anticipated.

The second thing is on the supposition that Hopkins's distinction

[1] Similar speculations are to be found in certain Early Fathers and ecclesiastical writers, commenting on the Old Testament theophanies and on the temporal generation of the Word. These speculations were materially heterodox and became obsolete. Cf. D'Alès, *De Deo Trino* (Paris, 1934), pp. 75–89.

between *ensarkosis* and *enanthropesis* were allowed as tenable, it might have an important bearing on the future. Space-travel and the discovery of other planets are now possibilities that have to be taken into account. In the event (however unlikely) of some form of rational life being found on another planet, the question of the redemption would be bound to arise. If Hopkins's distinction were valid, one would not have to suppose that the creatures of another planet had been deprived of the light of the Incarnation because they had had no historical knowledge of Christ's life and death on earth. The whole affair is too vague and problematical to be worth discussing further. But perhaps just that much was worth saying.

Hopkins's inspiration of 'the great sacrifice' by no means exhausts the interest of his spiritual writings. But the notes and appendix to this book are already so full that there seems little justification for adding anything here. There is, however, just one point which must be discussed because of its connexion with Part III of this Introduction, which returns to the biographical thread. It concerns Hopkins's psychology.

His introspective isolation of the self (in the great treatise included here as Chapter 1) and his relating of the self to the highest form of will-activity was in tune with the most advanced psychology of his time; there are several points where he anticipates William James. But just as Augustine and the mediaevals discovered a new psychology of personality in the light of the Trinity and the Incarnation, so Hopkins came to his original conclusions from the light shed by 'the great sacrifice'.

As has been said, he interpreted Philippians ii as a description of Christ's healing reparation of the sin of Lucifer which disrupted the universe. Lucifer's sin, as Hopkins says, was an exclusive 'instressing of his own inscape', that is, an excessive dwelling on his own likeness to God. He was right to adore God as mirrored in his own nature. At the same time he had the power to hold his will free and balanced in case an even truer image of God should be proposed for adoration. But he did the contrary. When the truer image was proposed he averted his will wholly from it and adored his own nature. (As Augustine has it: 'he preferred the likeness of God to the service of God'.) Christ repaired this primal sin for us all to see and understand at the agony in the garden of Gethsemane. He did not make his equality with God 'a snatching-matter'. All that was noblest in his human nature seemed to revolt from the Passion proposed; but he kept his free will balanced to follow the divine will. 'Let this chalice pass from me. But not as I will, but as thou willest.'

From these two prototypes, of obedience and disobedience, Hopkins derived his oft-repeated distinction between the 'elective will' (or *voluntas ut arbitrium*) and the 'affective will' (or *voluntas ut natura*). One of his recurring preoccupations is to show that St Ignatius proposed and required the same distinction in his *Spiritual Exercises*. The distinction may be said to be one between 'desire' and 'choice'. The point that is worth a brief discussion here—because of its bearing on his practical life—is whether Hopkins was right in sometimes taking for granted an inevitable opposition between the two.

By Scotus, no doubt, he was confirmed in his distinction. But Scotus, though he distinguishes between desire and choice in the higher or rational part of the soul, yet never thinks of them as *opposed* to each other in the way that the sensitive appetite of fallen man must sometimes be opposed to his rational appetite. Scotus's point is simply that, although the force of rational love is irresistible, the power of choice is not swamped by it; it rides the flood freely; for freedom does not consist in the presence of alternatives, it is an intrinsic power. 'The soul', he says, 'in her rational desire is wholly attracted to the supremely intelligible, just as the senses are attracted to the supremely delightful; but in her freedom she can check herself even as she elicits the act.'[1] He means that love is a free act, not a conditioned impulse. In his prologue to the *Scriptum Oxoniense* he uses, as Hopkins does, the terms *electiva* and *affectiva* of the will, but he treats them as two elements in the same act of love; he says that rational desire supplies the impetus for choice and that choice, as an expression of the whole man, would be impossible without it. This is the theme of St Augustine's famous passage commenting on Our Lord's words: 'Nobody can come to me without being *attracted* by the Father who sent me . . .' (John vi. 44).[2]

This too, in more prosaic language, was St Ignatius's view. He distinguished often (as Hopkins never failed to note) between desire and choice, but he always insisted that they should go together. This is the whole point of his insistence on what he called 'obedience of

---

[1] '. . . Inquantum est mere appetitus intellectivus, summe inclinaretur actualiter ad optimum intelligibile, sicut est de optimo visibili et visu, tamen, in quantum libera est, potest se refrenare in eliciendo actum' (*Oxoniense*, IV. xlix. 4).

[2] 'Noli cogitare te invitum trahi: trahitur animus et amore. . . . Quomodo voluntate credo, si trahor? Ego dico: Parum est voluntate: etiam voluptate traheris. Quid est, trahi voluptate? Delectare in Domino et dabit tibi petitiones cordis tui. Est quaedam voluptas cordis cui panis dulcis est ille caelestis. Porro si poetae dicere licuit: Trahit sua quemque voluptas: non necessitas, sed voluptas: non obligatio, sed delectatio: quanto fortius nos dicere debemus, trahi hominem ad Christum qui delectatur veritate, delectatur beatitudine, delectatur justitia, delectatur sempiterna vita, quod totum Christus est? An vero habent corporis sensus voluptates suas, et animus deseritur a voluptatibus suis? . . . Da amantem et sentit quod dico: da desiderantem, da esurientem, da in ista solitudine peregrinantem, atque sitientem, et fontem aeternae patriae suspirantem: da talem, et scit quid dicam' (see Roman Breviary for Wednesday after Whit Sunday).

the understanding'. It is often supposed that his teaching on obedience was summed up in the similes about the subject making himself
'like a corpse, or like the staff in an old man's hand'—passive and
supine. Such a supposition is quite wrong. These similes are neither
originally nor significantly Ignatian. They are well-worn images
from ancient times which he could hardly avoid using; but his own
contribution was something quite other. What he asked for and
advised (he did not attempt to *command* it) was obedience of the
understanding. He did not mean that the will should or could
constrain the understanding to go against the known truth; he
expressly excludes that as wrong and indeed impossible. What he
meant was that, when a man has chosen what he believes to be
right, he should not let his understanding (the desires, affections,
and sympathies of his rational nature) be separated from his choice.
When such a separation threatens, he should use his self-knowledge
to coax and incline his understanding back to the path of choice; 'if
you cannot desire,' he says, for example, 'then *desire* to desire . . . '.
For with the failure of joy and spontaneity all the goodness begins
to go out of service, and it cannot long remain loyal.[1] He also
recommends that if a man *is* commanded to do something which,
though not sinful, is against his better judgment, he should take
pains to put forward his point of view clearly and concisely to the
superior, so that the bitterness of doubt and self-reproach may not
be added to his dilemma.

Painful situations are bound to arise when desire and choice seem
irreconcilable, situations which may approximate in pain to what
St John of the Cross called 'the night of the understanding'. But as
long as the general intention to do God's Will is not lost, there will
always be a handhold on those cliffs—'hold them cheap may who
ne'er hung there'!—by which rational desire can struggle back to a
footing at a new level on the path of choice. The supreme example
was given by Our Lord in the garden of Gethsemane when desire
and choice seemed laid wide open and apart. At the end of his
prayer and bloody sweat they had come together again.[2]

It is to be understood, however, that such crises are very rare
and only for those who are made worthy by God to sustain them
victoriously. The general rule, as Hopkins says, 'is that consolation
should be our normal state and that when God withdraws it he

[1] 'Quod si forte quis aliquo temporis spatio obediat per communem illam
apprehensionem qua censetur perperam etiam praecipienti parendum esse, certe
id stabile ac fixum esse non potest: atque ita perseverantia deficit, vel saltem
obedientiae perfectio quae in prompte et alacriter obediendo consistit; nec enim
ibi potest esse alacritas ac diligentia ubi est animorum sententiarumque dissensio'
(*Epistola de virtute obedientiae*, par. 12).
[2] Suarez treats of this in his comment on the passage from which Hopkins took his
phrase *voluntas ut natura*. See note p. 292 (146. 3).

wishes us to strive to recover it'—consolation being the prevenient assurance that the object to be chosen is supremely desirable. One reason for this rule is clear, and it is stated most graphically by Hopkins. The irremediable divorce between desire and choice is the state of the damned in hell. The complete and utter union of desire and choice is true love, a pledge of heaven. (This applies of course to the married state, as a sharing in the Mystical Body, as well as to the religious, *mutatis mutandis*.)

It may be mentioned in passing that the deliberate refusal to allow desire and choice to be separated was the main inspiration of seventeenth-century religious art and poetry. As soon as the separation is sanctioned, the beauty begins to go out of religion and the certitude out of art.

All this, it is clear, Hopkins knew very well and kept deepening the knowledge of it. It represents his normal and considered position, and examples of his adhesion to it occur again and again in his poetry and his prose. Yet every now and again, both in his sermons and spiritual writings, there are signs of a dark opposing presupposition which he seems unable to exorcize wholly: the presupposition of the lonely will struggling grimly against *all* that is most attractive to his higher nature.

He says, for example,[1] that a man's personality and his nature are joined together by God in a wholly arbitrary manner—as if a man could be saddled with a nature fundamentally out of tune with his destiny. What he says in another place[2] is a logical consequence of this: that no initial impulse towards God the infinite can come from the spontaneous desire of the soul, all initiative comes from this isolated and mysterious *ego*, the *arbitrium* or 'self':

> But the tendency in the soul towards an infinite object comes from the *arbitrium*. The *arbitrium* in itself is man's personality or individuality and places him on a level of individuality in some sense with God; so that in so far as God is one thing, a self, an individual being, he is an object of apprehension, desire, pursuit to man's *arbitrium*.

This suggests the image of 'wrestling with God' in the sextet of *Poems*, 64, which disappoints somewhat after the unsurpassable first lines of the octet. It is an image which is somehow alien to Catholic spirituality.

In a seemingly different, but in fact connected, context he says in a sermon[3] that the mere fact of being esteemed makes a man proud. This is not true; esteem is a good which a man can use for the glory of God or misuse for his own. But the vanity of self-esteem

---

[1] See note p. 293 (146. 6).   [2] See note p. 291 (138. 4).
[3] See notes p. 275 (16. 1, 16. 2).

is in any case another and lesser danger than the lonely pride of self-satisfaction in self-will. To desire fame is more a folly than a crime, since it brings to most men—and it certainly would to a Jesuit—as much mockery and distress as soothing flattery. But a certain measure of esteem is the natural climate which a man's gifts require in order to operate fruitfully.[1] To desire a certain measure of esteem may be a mark of humility if a man knows he cannot work well without it; to reject it may be a mark of pride. Caught between Hopkins's exaggeration of the *arbitrium* and his horror of esteem lay his poetic genius.

His poetic genius was his very essence, his 'inscape', his special likeness to the Divine Essence. Yet Hopkins the Jesuit behaved to Hopkins the poet as a Victorian husband might to a wife of whom he had cause to be ashamed. His muse was a highborn lady, a chaste matron, dedicate to God; but he treated her in public as a slut, and her children as an unwanted and vaguely sinful burden. This is a dangerous thing to say because it raises biographical problems which can only be briefly indicated, but indicated they must be, in so far as they are bound up with his exaggerated distinction between the affective and the elective will.

It is certain that Hopkins was keenly and even agonizingly aware of his duty to these children, his poems, and that in secret he loved them passionately. This is clear from his letters, especially from the exchange with Dixon (November–December 1881) about 'the counterpoise'. A man, in order to manage his nature, has sometimes to lay far more stress in one direction than is ideally right, for fear that, if he tries merely to keep the balance, he will be overthrown. St Ignatius, for example, in the early days of his conversion committed certain 'pious follies' which he condemned in later years and would not allow his disciples to imitate. But in such cases a man is a surer judge of others' problems than of his own.

From this would arise the whole question of Hopkins's relations with his Superiors. If his Superiors attached no importance to his poetry, then he was aiming at the perfection of obedience in trying to make their attitude his own. But, on the other hand, if they had allowed him—as they probably would have done, had they been asked—to let Dixon publish some of his poems, was it not his duty to take this indirect means of enlightening them? One does not have to be cynical to know that to the practical mind an unpublished poem may seem a waste of time, but a published poem is, after all, an achievement. In Hopkins's reply to Dixon[2] it is not easy to

[1] This was Hopkins's own considered and very emphatic assertion in Oct. 1886. (*Letters*, i. 231.)
[2] *Letters*, ii. 29–31.

distinguish between his spiritual desire to be unknown and his sensitive horror of ridicule.

Now it is certain that Hopkins's stress on a naked, anti-natural, non-affective will does not come either from Scotus or from St Ignatius, the two main influences in his spiritual writings. But since that time there had been the Romantic Movement, Carlyle's 'Heroes', and the Victorian code of ethics. From the Romantic Movement came the notion of the poet as a rival priest and of poetry as a new and more revealing religion. As to the Victorian code, one does not have to be a social historian to know that in the days of one's grandparents the dichotomy between 'duty' and 'inclination' was taken for granted at every level—provided the inclination was conscious. The idea of duty itself being an inclination was unheard of; duty was a sort of Kantian categorical imperative. It would be surprising if something of this atmosphere had not invaded the training of an English Jesuit of that period. There is here a problem which all who aim at holiness have to solve. In the *Imitation of Christ*, which is prescribed reading for all Jesuits, a stark contrast is drawn between nature and grace, and in the writings of many of the saints, St John of the Cross, for instance, all creatures have to be denied. The Christian solution is not Manichæan, but undoubtedly in the nineteenth century a perhaps Jansenistic spirit crept at times into Catholic spirituality, which corresponded with the severe educational and religious ideals current in England at that time.

At any rate there were in the English Province at that time many men of great, even gigantic, moral stature—a surprising number of them converts, like Hopkins, from a strictly practised Protestantism. Hopkins had an intense desire to be worthy of his place among such men. It sometimes escaped him that this desire was entitatively the same as his desire to praise God through his poetry. Instead he tended to think of his love of beauty as a weakness to which stronger men than he were not liable, and to throw the whole weight of his indomitable will against it. So he exaggerated Scotus's distinction between nature and individuality; he assigned all his love of beauty to the *voluntas ut natura* and all his desire for holiness to the naked *arbitrium*, instead of remembering that the love of beauty is—as Scotus says it is—the initial impulse to the love of God. In this way, his psychological error about the *arbitrium* may be looked on both as a cause and an effect of his depreciation of his poetic genius.

Once more it must be stressed that this was not Hopkins's normal and settled poise. It was a kink which threatened him when he was off-balance. And even then, who is to say that, *under those circumstances*, he did not choose rightly? The 'counterpoise', though excessive in itself, may have been right for the whole. The criticisms levelled at him here are meant as investigators only. They are not in any sense conclusions. The only possible conclusion is that, mixed though his motives may have been both conscious and unconscious, he believed with complete sincerity that the sacrifice of his poetic gifts was a faithful imitation of Our Lord in 'the great sacrifice'. In reply to Dixon's simple but really unanswerable remark: 'Surely one vocation cannot destroy another', he wrote: 'Now if you value what I write, as I do myself, much more does our Lord. And if he chooses to avail himself of what I leave at his disposal he can do so with a felicity and a success which I could never command' (*Letters*, ii. 93).

As things have turned out, who dare say that he was not right?

CHAPTER ONE

FIRST PRINCIPLE AND FOUNDATION

Text of Exercises (*Principium sive Fundamentum*), Notes of GMH.
Further Notes of GMH on the Foundation.

Man was created to praise, reverence and serve God Our Lord,
and by so doing to save his soul. And the other things on the face
of the earth were created for man's sake and to help him in the
carrying out of the end for which he was created. Hence it follows
that man should make use of creatures so far as they help him to
attain his end and withdraw from them so far as they hinder him
from so doing. For that, it is necessary to make ourselves indifferent in regard to all created things in so far as it is left to the choice
of our free will and there is no prohibition; in such sort that we
do not on our part seek for health rather than sickness, for riches
rather than poverty, for honour rather than dishonour, for a long
life rather than a short one; and so in all other things, desiring and
choosing only those which may better lead us to the end for which
we were created.

ON *Principium sive Fundamentum*

'Homo creatus est'[1]—Aug. 20 1880: during this retreat, which I am
making at Liverpool, I have been thinking about creation and this
thought has led the way naturally through the exercises hitherto. I
put down some thoughts.—We may learn that all things are created
by consideration of the world without or of ourselves the world
within. The former is the consideration commonly dwelt on, but
the latter takes on the mind more hold.[2] I find myself both as man
and as myself something most determined and distinctive, at pitch,
more distinctive and higher pitched than anything else I see; I find
myself with my pleasures and pains, my powers and my experiences,
my deserts and guilt, my shame and sense of beauty, my dangers,
hopes, fears, and all my fate, more important to myself than anything I see. And when I ask where does all this throng and stack of
being, so rich, so distinctive, so important, come from / nothing I
see can answer me. And this whether I speak of human nature or of
my individuality, my selfbeing. For human nature, being more
highly pitched, selved, and distinctive than anything in the world,
can have been developed, evolved, condensed, from the vastness of
the world not anyhow or by the working of common powers but

only by one of finer or higher pitch and determination than itself and certainly than any that elsewhere we see, for this power had to force forward the starting or stubborn elements to the one pitch required. And this is much more true when we consider the mind; when I consider my selfbeing, my consciousness and feeling of myself, that taste of myself, of *I* and *me* above and in all things, which is more distinctive than the taste of ale or alum, more distinctive than the smell of walnutleaf or camphor, and is incommunicable by any means to another man (as when I was a child I used to ask myself: What must it be to be someone else?). Nothing else in nature comes near this unspeakable stress of pitch, distinctiveness, and selving, this selfbeing of my own. Nothing explains it or resembles it, except so far as this, that other men to themselves have the same feeling. But this only multiplies the phenomena to be explained so far as the cases are like and do resemble. But to me there is no resemblance: searching nature I taste *self* but at one tankard, that of my own being. The development, refinement, condensation of nothing shews any sign of being able to match this to me or give me another taste of it, a taste even resembling it.

One may dwell on this further. We say that any two things however unlike are in something like. This is the one exception: when I compare my self, my being-myself, with anything else whatever, all things alike, all in the same degree, rebuff me with blank unlikeness; so that my knowledge of it, which is so intense, is from itself alone, they in no way help me to understand it. And even those things with which I in some sort identify myself, as my country or family, and those things which I own and call mine, as my clothes and so on, all presuppose the stricter sense of *self* and *me* and *mine* and are from that derivative.

From what then do I with all my being and above all that taste of self, that selfbeing, come? Am I due (1) to chance? (2) to myself, as selfexistent? (3) to some extrinsic power?

(1) Chance in name no one acknowledges as a cause or principle or explanation of being. But to call things positive facts and refuse further explanation is to explain them by chance. What then is chance proper, not chance as we use it for causes unknown or causes beside a present purpose?—Chance applies only to things possible; what must be does not come by chance and what cannot be by no chance comes. Chance then is the ἐνέργεια, the stress, of the intrinsic possibility which things have. *A* chance is an event come about by its own intrinsic possibility. And as mere possibility, passive power, is not power proper and has no activity it cannot of itself come to stress, cannot instress itself. And in fact chance existence is a selfexistence. Chance is incredible or impossible by this *a priori*

consideration, but more strikingly is it incredible from experience. It is never verified and the more examined the less it is verified, the more is it out of the question. For if it is a chance for anything at any given instant to exist and exist as so-and-so it is so for the next. These chances are equal and in any finite time it is infinitely unlikely that it should continue being and being what it was, for there are infinite instants. It is incredible then that its continued existence should be due to chance. If you say that its being is the mental flush of a string of broken existences at very small average intervals, this is incredible because monstrous. Moreover its nature should quite change, for its parts might chance elsewhere and the parts of other things here, and the variation will be infinite. The most plausible, if anything is plausible here, is that virgin matter is due to chance, other things not. But as this does not affect the present case it may be let alone. No man then can believe that his being is due to chance.

(2) Can I then be selfexistent and even in some way necessary?— This is clearly not true of my body and that crowd of being in me spoken of above, but may it be true of some part of it or something in it, *aliquid ejus*, the soul, the mind and its consciousness?

The mind and all my being is finite. This is plain in its outward and inward operations. In its outward, for there is a resistance in the body and things outside the body which it cannot overcome; there is a degree of effort, pain, weariness to which it yields. And in the inward; it has a finite insight, memory, grasp of apprehension, power of calculation, invention, force of will.

Nothing finite can exist of itself. For being finite it is limited and determined in time and space, as the mind is limited and determined to particular dates of time and place by the body. And apart from the body it is determined. I say apart from the body because it may be maintained that the mind has no bound from space nor even from time, for it may exist after death and may have existed before birth. Nevertheless it is finite in its own being,[1] as said above, and determined. Its faculties compared one with another and compared with those of other minds are determined; they might be more, they might be less, they might be otherwise; they are then determined and distinctive. It is plain it might have more perfection, more being. Nevertheless the being it has got has a great perfection, a great stress, and is more distinctive and higher selved, than anything else I see, except other such minds, in nature. Now to be determined and distinctive is a perfection, either self-bestowed or bestowed from without. In anything finite it cannot be self-bestowed; nothing finite can determine its own being, I mean its being as a whole; nothing finite can determine what itself shall, in a world of being, be. For to determine is a perfection, greater than and certainly never less than, the perfection of being determined. It is a function of a nature, even if it should be the whole function, the naturing, the selving of that nature. It always in nature's order is after the nature it is of. Nothing finite then can either begin to exist or eternally have existed of itself, because nothing can in the order of time or even of nature act before it exists or exercise function and determination before it has a nature to 'function' and determine, to selve and instress,[1] with; how much less then when the very determination is what the determiner itself is to be and the selving what its self shall be like! And this is above all true of that inmost self of mine which has been said to be and to be felt to be, to taste, more distinctive than the taste of clove or alum, the smell of walnutleaf or hart'shorn,[2] more distinctive, more selved, than all things else and needing in proportion a more exquisite determining, selfmaking, power.

But is it as a last alternative possible that, though neither my body nor the faculties and functions of my soul exist of themselves, there should be one thing in the soul or mind, as if compounded or selved-up with these, which does? a most spiritual principle in some manner the form of the mind as the mind or the soul is said to be of the body; so that my mind would be one selving or pitch of a great universal mind, working in other minds too besides mine, and even in all other things, according to their natures and powers and becoming conscious in man. And this would be that very / distinctive self that was spoken of. Here we touch the *intellectus agens* of the Averrhoists[3] and the doctrine of the Hegelians and others.

Whether anything of this sort can be true or not, alike I find that I myself can not be selfexistent. I may treat the question from the side of my being, which is said to be compounded, selved-up, or identified with this universal mind, or from the side of the universal mind itself. And first from my side.

The universal mind being identified not only with me but also with all other minds cannot be the means of communicating what is individual in me to them nor in them to me. I have and every other has, as said above, my own knowledge and powers, pleasures, pains, merit, guilt, shame, dangers, fortunes, fates: we are not chargeable for one another. But these things and above all my shame, my guilt, my fate are the very things in feeling, in tasting, which I most taste that selftaste which nothing in the world can match. The universal cannot taste this taste of self as I taste it, for it is not to it, let us say / to him, that the guilt or shame, the fatal consequence, the fate, comes home; either not at all or not altogether. If not at all, then he is altogether outside of my self, my personality / one may call it, my *me*. If not altogether, if for instance there is something done or willed which I am wholly chargeable with and answerable for and he only so far as I am a part of him, a function or selving of his, then only so far is he answerable and chargeable, and this difference may make the difference of mortal and venial sin and of a happy or unhappy fate. Put it thus: suppose my little finger could have a being of its own, a personal being, without ceasing to be my finger and my using it and feeling in it; if I now hold it in the candle-flame the pain of the burning, though the selfsame feeling of pain, experienced by me in my finger and by my finger in itself, will be nevertheless unlike in us two, for to my finger it is the scorching of its whole self, but to me the scorching only of one finger. And beyond this, taking it morally, if I have freely put my finger into the flame and the finger is unwilling, but unable to resist, then I am guilty of my folly and self-mutilation, but my finger is innocent; if on the other hand my finger is willing, then it is more guilty than I, for to me the loss of a finger is but mutilation, but to my finger itself it is selfmurder. Or if again it were selfsacrifice the sacrifice would be nobler in the finger, to which it was a holocaust, than in me, in whom it was the consuming of a part only. Though then I most intimately share my finger's feeling of pain, for indeed it is to me and to it one and the same, I do not share its feeling of self at all and share little, if I share any, of its guilt or merit, fortune and fate. So then the universal mind is outside of my inmost self and not within it; nor does it share my state, my moral standing, or my fate. And for all that this universal being may be at work in mine it leaves me finite: *I* am selfexistent none the more for any part the selfexistent plays in me.

And the same conclusion follows if I look at the matter from the other side, that of the universal mind or being itself. For (1) the universal being too must have its self, its distinctive being, and distinctive more than mine. For if this is what I find myself to have above all other things I see, except only my peers in nature, other men, this self, in its taste to me so distinctive, how much more this greater being! Now if it, or he, has the same intimate feeling, consciousness, of all that goes on in me as I have of what goes on in my finger, so that even I were to him like a part or member, or not to speak of parts or members in what is infinite, as a feature or a selving, yet as my self was outside my finger's in the case supposed above and its self outside mine so must this infinite being's self be outside of mine as clearly as mine is outside of his: he must be able to think, mean, and say *I* and *me* as much as I am and when he says them he does not mean me who write this. Then too if, as said above, he does not (or not in the same degree) bear my guilt or merit or feel my shame, neither do I his: if e.g. it is ambition in him to want to be identified with or compounded or selved-up with all things, that is not my case nor my ambition, for I am compounded only with him and that by no choice of mine; if it is charity in him so to impart himself to all, that is not my case nor my merit either. And more generally (2) his *inlaw*, the law of his being is unlike mine, as the Ten of Hearts is unlike any one of the hearts in it: it is many or made of many, each of them is one. In fact his very composition with me, being a sample of his composition with other things, all things, makes him unlike me or any other one thing. If X is compounded with A, B, C, D etc so as to give AX, BX, CX, DX etc, then X has its being in a series, which is its inlaw, but A and B or AX and BX have not. And if it has besides a simple being X besides the series, that makes the matter no better. Whether then the universal mind by *me* and *myself* means his Being X or his Being in the shape of the series AX, BX etc he has another self than mine, which is, say, CX; either way self tastes differently to him and to me.

For, to speak generally, whatever can with truth be called a self—not merely in logic or grammar, as if one said Nothingness itself—, such as individuals and persons must be, it is not a mere centre or point of reference for consciousness or action attributed to it, everything else, all that it is conscious of or acts on being its object only and outside it. Part of this world of objects, this object-world, is also part of the very self in question, as in man's case his own body, which each man not only feels in and acts with but also feels and acts on. If the centre of reference spoken of has concentric circles round it, one of these, the inmost, say, is its own, is óf it, the rest are tó it only. Within a certain bounding line all will be self, outside of it nothing: with it self begins from one side and ends from the other. I look through my eye and the window and the air; the eye is my eye and of me and me, the windowpane is my windowpane but not of me nor me. A self then will consist of a centre *and* a surrounding area or circumference, of a point of reference *and* a belonging field, the latter set out, as surveyors etc say, from the former; of two elements, which we may call the inset and the outsetting or the display.[1] Now this applies to the universal mind or being too; it will have its inset and its outsetting; only that the outsetting includes all things, with all of which it is in some way, by turns, in a series, or however it is, identified. But then this is an altogether different outsetting from what each of those very things to its own particular self has. And since self consists in the relation the inset and the outsetting bear to one another, the universal has a relation different from everything else and everything else from everything else, including the universal, so that the self of the universal is not the self of anything else. In other words the universal is not really identified with everything else nor with anything else, which was supposed; that is / there is no such universal.

(In shewing there is no universal a true self which is 'fetched' or 'pitched' or 'selved' in every other self, I do not deny[1] that there is a universal really,[2] and not only logically, thus fetched in the universals,* but either it is selfless and they Selves, as may be the case in Man, or else it may be a true Self and they like its members only and not true Selves, something like which I am inclined to believe the species and individual in the brutes,[3] or at least that the specific form, the form of the whole species, is nearer being a true Self than the individual. But these universals are finite only.

In the case of such a universal as humanity these questions would arise: *first* of the attributes—say the merit or guilt—of each member, each individual by and to itself; *next* those of the universal collectively, the average morality; *thirdly* those of each member considered as a pitch of the universal and so of the universal morality and the degree in which each agrees or disagrees with, avows or disavows this average morality.

Neither do I deny that God is so deeply present to everything ('Tu autem, O bone omnipotens, eras superior summo meo et interior intimo meo')[4] that it would be impossible for him but for his infinity[5] not to be identified with them or, from the other side, impossible but for his infinity so to be present to them. This is oddly expressed, I see; I mean / a being so intimately present as God is to other things would be identified with them were it not for God's infinity or were it not for God's infinity he could not be so intimately present to things.

There is another proof that the universal being cannot be selved in or identified with all other things. Either the universal is selved not only in this world of things but in all possible ones or only in this one. If in all possible worlds then there is no difference between possible and actual and all possible and 'incompossible', incompatible, frames of being exist together or *are* together, for what coexist with a third thing (or are as true as a third thing) coexist with (or are as true as) one another. But this is absurd. Only then is this. Then this world must have been determined by the universal being out of all possible worlds, for, as shewn above, it could not determine its own being or determine itself into being. If so the universal exercises choice, is selfdetermining. But this is a great proof of self. It has then a self independent of its supposed selving in other things or, in other words it is not selved in or identified with other things.

No thing then, including myself, is in any sense selfexistent except this great being.

(3) The third alternative then follows, that I am due to an extrinsic power.

* Probably a slip for 'individuals'. See note p. 293 (146. 5) [Ed.].

(Remark that the assumption in no. 2 is to assume in oneself a hypostatic union.)[1]—Aug. 12 1882

FURTHER NOTES ON THE FOUNDATION

Dec. 19 1879—Reverence, praise, and service do not indeed mean faith, hope, and charity but are natural virtues due from man to God; still they would do in nature what the three theological virtues do. At least they may be ranked with them in this way—reverence, or right mind about God, with faith; praise, the joyfully welcoming God's manifestations of himself, with hope; service, that is / obedience to God's law, justice before God, with charity. And in all these points the heathen (Rom. i.) failed to do their duty: they did not praise him ('cum cognovissent Deum non sicut Deum glorificaverunt aut gratias egerunt' 21.) or reverence him ('non probaverunt Deum habere in notitia' 28.) but fell into idolatry ('qui commutaverunt veritatem Dei in mendacium et coluerunt et servierunt creaturae potius quam Creatori' 25.) and served him neither by worship (as just above) nor by good life ('cum justitiam Dei cognovissent non intellexerunt quoniam qui talia agunt digni sunt morte' 32.). They broke the law of nature and deserved death, nor did the Jews also keep the law from Sinai, as is said in the same Epistle

Aug. 7 1882—God's utterance of himself in himself is God the Word, outside himself is this world. This world then is word, expression, news of God. Therefore its end, its purpose, its purport, its meaning, is God and its life or work to name and praise him. Therefore praise put before reverence and service

See foot of p. 26 MS: the world, man, should after its own manner give God being in return for the being he has given it or should give him back that being he has given. This is done by the great sacrifice. To contribute then to that sacrifice is the end for which man was made (ibidem)

From against p. 26 n.[2] beginning 'Nov. 4 1878 Marie'—I have here changed *motion* to *movement*, which better represents the thought, an impulse in a particular direction

P. 27—'Sanitatem . . . divitias . . . honorem . . . vitam longam'— The things named may be used for good: mere objects of desire, pleasures, he does not name. Health is bodily wellbeing; riches are wellbeing in human society, amongst equals, peers, for to be rich is to be able to gratify desire for an equivalent, for a price, to exchange good possessed for good desired; honour, esteem is wellbeing in the minds of others; next comes power, which is the wellbeing of the will among other wills: its least but most precious part is freedom or independence. A long life is the wellbeing of bare life. Riches seem to be valued for three things: first and most simply they are plenty or *much* in good; next they are beyond everything else means, resources, *opes*, and so the equivalents of good; then they are a mark of or give esteem, status (this should rather be in the second place). But as what a man has is midway between himself, what he is, and the world which he is not and is like an extension of his being and a sphere of himself all round him so the love of having is called the desire of the eyes and reckons as belonging to the mind—Sept. 3 and later 1883.[1]

'Desiderando et eligendo': here distinction of affective and elective will—Sept. 3 1883.

Sept 1883 Beaumont Lodge

Sept. 3. Fundamentum 'Adeo ut non *velimus* . . . unice *desiderando et eligendo*'—dist. of elective and affective will.[2]

'Sanitatem'—goods of the body, desire of the flesh

'Divitias'—goods of fortune, mainly in the body—desire of the eyes

'Honorem'—goods of fortune mainly in the mind—desire of the eyes

'Vitam'—pride of life.

CHAPTER TWO

THE FIRST WEEK

THE FIRST EXERCISE

. . . The first point will be to apply the memory to the first sin, which was that of the angels, and next the understanding, by reasoning on it; and then the will, desiring to remember and understand the whole so that I may be the more ashamed and confounded, bringing into comparison with the one sin of the angels so many sins of mine; and while they have gone to hell for one sin, how many times have I deserved it for so many. I say, to apply the memory to the sin of the angels, how, being created in grace yet *not willing* to help themselves by means of their liberty to reverence and obey their Creator and Lord, falling into pride, they were changed from grace into malice and cast down from heaven into hell; and then to reason more in particular with the understanding and thus to move still more the affections by means of the will.

The second point, to do the same for the sin of Adam and Eve, to bring before the memory how for that sin they did such long penance and how great corruption came upon mankind, *so many men* going towards hell. I say, to apply the memory to the second sin, that of our first parents, how, after Adam had been created in the plain of Damascus and placed in the earthly paradise, and Eve had been formed out of his rib, being forbidden to eat of the tree of knowledge, yet eating of it and so sinning, and afterwards clothed in garments made of skins and driven out of paradise, they lived all their lives in toilsome labour and much penance, without original justice which they had lost; and in turn to reason with the understanding, making use of the will more in particular as has been said before.

The third, to do in like manner in regard to the third sin, that is, the particular sin of some one person who for one mortal sin has gone to hell; and many others without number for fewer sins than I have committed. I say, to do the same in regard to the third particular sin, bringing before the memory the gravity and *malice* of sin against one's *Creator* and Lord, reasoning with the understanding how, in sinning and *acting against the infinite goodness*, such a one has been justly condemned for ever; and to conclude with acts of the will as has been said.

Colloquy. Imagining Christ our Lord present and placed on the Cross, to make a colloquy (asking him) how, being the Creator, He has come to make Himself man, and from eternal life has come to temporal death, and this to die for my sins. Again, reflecting on myself, to ask what have I done for Christ, what am I doing for Christ, what ought I to do for Christ; and then seeing Him in such a condition, and thus hanging upon the Cross, to make the reflections which may present themselves.

The Colloquy is made properly by speaking as a friend speaks to a friend, or as a servant to his master, at one time asking for some favour, at another accusing oneself of some evil done, at another informing him of one's affairs and seeking counsel concerning them.

And to conclude with an *Our Father*.

'Nolentes' sqq.—It seems some scale—sloth, pride ('devenientes in superbiam'), hatred ('conversi fuerint in malitiam'). From notes made June 17 187(7?). Scotus[1] thinks that in Satan's contemplation of his own beauty was a sin of luxury. There was also ambition, avarice of a sort, and envy. Dec. 19 1879
St. Ignatius does not say this sin was in thought only

Secundum Punctum

'In campo Damasceno'—Said for the 'history's' sake, as 'a Nazareth', 'a Bethania', 'ex Monte Sion' etc in the contemplations on our Lord's life. So also about Eve.—It was in the same plain of Damascus that St. Paul *peccatorum princeps* was new-created, that is / regenerated, and from it raised to the third heaven. Damascus lies on the north, that is the cold and mournful side, of the Promised Land, in which some traditions, I think, place Paradise. Sister Emmerich at all events speaks of Adam and Eve coming down from Paradise to the after Garden of Gethsemane.—Caeterum injecta[2] mentione hujus campi Damasceni quasi individuatur Adam et ecceitate loci et materiae signatione—Nov. 5 1878

Tertium Punctum[1]

Sept 1883 Beaumont Lodge
  Sept. 3.

First Exercise—Sin of angels / 'nolentes', sloth, in some sense sin of frailty, inaction, only appearing not so much in non-resistance to evil as in non-execution of good; on the other hand, in third sin 'agendo contra bonitatem', action, sin of malice, ('gravitatem et malitiam peccati'). The sin of our first parents a sin of ignorance in the sense of fixing a false standard of right and wrong, ('arboris scientiae', the test-tree, criterion-of-right-and-wrong-tree); for Eve was deceived into thinking there was something morally beautiful in disobeying, that God had really meant her to disobey; Adam did not think that, but he too was deceived so far as to think God would admire the generosity of his self-sacrifice.

Hence 'justitia originali quam perdiderant', 'bidding' unbidden for a fresh covenant and contract of justice with God.

'Tam multis hominibus' etc—Fr R. must be wrong here:[2] angels lost every sinner for the common sin; man lost not every one for the common original sin; for in particular not Adam and Eve, yet through it many for particular *ones*; thirdly one sinner for his individual sin. For from corruption comes temptation, then with consent sin and from sin damnation.

'Contra suum Creatorem'—here the inordination, ugliness of sin in the frame and world of Creator and creature; 'ab homine', here the preposterousness, rebellion. *Malice* in English = *malignity, malitia* in Latin also = badness, nastiness, ungoodness.

Such a sinner banishes, excommunicates God, and dying finds himself from God banished and excommunicated—which is what he wanted but not the way he wanted it. There is a parallel 'contra Bonitatem infinitam' 'condemnatus in aeternum', the eternity of punishment is one side of the infinite of good sinned against. It is like an infinite removal of good, the removal of good to an infinite degree, which amounts to an infinite evil.

'Ejus attributa'—Remark that he names four attributes answering to the four cardinal virtues—'sapientiam' to prudence; 'omnipotentiam' to fortitude, for consider 'debilitate', frailty; 'justitiam'; 'bonitatem' to temperance, for goodness to us, not goodness in general but mercy, is meant: now mercy is a sort of selfcontrol by which the agent limits good, namely justice, by a greater or an equal good, as temperance is a selfcontrol by which the agent limits good at the point where it would cease to be good and become evil—Dec. 20 1879.

—*Malitia* here then may be, but it is not always elsewhere, the same as *malice*, that is / malignity; but badness and that in the special sense of corruption (and corruption appears especially in impurity) is especially opposed to God's holiness, which is the name we give to God's intrinsic goodness. From this we gather that the very virtue of goodness, which as holiness would most, one would think, incline God to punish, in the form of mercy inclines God to spare—Jan. 27 1882.—

If mercy tempers justice so does justice check indulgence and generosity, so that the control of one virtue by another is not a ground for pairing goodness (above) with temperance in particular

THE THIRD EXERCISE

After the Preparatory Prayer and the two Preludes, the first and second Exercises will be repeated, marking and dwelling on the points in which I have felt greater consolation or desolation, or greater spiritual relish; after which I shall make three Colloquies in the following manner:

The first Colloquy to our Lady, that she may obtain for me grace from her Son and Lord for three things: first, that I may feel an interior knowledge of my sins and an abhorrence of them; second, that I may feel the disorder of my actions in order that, abhorring it, I may amend and order myself rightly; third, to beg for a knowledge of the world in order that, abhorring it, I may put away from myself worldly and vain things; and then a *Hail Mary*.

The second, the same addressed to the Son, that He may obtain it for me from the Father; and then the *Anima Christi*.

The third, the same addressed to the Father that the same eternal Lord may grant it to me; and then the *Our Father*.

There is a way of thinking of past sin such that the thought numbs and kills the heart, as all this Week of the Exercises will do if care is not taken in giving it. It does not seem that we are to pray for this,[1] but for that feeling towards past sin which our Lady felt or would feel when sins were presented to her and shrunk from them instantaneously and which our Lord feels in His members and God Himself, who means us to copy His nature and character as well as we can and put on His mind according to our measure. For they turn from sin by nature (or our Lady as if by nature) and finding it embodied with a thing they love find it infinitely piteous: 'O the pity of it!' and why should it ever have been?—these are the sort of words that express it. So that we may pity ourselves in the same way, that such a thing as sin should ever have got hold of us.[1] This pure pity and disavowal of our past selves is the state of mind of one whose sins are perfectly forgiven. But as long as we are not certain this is the case, which is always,[2] as long as we have before God the status of penitents, which we should have till death, we must not wholly get rid of the shame of sin, for it is a part of penance. Disavowal of sin is the same thing as repentance; it is an act or state of mind the counterpart of the act of will by which a man sinned and the state of will which was induced by it. It is an election of the free will, *arbitrium*. It is unfolded into these three things—(1) penalty, penance (or *a* penance), pain (called *of sense*, though it need not affect the senses), and this corresponds to the material sin committed, the sinful act itself or evil executed, the *mischief* or damage done; (2) shame, which is nearly the same thing as penitence in its narrowest sense and corresponds to the dishonour done, which dishonour is measured by the disproportion between God and the sinner; (3) repentance proper or the change of mind from a resistance to God's will to an obedience to it, which is the counterpart of the rebellion or revolt made against God's precept and expressed will, the resistance of will to will which is in man malice or uncharity, in God reprobation

We are to hate disorder because it is the soil of sin, being by itself a negative thing without natural ugliness. You must consider its known consequences. It is like sleep in a pointsman, steersman, or sentinel. And the world is a frame of things consistent with and in part founded on sin—Understand the above *sensu diviso et composito*: sleep is a thing indifferent, but in a pointsman it is a crime. Disorder or *deordinatio* considered formally appears positive and naturally ugly, but the inordinate act or train of acts may be indifferent; will be so when you are contrasting disorder with sin (L. R., Nov. 27 1881).[3] However it will be true to say that *deordinatio* is a negative evil, because it is a want of subordination, of obedience to God's order; whereas sin is positive *insubordination* or disobedience

THE FIFTH EXERCISE

A MEDITATION ON HELL

Let the Preparatory Prayer be the usual one.

The first Prelude is the composition of place, which is here to see with the eyes of the imagination the length, breadth and depth of hell.

The second, to ask for that which I want. It will be here to ask for an interior *sense of pain* which the lost suffer, so that if I should through my faults forget the love of the Eternal Lord, at least the fear of punishment may help me not to fall into sin.

The first point will be to see with the eyes of the imagination those huge fires, and the souls as it were in bodies of fire.

The second, to hear with the ears the wailings, the groans, the cries, the blasphemies against Christ our Lord and all His Saints.

The third, to smell with the sense of smell, the brimstone, the filth and the corruption.

The fourth, to taste with the sense of taste of bitter things, such as tears, sadness and the worm of conscience.

The fifth, to feel with the sense of touch how those fires touch and burn the souls.

Making a Colloquy with Christ our Lord, to recall to memory the souls that are in hell, some because they did not believe in His coming; others, because, though believing, they did not act according to His commandments; making three classes: the first, before His coming; the second, during His life; the third, since His Life in this world; and therewith to give Him thanks because He has not permitted me to fall into any of these classes by putting an end to my life. In like manner, how until now He has always treated me with so great pity and mercy; ending with the *Our Father*.

'Poenae'—He speaks only of the pain of sense: the reason is the end proposed in this meditation, which is by sensible considerations to deter us from sin. Now he who is 'amoris Domini aeterni oblitus' how can he be brought to a better mind by being told that he will one day be without that which he is content to be without now? Also he speaks of the present condition of the lost, who are disembodied; therefore it is, I suppose, that he mingles without reserve or remark physical and figurative things, like brimstone and tears (which the disembodied soul cannot shed) and the worm of conscience. And as it is by the imagination that we are to realize these things so I suppose it to be by the imagination that the lost suffer them and that as intensely as by the senses or it may be more so. This simple explanation will never strike our[1] scholastics, because they do not see that there is an intellectual imagination. Our action leaves in our minds scapes or species, the extreme 'intention'[2] or instressing of which would be painful and the pain would be that of fire, sup-posing fire to be the condition of a body (and by analogy of any substance) *texturally at stress*.[3] The soul then can be instressed *in* the species or scape of any bodily action (whether this gives rise to a physical and quantitative extension of its substance or not) and so *towards* the species or scape of any object, as of sight, sound, taste, smell; and a high degree of such instress would in each case be the pain of fire, so that every other pain would be besides a pain of fire. How then is the soul so set at stress? As I suppose by some main stress from without, and that this is expressed by 'ingentes illos ignes' St Ignatius speaks of, as the current of air in the blowpipe casts or addresses a jet of flame this way or that. The seven gifts of the Holy Spirit are spoken of as seven spirits, seven jets or currents of breath; so it may be of 'the breath of the Lord that kindled Tophet of old', the stress of God's anger which first 'prepared' or* called into being fire against the Devil and his angels—that it was an intensification of or terrible instress upon the substance of one, Satan, first of all, casting that, with straining, in one direction (which is the being cast down to hell) and acting through that, by a sub-ordination or hierarchy (hence 'his angels', missionaries, subalterns), on the rest, so that their obedience to him is one of slavish fear and necessity. (So, I think, as a magnetic current is heightened needles and shreds of iron rear, stare, and group themselves, *se dressent*, at the poles. And this same fire I suppose to be called darkness and chains or imprisonment for these reasons. (2 Pet. ii. 4. σειροῖς ζόφου ταρταρώσας παρέδωκεν, εἰς κρίσιν τηρουμένους, Jud. 6. εἰς κρίσιν μεγάλης ἡμέρας δεσμοῖς ἀϊδίοις ὑπὸ ζόφον τετήρηκεν[1]): The fall from heaven was for the rebel angels what death is for man. As in man all that energy or instress with which the soul animates and other-wise acts in the body is by death thrown back upon the soul itself: so in them was that greater stock of activity with which they act, intellectually and otherwise, throughout their own world or element of spirit, which is perhaps, as I have thought, flushed by every spirit living in it. This throwing back or confinement of their energy is a dreadful constraint or imprisonment and, as intellectual action is spoken of under the figure of sight, it will in this case be an imprisonment in darkness, a being in the dark; for darkness is the phenomenon of foiled action in the sense of sight. But this constraint and this blindness or darkness will be most painful when it is the main stress or energy of the whole being that is thus balked. This is its strain or tendency towards being,[2] towards good, towards God—being, that is / their own more or continued being, good / their own good, their natural felicity, and God / the God at least of nature, not to speak of grace. This strain must go on after their fall, because it is the strain of creating action as received in the creature and cannot cease without the creature's ceasing to be. On the other hand the strain or tendency towards God through Christ and the great sacrifice had by their own act been broken, refracted, and turned aside, and it was only through Christ and the great

* *v.* Isa. xxx. 33.

sacrifice[1] that God had meant any being to come to him at all. But the perversion of their being in the first moment of their sin, when sanctifying grace died out in them, was not felt, because their natural activities still, till the obedient angels turned upon them and expelled them, played freely; it was felt as soon as these were violently restrained, as above; this violence was exercised by God through the Holy Angels his servants as instruments, as is read in the Apocalypse. The one stress or strain then encountered and clashed with the other; for instance the will addressed, 'at forepitch', towards beatitude, happiness, in God, with its own act of aversion, with the scape or species, indurated in it, of the act by which it turned aside; the understanding open wide like an eye, towards truth in God, towards light, is confronted by that scape, that act of its own, which blotted out God and so put blackness in the place of light; does not see God but sees that, so giving a meaning to something I remember in St Theresa's vision of hell, to this effect: 'I know not how it is, but in spite of the darkness the eye sees there all that to see is most afflicting'.[2] Against these acts of its own the lost spirit dashes itself like a caged bear and is in prison, violently in-stresses them and burns, stares into them and is the deeper darkened.

From the above it follows, geometrically, the greater the aversion the greater the pain and, morally, the greater the disobedience the greater the pain;

The keener the consciousness the greater the pain;

The greater the stress of being the greater the pain: both these show that the higher the nature the greater the penalty.

One sees that God could relieve this pain by diminishing consciousness. Hence also the diversion of consciousness is a relief and therefore the activity of the devils in this lower world, on this earth, to which they fell, is a relief and the higher the faculty employed the greater the relief, hence the tempting man; also possession. It would moreover seem that the concentration of the mind on the scapes of its own sin is some relief, as we act over to ourselves again and again the very scene which costs us shame as a relief to the shame, and that the pain of sense lessens while it conditions the pain of loss; so too in bliss the acts of virtue by which bliss was won, being finite in number and stress, condition beatitude, making it finite in the receiver. (Long Retreat, and later, 1881)

Sept. 5, 1883[3]

The memory, understanding and affective will are incapable themselves of an infinite object and do not tend towards it;[4] they are finite powers and can get each an adequate object. But the tendency in the soul towards an infinite object comes from the *arbitrium*. The

arbitrium in itself is man's personality or individuality and places him
on a level of individuality in some sense with God; so that in so far
as God is one thing, a self, an individual being, he is an object of
apprehension, desire, pursuit to man's *arbitrium*. There would be no
apprehension, desire, action, or motion of any kind without freedom
of play, that play which is given by the use of a nature, of human
nature, with its faculties; there would only be that inchoate positive
stress imperceptible in particular to itself; but with the use of a
nature and its faculties the strain of desire, pursuit, and also consciousness of self begins. The higher they the stronger it and therefore
the more grievous the balking of it.

Now during this life the faculties have their objects which are
adequate enough for the purpose and the self or *arbitrium* is not
disappointed or dissatisfied with them either, at least not instantly,
for to each of them as a single object or self, would-be and conventional self, at all events it can adequate itself. But after death the
soul is left to its own resources, with only the scapes and *species* of its
past life; which being unsupplemented or undisplaced by a fresh
continual current of experience, absorb and press upon its consciousness. But that this would necessarily be painful does not appear. For
though it is a weariness to us to be kept to one thing without change
while we perceive the flow of time and change going on past us, yet
where there is no such flow and change it does not appear that persistence would be painful, but only that the experience would be
pleasant or painful by its own intrinsic nature. It would seem that
there must be some revelation of himself by God to the soul to awake
the strain or *nisus* which is either to be gratified or denied. This
revelation takes place through the *species* of a past life, by means of
which, by instress of which, God testifies that he is pleased or dis-
pleased and varies in its intensity with them. But it is one of attraction or repulsion, of yes or no, in any case.

God is good and the stamp, seal, or instress he sets on each scape
is of *right*, *good*, or of *bad*, *wrong*. Now the sinner who has preferred
his own good, as revenge, drunkenness, to God's good, true good,
and God, has that evil between him and God, by his attachment to
which and God's rejection of it he is carried and swept away to an
infinite distance from God; and the stress and strain of his removal
is his eternity of punishment. How the instressing of the scope of the
sin is a mitigation of pain, and how at the same time it is a torment
I believe I have written elsewhere.[1]

Sept 7—But when I speak of the stress and strain of removal it
must be understood that the removal is primarily not a physical but
a moral thing, nor even moral in the sense that the affective will
is moral, but in a higher, applying to the self of things, and the

arbitrium, the highest sense in which one thing can equal or excel or fall below another in the scale of being, the scale or standard by which one thing is worth more or less than another. Pride lies in the claiming a high rank in this scale and the pride which is in all sin is essentially the matching of the sinner's self with God's and for himself preferring it, setting it higher in that scale; not his nature against God's, which even Satan could not do, but his bare self. And the true position of things between man and God appears by an immediate light at death, when man's self is set face to face with God's.

Why at death? Not by a physical necessity, as I think, but because life, being, by God's decree, one moral whole, namely a state of probation, it is befitting that some judgement on it should take place as soon as it is over. And yet this judgement is, as I suppose, in some manner unofficial, unformal, and its issue is rather the prisoner's plea allowed, not gainsaid, than the judge's own sentence. Or it is even formal but not a vindictive or punitive sentence formally, but of formal excommunication, non-communion, breaking off of inter-course, and detention till judgement.

'Primum punctum' etc p. 61—The 5 points are arranged so as to make a climax.

'Faciendo unum'[1] etc ib.—He makes 2 classes and again 3. What he means is to distinguish on the one hand the guilt of wilful in-fidelity from the guilt of those who sin *short* of apostacy or heresy and on the other the guilt of sinning against light and against precepts known by faith and that of sinning in ignorance, that is/ against reason only or reason even dulled by error. These are con-trary tendencies; the one makes infidels greater sinners, the other believers. This suggests to him the threefold division.

It is clearer if you say (Aug. 8 1882) that he is contrasting those who have and those who have not the blessings of redemption. The extreme cases of course are / on the one side the lost angels, who were not redeemed; on the other the elect among men, who were redeemed and are saved. These two classes are put aside, for we are dealing with men only and with the lost only. The class among the lost who come nearest the unredeemed and lost angels are un-baptised infants, who were indeed, like all men, redeemed but who have had no chance of availing themselves of the redemption, so that they are lost through no personal fault. Neither are these in question, for we are meditating not on the penalty but on the sorrows of hell and not on the pain of loss so much as on that of sense (I say not so much, for it may be maintained that there is an allusion to the pain of loss in 'planctus' and 'lacrimas, tristitiam'); though indeed we may thank God that we are not among their number.

Next to these come those heathen or untaught adults to whom the blessing of the redemption has never been offered, that is who are unbaptised and have not been offered the faith, for the offer of redemption comes to them in the shape of the offer of faith. (To avoid subtleties I put aside the question whether graces leading to faith have been offered and refused.) These are lost for their sins against the law of nature, lost by their own fault but unforgiven, unredeemed, by their misfortune. And though really such people are to be found now, not only the heathen but even in Christian countries, for simplicity's sake and as a type he calls them those who died before Christ's coming. Next come those who are offered the blessing of redemption and the forgiveness of their sins, are offered the faith, and refuse. These are lost not only for their sins against the law of nature but for their refusal of the law of grace or for the sin of unbelief; so that they are not only lost by their own fault but the misfortune of their not being forgiven is itself their own fault. These are those (or like those) who died in Christ's lifetime. Thirdly come those who have enjoyed the blessings of redemption, been Christians, Catholics, in God's grace, and have thrown it away and, to take the extreme case, apostatized. These are those who have died since Christ.

In the 2 classes then the first is the worst, for it is utterly to refuse obedience to God and always to have been his enemy; in the 3 the last, so far as it has most abused grace. It would appear also that in the 3 classes the first most offend God the creator; the second God the redeemer, whom they crucified; the third God the Sanctifier whom they outrage and expel.

'Secundum', 'quartum', p. 61—Though it is said that St. Ignatius speaks only of the pain of sense, yet, as remarked above, he may allude to the pain of loss. And between these there is something else, a link, so that we may call the evils which fall on the lost these three: *poenam damni, sensum poenae, poenam sensus.* Of course this *sensus poenae* is itself a *poena sensus poenae*; which leads to the thought that probably the sense of the penalty of loss is what of itself begets the (sort-of self inflicted) penalty of sense or, as I have often thought, that the *pain* (grief) of loss relieves itself by pain of sense. The first three Points seem to refer to this *sensum poenae*. (Scotus[1] thought that sorrow, *sensus poenae* in fact, was of the essence of penalty); the First to the intellectual sense of shame, driving the soul in hideous and fantastic shapes, to reenact its sins; the Second to the *affection* of grief and disaffection, that is / hatred, towards God and all things heavenly; the third to the consciousness of natural and like bodily degradation brought about by sin, especially impurity. The Fourth Point then will belong especially to the loss of God, the Fifth especially to the Penalty of sense. But these things are by way of suggestion or allusion, for primarily all five treat of sensible sorrow; certainly they are put before the exercitant in the most sensible shape. Aug 9 1882.

GENERAL EXAMINATION OF CONSCIENCE

Of Thoughts

There are two ways of gaining merit from an evil thought which comes from without. For example, a thought occurs to commit a mortal sin; I resist it promptly and it is conquered.

The second way of gaining merit is when the same evil thought comes to me and I resist; and it returns again and again, and I continue to resist it until it goes away conquered. The second way is much more meritorious than the first.

One sins venially when the same thought of sinning mortally comes and one listens to it, dwelling a few moments on it, or admitting some sensual pleasure, or when there is some negligence in rejecting such a thought.

There are two ways of sinning mortally. The first is when a person gives consent to an evil thought with the intention of acting afterwards in the way he has consented, or with the desire of acting if he could.

The second way of sinning mortally is when that sin is carried into action, and this is a more grievous sin for three reasons: first, on account of the greater length of time; secondly, on account of the deeper intensity; thirdly, on account of the greater injury to both persons.

'De Cogitatione'—By the will is meant that which decides action in us, *arbitrium*, or the faculty which is affected well or ill towards things, *voluntas*. If these are both one and the same faculty, then the first is the faculty at pitch, the other not, or it is the faculty at splay. The state of the will towards action beforehand, taking will in the second sense, the sense of affection, is desire, [*fairness*, the contrary of which is *lothness*, most hits it,][1] (see that threefold division of *concupiscentia, delectatio, consensus*), wish; at the time of action it is enjoyment (*delectatio*); after / it is *gaudium*, the being glad of it. There is something corresponding for the other sense of will: beforehand it is purpose (and other words are used, as determination, resolution, decision, intention); at the time it is something for which perhaps there is no ὄνομα κύριον—one may say consent, avowal, willingness, even *usus* in the sense of not having only but employing the power then acted on or *fruitio* in the sense of 'enjoying an income', not necessarily liking what one is said to enjoy; only *usus* might be said of any faculty and *fruitio*, even in the above sense, belongs rather to the will as affection; after action it is avowal, ratification: here again there is no proper word. All these three states of the will and that in either of its senses, but especially the sense of *arbitrium*, are consent. Of the third of them St. Ignatius does not speak. But it is this third nevertheless which most clearly shews that the consent of the will to right or wrong may be unaccompanied by action.

Then further we must distinguish in right or wrongdoing, but let us say wrongdoing, sin, only, for simplicity's sake, the evil forbidden, the *commission* (or omission; but here too let us treat only of commission) and the consent of the will to it, its approval of it. Evil is primarily in the commission, for that is primarily forbidden, as to eat of the tree of knowledge, and after that in the consent and the will. (It may further happen that evil is primarily in something prior to commission; as if for instance the forbidden fruit had been poisonous and forbidden on that account: then first would have been the physical evil of being poisoned, then the moral evil or at least the voluntary evil of poisoning oneself, then the distinctly moral evil of poisoning oneself against God's command to the contrary. But in this case there was no such direct physical evil.) On the other hand guilt is primarily in the will and its consent, next in the commission or act forbidden.

Now the consent to commit wrong and the commission itself may be completely separate, as when the king commands and the hangman or assassin kills, when the husband prostitutes his wife and she commits adultery. Or they may be distinct in time though in the same person; as if a man took poison or intoxicating drink or cantharides, which did not act at first and then acted suddenly, destroying reason, so that there was no renewal of consent nor pleasure in it nor consciousness of it nor even in the case of death fruition (in life) of the consequence. Yet it is the consequence, the commission— death, suicide; the being drunk, self-intoxication; the indulgence of lust—that is primarily forbidden: the taking the drink or drug is not strictly and necessarily sinful. One might take them five minutes before one was going to be hanged, which might be an hour, say, before they could begin to act. Or again one might not even take the means to action: a woman might take a narcotic from a profligate; but narcotics are no evil nor the taking them a means towards action other than that of going to sleep; only she consents to be violated thereby. Or one might consent to be killed in one's sleep. In these cases the guilt is purely in the consent, in the will. Therefore St. Ignatius says it is one way of sinning mortally 'quando homo

praebet consensum malae cogitationi ad operandum postea sicut con-
sensit [he is thinking of *morosam delectationem*: the man offers no resistance to or ceases resisting the impure thought and then follows the
enjoyment of it] vel ad eam opere exequendam si posset [here it is
question of a sin to be afterwards committed outwardly]'.

But if a man is conscious and free at the time when the consequence of such steps as taking cantharides comes, that is / when the
commission is come, then there will be one of three alternatives.
First suppose the cantharides were given to him without his knowledge by another, work their effect, and he freely commits an act of
lust: then he is guilty not of the means or purpose, (taking purpose
for previous consent) but only of the commission. Next suppose he
took it himself, but, from doing so often, forgets when he does and
in this instance imagines that it is unassisted nature that is prompting
him, and commits the act of lust: then there are two distinct sins,
one of purpose, the other of commission; but they are distinct in the
will only, for it was always this same act that was intended beforehand and is enjoyed now; there is one commission in outward act
but two sins of the inward faculty, *purpose* first and *permission* or
enjoyment after. Lastly he may remember his purpose and the purpose
persist: then there is but one sin in the will, but it has its phases and
features—first purpose, then permission or enjoyment; and this latter
will be a great aggravation, as St. Ignatius says, (1) because the
continuance or persistence of guilty consent, of a sinful state of will,
is one measure of its guilt: the longer we are sinning the greater the
sin; (2) because the consent is intensified at the time of commission,
in some sort renewed and at all events enjoyed; (3) because the
material act or commission is now in being, which is one element of
sin and the primary seat of the *mischief* of sin, with, as St. Ignatius
implies, all the further evil or *mischievous* consequences it may carry.
Besides, that must be a great aggravation of mortal sin which if I
only forgot my purpose would be a mortal sin by itself. This does not
however shew that such a sin is strictly as great as two; because it is
harder to withdraw the consent once given than to refuse it at first.

We are then to distinguish, according to St. Ignatius (and I think
Scotus has a distinction[1] amounting to it), the act of commission and
the act of consent. The first can never be guilty without the second,
without, I mean, the second physically existing before, or with or at
all events, after it (as in ratification, after-avowal) to give it guilt;
but the first, the act of consent, may exist in all its guilt without the
second. But this *without* is to be understood in different degrees.
There may be consent to sin without the commission of that sin by
oneself, yet it may be carried out, only by another; as murder by
commission (in quite a different sense of *commission*) or proxy. Or one

may be prevented from carrying it out oneself or may repent before the time comes. Or there may be no outward commission intended, but yet *morosa delectatio* in lust or, in a spiritual faculty, a thought of pride. This is in the will itself. The most inward and intimate kind of commission will be the intensity of the act of consent itself; for to consent implies no degree, it is a pure Yes or No; to intensify this consent then is to go beyond consent to an act of commission. And in fact physically bare consent, the act of the bare *arbitrium*, seldom or never exists: it would be a manifestation of bare personality, un-clothed in circumstance, which is impossible.

Applying this doctrine to what is said of merit pp. 42, 43, the first way of meriting is by simple dissent (= consent inverted), the second by dissent from or disavowal of the commission which is then in some sort taking place in the subject himself in his own despite; for the constant repetition, the continuity, of the bad thought is that actualising of it, that instressing of it, which he refuses himself to be guilty of but which is carried out by a power not his doing him violence.*

'Venialiter peccatur'[2]—There seem three distinct points here, as expressed by the three clauses disjoined by *vels*, and not two only. The first kind of venial sin will be an imperfect consent, *not* an act performed without consenting (or fully consenting), but the almost consenting to act; which may be, in the case of sins of the flesh, quite without *morosam delectationem*. This is a venial sin *of malice*; it being a tampering with the rebels to lend ear to temptation. The next is imperfect execution ('recipiendo aliquam delectationem sensus') and is material sin properly so called. Such a sin will sometimes only want full consent or full advertence to make it mortal. This is a sin of frailty, and it throws light on the nature of sins of frailty in general. The last is negligence and stands midway between formal consent, which is pride and rebellion, on the one hand, and mere cowardice and yielding, on the other, being passive towards both sides, neither consenting to the tempter nor yet rejecting the tempting thought. This negligence is dishonouring to the lawgiver. It is reducible to ignorance: that is / if one saw what one were doing one would wake up and bestir oneself.—Nov. 7 1878, but the matter belongs to some earlier date. It applies to sin venial *ex defectu formae* not *materiae*. It seems supported by what follows upon mortal sin, in which no one would think of a third member besides consent and execution and which therefore differs from venial sin in that respect, so that it was worth while to give a special instruction upon venial sin.

* I have expressed this doctrine more clearly and correctly in the rough draft of the Commentary for the Provincial.[1]

CHAPTER THREE

ON PERSONALITY, GRACE AND FREE WILL[1]

In looking into Suarez[2] *De Mysteriis Vitae Christi*[3] on Christ's Prayers this morning I happened to find in the article of St. Thomas embodied there this doctrine implied or expressed of the distinction of the will as *arbitrium* and, so St. Thomas speaks, as nature. No doubt it is to be found in him elsewhere.

Here I may put down some thoughts which throw light on and receive light from the above on personality. A person is defined a rational (that is / intellectual) supposit, the supposit of a rational nature. A supposit is a self. Self is the intrinsic oneness of a thing, which is prior to its being[4] and does not result from it *ipso facto*, does not result, I mean, from its having independent being; for accidental being, such as that of the broken fragments of things or things purely artificial or chance 'installs', has no true and intrinsic oneness or true self: they have independent existence, that is / they exist distinct from other things and by or in themselves, but the independence, the distinctness, the self is brought about artificially; naturally ivory is a tusk, the sphere of ivory meant to be a billiard ball is artificially made so, by turning. Now a bare self, to which no nature has yet been added, which is not yet clothed in or overlaid with a nature, is indeed nothing, a zero, in the score or account of existence, but as possible it is positive, like a positive infinitesimal, and intrinsically different from every other self.

For in the world, besides natures or essences or 'inscapes'[5] and the selves, supposits, hypostases, or, in the case of rational natures, persons / which wear and 'fetch' or instance them, there is still something else—fact or fate. For let natures be A, B, ... Y, Z and supposits or selves $a, b, \ldots y, z$: then if a is capable of A, B, ... Y, Z (singly or together) and receives, say, A, if b capable of the same receives also A, and if c capable of the same receives M, so that we have aA, bA, cM, these combinations are three arbitrary or absolute facts not depending on any essential relation between a and A, b and A, or c and M but on the will of the Creator.[6] Further, a and b are in the same nature A. But a uses it well and is saved, b* ill and is damned: these are two facts, two fates / not depending on the relation between a and b on the one hand and A on the other. Now as the difference of the facts and fates does not depend on A, which is the same for

* MS reads 'B' [Ed.].

both, it must depend on *a* and *b*. So that selves are from the first intrinsically different.

But this intrinsic difference, though it always exists, cannot appear except in a rational, to speak more to the point / in a free / nature. Two eggs precisely alike, two birds precisely alike / will behave precisely alike: if they had been exchanged no difference would have been made. It is the self then that supplies the determination, the difference, but the nature that supplies the exercise, and in these two things freedom consists. This is what I have before somewhere worked out in a paper[1] on freedom and personality and I think I used the terms *freedom of pitch* and *freedom of play*: they are good at all events and the two together express moral freedom.

Now if self begins to manifest its freedom with the rise from an irrational to a rational nature it is according to analogy to expect it will manifest more freedom with further rise in nature. Accordingly we find a more tremendous difference in fate between the good and the fallen angels than between good and bad or even saved and lost men. And this reasoning is of wide application. But the scale of natures is infinite up towards the divine. Now as the evil of venial sin is that if only the quantity of the matter were increased or the consent more perfect it would be mortal: so mortal sin itself seems to take its malice from an ideal sin worse and blacker than any that ever were or could be committed, in this way: he who breaks one commandment is guilty of all, St. James says, because he breaks *God's commandment*; murder is a mortal sin against God because if you will murder man you may come, as Caiphas and Pilate did, to *murder the man who is God*; and in general, if only God could be put into the position: the mortal sinner would have his way with him (the men of Sodom, Judas, and Caiphas are three typical cases), spoil him, sell him, or make away with him. Or to put it another way, if the sinner defiles God's image so he might God's person if he could; if he takes the limbs of Christ and makes them members of a harlot so he would Christ; if he could be, as Christ was, 'in the form of God' he would make God sin and do the deeds 'of a slave'. Sin seems to reach up to an, as it were, preposterous and wicked godhead: in this lies the infinity of its malice, so far as that is infinite, and the realising this is that pain, in the pain or penalty of loss, which is even relieved by the realising, in the pain of sense, the very act of sin which merited it.

But if this is so and guilt can grow greater with increase in perfection of nature how is it that every being might, if God chose, be saved? For it would appear that with higher opportunities Judas and Satan might have sinned more, not less. Here then we must consider that as there is a scale of natures, ranging from lower to higher, which height is no advantage at all to the evil self, the self which will give nature, and the higher the nature the more, a pitch to evil; so also there is a scale or range of pitch which is also infinite and terminates upwards in the directness or uprightness of the 'stem' of the godhead and the procession of the divine persons. God then can shift the self that lies in one to a higher, that is / better, pitch of itself; that is / to a pitch or determination of itself on the side of good. But here arises a darker difficulty still; for how can we tell that each self has, in particular, any such better self, any such range from bad to good? In the abstract there is such a range of pitch and conceivably a self to be found, actually or possibly, at each pitch in it, but how can *each* self have all these pitches? for this seems contrary to its freedom; the more so as if we look at the exhibition of moral freedom in life, at men's lives and history, we find not only that in the same circumstances and seemingly with the same graces they behave differently, not only they do not range as fast from bad to good or good to bad one as another, but, even what is most intrinsic to a man, the influence of his own past and of the preexisting disposition of will with which he comes to action seems irregular and now he does well, now he sins, bids fair to be a sinner and becomes a saint or bids fair to be a saint and falls away, and indeed goes through vicissitudes of all sorts and changes times without number.

This matter is profound; but so far as I see this is the truth. First, though self, as personality, is prior to nature it is not prior to pitch. If there were something prior even to pitch, of which that pitch would be itself the pitch, then we could suppose that that, like everything else, was subject to God's will and could be pitched, could be determined, this way or that. But this is really saying that a thing is and is not itself, is and is not A, is and is not. For self before nature is no thing as yet but only possible; with the accession of a nature it becomes properly a self, for instance a person: only so far as it is prior to nature, that is to say / so far as it is a definite self, the possibility of a definite self (and not merely the possibility of a number or fetch of nature) it is identified with pitch, moral pitch, determination of right and wrong. And so far, it has its possibility, as it will have its existence, from God, but not so that God makes pitch no pitch, determination no determination, and difference indifference. The indifference, the absence of pitch, is in the nature to be superadded. And when nature is superadded, then it cannot be believed, as the Thomists think, that in every circumstance of free choice the person is of himself indifferent towards the alternatives and that God determines which he shall, though freely, choose. The difficulty does not lie so much in his being determined by God and yet choosing freely, for on one side that may and must happen, but in his being supposed equally disposed or pitched towards both at once. This is impossible and destroys the notion of freedom and of pitch.

Nevertheless in every circumstance it is within God's power to determine the creature to choose, and freely choose, according to his will; but not without a change or access of circumstance, over and above the bare act of determination on his part. This access is either of grace, which is 'supernature', to nature or of more grace to grace already given, and it takes the form of instressing the affective will, of affecting the will towards the good which he proposes. So far this is a necessary and constrained affection on the creature's part, to which the *arbitrium* of the creature may give its avowal and consent. Ordinarily when grace is given we feel first the necessary or constrained act and after that the free act on our own part, of consent or refusal as the case may be. This consent or refusal is given to an act either hereafter or now to be done, but in the nature of things such an act must always be future, even if immediately future or of those futures which arise in acts and phrases like 'I must ask you' to do so-and-so, 'I wish to apologise', 'I beg to say', and so on. And ordinarily the motives for refusal are still present though the motive for consent has been strengthened by the motion, just over or even in some way still working, of grace. And therefore in ordinary cases refusal is possible not only physically but also morally and often takes place. But refusal remaining physically possible becomes morally (and strictly) impossible in the following way.

Besides the above stated distinction of freedom of pitch and freedom of play there is a third kind of freedom still to be considered, *freedom of field*. (This is the natural order of the three: freedom of pitch, that is / self determination, is in the chooser himself and his choosing faculty; freedom of play is in the execution; freedom of field is in the object, the field of choice.) Thus it is freedom of play to be free of some benevolent man's purse, to have access to it at your will; it is freedom of pitch to be allowed to take from it what you want, not to be limited by conditions of his imposing; it is freedom of field to find there *more than one coin to choose from*. Or it is freedom of pitch to be able to choose for yourself which of several doors you will go in by; it is freedom of play to go unhindered to it and through the one you choose; but suppose all were false doors or locked but the very one you happened to choose and you do not know it, there is here wanting freedom of field.

The *arbitrium* is indeed free towards all alternatives, even though one of them should be absolute evil, evil in itself; but not so the affective will: this must always be affected towards the stem of good and *malum quidem appetit sed sub specie boni*. Therefore all rival objects of desire being banished or sunk to insignificance and absolutely or practically emptied of their attractiveness, the will, still remaining free in itself as faculty or power, free to choose and even free of play, has no freedom of field and will choose necessarily the only object that attracts it.

Does this ever take place?—First distinguish prevenient or fore-stalling grace, grace accompanying, and consequent grace or grace of execution. It is prevenient grace which *rehearses* in us our consent beforehand, when for the moment we find ourselves to have con-sented, without finally consenting; and I suppose this to be a true and proper consent. For God having moved the affective will to an act (*actum exercitum*) of consent the *arbitrium* is passive. It cannot dissent, for want of motive; for the motives which may afterwards occur do not so instantaneously act and if they did are outweighed; this is *ipso facto*, for the affective will is moved towards the true good, therefore as a matter of fact and *actu exercito* the countermotives have been outweighed. And this absence of dissent alone would be enough consent morally. But probably there is also a positive and instanta-neous consent by way of ratification or after-avowal. Therefore what is called above the necessary or constrained act (of consenting to grace) is really necessary, and in the affective will is constrained, but in the elective will or *arbitrium* is free. But if after this we are left to ourselves for a leisurely and deliberate avowal or disavowal of this 'forestall' (as I shall call it), then as a *motus primo primus*, voluntary in itself, is treated as involuntary in comparison with our leisurely avowal or disavowal of it, so of these forestalls and our subsequent decision (the cases are not in all ways alike, for God's command of the faculties, his dominion over nature, being perfect, the consent to it is much truer and more perfect than what we give to a *motum primo primum*): they are to be considered physically free but morally constrained and irresponsible.

It is now plain that God has only to prevent, by a continuance of his own act, by death, by suspension of faculty, or by whatever means, a return of the creature to the old condition or rather to a condition near enough to it, which is all that is possible, for the wrong choice again to present itself; he has only, I say, to do this / in order to ensure a free and final correspondence with grace and choice of good.

I think, with God's help, the above is the truth about this very dark and disputed matter.—It is to be remarked that *choice* in the sense of the taking of one and leaving of another real alternative is not what freedom of pitch really and strictly lies in. It is choice as when in English we say 'because I choose', which means no more than (and with precision does mean) / I instress my will to so-and-so. And this freedom and no other, no freedom of field, the divine will has towards its own necessary acts. And no freedom is more perfect; for freedom of field is only an accident. So also *pitch* is ultimately simple positiveness, that by which being differs from and is more than nothing and not-being, and it is with precision expressed by the English *do* (the simple auxiliary), which when we employ or emphasise, as 'he said it, he did say it', we do not mean that the fact is any more a fact but that we the more state it. (It is also at bottom the copula in logic[1] and the Welsh *a*[2] in 'Efe a ddywedodd'.) So that this pitch might be expressed, if it were good English, *the doing* be, *the doing* choose, *the doing* so-and-so in that sense. Where there was no question of will it would become mere fact; where there is will it is free action, moral action. And such 'doing-be', and the thread or chain of such pitches or 'doing-be''s, prior to nature's being overlaid, is self, personality; but it is not truly self: self or personality then truly comes into being when the self, the person, comes into being with the accession of nature.

Is not this pitch or whatever we call it then the same as Scotus's *ecceitas*?[3]

Further on the same—As besides the actual world there is an infinity of possible worlds, differing in all degrees of difference from what now is down to the having nothing in common with it but virgin matter,[4] each of which possible worlds and this the actual one are like so many 'cleaves' or exposed faces of some pomegranate (or other fruit) cut in all directions across,: so there is an infinity of possible strains of action and choice for each possible self in these worlds (or, what comes to the same thing, in virgin matter) and the sum of these strains would be also like a pomegranate in the round, which God sees whole but of which we see at best only one cleave. Rather we see the world as one cleave and the life of each person as one vein or strain of colour in it.

This being so, God exercises his mastery and dominion over his creatures' wills in two ways—over the affective will by simply determining it so or so (as it is said the heart of the king is in the Lord's hand to turn it which way he will); over the *arbitrium* or power of pitch by shifting the creature from one pitch contrary to God's will to another which is according to it or from the less to the more so. This is that grace of correspondence of which mention is made in the passage quoted at p. 53.[5] It is plain that this is also to determine, but in another sense: the first is a change worked by God of something in man; the second an exchange of one whole for another whole, as they say in the mystery of Transubstantiation, a conversion of a whole substance into another whole substance, but here is not a question of substance; it is a lifting him from one self to another self, which is a most marvellous display of divine power.

Dec. 30 1881, from thoughts arising in the Long Retreat.—To make this clearer, we must say that the affective will is well affected towards, likes, desires, chooses, whatever has the quality and look of good and *cannot choose but* so like and choose; so that the affective will, taken strictly as a faculty of the mind, is really no freer than the understanding or the imagination. And in fact to say 'I will do' so-and-so, which belongs to the will is no more than to say (of things within our own control) 'I shall do it', which is a judgment of a fact, or to foresee oneself, forecast oneself (definitely) doing it, which is a simple apprehension or act of 'pure intelligence', of imagination in other words. Now when there is but one alternative, that is / no alternative, when there is no choice, no freedom of field, the elective will always, without effort, passively, ratifies the spring of the affective will to action. Its freedom of choice comes into play with freedom of field or choice of alternatives, all of which must have, though in different degrees, the quality of good. And it is in presence of the alternatives that the elective will has this freedom, for after their withdrawal it remains as fast as if it were frozen in its last choice. (How this freedom arises need not be treated here; but briefly it consists in this, that self can in every object it has see another self, personal or not, and taking the whole object not in its fulness and 'splay' but in this 'neap'[1] and foredrawn condition can treat any one thing how great or small soever as equal to any other thing how small or great soever.) The power therefore of going on from worse to better depends on the outward grace of God's ordinary providence, which brings fresh natural motives day by day before us and in the course of time, in the growing from childhood to manhood and youth to age, on the whole stronger ones. There will therefore always be a freedom to change in a year, month, week, or day, but for great changes there is practically no freedom within short spells of time, as days or hours: the physical freedom there always is, but this is of no use whatever for want of freedom of field. And, practically speaking, for any great change towards any great or important object of affection or disaffection, like or dislike, as the Christian religion, the Catholic Church, a political principle, and so on, a great change of circumstances, of point of view, either *taken* or *given* (which is like saying / a great change of perspective), is needed. For apart from grace who supposes that, without some accession of knowledge or self interest, a heathen will arbitrarily change from disliking to liking the Christian religion? and so of the rest. And if this never does happen then morally it cannot happen and morally speaking, practically speaking, men are not free—*not free to change,* for free they are—in such matters. For, applying here a pregnant principle which explains other difficulties, the continuance or persistency of a phenomenon may be no more than the splay, the quantita-tive, the time-long / *display*, of the oneness of a fact over against a number of other facts filling less time or more foredrawn, and so here the *going on* hating Christians is not the mere consequence of having once hated them and after that never having stopped: it is the attitude of mind freely taken by the man's self towards that other (so to call it) self (for bodies, principles, and so on have a oneness and a self either real and natural or else logical), Christianity, which arose from the mere contraposition of the two, as from positing 7 and 21 arises the ratio $\frac{1}{3}$, only not freely; and so while Christianity lasts and the man lives, till circumstances notably change this attitude of mind will continue. These attitudes of mind are so lasting, so like everlasting, because they are so nearly absolute.

For a self is an absolute which stands to the absolute of God as the infinitesimal to the infinite. It is an infinitesimal in the scale of stress. And in some sense it is an infinite, if looked on as the foredrawing of its whole being. For the foredrawing of a finite to the infinitesimal will give an infinite in the scale of stress, but only a relative infinite, as the world is only relatively infinite in the scale of extension. (Per-haps the divine Persons may be looked on as foredrawings of the divine nature: this will be like the exchange of the (true) infinite of magnitude for the true infinite of stress or of infinite *simpliciter* for absolute. However it is personality I should rather have said than person; neither do the other words express what is to be thought, for the divine nature is infinite in stress as much as in magnitude and absolute as much as infinite. I think I see how the truth should be stated but I leave this for the time.)

In so far then as the desire or affection we entertain towards any object comes nearer our true selves or bare personality in so far will it be the harder to change and if it were ever the relation of mere self towards that object it would be necessary and unchangeable, though free; neither of course would the subject wish to change it. And in fact the lost do not wish, do not will at all events, if it were even possible, to repent and love God.

From the above also may be seen, if the wills of all his children were contained in Adam's at the Fall and he could sway them and give them the pitch which his own took, in what sense they consented and in what sense not. But this point need not be raised here.

It has been shewn at p. 46 how God can always command if he chooses the free consent of the elective will, at least, if by no other way, by shutting out all freedom of field (which no doubt does some-times take place, as in disposing the hearts of princes; but whether in matters concerning the subject's own salvation we do not know: very possibly it does in answer to the subject's own or some other's prayer in his behalf). Therefore in that 'cleave' of being which each of his creatures shews to God's eyes alone (or in its 'burl' of being / uncloven) God can choose countless points in the strain (or countless cleaves of the 'burl') where the creature has consented, does consent, to God's will in the way above shewn. But these may be away, may be very far away, from the actual pitch at any given moment existing. It is into that possible world that God for the moment moves his creature out of this one or it is from that possible world that he brings his creature into this, shewing it to itself gracious and consenting; nay more, clothing its old self for the moment with a gracious and consenting self. This shift is grace. For grace is any action, activity, on God's part by which, in creating or after creating, he carries the creature to or towards the end of its being, which is its selfsacrifice to God and its salvation. It is, I say, any such activity on God's part; so that so far as this action or activity is God's it is divine stress, holy spirit, and, as all is done through Christ, Christ's spirit; so far as it is action, correspondence, on the creature's it is *actio salutaris*; so far as it is looked at *in esse quieto* it is Christ in his member on the one side, his member in Christ on the other. It is as if a man said: That is Christ playing at me and me playing at Christ, only that it is no play but truth; That is Christ *being me* and me being Christ.

It is plain then how true it is what is said at p. 53 about correspondence being a grace and even the grace of graces. For the momentary and constrained correspondence, being a momentary shift from a worse, ungracious / to a better, a gracious self, is a grace, a favour, and it is grace in the strict sense of that word; it is grace bestowed for the moment and offered for a continuance. But the continued and unconstrained correspondence is a greater blessing and therefore still more a grace and as it was only possible through the first or constrained one (the 'forestall'), the second multiplies the first and is a grace upon a grace or, as St. John says, χάρις ἀντὶ χάριτος, freer on man's part and also doubly free, unconstrained, gratis, grace / on God's.

What then does Marie Lataste (or Christ in speaking to her) mean by its being granted in answer to prayer?—First that salvation and every necessary grace is so granted. But taking the matter more in particular, I understand at bottom to be meant the simple act of *arbitrium*. For prayer is the expression of a wish to God and, since God searches the heart, the conceiving even of the wish is prayer in God's eyes (see Rom. viii 26, 27.). For there must be something which shall be truly the creature's in the work of corresponding with grace: this is the *arbitrium*, the verdict on God's side, the saying Yes, the 'doing-agree' (to speak barbarously), and looked at in itself, such a nothing is the creature before its creator, it is found to be no more than the mere wish, discernible by God's eyes, that it might do as he wishes, might correspond, might say Yes to him; correspondence itself is on man's side not so much corresponding as the wish to correspond, and this least sigh of desire, this one aspiration, is the life and spirit of man. For beyond this, all the work of actual correspondence, all whatever that has any score or 'afterleave' to any eye but God's, in the corresponding with grace needs fresh grace or the continuance of the offered grace, grace concomitant.

And remark that prayer understood in this sense, this sigh or aspiration or stirring of the spirit towards God, is a *forestall* of the thing to be done, as on the other side grace prevenient is God's forestall of the same, and it is here that one creature, one man, differs so much from another: in one God finds only the constrained correspondence with his forestall (as explained near the top of p. 220); in another he finds after this an act of choice properly so called. And by this infinitesimal act the creature does what in it lies to bridge the gulf fixed between its present actual and worser pitch of will and its future better one. For the forestall on God's part, in which the creature's correspondence is bound up, is a piece bodily taken out of the possible world, the 'burl of being', of that creature and brought into this actual one, which is, as has been said, one cleave of it; but the forestall on the creature's side, towards which of course God too plays his part, is in this actual world. Therefore though God can always, for the worst of creatures, for Satan, say, find a pitch at which the creature is in correspondence with his grace, nay any number of them, *by foreclosing the field*, it does not follow that he finds the same with the field open. For this is, as has been said above, to take away choice and freedom. Of this later.

It might be said that prevenient grace is no more than God's action in this world, that there is no ground for resorting to some world of possibility to explain it. And this may be true wherever there is not an absolute consent of the creature's will bound up with it, a consent not to the momentary affection but also to the action which is to follow. But what we experience sometimes in ourselves, and what will be most strongly experienced when the after-consent is most perfect, is a condition, an 'install' of ourselves in which we have consented to do, are doing, or have done that thing to which we feel God to be inviting us. This is a prophecy, a forecast, not of the certain future, for it leaves us free still to discard and unmake that future; therefore of a possible future, in which nevertheless God has already acted, nay we have done so too; hence it belongs to another creation. Let this now suffice, for I see that one might pursue some further subtleties and they weary the mind.

The sigh of correspondence links the present, with its imperfect or faulty pitch of will, to the future with its uprighter and more perfect one: it *begins* to link it, is the first infinitesimal link in the chain or step on that road which is to created power impassable. For this reason and from this point of view it may be called a forestall of the act to follow. For in so far as it passes into the act to follow it is not the forestalling but the stalling or lodging of that act. And even the sigh or aspiration itself is in answer to an inspiration of God's spirit and is followed by the continuance and expiration of that same breath which lifts it, through the gulf and void between pitch and pitch of being, to do or be what God wishes his creature to do or be. Cf. Eph. iii 16 'ἵνα δῷ ὑμῖν κατὰ τὸ πλοῦτος τῆς δόξης αὐτοῦ δυνάμει [the display of divine power] κραταιωθῆναι [like falling home into a fast bed] διὰ τοῦ πνεύματος αὐτοῦ [the aspiration on God's part] εἰς τὸν ἔσω ἄνθρωπον [known to God, the man created in Christ as ii 10.], κατοικῆσαι τὸν Χριστὸν διὰ τῆς πίστεως ἐν ταῖς καρδίαις ὑμῶν . . . ἵνα πληρωθῆτε εἰς πᾶν τὸ πλήρωμα τοῦ Θεοῦ.' This πλήρωμα τοῦ Θεοῦ is the burl of being in Christ, and for every man there is his own burl of being, which are all 'by lays' or 'byfalls' of Christ's and of one another's.

Now though it is true that God can raise anyone from any pitch of will and being however low to one in which he shall be gracious and consenting to God and in St. Paul's case wonderfully did so and though we cannot know why he does so to one and not to another, not to all, yet it is easy to see certain things which help to explain such cases as those of St. Paul or St. Matthew or of the penitent thief. St. Paul, if he was in sin and vehemently resisting the grace he then had at the time he was struck down, yet when he had been raised to his grace of conversion, even if that had been, which indeed it was not, a violence done to his will for that moment, corresponded most earnestly then and ever after. But if the will is always and even morally and practically free while in pilgrimage, *in via*, he need not have done so; he might still have come to be a cast away: he speaks so himself. And his former zeal of God had something certainly of good in it. So too St. Matthew was perhaps already a willing listener to Christ and the good thief had corresponded with lesser graces before he received his great one or was at the very least acting on natural charity. But it is rather the after use of the uplifting grace that ought to be looked at than the state of the soul before it came: here are the *praevisa merita*, and we must suppose at least that God is more willing to lay out his graces well than ill, to grant the greatest to those who will employ them the best rather than to those who will the worst, and this most of all in the case of the Blessed Virgin. Thus if the apostolic grace and dignity is the highest on earth below that of the Blessed Virgin and St. Joseph, why, of twelve Apostles there was indeed one traitor but there was only one; and to judge by what we see, fewer religious are lost than worldlings; fewer Catholics than other Christians, though in good faith; fewer Christians than heathen in the same. And yet it is the holiest that shews his freedom most, the wickedest that is most the slave of sin and carried with the motion of the flesh and of the world and of the Worldwielder. But what are we to say of those saints who, like St. Francis of Assisi, said that had the greatest sinners had the graces granted them they would have made a better use of them?—Perhaps it is the expression of their heaven-enlightened sense of their own shortcomings and yet it may not be in general true; that is / not true of the crowd of sinners, though here and there such sinners might be found. But all these last speculations are not for me, neither are they necessary towards my purposes.

God's forestalling of man's action by prevenient grace, which carries with it a consenting of man's will, seems to stand to the action of free choice which follows and to which, by its continued strain and breathing on and man's responding aspiration or drawing in of breath, it leads / as the creation of man and angels in sanctifying grace stands to the act by which they entered with God into the covenant and commonwealth of original justice;[1] further / as the infused virtues of baptism stand to the acts of faith etc which long after follow. This agrees well with the light I once had upon the nature of faith, that it is God / in man / knowing his own truth. It is like the child of a great nobleman taught by its father and mother a compliment of welcome to pay to the nobleman's father on his visit to them: the child does not understand the words it says by rote, does not know their meaning, yet what they mean it means. The parents understand what they do not say, the child says what it does not understand, but both child and parents mean the welcome.

The will is surrounded by the objects of desire as the needle by the points of the compass. It has play then in two dimensions. This is to say / it is drawn by affection towards any one, A, and this freely, and it can change its direction towards any other, as free, B, which implies the moving through an arc. It has in fact, more or less, in its affections a tendency or magnetism towards every object and the *arbitrium*, the elective will, decides which: this is the needle proper. But in fallen man all this motion, both these dimensions, κεῖται ἐν τῷ πονηρῷ; so that the uplifting action of supernatural grace takes place as if in a third dimension, motion, in which man is totally incapable. And here remark what now clearly appears, that the action of such assisting grace is twofold, to help man determine the will towards the right object in one field and at the same time from that field or plane to lift it to a parallel and higher one; besides all the while stimulating its action, in the right plane and in the right direction, towards the right object; so that in fact it is threefold, not twofold—(1) quickening, stimulating, towards the object, towards good: this is especially in the affective will, might be a natural grace, and in a high degree seems to be the grace of novices; (2) corrective, turning the will from one direction or pitting into another, like the needle through an arc, determining its choice (I mean / stimulating that determination, which it still leaves free): this touches the elective will or the power of election and is especially the grace of the mature mind; (3) elevating, which lifts the receiver from one cleave of being to another and to a vital act in Christ: this is truly God's finger touching the very vein of personality, which nothing else can reach and man can respond to by no play whatever, by bare acknowledgment only, the counter stress which God alone can feel ('subito probas eum'), the aspiration in answer to his inspiration. Of this I have written above and somewhere else long ago.

When man was created in grace, that is / in the elevated, the supernatural / state, and his will addressed towards God, the work of actual grace was all of the first sort. This may be called creative grace, the grace which destined the victim for the sacrifice, and which belongs to God the Father. After the Fall there came too 'medicinal', corrective, redeeming / grace, by the restrictions of the Law, by the exhortations of the Prophets, and by Christ himself. And all Christ's words, it seems to me, are either words of cure, as 'Veniam et curabo eum', 'Volo, mundare', or corrections of some error or fault; their function is always *ramener à la route*. This then is especially Christ's grace, it is a purifying and a mortifying grace, bringing the victim to the altar and sacrificing it. And as creative grace became insufficient by the Fall: so this grace of Christ's did not avail when he was no longer present to keep bestowing it or when its first force was spent. At Pentecost the elevating grace was given which fastened men in good. This is especially the grace of the Holy Ghost and is the acceptance and assumption of the victim of the sacrifice.

Light is thrown on the above points by Rom. viii 28 sqq. (29. 'οὓς προέγνω [by that touch which only God can apply and the response which only God can perceive] καὶ προώρισεν συμμόρφους τῆς εἰκόνος τοῦ υἱοῦ αὐτοῦ, εἰς τὸ εἶναι αὐτὸν πρωτότοκον ἐν πολλοῖς ἀδελφοῖς. οὓς δὲ προώρισεν, τούτους καὶ ἐκάλεσεν [*gratia vocans*, the first of the three graces above] καὶ οὓς ἐκάλεσεν, τούτους καὶ ἐδικαίωσεν [the second], οὓς δὲ ἐδικαίωσεν, τούτους καὶ ἐδόξασεν [raised to the state when their deeds should be the doing of God in them]') and ib. 38. 'πέπεισμαι γὰρ ὅτι οὔτε θάνατος οὔτε ζωὴ οὔτε ἄγγελοι οὔτε ἀρχαὶ [here add from

the Vulgate, which has 'neque virtutes', 'οὔτε δυνάμεις'] οὔτε ἐνεστῶτα
οὔτε μέλλοντα οὔτε δυνάμεις [read probably 'δύναμις', for the Vulgate
has 'fortitudo': *nor things possible*] οὔτε ὕψωμα οὔτε βάθος [that is / the
whole range of any one strain of personality] οὔτε τις κτίσις ἑτέρα [the
world of possibility, the burl] δυνήσεται ἡμᾶς χωρίσαι ἀπὸ τῆς ἀγάπης
τοῦ Θεοῦ τῆς ἐν Χριστῷ Ἰησοῦ τῷ Κυρίῳ ἡμῶν'. See also xi 12. 'εἰ δὲ
τὸ παράπτωμα αὐτῶν πλοῦτος κόσμου καὶ τὸ ἥττημα αὐτῶν πλοῦτος ἐθνῶν,
πόσῳ μᾶλλον τὸ πλήρωμα αὐτῶν;'

CHAPTER FOUR

THE KINGDOM OF CHRIST

Text of Exercises.
Notes of GMH (*De Regno Christi*).

The first prelude is the composition, seeing the place. Here it will be to see with the eyes of the imagination the synagogues, towns and villages through which Christ our Lord went preaching.

The second, to ask for the grace which I desire. Here it will be to ask grace from our Lord that I may not be deaf to his call but prompt and diligent to accomplish his most holy will.

The first point is to place before my eyes a human king, chosen by God our Lord himself, to whom all Christian men pay reverence and obedience.

The second is to consider how the king speaks to all his own saying: 'It is my will to conquer the whole country of the infidels; wherefore whoever desires to come with me must be content to eat as I eat, and likewise to drink and be clothed etc.; in like manner he must, as I do, labour by day and watch by night, etc.', in order that afterwards he may share with me in the victory according as he has shared in the toils.'

The third is to consider what good subjects ought to answer to a king so liberal and so gracious; and consequently if anyone were not to accept the call of such a king, how he would deserve to be despised by all the world and held as a recreant knight.

The second part of this Exercise consists in applying the above example of a temporal king to Christ our Lord according to the three aforesaid points.

And as regards the first point, if we pay attention to such a call of a temporal king to his subjects, how much more worthy of consideration it is to see Christ our Lord, the eternal King, and before him the whole of mankind, all of whom and each one in particular he calls saying: 'My will is to conquer the whole world and all my enemies, and so to enter into the glory of my Father. Whosoever, therefore, desires to come with me must labour with me in order that following me in suffering, he may likewise follow me in glory.'

The second point is to consider that all who have judgment and reason will offer themselves wholly for labour.

The third point is that those who wish to show greater affection and to distinguish themselves in every kind of service of their Eternal King and universal Lord will not only offer themselves for the work, but also by acting against their own sensuality and against their carnal and worldly love, will make offers of greater worth and moment, saying:

'Eternal Lord of all things, I make my oblation with thy grace and help, in the presence of thine infinite goodness, and in the sight of thy glorious Mother, and of all the Saints of the Heavenly Court (protesting) that I wish and desire and that it is my deliberate determination, provided only it be to thy greater service and praise, to imitate thee in bearing all injuries and all reproach and all poverty, as well actual as spiritual, if only thy divine majesty be pleased to choose and receive me to such a life and state.

DE REGNO CHRISTI[1]

'Secunda Hebdomada'—See Fr. Roothaan's note. St. Ignatius does not include this contemplation in the Second Week, in the same way as the Foundation is not included in the First, for the Meditation on the Three Sins is called the first Exercise. The present contemplation then is in like manner a foundation and first principle for the Week that follows. As in the Foundation man's relation and duty towards God is stated generally and abstractedly and without detail and then is meditated on in detail and historically and with examples in the Week that follows: so here our relations and duty towards Our Lord are seen in one view masked by a parable and afterwards we contemplate His Life and the example it sets in particular

'Praedicabat'—Nov. 15 1881 (L.R.) And nothing is said of Christ's passion and death. The call is that which Christ himself made from the first, when none but himself could know that he was to die a violent death, before he by degrees and to the Twelve unveiled the future. For he was not like a man who puts to another a dilemma hoping and expecting him to take one horn, at which he is prepared with an answer, and then if the other should take the other horn is at a loss and cannot go on; he did not entrap Pilate, Caiphas, and Satan into crucifying him, as though without that he could not redeem man; on the contrary he was all the time giving graces which his enemies might have used as well to their own justification as to the establishment of his kingdom. And he had all his plans ready, matured during his hidden life, and adapted for every case. As it was, we see that only baptism of his sacraments was instituted at leisure before his death; the Eucharist was like hurried forward, forestalled perhaps by the suddenness of that event; the others, which he had always meant to institute, were put off till after he rose again. He hid himself when the people wanted to make him king; yet he claimed to be their king and would in his own time have come to the throne: but everything was to be in its right time and natural order, which there was wanting. The Eucharistic Sacrifice was the great purpose of his life and his own chosen redemption: perhaps he would have instituted it and into it have disappeared— as at Emmaus. We must nevertheless suppose that he had won from his Father three years and a half as a minimum for his work. Even without divine knowledge he could for certain foresee his own early death, because he was sent to overthrow Satan's empire, who would certainly, if he were allowed, as he was, have his adversary's life. And as for the prophecies of his death, these are like histories written beforehand and are in nature[1] after the event they tell of. They contemplate (e.g. 'non erit ejus populus qui eum negaturus est' etc) this very thing, that Christ will offer his redemption and it will be refused.

The first class of Christ's subjects then, those who have 'judicium et rationem' are called on to follow him in his first design, which was a life of hardship; the other in his Passion.

'Proinde qui voluerit' etc—Directly, he asks *those who think of coming* to accept his terms; it is only indirectly he asks men to come at all. Just so Our Lord said *to His disciples* first, not to the public, 'Tunc Jesus dixit discipulis suis: Si quis vult post me venire abneget semetipsum et tollat crucem suam et sequatur me' Matt. xvi 24. And before this He had spoken so only to the Twelve ib. x 38. In Luke ix 23, 'ad omnes' seems to mean the other disciples besides St. Peter; however disciples proper or not, it matters little, for in Mark viii 34., which belongs to the same occasion as the above passages (Matt. xvi 24. and Luke ix 23.), namely one shortly after St. Peter's Confession and a week before the Transfiguration, it is said 'Et convocata turba cum discipulis suis dixit eis: Si quis vult me sequi deneget semetipsum et tollat crucem suam et sequatur me.' There were therefore at this time others following Christ besides His acknowledged disciples but they followed as disciples, learners, or enquirers; some pains they had taken and made some profession at least of interest and good intentions; and so the test of the true disciple must sooner or later be put to them. Again later than this (Luke xiv 25.) 'Ibant . . . multae turbae cum eo, et conversus dixit ad eos: Si quis venit ad me et non odit. . Et qui non bajulat crucem suam et venit post me non potest meus esse discipulus. Quis enim ex vobis volens turrim aedificare. . . ? . . Sic ergo omnis ex vobis qui non renunciat omnibus quae possidet non potest meus esse discipulus. Bonum est sal. . . Qui habet aures audiendi audiat.' But this seems a call to the discipleship proper and belongs therefore to Point 3 in the Application, 'Tertium ii qui magis affici' etc. What then is important to bear in mind throughout is that the king's call is to those directly who have already committed themselves to something, are *equites* (remark the word), knights, follow the profession of arms and having been knighted are bound by allegiance, fealty, loyalty, chivalry, *knighthood* in a word, to live up to a standard of courage above the civilian and even above the private soldier. And an adult Christian is such, being not only baptized but confirmed (for Confirmation is spiritual knighthood), and at least the exercitant is, who must at this point advert to his sacramental promises, his engagements and bounden duty. Cowardly it would be and a wretched inconsistency in a knight ('perversus . . . eques') to decline a glorious campaign from dislike of the hardships to be borne in securing its success, dislike of being obliged *to share his general's lot*: St. Ignatius appears to apply this to all adults, Christian adults at least, that is confirmed Christians, 'qui habuerint judicium et rationem'.—What of those who are not confirmed? Let them get confirmed without delay.

Many would be unable to accept the king's terms and come, and these are all excused; as children, who are like reserve forces and their time yet to come; women; the clergy; the aged, sick, and infirm; all engaged in necessary work at home, as tillers of the ground and others whose employments are indispensable. But all these would be called on according to their state and means to support the war, they would be engaged in it in the sense that the whole kingdom was, and would justly share the joy, triumph, and prosperity of the victory. And these correspond to all baptized Christians who, not through their own fault, are not fully entered in the warfare of the Christian life, those namely who have not and so far as they have not the use of reason

But what of those who refused to come not from dislike of the king's terms, the particular hardships of this campaign, but from dislike of soldiering altogether, from complete cowardice, and yet able-bodied men?—Not only they would be despised for cowardice but in the general movement of the commonwealth towards the great war this would be held disaffection and they would be disfranchised in the hour of triumph. Nevertheless these people are quite in the background in this Contemplation, as has been said above

The Application consists not in repeating the three Points over again, only substituting Christ for the temporal king in the First, Christ's teaching for the king's address in the Second, and the disgrace of putting the hand to the plough and looking back in the kingdom of heaven for the recreant knight in the Third, but, after once for all fitting the meaning to the Parable and unmasking the king to find Christ, then without delay acting on Christ's example as proposed to us in the three Points and responding to it point by point

First set before your eyes the case ('exemplum') of a temporal king sovereign in the way described and realise the stress and importance the sight or thought of him should and would have on his subjects ('consideramus' etc); then open the eyes of your mind and see that Christ is this king; that he makes a like offer and that we are much more bound to listen and obey; that the question of honour and disgrace, generosity and niggardliness is much more truly involved than in the Parable. If so then under the First Point let us respond by realising His Person and ours, His claims and our duty ('quanto magis res est digna consideratione'); in the Second by listening to, in the sense of obeying, His call; in the Third by acknowledging and rising to the note of Honour

'Mea voluntas'—The point is that we are in duty and loyalty bound to follow Him ('Regis', 'Christum Dominum nostrum, Regem aeternum') and it is for Him to choose what or where. Now as a fact He has chosen etc. It is therefore of precept to choose (but still to choose, for in this life we are free) *what* He has chosen, labour, and it is of counsel to choose *as* He has chosen, namely, the better part or the more laborious way of perfection, for this is a more deliberate and positive choice of good, taking it not anyhow but by the forelock or the handle; since he who from duty chooses the right prefers good to evil but he who for zeal selects the best good loves good not by contrast but for its own sake purely. Observe therefore the words 'Ego volo et desidero'[1] sqq. It is well here to cite Phil. ii 5–11, Heb. xii 2. sqq.[2]

'Offerent se totos ad laborem' / *will offer themselves without reserve to all laborious* DUTY—that is / will give in a particular allegiance and accept a particular obedience for the campaign, to do all, however laborious, that it involves, but not more. And here on obedience, allegiance, indifference, and morality in general—

The sovereign and the subject enter (by free contract or otherwise) into relations and this makes a polity or commonweal, commonwealth.[3] There is joint action, a common end in view, and a common good. The common good is shared either according to some constitution or terms of the contract or else by the disposal of some judge, usually the sovereign power; in the case of God and man altogether by the disposal of the sovereign. It is equitable that it should be in proportion to the work done. Besides the common good to be attained by common action there is status, the status of sovereign and the status of subject. To the status belongs duty or function, in the sovereign to legislate, command; in the subject to obey, but in the sense of consenting. This consent is primary, I mean that in it consists obedience rather than, or prior to, the execution (and Matt. xxi 28 sqq., the parable of the Two Sons sent into the vineyard, is not against this, for the first was 'paenitentia motus': in itself his offence was greater). This status arises immediately from the first compact or entry into relation and is confirmed or supported at each fresh command and obedience. It may be said to consist in citizenship or, to take a good which will include the sovereign, in statemembership, and again it is the being in one's rights, in one's duty, it is justice, and it is charity—charity because it is the friendliness which holds all together who are working for a common good and where one's good is all's good, in subject towards sovereign loyalty, in sovereign towards subject a sort of fatherly or patriarchal piety, in subject towards subject something rudely expressed by 'civil terms', 'civility'. It is compared to membership in the human body; and every one says / body politic.

The general rule for all such commonwealths is 'Qui fecerit ea [quae legis sunt] vivet in illis' (Gal. iii 12., quoting Lev. xviii 5.). This has a narrower and fuller sense of *live*. So far as live is barely live, not die, the keeper of the law, that is / he who does not break the law (understand, for simplicity's sake, in extreme, mortal matters and consider these only) shall be allowed to live; *for the law*, for anything the law does to him, he may live. In the higher sense of live he who keeps the law is to thrive by the law, have the blessings he would not have but for the law, his citizenship, status, the peace and prosperity of the state, the common weal and wealth, the fulness of *civil life*.

Death is to the individual the extreme of civil punishment. Banishment is a sort of civil death, disfranchisement another. But when we are speaking of religion, of the world as a commonweal where God is the sovereign, banishment and death will be the same thing.

The above on 'vivet in illis' is important as explaining St. Paul's meaning in the text quoted, and the Romans and Galatians in general, about the living by the Law and by faith. His remark applies to all law.

God first entered into relations (or what I used to call bidding) with man in Adam and a commonweal arose—with its sovereign and one subject; its membership (and perhaps it was to make a palpable reality of this membership, this headship, that God in some sensible form walked in Paradise); its distribution of the common goods, in which distribution the Tree of Knowledge was reserved to the sovereign; its justice, *original justice*; and so on. This commonweal may be looked on as not only a polity of sovereign and subject

but also in the light of property, where God is the landlord, man
the tenant, and this indeed not only as touches property strictly so
called but also life and other *bona* or blessings. Then sacrifices, tithes,
and so on will be rents, real or conventional; acknowledgments of
dependence; life will be a lease, with its terms; breaches of the
divine law will be encroachment on the landlord's or on a fellow
tenant's right; death will be ejectment and *now*, after the Fall, men
will be tenants at will. Property indeed is called substance, *substantia*,
οὐσία, and power ἐξουσία (but from an impersonal) as though to
mark that our subjection to God in both respects immediately followed from our creation. There is besides a third point of view
according to which God is lord of life and death to us not here by
way of justice and judgment but as a providence concerned with
our health, food, generation, and pleasures. From this point of view
marriage, which is called a Law, a constitution Rom. vii, 1, 2., will
be the prominent feature in the divine commonweal, City of God,
or Kingdom of heaven. In these three lights the three roots of action,
now after the Fall the three concupiscences, were subject to the law
of God. In the laws or terms of this constitution, more shortly by this
Law, man lived and saved his soul, that is / was in God's favour and
enjoyed the blessings of the commonweal, God's disposal or testament, the First and Oldest Testament; God also enjoyed from man
praise, reverence, and service.

Morality is divided into the binding and the free. By the binding
I mean what is commanded or forbidden. What is commanded is
duty, what is forbidden is offence or sin. The bindingness or obliga-
tion depends on the strength of the sanction, which in the divine
law is twofold, under pain of mortal or of venial sin, and these two
sanctions must be supposed to have degrees varying with the degrees
of good in the thing commanded and evil in that forbidden. Between
the commanded and the forbidden, between duty and sin, both
limits of man's right and freedom, stood his field of freedom or his
exercise of right. Now the things in which right could be exercised, for
instance leisure time, were some of them intrinsically indifferent,
others intrinsically good, none intrinsically bad. To praise God
oftener than what duty or even the becoming called for was a thing
good in itself but not a duty. But to admire the stars is in itself
indifferent. *Both classes were indifferent in point of sanction.** I think this
is the truth and that there is no *deordinatio* in the absence of all
special *ordinationem*, otherwise there is no real freedom left, I mean
option, and no exercise of right nor yet exercise of generosity. To say
/ I do this because I am allowed, because I am not forbidden, because
it is left open / is a submission as much as to say / I do this because

* But see next leaf. [a note in the margin. Ed.]

it is commanded, I shun that with all my might because it is forbidden strongly, the other as far as human frailty allows because it
is forbidden as far as human frailty allows. Such free action in
things in themselves indifferent was an exercise of right though not
of duty, it was *justified*, it was in the sense of the Psalmist a *justificatio*,
an acquittance of himself by man (for *justificari* is to acquit oneself).

Here I remark that we must distinguish in moral acts first the
nature of the act in itself, which will be good (as to shew mercy, to
praise God), bad (as to steal, to murder), or indifferent (as to eat or
fast) / and this is like matter to which a form may be added; next
the exercise and its conditions, that it is commanded or forbidden,
in other words matter of duty, that it is permitted, and lastly, which
is obscurer, that it is accepted.[1] Whatever is either commanded,
permitted, or accepted is justified, and in this sense no act can be
indifferent positively, that is / it must have its positive rightness or
justification, which may however be without quantity, e.g. without
merit. But intrinsically and also in point of being neither commanded nor accepted, that is neither of duty nor of grace (using
grace in a primary, not in a strict theological sense) it may be indifferent, gaining no goodness from the instress of the lawgiver (and
morality-maker, right-maker, justifier) to which the subject has
given his consent or obedience nor yet from the consent or correspondence of the lawgiver in accepting the instress of the subject.
So that acts may be indifferent in point of quantity but not positively
(or to speak mathematically, in point of sign)

The making of intentions, on which ascetically we lay so much
stress, turns altogether on the property of acceptance[2] and, given
acceptance, intentions may be made upon acts free and indifferent,
acts of necessity, and acts of duty as well as upon acts of grace or
generosity or supererogation.

What is written on the last leaf and underscored about sanction
must be understood not as we call permission sanction but of sanctions as stresses of the lawgiver's will given as motives to action. In
duty the lawgiver originates, the subject accepts; in free exercise of
right the subject originates, the lawgiver neither originates nor
accepts; in grace or supererogation the subject originates, the lawgiver accepts. If the lawgiver's will should ever be without sanction it
would seem to be without stress and not to constitute duty. Of that
hereafter, but on second thoughts I see that the word *sanction* in the
sense of permission and in that of enforcement is really the same,
being the genus of those two species. For there is a negative and a
positive permission: the positive only is sanction. I conclude then
that all moral action is either sanctioned or unsanctioned and in that
sense good or bad and none indifferent, but that this sanction may

be 'at balk' and the action positively good but quantitively nothing, that is, indifferent. There may also be an unquantified acceptance and hence indifference in point of merit, since merit is understood to have quantity.

Obedience or the subject's correspondence to the sovereign's commandments or instress and initiation[1] is in general nothing else than the relation, the compact in which the commonwealth consists and to it seems in equity or in justice to answer a correspondence, a compliance of the sovereign to the subject's instress of initiation:[2] it does not merit anything but the substantial or essential good which belongs to the commonwealth, the common weal itself. But to execution are due wages, an additional recompense, and this whether the execution of duty or of supererogatory work. However in so far as the issuing of fresh and incidental commands or laws calls forth a fresh submission on the subject's part and further abridges his liberty and field of right so far it does deserve a fresh reward[3]

July 14 '83—Isocrates[4] Πανηγυρικός, which I have been reading, may be used as an illustration of this exercise. At the end cap. 185 he says: καὶ μὴν οὐδὲ τὰς πόλεις λυπήσομεν στρατιώτας ἐξ αὐτῶν καταλέγοντες, ὃ νῦν ἐν τῷ πολέμῳ τῷ πρὸς ἀλλήλους ὀχληρότατόν ἐστιν αὐταῖς· πολὺ γὰρ οἶμαι σπανιωτέρους ἔσεσθαι τοὺς μένειν ἐθελήσοντας τῶν συνακολουθεῖν ἐπιθυμησόντων. τίς γὰρ οὕτως ἢ νέος ἢ παλαιὸς ῥᾴθυμός ἐστιν ὅστις οὐ μετασχεῖν βουλήσεται ταύτης τῆς στρατιᾶς τῆς ὑπ' Ἀθηναίων μὲν καὶ Λακεδαιμονίων στρατηγουμένης, ὑπὲρ δὲ τῆς τῶν συμμάχων ἐλευθερίας ἀθροιζομένης, ὑπὸ δὲ τῆς Ἑλλάδος ἁπάσης ἐκπεμπομένης, ἐπὶ δὲ τὴν τῶν βαρβάρων τιμωρίαν πορευομένης; φήμην δὲ καὶ μνήμην καὶ δόξαν πόσην τινὰ χρὴ νομίζειν ἢ ζῶντας ἕξειν ἢ τελευτήσαντας καταλείψειν τοὺς ἐν τοῖς τοιούτοις ἔργοις ἀριστεύσαντας; etc

Furthermore, we shall not even trouble the several states by levying soldiers from them—a practice which now in our warfare against each other they find most burdensome. For it is my belief that those who will be inclined to remain at home will be far fewer than those who will be eager to join this army. For who, be he young or old, is so indolent that he will not desire to have a part in this expedition—an expedition led by the Athenians and the Lacedaemonians, gathered together in the cause of the liberty of our allies, dispatched by all Greece, and faring forth to wreak vengeance on the barbarians? And how great must we think will be the name and the fame and the glory which they will enjoy during their lives, or, if they die in battle, will leave behind them—they who will have won the meed of honour in such an enterprise?

CHAPTER FIVE

THE SECOND WEEK

Text of Exercises (The Incarnation), Notes of GMH.
Text of Exercises (The Nativity: the Preludes), Notes of GMH.
Text of Exercises (The Nativity: the three Points), Notes of GMH.
Text of Exercises (The Nativity: Repetition by means of the five Senses),
Notes of GMH.
Notes of GMH (The Hidden Life).

THE INCARNATION*

The first prelude is to bring to mind the history of the thing I am to contemplate, which is here: how the three divine Persons were looking at the great plain of the whole world and the circuit of it full of men; and how seeing that they were all on the way down to Hell, it is decreed by the most holy Trinity *in its eternity* that the second Person *become man* to save the human race, and thus, when the fulness of time is come, They sent the Angel St Gabriel to Our Lady.

Second, the composition, by seeing the place. Here it will be to see *the great capacity and circuit of the world*, where there dwell so many and such diverse peoples. And thereafter to see the house and the room of Our Lady, in the township of Nazareth in the province of Galilee. . . .

The first point is to *see the persons*, one after the other, and first those who are scattered over the face of the earth in such great diversity. . . .

Secondly, to see and consider the three Divine Persons, as it were *upon their royal throne*. . . .

Thirdly, to see Our Lady and the Angel . . . the Angel *confirms* what he said to Our Lady by announcing the conception of St John the Baptist. . . .

Observe 'in sua aeternitate'. The divine Persons see the whole world at once and know where to drive the nail and plant the cross. A 60-fathom coil of cord running over the cliff's edge round by round, that is, say, generation by generation, 40 fathom already gone and the rest will follow, when a man sets his foot on it and saves both what is hanging and what has not yet stirred to run. Or seven tied by the rope on the Alps; four go headlong, then the fifth, as strong as Samson, checks them and the two behind do not even feel the strain. And so on. — See this confirmed by Fr Roothaan's note

---

* Only those parts of the text of the Exercises that are here relevant are quoted. The words commented on by GMH are italicized. [Ed.]

13 p. 79. In fact, *tota planities vel ambitus totius mundi plenus hominibus* is a graphic expression for the field in which man or humanity is seen by the divine mind from the beginning to the end of time. Therefore also he says *all*, for all men but the Blessed Virgin are by original sin lost as soon as conceived and we are here to consider the crying need of redemption. Otherwise one would not be able to explain how St Ignatius should make no exception of holy Simeon and Anna and all other just men and women living or dead, Jew or Gentile

'Homo fiat'—If Adam had not fallen it seems that Christ and his Mother would not have been born among his descendants.[1] But as the Blessed Virgin, who bore Christ in the flesh without birthpangs, is with great birthpangs the mother of all men in the spirit, so she would then have been their mother in the spirit but without sorrow. She would have been mother of man but not daughter of man and Christ would have been Son of Mary but not 'Son of Man', but Christ and Mary would have belonged to what those revelations made to a Dominican nun which Fr Le Gonidec[2] had seen called 'the hypostatic order'. Christ would have been in some *specie Mariana* and this would then have been his *forma servi* (which well agrees with what seems to me the true punctuation of Phil. ii. 7, 8.).[3] Man therefore gained by the Fall and Christ's redemption was a richer one, as bloodred is richer than white and bloodshed costlier than to heave a sigh, and this fully satisfies 'O felix culpa'[4] etc. Christ then is the redeemer in three or four senses: of his own created being, which he retrieves from nothingness, when it becomes divine and of infinite worth; of the Blessed Virgin not only from nothingness but also from the worthlessness towards God or unworthiness of God which is in every pure creature, and this he retrieves to divine motherhood, a status in kind and not in degree higher than what is attainable by any other creature's correspondence with grace; of the angels not only from nothingness and from worthlessness but also from that shortcoming which all creatures but the Blessed Virgin would seem to have from their want of correspondence with grace, and these, as the *Redemptor Saeculorum*, he relieves from imperfection; of fallen man, whom he reprieves from original and actual sin. As unfallen Adam's redeemer he would fill an office like that towards the angels; but perhaps in Adam unfallen there was venial sin strictly possible or even actual and in the Holy Angels only imperfection (L. R. Nov. 17 1881).

And this grace of the 'hypostatic order'[5] will be that sunlight with which the woman, that is / she-being, not she-man, of the Apocalypse is clothed,[6] her flesh or earthly but pre-human being is clothed; the incorruptible world of the angels is in attendance on her above, being by nature higher, as purely spiritual; and mortality and the world of corruption awaits her below, if she should choose, as she did, to descend onto it. Further, I suppose Melchisedech[1] to be a theophany of Christ in human shape out of this pre-human being of his and to differ from other theophanies[2] in that when Christ appeared as an angel he might be 'installed' or 'steaded' in some real and personal angel, as St Michael or St Gabriel, and this was their dignity to be vessels of Christ, but that there was no man Melchisedech, no such person but in person Christ. Incarnation then, ἐνσάρκωσις, is not the same thing as ἐνανθρώπευσις.[3]

Also out of this same world or stead of things in which Christ lived before he became man I suppose to have been made the earthly paradise planted by God from the beginning, that is perhaps / when the angelic world was brought into being, so that spirit and flesh started together, flesh being the name for a condition of matter. About this no doubt light may be had from the book of Genesis.[4] In this Christ *deambulabat ad auram post meridiem*, which seems to describe a ranging in the spirit through a world of his own. So that man lived at first rather in Christ and his mother, who came afterwards to live among men.

The above explains how it was that Satan could not recognize either Christ or his mother when he saw them in human shape, though he had seen them in heaven.

'Magnam capacitatem et ambitum mundi' — This suggests that 'pomegranate', that *pomum possibilium*. The Trinity saw it whole and in every 'cleave', the actual and the possible. We may consider that we are looking at it in all the actual cleaves, one after another. This sphere is set off against the sphere of the divine being, a steady 'seat or throne' of majesty. Yet that too has its cleave to us, the entrance of Christ on the world. There is not only the pomegranate of the whole world but of each species in it, each race, each individual, and so on. Of human nature the whole pomegranate fell in Adam (Aug. 26 '85)

'Videre Personas'—See for this pp. 121, 122 MS.[5] The Trinity made man after the image of Their one nature but They redeem him ('*faciamus* redemptionem') by bringing into play with infinite charity Their personality. Being personal They see as if with sympathy the play of personality in man below Them, for in his personality his freedom lies and this same personality playing in its freedom not only exerts and displays the riches and capacities of his one nature (see Fr Roothaan's note . . . 'unam eandemque' sqq) but unhappily disunites it, rends it, and almost tears it to pieces. One of Them therefore makes Himself one of that throng of persons, a man among men, by charity to bring them back to that union with themselves

which they have lost by freedom and even to bring them to a union
with God which nothing in their nature gave them

'Solio regali' etc—To shew the peaceful majesty which Our Lord
quitted to enter the miserable turmoil of mankind

'Omnes descendebant ad infernum'; 'morientes'—He harps on
this string, their miserable end at last—'omnes . . . moriantur et
descendunt ad infernum', 'occidunt, eunt ad infernum'—to shew
the necessity of the Redemption. One may also dwell on 'gestibus',
many of them sinful; 'nigros', under the curse of Canaan; 'in bello',
the scourge of war hurrying men untimely to death; 'plorantes',
'infirmos', 'morientes', miseries and consequences of the Fall.

The first object, I think, is that the mind may touch and appre-
hend the historical reality of the scene; then, as the note says, that
we may understand the need of the Redemption and the zeal of the
Trinity to bring it about and so may conceive a like zeal after our
measure. The different conditions of men serve to shew their need:
they are divided and estranged man from man by death, difference
of age, difference of health even in one family; family from family
by merriment or mourning; class from class by employment ('gestibus'), nation from nation by war; race from race by colour; and so on.
Tradition is almost wholly falsified among them; the division of race,
language, and interests makes the Old Law of almost no use to the
rest of the world. They are not held together by one worship and one
divine charity nor yet by human charity and natural ties, for these
bind them only into small, soon broken, and ever changing knots, all
more or less selfish. This then is why he dwells on their diversity ('in
tanta diversitate'): towards one another they are selfish and being
given up to their own purposes towards God they are blind ('in tanta
caecitate'). Each of these *persons*, for in the first Point he insists on
their personality, wants to be the world to himself; he hates his
brother whom he sees and therefore the God whom he does not see
and the not seeing, the blindness, is part of the hatred. Therefore in
the other points the vices St Ignatius dwells on are those of hatred:
they swear at one another, only naming God to their neighbour's
harm; God Himself they blaspheme. This for their words, and for
their deeds they strike and kill. See Romans iii 9–18 etc.

'Confirmat'—How, if she doubted him, could he confirm one uncertainty by another? It was not that she doubted his truthfulness
but that the promise 'concipies' etc was a free offer, depending on
her consent, and she was doubting whether she ought to give it,
wondering what was best before God. But by telling her of her
cousin Elizabeth's having already, by a less but like miracle, conceived, the angel shewed her what God's will was and that the
preparations for that event had already been begun for which only

her consent was wanting; so that she is no sooner thus determined and set at rest (confirmata) about God's will than she gives her submission to it: 'Ecce Ancilla' etc[1]

DE NATIVITATE

NOTES ON CONTEMPLATION

A. The Preludes:

The first prelude is the history; and here it will be how Our Lady came out of Nazareth, nearly nine months gone with child, mounted upon an ass (*as we may devoutly think*), with Joseph and a serving-maid, leading an ox, on their way to Bethlehem to pay the tribute which Caesar had imposed on all those regions. . . .

The second is the composition. It will be here to see with the eyes of the imagination the road from Nazareth to Bethlehem, *considering* its length and breadth, and whether it is a straight road or by cliffs and valleys; and considering the place, the cave of the nativity, how big it is or small, how high or lowly, and how it was prepared.

The third will be to ask for what I want, and here it will be to ask for an intimate knowledge of the Lord who for me is made man, that I may love him the more, and follow him.

Henceforward all the Exercises have these 3 preludes. And all are called Contemplations, with two exceptions only, those on the Two Standards and the Three Couples, which he calls Meditations; otherwise he uses that word no more. See p. 154, where he implies that the Mysteries of Christ's life may be meditated *or* contemplated. The first Week is the one in which he makes use of Meditations.— Nevertheless the word 'meditando' occurs pp. 82, 85[2]

'Ut pie meditari licet'—This is the conclusion, he means to say, to which pious *reasoning* will lead us, that they mounted Our Lady on the ass which, according to tradition, they brought with them. 'Meditari' refers to reasoning. See pp. 77, 85

'Considerando . . an . . an . . quam . . quam' etc—Not that the exercitant, if he has not been over the ground, will make much of it, but that, even by the realising—I mean more as we speak of realising a sum, a fortune—his ignorance or the small knowledge he has, he may reach the reality of the facts; something as to have been on pilgrimage to Jerusalem in the dark would be more full of devotion than to see it in the best panorama

B. The Points.

The first point is to see the persons, that is to see Our Lady and Joseph and the serving-maid, and the baby Jesus after he has been born, making myself a poor little unworthy serving-boy, watching them, contemplating them, and *ministering to them* in their needs, *as if I was there present*, with all possible dutifulness and reverence, and then to *reflect on myself so as to gain some fruit*.

Secondly, *to attend to, to take heed of, and to contemplate* the things that they are saying, and by reflecting on myself to gain some fruit.

Thirdly, *to watch and consider* what they are doing, the journey they make, the hardships they are undergoing, in order that Our Lord may be born in extreme poverty, and that after so many hardships, after hunger and thirst and heat and cold, after so much ill-usage and reviling, he may die at last upon the cross, *and all this for me*. Then by reflecting to gain some spiritual fruit.

On the contemplating Persons, Words and Actions—These three points belong to the three powers, memory, understanding, and will. Memory is the name for that faculty which towards present things is Simple Apprehension and, when it is question of the concrete only, γνῶσις, ἐπίγνωσις, the faculty of Identification; towards past things is Memory proper; and towards things future or things unknown or imaginary is Imagination.[1] When continued or kept on the strain the act of this faculty is attention, advertence, heed, the being *ware*, and its habit, knowledge, the being *aware*. Towards God it gives rise to *reverence*, it is the sense of the *presence* of God. The understanding, as the name shows, applies to words; it is the faculty for grasping not the fact but the meaning of a thing. When the first faculty just does its office and falls back, barely naming what it apprehends, it scarcely gives birth to the second but when it keeps on the strain ('attendere, advertere, et contemplari') it cannot but continuously beget it.[2] This faculty not identifies but verifies; takes the measure of things, brings word of them; is called λόγος and reason. By the will here is meant not so much the practical will as the faculty of fruition,[3] by which we enjoy or dislike etc, to which all the intellectual affections belong. For all three faculties are the mind, the intellect, νοῦς. I ought to have added that the second faculty ends in admiration, which issues in *praise*, and the third in enjoyment, which issues in love, which issues in *service*. But practice or action[4] properly so called may follow from any of the three, as St Ignatius implies by adding to each point 'reflectere' etc and 'ad capiendum fructum'; indeed he makes the first, you would say, more practical here than the last—'serviendo illis' etc. Besides this all voluntary exercise of faculties is in such a case practical; it is not mere speculation, whatever its name.

To confirm the above see in the present case in the first Point 'ac si praesens adessem', 'obsequio et reverentia'; in the second 'attendere, advertere, et *contemplari*' [as the term and climax]; in the third 'et omnia haec propter me', an appeal to the affections.

It should have been added that as the first faculty directed towards God is the sense of God's *presence* the second is that of His *essence*; the third that of His *power*, that is / the display of His hand or finger working in the world

'Postquam natus fuerit'—said out of reverence

'Serviendo illis' etc—So Sister Emmerich would say she had been that day to Bethany etc and had made herself useful in scouring the dishes and in other ways[1]

'Attendere, advertere, et contemplari' / *to be on the watch for, take notice of, and dwell on* what they say. In the First Point it is enough to say 'videre personas', for sight is a continuous sense, but hearing is intermittent mostly and in looking at the persons and the scene we might overlook that they spoke now and then; therefore he tells us by fresh casts of the mind to renew our realisation of the scene, not only taking note of the persons and watching ('spectare et considerare') what they do but also by imagination catching the words they say, not that we need know what they are, except the song of the Angels (see the *Mysteria*),[2] but this is of a piece with what has been said over leaf on 'considerando' and elsewhere.

C. Repetition of the exercise by means of the five senses.

'The first point is to see the persons with the eyes of the imagination, *meditating and contemplating in particular their circumstances*, and from the seeing of them to get some fruit.

Secondly, to hear with my hearing what they say, or might say, and by reflecting on myself to get some fruit.

Thirdly, *to savour and to taste*, by smell and by taste, the infinite delicacy and sweetness of the divinity, of the soul and of the virtues and of the rest of the things that belong to the person whom I am contemplating, and by reflecting on myself to draw hence some fruit.

Fourthly, *to touch* by touching, that is to say to kiss and to embrace the ground where such persons leave their footprints and the places where they recline, always with a view to the fruit that I may draw from thence.

'Meditando .. circumstantias earum' / inferring what they must have been, 'contemplando' / observing what they are. See notes on pp. 77, 82[3]

'Odorari' etc—Here he speaks of metaphorical taste and smell. You may suppose each virtue to have its own sweetness—one rich, another fresh, a third cordial, like incense, violets, or sweet-herbs, or, for taste, like honey, fruit, or wine.

'Tangere' etc—I suppose that St Ignatius means us to do what we might have done if present and not to do what we should not have ventured to have done, and this also shows how strongly he means us to realise the scene

THE HIDDEN LIFE

The Life of Christ Our Lord from the Twelfth to the Thirtieth Year

'De vita'—Nov. 19 1001 (Long Retreat)—Fr. Whitty gave last night the following pregnant thoughts: (1) *Erat subditus illis*: the hidden life at Nazareth is the great help to faith for us who must live more or less an obscure, constrained, and unsuccessful life. What of all possible ways of spending 30 years could have seemed so ineffective as this? What might not Christ have done at Rome or Athens, Antioch or Alexandria! And sacrificing, as he did, all to obedience his very obedience was unknown. Repulsiveness of the place: a traveller told him, who had been twice to Nazareth, that even now it keeps its fame for rudeness and worthlessness. But the pleasingness of Christ's life there in God's eyes is recorded in the words spoken when he had just left it: 'This is my beloved Son' etc.

(2) What was his life there?—One of devotion, saying or singing the psalms of David, which St Jerome used still to hear in the fields of Palestine; also one of labour; and of obedience: in every way it looked ordinary, presented *nothing* that could attract the world, not even austerities like those of St John in the wilderness.

(3) Our Lady's life at the same time—She was watching all he did. Twice St Luke tells us 'she laid up all these things in her heart' which therefore is a sort of fifth Gospel (cp. 'Is it not written in the book of' etc) and to it we must apply to know what Christ then was

The Coming of Christ to the Temple when He was Twelve Years Old

'De adventu'—On this occasion Christ manifested himself in his office of prophet, that is / teacher from heaven, and that as a boy. For at his birth he was manifested as king and yet as an infant. These strange circumstances were to leave room for faith. And thirdly at the baptism and at Cana he manifested himself as priest. And remark that in each of these three mysteries is again something three-

fold. For at his birth he was manifested (1) by angels to the shepherds, as a king from heaven; (2) by the star to the Magi and by
them to Herod and the Jews and again by these Jews to Herod and
the Magi as the King of prophecy and of David's race; (3) by inspiration to Simeon as the King who fulfilled the Old Law and
should enact the New: hence '*lumen* ad revelationem Gentium et
gloriam populi tui Israel' and 'signum cui contradicetur', the rallying
point of loyalty, touchstone of allegiance. In the manifestation in the
Temple, made to the learned, I see just the indication of the triad
in the three days, which may stand for the loss of the presence of
Christ by the Fall, the search for him under the Law of Nature, and
the finding him at last under the Law of Moses. At the baptism (1)
Christ was manifested by the descent of the Holy Ghost and the voice
of the Father and marked out as the 'pontifex ex hominibus assum-
ptus' mainly to St John; (2) by St John he was pointed out as the
Lamb of God, the victim, to St Andrew, by Andrew to Philip, by
Philip to Nathanael (in which things 3 days passed: see the place);
(3) he was, so to say, betrayed by his mother at Cana as the miracle
worker and good magician (which is a priestly office) to the marriage
party, when he might have seemed but a feaster and like the other
guests (L. R. Nov 21 1881)[1]

How Christ said Goodbye to His Blessed Mother and came from
Nazareth to the River Jordan where St John the Baptist was

'Valedicto'—The Baptism symbolical of Christ's descent into
human nature and that not only from the heaven of the Godhead,
to whose glories he had said farewell before, but also from that
heaven or aeon of Mary in which he had lived and been manifested
to the angels. (And here remark that his birth and the Gloria in
excelsis, the persecution by Herod, the flight into Egypt, the massacre of the innocents, the return to Nazareth and life of toil there,
all symbolise the manifestation of the eucharistic victim to the
angels, Satan's attack on it, its disappearance from his eyes in the
world of matter, the ruin of man—which reminds one again of that
river that after all did not drown the woman in the vision—and the
theophanies and preparation made for Christ's coming.)[2] (L. R.
Nov. 21 1881)

CHAPTER SIX

THE SECOND WEEK (*Continued*)

Text of Exercises (Two Standards), Notes of GMH, How Christ was tempted.
Notes of GMH ('Three Classes of Men': Three Kinds of Humility).

The first prelude is the history: it will be here how Christ calls and desires all to come under his standard, and Lucifer, on the contrary, under his.

The second is the composition, seeing the place. It will be here to see a vast plain embracing the whole region around Jerusalem where the supreme Captain-General of the good is Christ our Lord; and another plain, in the region of Babylon, where the chief of the enemy is Lucifer.

The third is to ask for what I want; and it will be here to ask for knowledge of the deceits of the wicked chieftain, and help to guard myself against them; and for knowledge of the true life which the supreme and true Captain points out, and grace to imitate him.

The first point is to imagine the chieftain of all the enemy as seated in that great plain of Babylon, as on a lofty throne of fire and smoke, horrible and terrible to behold.

The second to consider how he summons together innumerable devils, and how he disperses them, some to one city, some to another, and so on throughout the whole world, omitting no province, place or state of life, nor any person in particular.

The third is to consider the address which he makes to them, and how he admonishes them to lay snares and chains; that they are first to tempt men with the lust of riches, as he is wont to do in most cases, so that they may more easily come to the vain honour of the world, and then to unbounded pride; so that the first step is that of riches, the second of honour, the third of pride; and from these three steps he leads them to all other vices.

In like manner on the other hand we are to imagine about the supreme and true Captain who is Christ our Lord.

The first point is to consider how Christ our Lord takes his stand on a great plain near Jerusalem, in a lowly place, in aspect beautiful and attractive.

The second point is to consider how the Lord of the whole world chooses so many persons, Apostles, Disciples, etc., and sends them throughout the whole world to spread abroad his sacred doctrine through all states and conditions of persons.

The third is to consider the address which Christ our Lord makes to all his servants and friends whom he sends on this expedition, recommending them that they should desire to help all by drawing them first to most perfect spiritual poverty, and if it pleases his Divine Majesty and he should desire to choose them, even to actual poverty; secondly, to a desire of reproaches and contempt; because from these two things, humility results. So that there are three steps; the first, poverty, opposed to riches; the second, reproaches and contempt, opposed to worldly honour; the third, humility, opposed to pride; and from these three steps let them lead them on to all the other virtues.

Colloquy with our Lady . . . the Son . . . the Father . . .

Secunda Hebdomada. De Duobus Vexillis.

'Historia' / a historical fact—Dec. 22 1879. It is a real thing he means but he couches it in an imaginary shape—imaginary, for the real Jerusalem is not in a great plain. It is the same thing with the composition of place in the first meditation of all. The composition of place is always a reality, even when the story, the *historia*, is not history: for this see the Kingdom of Christ and the Three Pairs of Men. See also the Contemplation for Divine Love. Here it seems the heavenly Jerusalem that is meant and the infernal Babylon. The teaching of the two leaders to their soldiers is not one historical moment but the continual though actual system they keep at work and influence they exert upon it.

Dec. 22 1879—The heavenly Jerusalem and infernal Babylon but not heaven and hell but Christ's and Lucifer's kingdoms, which are partly on earth. 'Campum magnum' / great plain, suggests grand *plan*, *platform*, field of action

'Imaginari ac si sederet' and later 'Similiter ex opposito imaginandum est de . . . vero duce'—The imagination is employed to realise truth, not error, but under its own imagery, without which 'pro hoc statu' the truth cannot be reached (Nov. 20 1881, L. R.)

'Cathedra ignis'—This was perhaps an image in use at the time, for cp. Shakespeare 'And let the Devil Be sometime honoured for his burning throne.[1] (L. R.)

'Reliqua vitia'—that is / besides pride, for riches and honours are not vices, though the inordinate love of them may be. So of 'reliquas virtutes' lower (Nov. 20 1881, L. R.)

This was the process of his own fall.[2] For being required to adore God and enter into a covenant of justice with him he did so indeed, but, as a chorister[3] who learns by use in the church itself the strength and beauty of his voice, he became aware in his very note of adoration of the riches of his nature; then when from that first note he should have gone on with the sacrificial service, prolonging the first note instead and ravished by his own sweetness and dazzled, the prophet says, by his beauty, he was involved in spiritual sloth ('nolendo se adjuvare') and spiritual luxury and vainglory; to heighten this, he summoned a train of spirits to be his choir and, contemptuously breaking with the service of the eucharistic sacrifice, which was to have a victim of earthly nature and of flesh, raise a hymn in honour of their own nature, spiritual purely and ascending, he must have persuaded them, to the divine; and with this sin of pride aspiring to godhead their crime was consummated.[1]

The point of laying the train of things, as Fr. Roothaan says, in themselves indifferent is to be able to approach and attack everyone, even the innocent, the virtuous, and so on; for Lucifer was innocent and virtuous and enlightened and high in grace when he entered on the first of these degrees.

The 'nets and chains' have reference to that very hierarchy and subordination, that web of functions, and concerting of voices by which Lucifer had first entangled and 'with his tail swept down', as the Scripture says, his angels themselves.

Remark also the 3 degrees of selfishness—love of our goods, which are wholly outside ourselves; love of our good name ('vanus honor mundi'), which is ourself indeed, but in others' minds; love of our own excellence, of our very selves, pride. And therefore intellectual goods, as learning, still more / talents, and moral goods, as virtues, merits, graces, are more dangerous to be attached to and proud of.

Apostacy[2] is the crowning sin of pride. The hold an apostacy or heresy has on those who find themselves in it is mainly due to worldly goods and public opinion. But personal pride will be stronger still.

Language acknowledges the truth of the series. Goods are estate; estate / status; status / rank; rank / honour or estimation, esteem; self esteem / pride

'S. P. Mentionem'[3] etc—For it is question of Christ's historical coming upon earth and calling men who should call other men. Lucifer, who was never incarnate, can only call men by devils; yet he would set up, as Christ has, an earthly power and kingdom and so enthrones himself now at Rome, by Nero and Diocletian to persecute the early Christians; now at Bagdad; now at Stamboul. For he is always being brought to confusion and vice, which is $\phi\theta\alpha\rho\tau\iota\kappa\grave{\eta}$ $\dot{\alpha}\rho\chi\tilde{\eta}s$, cannot be consistent like virtue. And God is continually confounding the builders of Babel or of Babylon (Nov. 20 1881, L. T.)—and so dividing Satan's kingdom against itself. And here I see an answer to the difficulty I have often felt about that very text. When Mahomet overthrew idolatry Satan was divided against himself, but it was a weak and ineffective empire he overthrew to found a strong and central one, it was a sacrificing of the tail to the head; whereas to cast out devils is to overthrow Satan's empire in its head, the dominion of the body and even of the mental faculties of man—which if Beelzebub ever did / it would be to send mightier devils in their place

'Ita ut'—And there are 3 degrees in Christ himself; 'qui cum in forma Dei [the riches, as St Paul calls them, of the godhead] non rapinam[1] ['no booty for *him*': here is the poverty] arbitratus est esse se aequalem Deo [and so put aside the status and honour of godhead], sed semetipsum exinanivit [made himself poor], formam servi accipiens [and contemptible, which is humility,]; in similitudinem hominum factus et habitu inventus ut homo [and then all over again, when he was now actually man and born in poverty], humiliavit semetipsum, factus obediens usque ad mortem, mortem autem crucis [that is / the most ignominious of deaths]'. This process took place in its own fashion (1) in the procession of the godhead; (2) in his entrance into creation, his incarnation proper; (3) on earth, in the ἐνανθρώπευσιν, the becoming man[2] (Nov. 21 1881. L. R.)

HOW CHRIST WAS TEMPTED

'*QUOMODO*'—On the Temptation—Satan was quite ignorant of the Incarnation, of what the mystery was, but suspected some mystery, and was no doubt ready with every alternative about Christ, from that of his being a fallen man up to that of his being a theophany of the Trinity; everything that was afterwards tried in the shape of heresy on the Incarnation and more. His pride especially made this mystery of humiliation dark to him. He hoped that if the worst happened, which was that he should be driven away with indignation for his presumption, at least it would be proved that Christ was God and he should know who he was dealing with. And in fact the issue of the first temptation confirmed him somewhat in the belief that he was not dealing with God. (See later at p. 208)[3]

Christ's Temptation—The historical order of events, that in St Matthew. This appears by the way in which Christ's answer to the first temptation serves as a suggestion for the second, namely to quote Scripture and to put forward trust in providence, and by other circumstances.

In these three temptations many things must be borne in mind, as (1) the process of Satan's own fall; (2) that of his angels; (3) that of Adam and Eve; (4) the three concupiscences; (5) the three phases of actual sin (desire, consent, enjoyment or, as St Gertrude has it and applies them to Christ's temptations in this order, *delectatio, consensus, concupiscentia*); (6) Christ's offices of prophet, priest, and king. And I have no doubt there is more. And each temptation was composite; there were several strands, any one of which Satan could draw upon, who like the spider 'lives along the line'.

First then, after witnessing what had happened at the Baptism, in which Christ had hallowed water and driven him out of it and had been borne witness to as God's wellbeloved son, Satan treats Christ as a 'pontificem ex hominibus assumptum, pro hominibus constitutum in iis quae sunt ad Deum, ut offerat dona et sacrificia pro peccatis' (Heb. v 1.) and asks of him to use his sacramental or, so to call it, magic power, and that not for a common meal's sake but for a sacrificial one, a sacramental, nay a eucharistic; for something of this mystery, it is likely, he was experimenting upon: Christ was to eat it in thanks for his preservation through the fast and Satan, disguised perhaps as Milton[1] makes him, like a poor hermit or something of that sort was for pity's sake ('qui condolere possit iis qui ignorant et errant, quoniam et ipse circumdatus est infirmitate' ib. 2.) to be allowed to partake. It might be proposed as a sin offering too ('et propterea debet, quemadmodum pro populo, ita etiam et pro semetipso offerre pro peccatis' ib. 3.: see the whole place) and that would discover what Christ was.

The yielding to the temptation would not necessarily be more than the least of imperfections, the doing a necessary and prudent thing before the positive inspiration to do it; but from that little beginning Satan was prepared to lead things on to devil worship, by suggesting that he was a theophany such as Abraham had and that the bread should be offered to him. And there is something of this process in the other temptations: the throwing of himself from the pinnacle was to be a safe act; for the angel, Satan disguised, at his side was himself to be answerable and the imprudence would be reduced to that of not ascertaining what the angel was, which imprudence must, it would seem, be small, so subtly did he disguise himself as a good one. And then his best hope was that his victim would kill himself; the next that unaided by God he would have to call on himself / Satan to help him; the next that he would have to put out some miraculous power, which would at least shew the folly of the act in itself; at the least that that should happen which he himself had suggested, angels bear Christ up, and then he would press a temptation of vainglory. He would likewise then too pass himself off as a theophany, this time in angel form, and draw the leap into an act of adoration, of self immolation, at least of obedience to him. The order of things then I suppose to be

'*DE VOCATIONE*'[1]—He points out there were in the case of the
Apostles three sorts of vocation. The first was gradual: by this were
called St Peter and St Andrew and, though he does not say so, the
two sons of Zebedee, and not as the Vulgate says[2] 'secundo': in the
case of St Peter and St Andrew he distinguishes three steps in it, three
calls. In John i. it is likely that the other disciple besides Andrew was
St John himself, for cp. 38 with xxi. 20.; also that St John brought
his brother to Christ as St Andrew did his. These in some sort presented themselves to Christ and were accepted, I mean St Andrew
and St John (see Joan. i 37, 38.), and then presented their brothers,
and these were accepted. And they were themselves in some sort presented by St John the Baptist.

The second sort is that of a single and sudden call and without
any presentation. And here it should be remarked that St Philip
presented Nathanael and Christ, who praised him so highly, did not
accept him as an Apostle.

Of the third sort St Ignatius tells us nothing or tells us the Gospel
tells us nothing particular. It is that of those who having followed
Christ as disciples were formally chosen Apostles after Christ's
night of prayer (Luc. vi 13.)

This third call then all had: this is the hierarchical call. Some had
the second besides, the prophetical; and of these the two pairs of
brothers had besides the first, the royal call or call to allegiance. St
Paul was called by the second sort; so also the rich young man and
two others, and these refused it. Our vocation is strictly of the third
sort but God's inward dealings may bring it under the others (Nov.
25 1881, L. R.). And as St John Baptist representing the Law and
Prophecy, the Old Testament, presented his disciples to Christ:
so there is a machinery of presentation with us and the first sort
resolves itself into the third. For first there must be allegiance, but
given allegiance, then hierarchy or political order and organism can
do its work.

Compare the three times for making an Election p. 114.[3] The first
answers to the prophetical call; the second to the call to allegiance
or royal call (cp. 'per experientiam' there with 'ad quandam notitiam' opposite); the third to the hierarchical (see 'eligit ut medium
vitam aliquam seu statum intra limites Ecclesiae' etc, like saying /
makes use of the appointed machinery of the Church).

NOTE ON THREE CLASSES OF MEN[4]

'Historia' — as in the Two Standards (v. ad p. 94), a fact of
history, and the six men are the exercitant himself and five other
such exercitants who have been before him or will be after, but

clothed in this much parable, that it is made question of 10,000 ducats. That this is so appears from the composition of place which follows (Nov. 20 1881, L. R.)—Or say rather five men to whom the offer of the Spiritual Exercises has been made, for to accept that offer is to take a great step, which the first Pair never did; or anything equivalent, any call from God (Aug. 12 1892).

Remark that all six begin with an *affectus* or disposition of avarice; for it is avarice to make money not for God's service. And the question is about getting rid not of the money but of the affection or vice. They also begin with a counter-affection, the wish to serve God. (It is of little use in English to say *velleity*: *wish* expresses the thought and better for the most part.) Now wish is the condition of the affective will before action; whether action shall follow depends on the *arbitrium*. With the first pair none follows; they take no step, not even against the affection for the money. The second pair try to lay aside the unruly affection, but under impossible conditions; not that it is impossible to keep money without loving it, but that they want to keep it in reality only because they love it and so propose to love it and not love it too. The third pair wish to lay aside not only the direct love of the money but also that secondary love, the desire to keep it, which is in fact only the old love disguised, one remove away. They therefore now resolve to leave the money as soon as they shall know that to be God's will, which they will go on to ascertain by the Election; meantime they do leave it in affection.

'Cur bini,'[1] etc (overleaf)—And that the exercitant in whichever mind he should find himself may know that there has been another like him, another in the same; that it is an old story; 'quid est quod factum est? idem quod futurum est' etc (Aug. 12 1882)

'In affectu'[2]—The reading seems right and the meaning to be: meanwhile he wishes it to be an understood thing that as far as affection towards it goes he has quite given the money up and that if at present he takes no step and lets it lie in his hands it is only because he is waiting for and has not yet felt that impulse from God and heaven-inspired desire which is to decide him whether to keep it or to leave it in reality (L. R.)—And, if the others would but see it, this is to do all. Before God the third Pair have taken the decisive step—given up the inordinate affection; for the money is neither here nor there

NOTE ON THREE KINDS (OR DEGREES) OF HUMILITY

'Primus Modus' etc—The First Degree is for no consideration to consent to sin mortally. The Second is for no consideration to consent to sin venially and in that and in other respects to fulfil perfectly God's naturally known or revealed will, apart from the work of redeeming mankind. The First is the mind of the first Adam before he fell. The Second is the mind of a follower of the second Adam as we see him apart from his Passion, i.e. in that character or *role* which Marie Lataste[1] speaks of not very clearly, his character or *role* of the ideal man, God's meaning in man realized;—which life though he lived[2] it in Galilee and on earth he might have lived in some earthly or other Paradise. But with it Christ had undertaken the work of redemption, the undoing of the evil done and not only the doing of the work that was to be done better; in other words the Cross and Passion (for otherwise the merits of his ideal or perfect life might by concomitance have redeemed man too). This is the force of 'actu similis' what Christ *as a fact* was and did (Aug. 12 1882)

CHAPTER SEVEN

THE THIRD AND FOURTH WEEKS

The Passion, Notes of GMH (Compositions of Place).
Text of Exercises (Additional Points on Sorrow), Notes of GMH.
Notes of GMH (Pilate).
Text of Exercises (The Resurrection), Notes of GMH (Appearance to Our Lady,
   Appearance on Mount Tabor).
Text of Exercises (Contemplation for Obtaining Love), Notes of GMH.

THIRD WEEK

THE PASSION

COMPOSITIONS OF PLACE

The Supper Room

'Videre personas': see on 'videndo locum'[1]—As all places are at
some point of the compass and we may face towards them: so every
real person living or dead or to come has his quarter in the round of
being, is lodged onewhere and not anywhere, and the mind has a real
direction towards him.[2] We are to realise this here of 'the persons of the
Supper': as we have got the orientation of the room, its true measurements and specifications, properly furnished it and so on, so now we
are properly to people it and give it its true personallings. It is in
this way that Scotus says[3] God revealed the mystery of the Trinity
that His servants might direct their thoughts in worship towards,
determine them, pit them, upon the real terms, which are the Persons,
of His being the object of that worship. 'Fructum': we shall look on
Christ with adoration, on St. Peter with reverence as our foundation,
St. Matthew and St. John as our informants, on Judas with grief,
and so forth

The Garden

'Relinquens octo' etc—This posting and localising of the persons is
a part of his preparation of the board or stage for the scene and is, as
elsewhere, all directed to help us to realise it.—Dec. 23 1879 And
remark the 'per vallem deorsum ac dein per declivum sursum'

ADDITIONAL POINTS ON SORROW[4]

. . . The fourth, to consider what Christ our Lord suffers in
his humanity and wishes to suffer, according to the passage which

is being contemplated; and here to begin with much force to strive to grieve and bewail and lament, and in the same way to continue striving through the other points which follow.

The fifth, to consider how the Divinity hides itself, that is to say, how it could destroy its enemies and does not do it; and how it allows the most holy humanity to suffer so cruelly.

The sixth, to consider how he suffers all these things for my sins, etc., and what I ought to do and suffer for him. . . .

The special grace to be asked for in the Passion is sorrow with Christ in his sorrow, a broken heart with Christ broken-hearted, tears and interior pain for the great pain that Christ has suffered for me.

These 3 points are (1) Christ's human nature and how it suffers: the victim; (2) his godhead and how (A) it spares or lets do, (B) forsakes and lets be done to: the priest or the giver of the victim; (3) me, the culprit, the lost sheep, the redeemed. Then further we are (1) to suffer with Christ suffering, (2) keep sight of the godhead hiding, (3) repay if we can the price of our redemption. See at p. 135 (L. R.)[1]

'Hic incipere'—viz. doing what we are to pray for in 'Tertium, petere id quod volo'. He says we are to strain for it: this straining is becoming and suitable here, it gives us some likeness to Our Lord's condition and is some sort of homage to that—See also on 'adnitar' at p. 125.

'Dolorem' grief for Christ's sake, 'afflictionem' as if it concerned myself, 'et confusionem' plainly 'eo quod ob mea' etc—Dec. 23 1879 *Dolere*, to be sorry, is to wish an evil undone—when of our own doing it is penitence or repentance; *afflictio*, affliction, properly *wrecking*, is the material side of evil, the mischief, the havoc done—or the havoc of mind answering to it; thirdly (see more plainly p. 125 'poenam internam' sqq.) there is what answers to the formal evil, the badness or evil quality, the *malitia*, of the evil and it consists of two things commonly—shame and sadness. See note to p. 58 and to p. 125.[2]

'Confractionem'—See the remarks on 'afflictionem' in the note beginning 'dolorem' at p. 122 (L. R., Nov. 27 1881)—Supposing, what I found in St. Gertrude, that there are in sin the three stages or features, *concupiscentiam, consensum, delectationem*, / *dolor*, the wishing a thing undone, will answer to *concupiscentiam*, the wishing to do it; *confractio*, the being wrecked by the havoc or mischief of sin, to *consensum*, taken in the sense of commission, the fatal blow itself; tears and *poena interna* to *delectationem*, the pleasure taken in the sin. The three things named are all in the agent and in his mind; besides these there is the outward or objective mischief done and between the agent and the harm done the act of execution by which he does it. I have more on this subject to enter under the instructions on the General Examination of Conscience at pp. 42, 43.

'Adnitar'—See on 'hic incipere' at p. 122.

PILATE

'*A DOMO CAIPHAE*'—Harmony: The Council or Sanhedrim in a body take Christ to Pilate, who, it being the feast, was perhaps not sitting in court at the time. They do not enter the praetorium, for fear of defilement, but perhaps some outer court of the building reckoned extrajudicial. They send in to Pilate that the Council desires formally to deliver into his hands the prisoner Jesus of Nazareth, who claims to be the Christ or independently anointed King of the Jews. (This expectation of the Christ must have been known to Pilate and he must have had some knowledge about our Lord's life.) Pilate goes out to the Council and asks a more definite charge: 'Quam accusationem affertis adversus hominem hunc?' (Joan. xviii 29.), almost = What is the meaning of the charge? I want it put in some shape that brings it within my cognisance. They answer that it means the refusal of taxes to Caesar and a revolution, to which he has been convicted of exciting the people. That is to say / it is not a mere question of religion and touching themselves the Jews only; it is a public crime and the man a common malefactor and as such they have felt themselves bound to make his case over to the secular tribunal (Luc. xxiii 2. 'Hunc invenimus [formal, *we have convicted*] subvertentem gentem nostram [as if their very patriotism here seconded their loyalty to Rome] et prohibentem tributa dare Caesari et dicentem se Christum regem esse'; Joan. ib. 30. 'Si non esset hic malefactor non tibi tradidissemus eum'). Pilate says that as they understand the case he wishes it to be left in their hands. They answer that with them it is a question of a capital charge, that the man has been found guilty, and that no more remains to be done but to execute him; which is not in their power. And this answer, being complete, baffled Pilate's first unjust attempt to be rid of the duty of discharging an innocent man, for from the first moment he knew that Christ was innocent (Marc. xv 10.): if it had been otherwise he would have known independently. He was therefore unjust in entertaining the charge, in giving it a hearing, as Caiphas was unjust in the opposite, in not giving Christ a hearing but condemning him *for claiming*, not unfoundedly claiming, to be the Christ. For the man must be to come who should be the Christ and claim to be. Pilate therefore called Christ into the praetorium and

examined him on the only count he could make out of the accusation. The charges seem not to have been made in Christ's hearing, as
appears by his question: 'A temetipso' etc Joan. ib. 34. Pilate asks an
ambiguous question: 'Art thou *the* king of the Jews?' which may
mean: Dost thou claim royalty against my sovereign? or / Art thou
the Messias the Jews expect; so that Pilate hoped from the first to
save himself in one of two ways, either of sentencing Christ on a
genuine Roman criminal charge or of throwing him back upon the
Jews again, as being rather a benefactor of than an offender against
their nation. Christ cuts off the ambiguity by the question: 'A
temetipso hoc dicis an alii dixerunt tibi de me?' —that is / Art thou
going to try me on a charge touching thee or only to carry out the
sentence of the Jews? It was to avoid this kind of check that the Jews
had not at first made their charges in Christ's presence. Pilate is
forced to take a side: 'Numquid ego Judaeus sum? Gens tua et
pontifices tradiderunt te mihi: quid fecisti?' / like saying / the claim
to be their Messias is of itself no crime: where is thy criminality? He
still hopes to get hold of something from the prisoner's confession.
But the only thing which could concern Pilate must be a state-
charge: to that Christ replies. His kingdom is not of this world or his
servants would have fought; that is / it is not founded on an earthly
title nor on earthly force; not on an earthly title, for if it were he
would maintain it against Pilate, which he does not—he did maintain his title before the high-priests, but that was a heavenly one;
not on earthly force for the reason he gives, and he says *to the Jews*,
because they were his first assailants and that he may in no way seem
to clash with Pilate's power. Then he shews in what sense he is a king,
but Pilate was satisfied and more, at once wearied: he had got on
the one hand the acknowledgment he wanted, to be used as need
should require, and on the other the proof that the charge did not
concern him. 'What is truth?' like saying / Kingdom over Truth!
never mind *that* kingdom: I have no time for trifling. He therefore
goes out again and saying that he finds no case tries to get rid of the
affair at once. But the Jews renew their accusation or bring new
ones, which are the old one in various shapes. This is now in
Christ's hearing (Luc. xxiii. 5, Marc. xv. 3, Matt. xxvii. 12), who
makes no answer, for witnesses are not brought and above all Pilate
has refused to entertain the charge or has entertained it and found
it baseless and yet the case goes on. Therefore when Pilate asks him
if he has nothing to say he says nothing even to that question, which
embarasses Pilate and puts the truth before him more clearly than
anything could. At this point the mention of Galilee is made. The
fresh charges are to shew that the case *is* one which concerns the
state: Galilee has to be named, for Pilate could answer for it well

enough if Judaea only were concerned. He takes hold of this admission and sends Christ to Herod. This is his second attempt to get rid of the case unjustly. For Christ being innocent why should he even endanger him? Herod could manage his own business in Galilee.

FOURTH WEEK

THE RESURRECTION

The first Prelude is the history,[1] which is here how after Christ had expired on the Cross, and his body remained separated from the soul yet always united to the Divinity, his blessed soul likewise united to the Divinity descended into hell, whence releasing the souls of the just and coming to the sepulchre and rising again, he appeared in body and soul to his Mother.

Additional Points for the Fourth Week

The first, second and third points are the same that we have had in the Supper of Christ our Lord.

The fourth is to consider how the Divinity, which in the Passion seemed to hide itself, now appears and shews itself miraculously in the most holy Resurrection by its true and most holy effects.

The fifth is to regard the office of Consoler which Christ our Lord exercises, comparing it with the manner in which friends are wont to console one another.

The Ninth Apparition (Matt. xxviii, 16–20):

The disciples at the command of the Lord go to Mount Thabor....

The Tenth Apparition (1 Cor. xv, 6):

'Afterwards he was seen by more than five hundred brethren at once.'

APPEARANCE TO OUR LADY

'In corpore et anima'—On the pregnant principle expressed in the Mysteries and in this very one (p. 173)[2] we cannot doubt that at the Last Supper Christ invisibly but sacramentally communicated his Blessed Mother (as many ecstatics and others have been communicated) by the hands of angels or otherwise. After this she would have fasted till the Resurrection and the Sacred Host have lain in her breast unconsumed.[3] In her then as well as on the cross Christ died and was at once buried, her body his temple becoming his sepulchre. At his rising the soul entered the body in her as in the sepulchre and, issuing from her breast, the two presences passed into one. And at the same time the windingsheet left empty fell in upon itself in the sepulchre and the empty accidents were consumed in the Blessed Virgin. St. Ignatius seems just to hint this mystery in the words above (L. R., Dec. 4 1881)

'Primum punctum' etc—namely Persons, Words, and Actions respectively.

'Quartum' etc—This and the 5th Point correspond to those for the Passion Week on p. 122.

[You would expect therefore a 6th, as to consider how all this Christ does for my encouragement and how I ought to respond to it. He does allow you to make such a point at your discretion, see p. 137,[1] remark 3, where he especially speaks of *five* points.]*

(What is crossed out contained a strange blunder). There is nothing corresponding to the 4th Point in the Passion Week, viz. What it is that Christ is suffering in this part of his Passion, but it was not necessary: what would correspond would be the particular Apparition and its object, which was in some way to console, as in Point 5—Dec. 23 1879—See at p. 122. It is no wonder the 3 points become 2, for whereas in the Passion we were to contemplate the withdrawal and hiding of the godhead,[2] the deep severance between it and the manhood, now we are to contemplate the union between them (L. R., Dec. 4 1881)

APPEARANCE ON MOUNT TABOR

'Thabor'—traditional—'Et videntes eum adoraverunt, Quidam autem dubitaverunt. Et accedens Jesus' etc Matt. xxviii 17, 18. Either understand *dubitaverunt*, ἐδίστασαν, *had doubted* (the aorist often is a pluperfect) or else join closely 'Quidam autem dubitaverunt, et accedens' etc / Yet some doubted: then Jesus coming up . . all doubt was over: cf. Luc. xxiv 41. And remark that St. Matthew tells of this apparition only, after the one in which he bid the women appoint this very meeting on the mountain: his account is foreshortened and he does not say the women were not believed. But see below.

Our Lord had a Church of his lifetime, that of the Circumcision and to this alone he said he was sent: this he opened formally, so to say, at the Sermon on the Mount. The Church Catholic he opened formally on another mount, Thabor. (However its being was not perfect until Pentecost). This is the meaning of choosing the mountain in Galilee—Dec. 24 1879

* The sentences in square brackets are crossed out in MS. [Ed.]

This apparition must, one would think, have taken place between Easter Sunday and Low Sunday and the disciples must have been to Galilee and back. In that case St. Thomas is meant in *quidam autem* (L. R.). St. Paul 1 Cor. xv 5–8, mentions 5 apparitions besides that to himself, the 2nd τοῖς δώδεκα: this means the College but not all assembled; then that to the 500; then to St. James;* then τοῖς ἀποστόλοις πᾶσιν, that is / the eleven, including St. Thomas. This makes it still more likely that St. Ignatius' 9th and 10th apparitions are the same.

'DE DECIMA'—generally believed to be the same as the foregoing. —And as Mt. Tabor is more than 60 miles from Jerusalem, so that 4 days would be required for going and returning, and they could not start before Easter Monday nor travel on Saturday, it must have taken place on Easter Wednesday (L.R.) But by comparing Matt. xxviii 7, 'καὶ ταχὺ πορευθεῖσαι εἴπατε τοῖς μαθηταῖς αὐτοῦ ὅτι ἠγέρθη ἀπὸ τῶν νεκρῶν καὶ ἰδοὺ προάγει ὑμᾶς εἰς τὴν Γαλιλαίαν· ἐκεῖ αὐτὸν ὄψεσθε· ἰδοὺ εἶπον ὑμῖν', where, though we might understand ἠγέρθη to the end as a quotation, the message sent, yet considering both the words and the context it seems more reasonable to include the women in 'ὑμᾶς' and 'ὑμῖν'; and again 10. 'ὑπάγετε, ἀπαγγείλατε τοῖς ἀδελφοῖς μου ἵνα ἀπέλθωσιν εἰς τὴν Γαλιλαίαν κἀκεῖ με ὄψονται,' where, though 'ἀδελφοῖς' might mean the Apostles only, yet on the whole it seems more reasonable to include all the disciples; comparing then these places (and Mark xvi 7.) with inf. 16 'οἱ δὲ ἕνδεκα μαθηταὶ ἐπορεύθησαν εἰς τὴν Γαλιλαίαν εἰς τὸ ὄρος οὗ ἐτάξατο αὐτοῖς ὁ Ἰησοῦς', we may suppose perhaps that the appearance of the 500 was to the body of the disciples, the Christian community, travelling together (as people went to and from the feasts in caravans) down to Galilee, but not to the Apostles or not to all of them, and that the appearance on the mountain was later. And in this appearance too it may be that Christ shewed himself to many, but, as at the Sermon on the Mount, had a special audience of the Twelve in a place higher and more retired. The Apostles then need not have been to Galilee and back in Easter Week.—St. Jerome however assumes that they did (Comment. in Matt. lib. 4 quoted in the Breviary / Friday in Easter Week)

CONTEMPLATION FOR OBTAINING LOVE

In the first place two things are to be noted here. The first is that love ought to show itself in deeds more than in words. The second, that love consists in mutual interchange on either side,

* St. Paul *loco citato* shews that this took place between Easter Wednesday and the evening of Low Sunday (L.R.). As St. James the Great was dead when St. Paul wrote and he is quoting accessible witnesses he must mean St. James the Less (L. R.).

that is, in the lover giving and communicating to the beloved that which he has, or of that which he has or can give, and so in turn the beloved to the lover. So that if one has knowledge he gives it to him who has it not, and likewise if he have honours or riches; and the other in turn does the same.

The usual preparatory prayer.

The first prelude is a composition of place, which is here to see how I stand before God our Lord, before the Angels and Saints who are interceding for me.

The second to ask for that which I want. It will be here to ask for an interior knowledge of so much good I have received, so that acknowledging it to the full, I may be able to love and serve his Divine Majesty in everything.

The first point is to call to mind the benefits received, of creation, redemption and particular gifts, pondering with great affection how much God our Lord has done for me and how much he has given me of what he has; and consequently how much the same Lord desires to give me himself in so far as he can according to his divine ordinance: and then to reflect upon myself what I on my part, with great reason and justice, ought to offer and give to his Divine Majesty, that is to say, all things that are mine and myself with them, as one who makes an offering with great affection, saying:

'Take, O Lord, and receive all my liberty, my memory, my understanding, and all my will, whatsoever I have and possess. Thou hast given it to me; to thee, O Lord, I return it: all is thine, dispose of it entirely according to thy will. Give me thy love and thy grace, for this is enough for me.'

The second point is to consider how God dwells in creatures: in the elements giving them being; in the plants giving them growth; in the animals giving them sensation; in men giving them understanding; and so in me giving me being, life, sensation, and causing me to understand; making likewise of me a temple, since I am created to the likeness and image of his Divine Majesty; and then to reflect on myself in the same way as has been said in the first point, or in any other way that I may feel is better. And the same method shall be followed in each of the points that follow.

The third point is to consider how God works and labours for me in all created things on the face of the earth, *habet se ad modum laborantis*, as in the heavens, elements, plants, fruits, flocks, etc., giving them being, preserving them, giving them growth and sensation, etc., and then to reflect on myself.

The fourth point is to see how all good things and gifts descend from above, as for example my limited power comes from the supreme and infinite power on high, and in the same way justice, goodness, pity, mercy, etc., just as the rays descend from the sun and the waters from the spring. Then to conclude by reflecting on myself as has been said.

To finish with a colloquy and the *Our Father*.

'Contemplatio'—This last exercise of the book corresponds to the Foundation. Cp. e.g. 2nd Prelude 'amare et servire' with 'Homo creatus est ut laudet . . . serviat'. But there there is no mention of love; everything is of bounden duty, the duty of a servant: here everything is of love, the love and duty of a grateful friend.—And it serves as a foundation for the rest of life. (Dec. 8 1881)

'Primum' Cp. 'ut laudet', Man's praise is good and highly prized by God if it corresponds to his works or true intentions; hence St. Ignatius says 'magis . . quam', not 'non'.[1] Otherwise it is worth little or nothing. What is meant on God's side is the promises He makes, He has created us for bliss and He will give it, or the failure will be ours; He has paid the price of our redemption and it has been accepted; He has said 'Quaerite . . . primum regnum Dei' etc, 'Centuplum accipiet', etc and He will fulfil. In particular He has suffered in the flesh as man, the *Word* but really made flesh. Then under the other points—(2) His presence is a reality though invisible; (3) Nature has a real stability, His providence is active, air, food, and clothing etc will not run short during our lifetime; (4) these copies of His perfections are the merest shadows, the reality beggars expectation. Hence we are led on to the second remark, for it turns out that though God gives us His Word and Image, the Word and Image has with it the divine substance

'Non habet'—God has not got, is without, the praise, honour, and service which man can give or refuse him. Nevertheless, He is glorified even in the reprobate. But what He loses absolutely is glory *freely* given; hence 'omnem meam libertatem'

'Interpellantibus'—As at Pentecost for the Holy Ghost to be sent upon the Church (Dec. 8 1881)

'Quatuor puncta'—The First is that all God gives us or does for us He gives and does *in love* and therefore that all we do towards God we should do in love. The rest evolve this thought: the 2nd refers to God's being in things by His Presence, the 3rd by His Power, the 4th by His Essence. Suppose God shewed us in a vision the whole world inclosed first in a drop of water, allowing everything to be seen in its native colours; then the same in a drop of Christ's blood, by which everything whatever was turned scarlet, keeping nevertheless mounted in the scarlet its own colour too.—Observe also that the first Point speaks in the past—'quantum fecerit, . . quantum . . dederit'

—and gathers from this how much 'idem Dominus desideret dare seipsum mihi' etc; then how he does give himself is shewn in the detail in the points which follow.[1]

God's Power or Operation, which is attributed especially to the Third Person, is put in the second instead of the third place (the 3rd instead of the 4th Point) because St Ignatius is dwelling on the thought of communication, and the Holy Ghost is the communication or the communion of the Father and the Son. It is by communication of his power that God operates the likeness of himself in things, so that this exertion or operation comes between[2] his presence and his essence (or nature)—Aug. 14 1882

'Intellige non liberum arbitrium'[3]—Contra, intellige. Liberty applies properly to no faculty but to the whole man

'Faciens me templum, cum creatus sim ad similitudinem et imaginem'—The word Temple at first sight hides the thought, which is, I think, that God rests in man as in a place, a *locus*, bed, vessel, expressly made to receive him as a jewel in a case hollowed to fit it, as the hand in the glove or the milk in the breast (Dec. 8 1881). And God *in forma servi* rests *in servo*, that is / Christ as a solid in his member as a hollow or shell, both things being the image of God; which can only be perfectly when the member is in all things conformed to Christ. This too best brings out the nature of the man himself, as the lettering on a sail or device upon a flag are best seen when it fills[4]

'Laborat'—'Ipse Spiritus postulat pro nobis gemitibus inenarrabilibus' Rom. viii 26 (Dec. 8 1881)

The last mystery meditated on in the Spiritual Exercises is our Lord's Ascension. This contemplation is that which comes next in order, namely the sending of the Holy Ghost; it is the contemplation of the Holy Ghost sent to us through creatures. Observe then it is on love and the Holy Ghost is called Love ('Fons vivus, ignis, *caritas*'); shewn 'in operibus', the works of God's finger ('Digitus paternae dexterae'); consisting 'in communicatione' etc, and the Holy Ghost as he is the bond and mutual love of Father and Son, so of God and man; that the Holy Ghost is uncreated grace and the sharing by man of the divine nature and the bestowal of himself by God on man ('Altissimi donum Dei'): hence we are to consider 'quantum . . . Dominus desideret dare seipsum mihi in quantum potest'; hence also the repetition in pt. 2 of 'dans'. Remark also how after the benefits of creation and Redemption he does not add, he means *us* to add, that of sanctification. Again in Pt. 2 'templum', in 3. 'operatur' as above, in 4. 'a sole . . radii, a fonte aquae' ('*Fons* vivus, *ignis*') (Dec. 8 1881). All things therefore are charged with love, are charged with God and if we know how to touch them give off sparks and take fire, yield drops and flow, ring and tell of him.[5]

CHAPTER EIGHT

CREATION AND REDEMPTION
THE GREAT SACRIFICE

NOV. 8 1881 (*Long Retreat*)

Time has 3 dimensions and one positive pitch or direction. It is therefore not so much like any river or any sea as like the Sea of Galilee, which has the Jordan running through it and giving a current to the whole.[1]

Though this one direction of time if prolonged for ever might be considered to be parallel to or included in the duration of God, the same might be said of any other direction in time artificially taken. But it is truer to say that there is no relation between any duration of time and the duration of God. And in no case is it to be supposed that God creates time and the things of time, that is to say / this world, in that duration of himself which is parallel with the duration of time and was before time.[2] But rather as the light falls from heaven upon the Sea of Galilee not only from the north, from which quarter the Jordan comes, but from everywhere / so God from every point, so to say, of his being creates all things. But in so far as the creation of one thing depends on that of another, as suppose trees were created *for* man and *before* man, so far does God create in time or in the direction or duration of time.

There is therefore in the works of creation an order of time, as the order of the Six Days, and another order, the order of intention,[3] and that not only intention in understanding and intention in will but also intention or forepitch of execution,[4] of power or activity. In the order of intention 'other things on the face of the earth' are created after man; the more perfect first, the less after. From this it follows that the more perfect is created in its perfection, that is to say / if perfectible and capable of greater and less perfection, it is created at its greatest. And thus it is said 'Ipsius enim sumus factura, *creati in Christo Jesu* in operibus bonis, quae praeparavit Deus ut in illis ambulemus' (Eph. ii 10., and he had already dwelt on these Gentiles and on himself too as having been children of wrath, dead in sins, and so on). And further it follows that man himself was created for Christ as Christ's created nature for God (cf. 'omnia enim vestra sunt, vos autem Christi, Christus autem Dei' 1 Cor. iii 22, 23.). And in this way Christ is the firstborn among creatures. The elect[5] then were created in Christ some before his birth, as Abraham, some before their own, as St. Ignatius; that so their correspondence with grace and seconding of God's designs is like a taking part in their own creation,[1] the creation of their best selves. And again the wicked and the lost are like halfcreations and have but a halfbeing.

The first intention then of God outside himself or, as they say, *ad extra*, outwards, the first outstress of God's power, was Christ; and we must believe that the next was the Blessed Virgin.[2] Why did the Son of God go thus forth from the Father not only in the eternal and intrinsic procession of the Trinity but also by an extrinsic and less than eternal, let us say aeonian[3] one?—To give God glory and that by sacrifice, sacrifice offered in the barren wilderness outside of God, as the children of Israel were led into the wilderness to offer sacrifice. This sacrifice and this outward procession is a consequence and shadow of the procession of the Trinity, from which mystery sacrifice takes its rise; but of this I do not mean to write here. It is as if the blissful agony or stress of selving in God had forced out drops of sweat or blood, which drops were the world, or as if the lights lit at the festival of the 'peaceful Trinity' through some little cranny striking out lit up into being one 'cleave' out of the world of possible creatures. The sacrifice would be the Eucharist,[4] and that the victim might be truly victim like, like motionless, helpless, or lifeless, it must be in matter. Then the Blessed Virgin was intended or predestined to minister that matter. And here then was that mystery of the woman clothed with the sun which appeared in heaven. She followed Christ the nearest, following the sacrificial lamb 'whithersoever he went'.

In going forth to do sacrifice Christ went not alone but created angels to be his company, lambs to follow him the Lamb, the flower of the flock, 'whithersoever he went', that is to say, first to the hill of sacrifice, then after that back to God, to beatitude. They were to take part in the sacrifice and he was to redeem them all, that is to say / for the sake of the Lamb of God who was God himself God would accept the whole flock and for the sake of one ear or grape the whole sheaf or cluster; for redeem may be said not only of the recovering from sin to grace or perdition to salvation but also of the raising from worthlessness before God (and all creation is unworthy of God) to worthiness of him, the meriting of God himself, or, so to say, godworthiness. In this sense the Blessed Virgin was beyond all others redeemed, because it was her more than all other creatures that Christ meant to win from nothingness and it was her that he meant to raise the highest.

Christ then like a good shepherd led the way; but when Satan saw the mystery and the humiliation proposed he turned back and rebelled or, as that Welsh text[5] says, flung himself direct on beatitude, to seize it of his own right and merit and by his own strength, and so he fell, with his following.

Here I have thought of a parable of a marriage cavalcade, in which some as soon as they see the bride's lowly dwelling refuse to go further, are themselves disowned by the bridegroom and driven off, but keep attacking the procession on its road.

The mystery remained in some sort a mystery. When Satan saw Mary and Christ in the flesh he did not recognise them. This may be the meaning of the woman's hiding in the wilderness, that is / the material world. The river that the dragon vomited to sweep the woman away perhaps means that Satan, who is the κοσμοκράτωρ, the worldwielder, gave nature all an impulse of motion which should destroy human life, and the earth's helping the woman and swallowing the river that nature absorbed this motion and was overruled to digest and distribute it throughout, making it still habitable by man. I understand the sun, moon, and stars to mean two things— first to compare the woman to the earth, this planet, which is clothed in sunlight, ministered to more humbly by its satellite, and graced by the beauty of the zodiac and other signs of the firmament, and then to her being adorned with God's grace, the service of material nature below, and the service of angels above. By the 'other sign that appeared in heaven', of the red or fiery dragon I understand the counterpageant or counterstandard set up by Lucifer which reduced a third of the angels and he is said with his tail to have swept the third part of the stars down to the earth because he drew them in his train and they were involved in his fall, not that he cast them down before himself. As the woman is compared to the earth in the solar system so the dragon is to the constellation Draco,[1] the tail of which sweeps through 120° or a third of the sphere and which winds round the pole (the polestar was once in the head of Draco, I mean a star in the head of Draco was then the polestar), this world's seeming axis and the earth's real one, so as to symbolise how Satan tried to possess himself of the sovereignty of things, taking 'The mountain of the North', that is to say / the culmination of the firmament towards the pole, as a throne and post of vantage and so wreathing nature and as it were constricting it to his purposes (as also he wreathed himself in the Garden round the Tree of Knowledge); though he was foiled, cast from heaven, and left master only of the material world, by a figure the earth.

A coil or spiral is then a type of the Devil, who is called the old (or original) serpent, and this I suppose because of its 'swale'[2] or subtle and imperceptible drawing in towards its head or centre, and it is a type of death, of motion lessening and at last ceasing. *Invidia autem diaboli mors intravit in mundum*: God gave things a forward and perpetual motion; the Devil, that is / thrower of things off the track, upsetter, mischiefmaker, clashing one with another brought in the law of decay and consumption in inanimate nature, death in the vegetable and animal world, moral death and original sin in the world of man. This seems to expand the meaning of that river explained on last leaf and also of the river running through the lake spoken of against p. 37.[1]

The snake or serpent a symbol of the Devil.[2] So also the Dragon. A dragon is or is taken to be a reptile. And first a dragon is a serpent with any addition you make, as of feet or of wings or something less. I found some Greek proverb 'The serpent till he has devoured a serpent does not become a dragon' and the snakes found in China and preserved in temples for adoration are called dragons in virtue of some supposed incarnation which has taken place in them, but they are and look ordinary snakes. So that if the Devil is symbolised as a snake he must be an archsnake and a dragon. Mostly dragons are represented as much more than serpents, but always as in some way reptiles. Now among the vertebrates the reptiles go near to combine the qualities of the other classes in themselves and are, I think, taken by the Evolutionists as nearest the original vertebrate stem and as the point of departure for the rest. In this way clearly dragons are represented as gathering up the attributes of many creatures: they are reptiles always, but besides sometimes have bat's wings; four legs, sometimes those of the mammal quadrupeds, sometimes birds' feet and talons; jaws sometimes of crocodiles, but sometimes of eagles; armouring like crocodiles again, but also sturgeons and other fish, or lobsters and other crustacea; or like insects; colours like the dragon-fly and other insects; sometimes horns; and so on. And therefore I suppose the dragon as a type of the Devil to express the universality of his powers, both the gifts he has by nature and the attributes and sway he grasps, and the horror which the whole inspires. We must of course remember how the Cherubim are in Scripture represented as composite beings, combinations of eagles, lions, oxen, and men, and that the religions of heathendom have sphinxes, fauns and satyrs, 'eyas-gods', 'the dog-Anubis', and so on. The dragon then symbolises one who aiming at every perfection ends by being a monster, a 'fright'.

The word Throne, one of the nine choirs, suggests that the rebel angels might claim that the sacrifice should be offered in them as living altars, not on earth or in anything earthly. Satan sets up a rival altar and sacrifice, which did not please, any more than those of Cain or of Core, and fire, as with Core, broke out from below. Whereas the manchild to whom the woman gives birth is, like a pleasing sacrifice, caught up to God's throne.

Nov. 14—And this morning I had more light on this mysterious subject. The angels, like Adam, were created in sanctifying grace, which is a thing that affects the individual, and were then asked to enter into a covenant or contract with God which, as with Adam, should give them an original justice or status and rights before God.[1] The duties of this commonwealth were, for them, to contribute each in his rank, hierarchy, and own species, towards the Incarnation and the great sacrifice. Sister Emmerich saw this under the figure of the building of a tower: it might perhaps also be called a temple and a church. It was in fact the Church and the heavenly Jerusalem. It is also compared to a concert of music, the ranks of the angelic hierarchies being like notes of a scale and a harmonic series: the working of the commonwealth and building of the tower or temple would be like the playing on these notes, like the tune, the music. They are also compared to heavenly spheres, planetary distances, and so on; and indeed these things, music and astronomy, are compared among themselves (in the Music of the Spheres and the morning stars singing for joy)[2]—(Dec. 13) And lastly they are compared to a pedigree, to generations; and through such a pedigree or tree of generations in some sort it is likely that Christ passed, taking the stead but not the true nature of a race or series of angels. Into such pedigrees or genealogies St Paul discouraged St Timothy from enquiring, St Ignatius the Martyr[3] says that he could if he chose explain them, and out of them sprang the Gnostic heresies (in which the place of Sige, silence should be remarked).

The term of these generations was the victim of the great sacrifice, a victim in a material or, to speak more strictly, earthly nature. And I suppose that Christ reached this term during the time of probation, the *via* or pilgrimage, of the angels; nay instantaneously and from the first, for reasons given above. This took place by means of some dimension counter to the leading dimension of the angelic action:[4] the matter is most recondite and difficult.[5] At any rate I suppose the vision of the pregnant woman to have been no mere vision but the real fetching, presentment, or 'adduction'[6] of the persons, Christ and Mary, themselves; though this need not have been known to the angels then. And I cannot help suspecting that the attack on the woman which the dragon makes was, though I cannot yet clearly grasp how, the actual attack which he made, is making, and will go on making on the human race.[7]

But first I suppose that Christ, in his first stead of angelic being, led off the angel choir (and in this the Babylonian and the Welsh text agree),[8] calling on all creatures to worship God as by a kind of *Venite adoremus*. They obeyed the call, which indeed was a call into being. For what followed see at p. 96.[9] This song of Lucifer's was a dwelling on his own beauty, an instressing of his own inscape,[1] and like a performance on the organ and instrument of his own being; it was a sounding, as they say, of his own trumpet and a hymn in his own praise. Moreover it became an incantation: others were drawn in; it became a concert of voices, a concerting of selfpraise, an enchantment, a magic, by which they were dizzied, dazzled, and bewitched. They would not listen to the note which summoned each to his own place (Jude 6.)[2] and distributed them here and there in the liturgy of the sacrifice; they gathered rather closer and closer home under Lucifer's lead and drowned it, raising a countermusic and countertemple and altar, a counterpoint of dissonance and not of harmony. I suppose they introduced a pathos as of a nobler nature put aside for the higher and even persuaded themselves that God was only trying them; that to disobey and substitute themselves, Lucifer above all, as the angelic victim of the world sacrifice was secretly pleasing to him, that selfdevotion of it, the suicide, the semblance of sin was a loveliness of heroism which could only arise in the angelic mind; that it was divine and a meriting[3] and at last a grasp of godhead.

Meanwhile as they drew back from their appointed lots the score of their disobedience rose as in a mirror in the vision of the woman with child: she felt it as birthpangs and cried aloud. For this they despised her the more and hated the presumption of so weak a creature, not knowing the weakness was their own sin. And Lucifer who had drawn so many of the angels into his train prepared to consume, absorb, the woman's offspring too. But this hope and all their hopes of acceptance must have been dashed to the ground by the assumption and acceptance of the newborn child. Was it at this point then that they broke out into open rebellion? on which followed the war in heaven and their expulsion, which was not *ipso facto*. See against pp. 61 and 204.[4] It was St. Michael and his angels who attacked them, not they St. Michael; it was a sort of crusade undertaken in defence of the woman in whom the sacrificial victim had lain and from whom he had risen, a sort of Holy Sepulchre[5] and a heavenly Jerusalem, and this is perhaps the explanation of the curious construction in the Greek: 'καὶ ἐγένετο πόλεμος ἐν τῷ οὐρανῷ. Μιχαὴλ καὶ οἱ ἄγγελοι αὐτοῦ πολεμῆσαι [Vat.: Alex. τοῦ π.] μετὰ τοῦ δράκοντος, καὶ ὁ δράκων ἐπολέμησε καὶ οἱ ἄγγελοι αὐτοῦ' / And war arose in heaven; that is to say he whose name is called *Who is like God?* raised that warcry and other angels rallied to it and with that cry they declared war upon the dragon and his, and the dragon and his adherents, théy raised théir answering warcry (say of *Non serviemus* / We will not be slaves); but it would not do, 'καὶ οὐκ ἴσχυον'. It would seem that their fall was at once the attack of Michael and

202 SERMONS AND WRITINGS OF G. M. HOPKINS

their own act: Michael and his angels instressed and distressed them with the thought of their unlikeness to the Most High; they from their selfraised pinnacle and tower of eminence flung themselves, like the sally of a garrison, with the thought of / We are like the Most High, thinking in their madness their heroism, which was the divine in them, would declare itself as the godhead and would bear them up and its splendour dismay and overwhelm their enemies; but it was a blow struck wide, a leap over a precipice, and the weight of that other word bore them headlong down.

Further I suppose that the procession or liturgy of the angelic host was to have its score upon the world of matter and the angels thus to unfold and by cooperating create the species and the order of the lower world; which in consequence is marked everywhere with the confusion, clashing, and wreck which took place in the higher one and was there repaired at once but here not all at once. If this is so and the beginnings at least of every form were in the first *move* of the heavenly hierarchy made / one can see how it was possible for Satan to attack man even before his fall,[1] that is / before it was complete. In Cassian Germanus (Conf. 8 cap. 9) is corrected by Abbot Serenus for supposing that the temptation of Eve was the Devil's first sin and the cause of his fall. But he may have tried to destroy by violence before he succeeded in ruining by fraud.

CHAPTER NINE

FURTHER NOTES

Text of Exercises (Rules for the Discernment of Spirits), Notes of GMH.
Notes of GMH (Three Ways of Praying).

RULES FOR THE DISCERNMENT OF SPIRITS[1]

I

RULES TO PERCEIVE AND KNOW, IN SOME MANNER, THE
VARIOUS MOVEMENTS EXCITED IN THE SOUL—THE GOOD,
THAT THEY MAY BE ADMITTED; THE BAD, THAT THEY MAY BE
REJECTED—AND ARE MORE SUITABLE FOR THE FIRST WEEK.

I. In the case of those who go from mortal sin to mortal sin
the enemy is generally wont to set before them apparent
pleasures, causing them to imagine sensual gratifications
and pleasures, in order to keep them fast, and to plunge
them deeper, in their vices and sins. The good spirit acts in
such persons in a contrary way, pricking and stinging with
remorse their conscience by the judgment of reason.

II. In those who go on earnestly purifying themselves from
their sins, and advancing from good to better in the service
of God our Lord, the contrary to what is set down in the
first rule takes place; for then it is peculiar to the evil spirit
to cause anxiety and sadness; and to place obstacles in the
way, disquieting the soul by false reasons so that it makes no
further progress; and it is the distinguishing mark of the
good spirit to give courage and strength, consolation, tears,
inspirations, and peace, making things easy, and removing
every impediment, in order that the soul may make further
progress in good works.

III. Of spiritual consolation. I call that consolation when there
is excited in the soul some interior movement by which it
begins to be inflamed with the love of its Creator and Lord,
and when, consequently, it can love no created thing on the
face of the earth in itself, but only in the Creator of them
all. Likewise when it sheds tears, moving it to the love of its
Lord, whether it be from grief for its sins, or for the Passion
of Christ our Lord, or for other things expressly ordained to
His service and praise. Finally, I call consolation any increase of hope, faith, and charity, and any interior joy

which calls and attracts one to heavenly things and to the salvation of his own soul, rendering it quiet and at peace with its Creator and Lord.

IV. Of spiritual desolation. I call that desolation which is contrary to what is set down in the third rule, such as darkness and confusion of soul, attraction towards low and earthly objects, disquietude caused by various agitations and temptations, which move the soul to diffidence without hope and without love, so that it finds itself altogether slothful, tepid, sad, and as it were separated from its Creator and Lord. For as consolation is contrary to desolation, so the thoughts that spring from consolation are contrary to those that spring from desolation

V. In times of desolation we must never make a change, but stand firm and constant in the resolutions and determination in which we were the day before the desolation, or in the time of the preceding consolation. For as in consolation it is the good spirit which guides and counsels us, so in desolation it is the evil spirit, by whose counsel we cannot find the way to any right decision.

VI. Although in desolation we ought not to change our former resolutions, it is nevertheless very profitable greatly to change ourselves in opposition to the said desolation; as, for example, by insisting more on prayer and meditation, by making our self-examination more searchingly, and by increasing in some suitable manner our penance.

VII. Let him who is in desolation consider how our Lord, to try him, has left him to his own natural powers to resist the various agitations and temptations of the enemy; and to do so is always in his power, with the divine help, which remains always to him, though he may not clearly perceive it, because our Lord has withdrawn from him His great favour, ardent love, and intense grace, leaving him, however, grace sufficient for eternal salvation.

VIII. Let him who is in desolation strive to remain in patience, which is the virtue contrary to the troubles which harass him; and let him think that he will shortly be consoled, making diligent efforts against the desolation, as has been said in the sixth rule.

IX. There are three main causes on account of which we find ourselves in desolation. The first is because we are tepid, slothful or negligent in our spiritual exercises; and thus through our faults spiritual consolation is removed from us. The second is that God may try how much we are worth, and how much we progress in His service and praise, without such bountiful pay of consolation and special graces. The third is that He may give us a true knowledge and understanding whereby we may intimately feel that it is not in our own power to acquire or retain great devotion, ardent love, tears, or any other spiritual consolation, but that all is a gift and grace of God our Lord; and to teach us not to build our nest in another's house, by allowing our intellect to be lifted up to any kind of pride or vainglory, by attributing to ourselves the devotion, or other kinds of spiritual consolation.

NOTES ON THE RULES FOR
THE DISCERNMENT OF SPIRITS

Opposite the 1st Rule.

'Imaginentur'—Here St Ignatius does speak of the lower, not the intellectual, imagination. See 'synderesin *rationis*'. And perhaps the impediments which (in the next Rule) the two spirits put in or out of the soul's path are imagined impediments, not resistances, so to say, in the functions themselves. The devil also uses reasons— Dec. 24 1879—Nov. 14 '81 (L.R.) He may be but need not be speaking of the lower imagination. Or the Devil may offer those seeming pleasures to the lower in order to excite the higher. Nothing, I think, decisive can be shewn from this place.[1]

The purport of this body of rules, Fr. Whitty says,[2] is that consolation should be our normal state and that when God withdraws it he wishes us to strive to recover it/. Cf. 'da nobis in eodem Spiritu recta sapere et *de ejus semper consolatione gaudere*'[3]

But here there seems to be no question of tepidity.[4] The only class of people St Ignatius contemplates as making the Exercises or as reading these rules are the second, *illi qui intense procedunt in purgandis suis peccatis*: they are in the Purgative Way and penitents at any rate now. Rule 3. and all the rules that follow are commentaries on Rule 2. and nothing further is said about Rule 1.

Opposite the 12th Rule.

'Quis enim' etc[5]—In that case the Devil ought not to have been compared to a woman, for woman is naturally weaker than man. But we are considering things as they now are, not comparing the original endowments of men and angels. The Vulgate rendering therefore seems best. But if 'per vim' means 'perforce', then it is God's force in restraining the Devil, not man's in resisting him.

Opposite '*Regulae Aliae*'.[1]

From Blessed Peter Favre's *Memoriale* April 1543—'Alio quodam die, dum visitassem Magistrum Petrum Gueldriensem qui exercebatur juxta modum exercitiorum nostrorum, ego habui quaedam argumenta [grounds] magnae evidentiae quibus clarius quam unquam intellexi quam plurimum referre ad discretionem spirituum an cogitationes ac locutiones internas attendamus an ad ipsum spiritum, qui per desideria, per affectus, per fortitudinem animi vel debilitatem, per tranquillitatem vel inquietudinem, per laetitiam vel tristitiam, et similes affectus spirituales, sese prodere solet. Per haec sane facilius potest judicari de anima et ejus spiritibus quam per ipsas cogitationes. Quidam autem sunt qui per multas ac varias diversorum exercitiorum spiritualium contemplationes aut orationes vix possunt deprehendere varietatem spirituum diversorum sed semper videntur agitari uno et eodem spiritu, licet hoc fiat secundum magis ac minus. Efficacissimum autem medium ad excitandam hanc distinctionem [to bring out this difference] est propositio electionis vitae et status; deinde in eodem varii gradus ad perfectionem tendentes; et generaliter quo quis altiorem ad agendum vel sperandum vel credendum aut amandum rem proposuerit vel ad ipsam sese applicuerit affectualiter et effectualiter eo facilius dederit argumenta excitandi differentiam spiritus boni ac mali. In quibusdam quoque ideo non agnoscitur spiritus malus, et maxime in piis et diu versatis in devotione et extra peccata, quia non habeant cogitationes extra limites veritatis et bonitatis neque affectus manifeste inordinatos. Hos tamen, quantumlibet sancti sint, si induxeris ut sese examinent, in aliquo gradu perfectioris vitae et conservationis in statu proprio (si immutabilis fuerit) aut in alio statu magis perfecto facile erit videre utrumque ipsorum spirituum, confortatorem ac debilitatorem, illuminatorem et offuscatorem, justificatorem et maculatorem, id est bonum et eum qui est bono adversarius.'

Ibid. Feb. 14 'In hoc die, dum considerassem diversitatem spirituum qui me frequenter agitarunt, et varium esse fecerunt circa possibilitatem faciendi fructum in Germania, notavi non esse adhaerendum ullo modo verbis illius qui omnia facit impossibilia et semper adducit inconvenientia, sed potius verbis et sensibus illius qui ostendit possibilitatem et dat animum; sed tamen etiam cavendum ne nimium curramus in dexteram. Sumenda enim tandem est discretio, ut in medio quodam consistamus inter dextrum et sinistrum, sic videlicet ut nec in nostra spe misceatur inanis abundantia nec in metu nostro aggravetur penuria. Quod si nequeat fieri quin vel in hanc vel in illam partem declinetur, tutius et minus periculosum est si juxta tempus potius abundantiae ambulemus ac speremus quam si juxta modum tristitiae nos adaptaverimus, ubi mille errores ac deceptiones, mille sursum germinantis amaritudinis labyrinthi, etc. Qui autem noverit spiritum abundantiae et verba ejus, item spiritum tentantem et turbantem et verba ejus, is poterit ex utraque parte doceri. Sumendus enim erit et retinendus et dum amissus fuerit semper requirendus spiritus abundantiae, servanda erit illa laetitia et consolatio ac confortatio et tranquillitas et reliquae dispositiones quae se tenent ex parte boni affectus, et ad has redeundum erit ut tandem firmius haereant; verba autem omnia quae accidunt non ita sumenda erunt quin possent quaedam admisceri non vera, propterea quod et malus spiritus possit induere speciem lucidi angeli. Circa spiritum autem contrarium et verba ejus contradictorio modo faciendum est: spiritus quidem iste quantum ad omnes partes suorum sensuum expellendus est ac fugiendus, non autem omnia verba; quia multa posses accipere ad multas cautelas et ex ipsis reddi circa res humanas prudentior: quia sunt multa vera et utilia, si postea informata fuerint alio spiritu'

'Quid erit' etc[1]—It is not really necessary for the soul to know this object. Even natural 'consolation' or good spirits come and go without any discoverable reason and certainly God *could* make us most happy without our knowing what we were happy about,[2] though of course the mind would then turn with pleasure to any, the first pious thought that came, as its object. Neither need the other consolations here spoken of, those which come from good or bad angels, be in proportion to the objects which first gave them rise; on the contrary if they were they might as well be wholly natural and our own; what part would the stranger spirit, the angel, play in them at all? But the greater the disproportion the greater the likelihood of the consolation being from God.

See note to p. 179.[3] In this Rule is the first allusion to the lukewarm. The lukewarm are those *qui procedunt de malo in pejus*, which = *de bono in pejus* perhaps. For in the Second Week the question is between lukewarmness and fervour, not between mortal sin and grace. Perhaps one may say that he assumes the readers of this Rule, the people who have come thus far in the Exercises, to be of the fervent, only not quite so decidedly as he assumes the readers of the first set to be penitents, and in grace, as is natural. 'In iis qui procedunt' etc almost = when people are proceeding, when the soul etc: it seems less to mark two sorts of people than two conditions of the same people. For the distinction between fervour and lukewarmness is not so definite as that between sanctifying grace and mortal sin—

(Nov. 25 1881, L. R.) The above doctrine seems true. Spiritual tepidity then is not the being between hot and cold, for in that state every soul must be that has neither perfect charity nor mortal sin, taking these terms or limits to be what the metaphor means by heat, that is / the boiling point of heat, and by cold or the freezing point: but it is the passage downwards only from hotter to colder, it is to be cooling or to have cooled. And since the water must always be getting hotter, never cooler, while the pot is on the fire, it is implied, to keep up the figure, that the pot has been taken off, that is to say / that the soul is no longer acted on by grace but is left to nature. And this is what Father Whitty says[1] is the meaning of tepidity, the state of a soul that, being in God's grace, is content to live not according to grace but according to nature. So that while we strive, though we commit faults, we are not lukewarm; when we give up struggling and let ourselves drift, then tepidity begins. Fervour, ζεστότης (Apoc. iii 15, etc.) is properly the being on the boil, the shewing the stir of life, of a life not shared by all other things, and the being ready to pass, by evaporation, into a wholly spiritual condition. Freezing is the earthly blockish insensible condition of a soul which may indeed be melted by warm breath but must first be so melted before it can sway to it. Between the two extremes of freezing and evaporation lie the two 'swales'[2] or phases of fervour, which is like when the liquid however cold is on the fire, and of tepidity. Remark that ζεστόν seems akin to ζῆλος.[3]

Further on the figure used in Apoc. iii. Either hot or cold water would be welcome; the hot as cheering, as cordial: with wine and spice it would serve the Master for his festivity; the cold as refreshing: it would slake his thirst for souls, for cold and sinful souls, and would take the temperature of the drinker's mouth. Only the lukewarm brings on disgust and vomiting.

Cassian (Conf. 4) makes Abbot Daniel say the lukewarm are the ψυχικοί, the animales, of 1 Cor. ii 14. This word ψυχικόν is also found iii. 15. and Jude 19. ('ψυχικοί, πνεῦμα οὐκ ἔχοντες'),[4] from which passages we see that the soul taken from the fire of divine love may yet be set upon the coals of earthly passions and boil with a bitter zeal instead of zeal inspired by God. Abbot Daniel takes the fire for that of tribulation and carnal temptation and the stir for the struggle or wrestling of the flesh with the spirit: this is the subject of that Conference and he points out the advantages of it to man.

The spiritual man is the subject and, so to say, patient (in reality rather agent) of the Spiritual Exercises. Mortal sin is his death, lukewarmness his state of disease or languor. (Aug. 13 1882)

THREE WAYS OF PRAYING[5]

'TRES MODI'—These three ways of praying correspond to the purgative, illuminative, and unitive stages respectively in a general sense. The third is prayer of the affections. (L. R.)

'[ad exercitia facienda]'[1]—No, this should be left out. 'Illis' refers
to 'potentias' and 'sensus' above. St Ignatius means that this First
Method is nothing but *practice in praying well* and in the use of one's
natural powers in praying. Cp. what he says of the *exercises* in general
Annot. 1—It makes little difference whether you refer 'illis' to
'potentias' etc—the list of things beginning 'decem praecepta', that
is—or to 'formam, modum, et exercitia', for the 'exercitia' there are
the things named above, the Ten Commandments and the rest. (It
is not easy to see what Fr Roothaan took the words to mean: he
writes the first *exercitia* with a capital, whereas it seems to mean
exercises simply and not to want one, and the second, in the brackets,
without one, whereas it seems to mean *the* Spiritual Exercises and to
need one.) And as the Spiritual Exercises though called exercises
only become really πρᾶξις[2] proper or a course of conduct when made;
for in them the exercitant reforms his life, listens to Christ's call, and
so on, / so with this first way of praying (which St. Ignatius says can
scarcely be called a 'method of prayer'): it is practice for prayer,
practice in praying, but it is also meant to give rise to penitence,
acts of contrition, and amendment of life, and will thus be the most
efficacious prayer (L. R.). 'Quomodo' etc then means: 'By using
which the soul may prepare itself to pray, may earn merit or do
itself spiritual good in such preparation, and may learn to offer prayer
which *shall* be acceptable to God'; the thought being that the soul
in mortal sin or but little contrite for its sins ('decem praecepta'),
subject to passions ('septem peccata'), that has scarcely any habit
or custom of employing the memory, understanding, and will on
spiritual things ('tres potentias'), and unmortified in the use of the
senses ('quinque sensus') is as yet much unfitted for union with God
and raw in spirituality.

This method if made on the Ten Commandments will take about
12 minutes in all or at most a quarter of an hour, reckoning a minute
of prelude, rather more than a minute to each Commandment, and
the rest colloquy. The others (on the Seven Sins etc) will be shorter.
One difference then between the three Methods is the time they
take, for the 3rd takes at the longest half an hour, while the second,
which he calls contemplation, he seems to mean to take an hour.
But all three allow of being shortened.—See Annotation 18 p. 19,
where he speaks of the First Method as taking half an hour and suggests fresh matter.

PART THREE

ISOLATED DISCOURSES AND PRIVATE NOTES

INTRODUCTION

THE isolated pieces gathered together in Part III of this volume contain items of great and varied interest. But the only ones which call for comment outside the notes are those which cover—very sparsely and spasmodically—the years 1883–9. To appreciate these fragments in their biographical setting, the thread of Hopkins's life must be resumed from the end of the Introduction to Part I, and with the Introduction to Part II as a background in the mind.

During his year of tertianship, which ended in July 1882, Hopkins had been flooded with light on religious subjects which boded well for his poetry. In several of his letters to Bridges of the following year there are impromptu explanations of Catholic mysteries, both beautiful and profound. He was standing at a focal point from which he could see the origin and progress of many possible creations. He had, in fact, at least five works in mind: three in prose and two in verse. In prose there were: his commentary on the Exercises already begun; a treatise on the idea of sacrifice in ancient religions; and a work on Greek Lyric Art which would have included a revolutionary principle of criticism, 'the undercurrent of thought governing the use of images'. In verse there were his 'great ode' on Edmund Campion, and the drama of St Winefred; the inspiration of both of these, which went back to autumn of the previous year, had received fresh impetus from his insight into 'the great sacrifice'.

The Provincial, to whom he had just made his Last Vows and to whom he outlined some of these projects, gave him a discreet measure of encouragement. He had appointed him to teach classics at Stony-hurst to the 'philosophers'—young men who had finished their schooling but were still more or less precluded from Oxford and Cambridge. His duties were not onerous: he liked his pupils and was proud of the place with its history and its animation; and he found the company congenial. Among his colleagues were men of such intellectual stature as Fr Perry the astronomer, Fr Harper the meta-physician and friend of Newman, Fr John Gerard of 'gunpowder plot' fame, and Fr Forbes-Leith the Scottish historian. Of Forbes-Leith Hopkins wrote enviously: 'He never lets a minute go idle and after his teaching-work returns at once to his own studies.' This was what the Provincial had recommended to Hopkins, and what he sincerely hoped to do. The omens seemed propitious for at least one work that might have been a classic today. By October he had writ-ten the choruses for *St Winefred's Well*, and by December the speech of Beuno. It was at Stonyhurst, moreover, that he was to meet and gain the respect and interest of Coventry Patmore, whose example of individual inspiration in Catholic verse should have been a spur and a help.

Yet by January 1883 he was writing to Baillie that he had time on his hands but could do nothing with it. This was not a temporary setback. He repeated it more desperately to Bridges in March and to Dixon in June:[1]

> My time, as I have said before, is not so closely employed but that some-
> one else in my place might not do a good deal, but I cannot, and I see no
> grounded prospect of my ever doing much not only in poetry but in any-
> thing at all. At times I do feel this sadly and bitterly, but it is God's will and
> though no change that I can foresee will happen yet perhaps some may that
> I do not foresee.

To be accurate, the shadow of this frustration can be traced back to a letter of September 1882, following on his interview with the Provincial. The Provincial had been courteous and considerate, he wrote to Bridges, about where he might stay during the holidays— but he had decided not to take advantage of the permission. The Provincial had further added that his spare time could be spent on one or other of the books projected—but he did not think he would have any spare time. This fear turned out to be groundless, but already a foreboding of failure seems to have been upon him.

The Provincial was not any of the four Provincials who had, in succession, influenced Hopkins's previous career: Fr Weld, an ardent and percipient soul, who had admitted him to the Society; Fr Whitty, on whose spiritual wisdom he placed such reliance; Fr Gallwey, who once 'sitting by the bedside took my hand within his and said some affectionate and most encouraging words'; Fr Jones, the warmhearted Welshman who, as Rector of St Beuno's, had sug-gested *The Wreck of the Deutschland*.

The Provincial from 1880 till 1888 was Fr Edward Ignatius Pur-brick. The name Ignatius had been taken on his conversion from Anglicanism. Of noble, ascetic and commanding appearance (at Rome, when all the Provincials of the Society were assembled to-gether, he had been styled *Rex Congregationis*), he had characteristics in common with Cardinal Manning. At school his inseparable com-panions had been two boys called Benson and Lightfoot.[2] Great careers had been prophesied for all three. Though Fr Purbrick's intellectual abilities were solid, his scope and talent as Provincial lay in the administrative order. Under him the English Province

---

[1] A further disappointment may have been Newman's refusal in regard to *The Grammar of Assent*. See note p. 312 (209. 2).

[2] Edward Benson, Archbishop of Canterbury; Joseph Lightfoot, the New Testa-ment scholar and Bishop of Durham.

reached a climax of material expansion. One of his earlier achievements had been the complete south front at Stonyhurst, of which
Hopkins wrote in the same letter: 'The new college, though there is
no real beauty in the design, is nevertheless imposing and the furniture and fittings are a joy to see.' Fr Purbrick's reputation and
achievements, then, are solid enough to stand the slight burden of
the following supposition.

Confronted with the perfect neatness of the Provincial's mind,
with his massive and smoothly-moving deliberation, a wave of
diffidence amounting almost to despair seeped up in Hopkins. It was
borne in upon him that he must look on his poetic genius as an
amiable weakness which a hard-working Jesuit might indulge for
an hour or two occasionally. And he grasped, half-consciously but
once and for all, that the secret 'wildness' of his inspiration could
never be channelled in that manner.

There was no decisive renunciation as yet. '. . . I cannot get forward with my ode,' he wrote to Bridges in the same letter, 'But one
must hope against hope.' It may well have been Bridges himself who
delivered the *coup de grâce*.

A week or two after the September letter, 'hoping against hope',
he had written the choruses for *St Winefred's Well*, reproducing, as he
rather quaintly said, 'the thoughts of a good but lively girl'—which
reminds one of Henry James's remark that a lively girl could repro-
duce the thoughts of a Guardsman after one glance through a mess-
room window. These choruses represented in fact the perfect fusion
of his spiritual sensuousness and his religious ideals; they were in the
high tradition of the seventeenth-century refusal to let beauty and
morality go different ways. But from Bridges they elicited only some
maladroit remark about 'imitating Walt Whitman'. Galled by the
insult, but ruthless to himself, Hopkins wrote back in the course of a
long reply:

> But first I may as well say what I should not otherwise have said, that I
> always knew in my heart Walt Whitman's mind to be more like my own
> than any other man's living. As he is a very great scoundrel this is not a
> pleasant confession. And this also makes me the more desirous to read him
> and the more determined that I will not.

No two *personalities*, surely, could have been more different than
Hopkins and Whitman. But it was not his personality that Hopkins
was thinking of; he was thinking of his mind in the sense of Aristotle's
phrase, *mens est quodammodo omnia*. He was thinking of his *nature*, which
made him kin with all nature and was the source of his poetic
genius. His exaggerated distinction between *voluntas ut natura* and
voluntas ut arbitrium is highly relevant here, but has already been

sufficiently discussed in the Introduction to Part II. It need only be added that what he was particularly afraid of—though it is hard to see the reason why—was that the beauty of his poetry might lead anyone astray in faith or morals.

> For good grows wild and wide,
> Has shades, is nowhere none,
> But right must choose its side,
> Its champion, and have done.

Attention should also be drawn to another piece of writing in Part II, different in context but closely connected with the foregoing. In the latter part of Chapter 4 Hopkins discusses the morality of acts and in particular the use of spare time. He considers how a man may, in his own rather jarring phrase, '*justify himself*' before God. We may see here the distorted effect of one of Scotus's less beneficent teachings—upon 'indifferent acts'. It is a difficult subject, and Hopkins's reasoning is not altogether clear. But the conclusion as regards himself seems to be that, unless he can get a positive command from a superior or a special light from God to sanction his verse-writing, any time that he spends on it will be time wasted, not wasted in a sinful sense, but wasted as regards laying up merit in heaven. This passage was written probably much earlier in 1882; and it may be unjust to Hopkins's intellect to apply it thus crudely to these later circumstances. But it does seem very likely that he was hoping for some such positive sanction from the Provincial, and that this hope was dashed. It is possible that at the same time his Scotist treatise on 'the great sacrifice' (which had a good deal to do with his projected poems) was shown by him to the Provincial and received by the Provincial with marked reserve;[1] but this can never be anything more than a conjecture.

On 4 November, three weeks after his long letter about Whitman, Hopkins wrote again to Bridges, 'My mind is dull and museless . . .'. It might be only a casual remark, but the word 'museless' is ominous; and the omen was borne out by the letters of the following six months which have been already mentioned.

This background may be helpful in studying the retreat he made at Beaumont that autumn (Part III, sec. 5). Two things stand out from it. First, he received a very strong desire from heaven to reach a higher state of holiness and saw clearly that this would mean a

---

[1] Fr Purbrick's obituary in *Letters and Notices*, though mostly laudatory, has the following:

'By some he has been accused, not altogether with cause, of being intolerant. There were, as almost always happens with strong characters, certain ideas which are not easily changed. He was, we may think, too Roman in some of his ecclesiastical tastes. He was so Ultramontane that everything Cisalpine, even old Catholic customs, savoured to him of national independence.'

greater sacrifice on his part. The second thing was that, without committing himself to an *effective* renunciation of his poetry, he achieved (or thought he had achieved) a complete *affective* detachment from it—in the manner of the 'Three Classes' consideration (see Part II, ch. 6). In return he had, as he believed, a clear light from heaven that, whatever happened to his poems, they would never be a cause of hurt to himself or scandal to others. At the same time there remained in him, against his will, a natural bitterness which he could not eradicate.

It will be noted that Hopkins was advised in this retreat to break off the consideration of his own sins. It was a misfortune that he could not make the exercise, *De Processu Peccatorum*, without undue self-laceration. It is a meditation in which terror yields to pity; it ends with an *exclamatio admirativa cum ingenti affectu*, a cry of wonder and passionate gratitude at God's gentle forbearance. Its effects, when it has settled into a matter of conviction rather than of sentiment, are beneficently peaceful and stabilizing. The continual awareness of one's native *defectibility* destroys the illusion that holiness can be achieved by one's own efforts; self-preservation by a blind trust in God's pity is grasped as a deeper essential than furious self-examination and self-reproach. Such a blind trust might degenerate into fatalistic complacency; but the previous meditation, the grand structure *De Tribus Peccatis*, should prevent this because it links one's inner history with the struggle that is now going on in the universe. On the other hand, if the *De Tribus Peccatis* is *not* followed by the *De Processu Peccatorum* it might tend of itself to be academic and comfortless. Two extremes are observable in Hopkins: he made the *De Tribus Peccatis* too much of a speculative exercise, and he made the *De Processu Peccatorum* too much of an examination of conscience —which it is not meant to be. He had, as one or two of his sermons show, a slight—*but fatal*—sympathy with the Pharisee rather than with the Publican. These things must be borne carefully in mind in passing from the retreat of 1883 to that of 1889.

The triple pattern of the 1883 retreat should also be noted. There is a period of desolation in the 'first week', followed by an abundance of light and strength in the 'second week'; but his final resolution from the 'third and fourth weeks' is that his joy must be wholly objective, the joy of the Lord, not the fruition of his own spiritual desires. Thus high he pitched his elective will and left his affective will to follow as best it could.

The notes of the next two years, 1884–5, show him struggling to reconcile his elective will, nailed to the cross, with his rational affections which have found reason to revolt. The notes are so scarce that they cannot be considered an adequate story of his interior life. But they have a special interest in that they cover the period, 'that year of now done darkness', when his five or six famous sonnets of desolation were composed, as well as others of his most striking poems.

His transfer to Dublin and the events that followed might be read as an acceptance of his offer of a greater sacrifice for a closer union with Our Lord. But it could also be read as a rejection of that offer, as a sign that he had presumed beyond the measure of grace that was due to him. He himself insisted perhaps too strictly upon justice in his dealings with God; and doubts as to the acceptance of his sacrifice, accompanied by involuntary doubts about God's justice, were possibly at the root of the misery that now entangled him. Instead of being lifted to a closer union in prayer, he found himself deteriorating not only physically and mentally, but spiritually as well. There was not the faintest suggestion of martyrdom in the outward circumstances of his life, which were pleasant enough. The war was all within.

There are indications in the notes how his outraged nature (that is, his poetic genius) wreaked its revenge. It curled itself around his beloved country, 'England . . . wife to my creating thought', and enlisted his patriotism and sense of justice against his vow of obedience. It entangled itself demonstratively in the endless labyrinth of examination papers, emphasizing the slavery to which it was being subjected. It spread tantalizing prospects of the great poems he could write for the glory of God, if he could only get back to England or Wales. It took ugly forms of threatened self-destruction. In these last forms—since, after all, there was no real distinction between his nature and himself—it may be said to have crept into the very selfwill with which he was suppressing it. For example, he suffered terribly from his eyes and feared they were threatened by an incurable disease. Yet years later, in October 1888, he found that there was nothing really wrong with his eyes; all he had needed was a pair of spectacles.[1] But why did he not go and see an oculist three or four years earlier? The answer presumably is that his mental darkness and confusion was of that sort in which the most obvious remedies seem the most useless. This he knew well enough, but the knowledge did not help. 'Pray not to be tormented' is one of the most revealing and piteous of the entries in these notes.

During these years and under these assaults, his will—as he was able to aver with the complete truthfulness which was his constant characteristic—'never wavered'; nor was his essential judgement of his state ever impaired. His only complaints were in the nature of involuntary gasps and groans. They occur chiefly in the letters to

[1] *Letters*, i. 296.

Bridges, interspersed with horrific casualness amid congratulations to Bridges on his engagement and marriage: he has nearly died, he is being driven mad, he fears for his eyesight—but there is nothing to worry about, Bridges must not be disturbed on his account. It is no wonder that Bridges thought bitter thoughts about the Jesuits. There were Jesuits themselves among Hopkins's contemporaries who felt that he was being wasted and misused.[1] But it does not seem possible to lay any blame at any particular door. The most that can be said is that if the Society *had* managed to find him a field of long and fruitful labour, its reputation as a cultural force would have been confirmed or repaired, according to the point of view. At the same time it is hard not to believe that Hopkins's trials were part of a predestined process of sanctification. Even if it is granted that they were due to his own wilfulness, such noble wilfulness seems to be always allowed for by God in the sanctification of proudly courageous men like Hopkins.

The period of most savage stress ended with the beautiful sonnet of desolation:

> My own heart let me have more pity on; let
> Me live to my sad self hereafter kind . . .

His experience bore fruit also in Caradoc's soliloquy—transcribed in the same book as these notes—surely one of the grandest bits of English verse ever written.

> But will flesh, O can flesh
> Second this fiery strain? Not always; O no no!
> We cannot live this life out; sometimes we must weary
> And in this darksome world what comfort can I find? . . .

> I all my being have hacked in half with her neck . . .

Hereafter he did live to himself more kind. He accepted the holidays and relaxations that were offered him by his superiors in generous abundance. On a deeply-enjoyed vacation in Wales in the autumn of 1886 he even got forward with his drama on St Winefred, who had always symbolized for him the sweet union of election with affection—like the water of her well, 'the sensible thing so naturally and gracefully uttering the spiritual reason of its being (which is all in true keeping with the story of St Winefred's death and recovery) and the spring in place leading back the thoughts by its spring in time to its spring in eternity'.

But it was too late to recapture 'the roll, the rise, the carol, the creation'. At the same time it was too soon for him to have completed the transition at which he was now consciously aiming—a transition which seems common to all great English poets in middle

[1] Private letters to Fr Keating, at Farm Street.

age, from the delight of self-expression to a graver and more detached labour of creation. The inevitable barrenness of transition was accompanied in his case by a continued inability to pray, as he was used to, with the aid of his poetic understanding and sensibility. Illuminative prayer, the prayer of *intima cognitio*, was closed to him because of the ever-present threat of self-torment. He had to be content with a blind attachment of the will which brought strength but no inspiration. He wrote to Dixon in July 1886, not meaning to speak of himself, but unconsciously doing so:

> Great gifts and great opportunities are more than life spares to one man. . . . Above all Christ our Lord: his career was cut short and, whereas he would have wished to succeed by success—for it is insane to lay yourself out for failure, prudence is the first of the cardinal virtues, and he was the most prudent of men—nevertheless he was doomed to succeed by failure; his plans were baffled, his hopes dashed, and his work was done by being broken off undone. However much he understood all this he found it an intolerable grief to submit to it. He left the example: it is very strengthening, but except in that sense it is not consoling. (*Letters*, ii. 137–8.)

The unspoken reference is to the clash of elective and affective will at Gethsemane. An 'intolerable grief' was still lurking in Hopkins's nature, compounded of many submerged anxieties and resentments, coiled like a dragon waiting for the moment when he should be tempted to challenge it once more.

The moment came in January 1889 when he spent the first three days of his annual retreat in ruthless self-examination. The result was a hideous struggle and a painful, glittering victory. Written only six months before his death, these are the last of his spiritual notes that are extant.

Emotionally, they are unnerving; but intellectually they present the spectacle of a classic ascent according to the rules—though whether he was right to choose so steep a cliff-face is another matter. For three days he gives clear, trenchant expression to all his lurking griefs—politics, illness, scruples, failures; he explores every crevice unflinchingly, and the result is apparently complete abandonment —'helpless loathing'.

Then on the fifth day is felt the grinding application—'We hear our hearts grate on themselves'—of Fr Whitty's rule, to concentrate on the immediate duties of one's state:

> I am not willing enough for the piece of work assigned me, the only work I am given to do, though I could do others if they were given. This is my work at Stephen's Green. And I thought that the Royal University was to me what Augustus's enrolment was to St Joseph: *exiit sermo a Caesare Augusto*; so resolution of the senate of the R.U. came to me, inconvenient and painful, but the journey to Bethlehem was inconvenient and painful. . . .

On that same day came the deliverance, the promised 'illumination' of the Second Week: 'Yesterday I had ever so much light . . . and last night . . . and today . . . more than I can easily put down.'

It may be asked whether this intellectual light was the light he had asked for, 'a light shed on our way and a happiness spread over our life'. It would seem that it was. It was the light of the Epiphany broadening out, in the wonderful first chapters of St John's gospel, into the coming of Christ, the Way and the Light, to carry with him the sons of men. Moreover there is a change observable in his letters after this date. His health gets worse but his spirits get better.

He wrote to Bridges four days after this retreat: 'I have been a little ill and am still a little pulled down; however I am in good spirits' (*Letters*, i. 271).

And again forty days before his death: 'I am ill today, but no matter for that as my spirits are good' (*Letters*, i. 303).

But these considerations are outside the scope of an edition which ends with January 1889. In any case, as has been said already, the autobiographical element in Hopkins's spiritual writings is less important than their intrinsic interest. In these last notes all is juice sucked from the words of the gospel, nothing is spun from fancy.

They end with the cliff-face scaled and his mind and heart at one, striding forward with great strides on a high plateau of light; of light, or rather of bright shadow, in which the beloved shapes of Galilee and Judaea return once more and take their places around the radiant centre where Christ is.

How busily and devotedly, with what detective ingenuity, his mind runs here and there to reconstruct the wise men's journey: how grandly the figure of St John the Baptist arises, haughty and gentle, by the wild river-side: with what a sudden inspiration Nathanael comes to life between the sun-dappled leaves of the fig-tree: with what consummate delicacy, with what patristic verve the poet and scholar delineates the part played by Our Blessed Lady at the marriage feast of Cana: 'She knew he did not need reminding, but she did not know he might not need requesting.'

In the contemplation of that Marriage Feast the notes break off— with a sentence that might stand for posterity's estimation of him as well as the steward's of the wine: 'there has been no stint, but there has been an unwise order in the serving'.

TRANSLATION FROM CHRYSOSTOM ON EUTROPIUS

A. M. D. G.[1]

OPENING OF ST. JOHN CHRYSOSTOM'S HOMILY ON THE FALL OF EUTROPIUS[2]

It is always in season but now more than ever is it seasonable to say: Vanity of vanities and all is vanity. Where now are the bright keepings of the consulship?[3] Where is the gay torchlight now? Where are the clapping hands and the dances and the assemblies and the festivals? Where the green garlands and the curtains floating? Where the cry of the town and the cheers of the hippodrome, and the noisy flattering lungs of the spectators there? All that is gone: a wind blew and on the sudden cast the leaves and shewed us the tree bare and all that was left of it from the root upwards shaking—the gale that struck it was so fearfully strong and threatened indeed to tear it up root-whole, or shatter it this way and that, even to the rending of the grain of the timber. Where now are the friends, the make-believes, followers of the fashion? Where are the suppers and feasts? Where the swarm of hangers-on? the strong wine decanting all day long, the cooks and the daintily dressed table, the attendants on greatness and all the words and ways they have to please? They were all night and dreaming: now it is day and they are vanished. They were spring flowers, and, spring over, they all are faded together. They were a shadow, and it has travelled on beyond. They were smoke, and it has gone out in the air. They were bubbles, and are broken. They were cobweb, and are swept away.[4] And so this spiritual refrain is left us to sing, coming in again and again with: Vanity of vanities and all is vanity. O this is the verse that should be written on walls, and in clothing and at markets and at home and by waysides and on doors and over entries and above all in the conscience of each, written wherever we look that we may read it whatever we do. While this swindle of the business of life and this wearing of masks and playing of characters is taken for truth by the many, this is the verse that every day, at dinner and supper, and every meeting between men I wish that each one of you could be bringing to his neighbour's ear and hearing from his neighbour's tongue: Vanity of vanities, all is vanity.

Did I not tell you that wealth was a runaway? But you could not have it. Did I not keep saying it was a thankless guest? But you could not hear. See, the experience has come and the fact has taught you, it is not only a runaway and unthankful but that it is a murderer. Did I not tell you, every time when you rebuked me for speaking the truth: I love you better than those that flatter you: I, who bring your faults home to you, care for you more than your obliging friends? Did I not add to these words how *wounds from a friend are faithful more than the offered kisses of an enemy*? If you had put up with my wounds then their kisses would never have been father to this death; for my wounds carry health in them, but their kisses have developed disease past surgery. Where now are those who poured you out the wine? Where those who looked important in the market-place and spoke of you ten thousand praises in every ear? They have run, they have said No to friendship, they are looking for their own safety while you are in your deadly pangs.

Not so we, not so we. We would not fling away from your displeasure then, and now, see how we try to gather you home, to recover you in your fall. And the Church you yourself made war on once, has opened her breast and welcomed you in, and the theatres that courted you, in whose behalf many times you were indignant with us, they have betrayed and undone you. And yet we said, we never ceased saying: What is it you are doing? You are making havoc of the Church, and it is yourself you are hurrying over the cliff's edge—but you pushed by me, not to hear. And the hippodromes that your riches were drained upon have whetted the sword, and the Church that drank of your anger, your untimely anger, is running round you everywhere, trying and trying to have you from the net.

And all this I say now not to trample on the fallen but because I want to make those who stand stand firmer; not to rip open the sores on the bleeding back, but to keep the unhurt in their soundness of limb; not to sink the boat the seas break over but to signal those who scud before the wind, that they may never feel the waters rolling overhead. And how will that be done? It may be done if we will only think of the reverses of human life. Here was a man who if he had feared a fall would not have suffered a fall. But since *he* neither from his own thoughts nor yet from others' warnings has gathered what could have done him good, you at least that wear the pride and plume of wealth make your gain by his misfortune: for nothing, no nothing has so little strength to stay as the things of man. And this is why, whatever name you choose to call their cheapness and their poorness by, you will still fall below the truth: call them smoke, call them grass, call them dreams, call them flowers in spring, call them what you like: they are so wholly on the turn of hazard, they are such nothingness beyond all that goes for nothing. But that is not all: besides their nothingness there is headlong falling in them— and it is plain from him. For who stood higher than this man stood? Did he not in wealth outgo the whole world? Did he not tread to the very crests and crags of honour? Did not all fear him, tremble at him? And O look, he is more helpless than men in dungeons, more pitiable than poor slaves, in need more utter than wretches thin with hunger, seeing all day long but swords whetting and the pit and the executioners and the march to the scaffold; and the pleasure he basked in once, he forgets if it was, he cannot tell that he was ever there; and does not see these sunbeams even, but at broad mid-day as if it were the dead of night, sits there dark between walls, as lost to eyesight as a blind man. No, the truth is strive as we may we shall find words will not do to represent his condition as it must truly be, the life a man lives that every hour thinks he is going to be killed. After all, what need is there of words of ours? Why he himself has drawn clearly enough the picture we are to look at. Yesterday when some came for him from the palace to arrest him and he fled to the sacred vessels for sanctuary, his face was yellow like a thing in box-wood, and even now it is no fresher than the face of a corpse; then there were the chattering teeth and knocking knees and a trembling in the whole body, and a voice that broke off and could not finish the word and a tongue paralysed that would not do its office and the whole look of him such that if a man in stone could have a soul it might show such life as he showed then.

L. D. S.

SECTION TWO

THE 'DOMINICAL'—11 MARCH, 1877

A.M.D.G.
March 11 1877
See at the end[1]

Dixit ergo Jesus: Facite homines discumbere—Then Jesus said: Make the men sit down—John vi 10.

And now, brethren, you have heard the Gospel of Christ feeding 5000 men with five loaves in the wilderness and how they would have made Him king. Let us do as we are accustomed—return to the story, turn it over and dwell on it, go in mind to that time and in spirit to that place, admire what Christ says as if we heard it, and what He does as if we saw it, until the heart perhaps may swell with pride for Jesus Christ the king of glory. Being a number here together we can do much, we can do what one could not do; I beg of you to lend me your ears and go along with me, in mind, I say, and in spirit, not in the body, for you are as when Our Lord said: make the men sit down; and at the end of all we will crown Christ king—how and where are we to crown Him? in our hearts and souls: He will not make away to the mountain, He wishes for that crowning, He requires it. And in the meanwhile let the men sit down, that is / be at rest, be still, be attentive, listen for what is to come: our Lord by this gospel gives out the living bread of His teaching, I will hand it on to you.

First of all then when was the time of this miracle? It was, St John says, near the Pasch, the feast of the Jews. The Pasch is Easter. It was therefore as it might be now, in Spring-time, not long before Easter; for which reason we read this gospel this Sunday and St John's gospel, for the other gospels do not tell the time. The Pasch was the last before the one at which Christ suffered. And what was the time of day? Towards evening. And so much for the time.

And now where was the place? It was beside the sea of Galilee or the sea of Tiberias, which lake is 12 miles long and 7 wide at the broadest, and the Jordan running through it with a strong stream; so that if it were in this valley it would stretch from Rhuddlan to beyond Llanrhaiadr or from St Asaph to Ruthin, let us say that —from St Asaph to Ruthin, and would fill the valley from hill to hill,—only the Jordan runs from north to south, not like the Clwyd from south to north. And here I will say what may be useful to you in thinking of places where our Lord often was. The lake is shaped something like a bean or something like a man's left ear; the Jordan enters at the top of the upper rim, it runs out at the end of the lobe or drop of the ear. One Bethsaida—Bethsaida Julias—stands by the Jordan as it were above the ear in the hair; Capharnaum on the bow or rim nearer the cheek; the other Bethsaida, where Peter and Andrew and Philip lived, against the cheek where the bow of the ear ends; Tiberias on the tongue of flesh that stands out from the cheek into the hollow of the ear; Chorozain[1] and Gergesa outside, on the outer bow. So that in this valley, St Asaph would be where the Jordan enters the valley; Bethsaida Julias would be Rhuddlan; Capharnaum would be near Llannefydd standing high; but Bethsaida near Hen-llan; Tiberias would be Denbigh; Chorozain might be Bodfari; and the place of the miracle seems to have been at the north end of the lake, on the east side of the Jordan, as it might be at this very spot where we are now upon the slope of Maenefa.[2] The place was desert, not barren or sandy at all, for there was much grass there, but it was not lived in or tilled; why I cannot say—certainly not for want of people, for the Holy Land was thickly peopled, full of prosperous towns and villages, of rich vineyards and farms. This spot was however wilderness. And so much for the place.

Who were the persons there? They were our Lord, His apostles, His disciples above on the mountain; the crowd it was below. But how had they come there? This way. The apostles had just come back from preaching and had told Christ what they had taught and done. He said to them: Come apart to a lonely place and rest awhile. For there were many coming and going and they had not a moment to get even a meal: so St Mark says. My merciful master would give His good apostles rest, that had been doing His work.

But it could not be, they could not get that rest. For the apostles had done their work too well and all the country was astir about Jesus. So now they lift up their eyes from the mountain side where they are resting and lo they are not alone even here! A crowd is streaming in below—men, women, and children, and sick folk brought to be cured. So our Lord welcomed them, since the thing must be, taught them and cured the sick. And now it was late and the people faint and no shops near, the apostles wanted our Lord to stop teaching and send the crowd off while there was daylight to spare to the nearest villages to buy food. No, said He, but you give them food to eat. All this is in the other gospels and I have put it in: but what says the gospel of today? for on that we are to dwell. *Jesus said to Philip*, writes St John, *where are we to buy bread that these may eat? Where*, said the Word of God, *where*, said the uncreated wisdom speaking to His creature, *shall we buy bread for these to eat? This He said to try him for He Himself knew*, had made up His mind,

A Map Illustrating Hopkins's Comparison of the Clwyd Valley and the Sea of Galilee

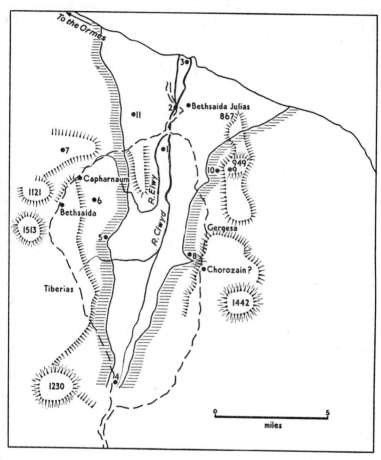

```
                    ↑ CLWYD NORTH
——— SEA OF GALILEE  ≣ CLWYD VALLEY  ↑ GALILEE NORTH
```

1. St. Asaph   2. Rhuddlan   3. Rhyl   4. Ruthin   5. Denbigh   6. Henllan
7. Llannefyd   8. Bodfari   9. Maenefa   10. St. Beuno's   11. Bodelwyddan

what He was going to do. He said it to try him—to try his patience, his
charity, humility, obedience, to try his faith. This is what He
means: Send them away to get food? No. You were right to be
thoughtful for them, they are indeed fasting, they are faint, they by
all means need food. Give it them, you give them food. You seem at
a loss: if you have not enough get more. Are you *sure* you have not
enough; just think; perhaps there is some help here, someone who
can multiply food if need be, who turned water into wine at Cana
for instance. Go and see what you have got. *If* we have not got
enough, if we cannot get it any other way, we must buy it. How
much do we really need? Philip has a good eye: how many are there
here, Philip? How much bread should we want? If we must buy it
where shall we buy it? Think and tell me for there is no time to be
lost. Philip, what do you say? Such thoughts, I say, our Lord's
question should have awakened in St Philip's mind, though these
were not His words: for it is not for me, it is not for men to put their
prattle into the mouth of their Maker. Where shall we buy bread?—
He said it to try him. Why to try St Philip. Here, brethren, remark
a mystery. Philip is a Greek, not a Jewish, name; it has a noble air;
it suits noblemen, like Guy or Marmaduke or Perceval—with us. It
means fond of horses, proud of his stud; not fond as a groom is of the
horse he grooms or a ploughman or a coachman of his team but as
a wealthy man is of his stud, his show of cost and wealth and pride.
The name then means one who has an eye to the pomp and beauty
of this world. St Philip was but a poor man but he was a heaven-
enlightened apostle of Jesus Christ: Christ would give him, instead
of the contemplation of this world's studs and steeds and splendour,
its chivalry and chariots and chargers, an eye to dwell on the glory
of the kingdom of heaven. We find this saint what is called contemplative: wherever we hear of Philip there is question of *seeing*
Christ or *seeing* God. His friend St Andrew first called him and
brought him to Christ, one look was enough for Philip. He went in
his turn and called his friend Nathanael: can any good, said Nathanael, come out of Nazareth? No wrangling, no reasoning: come
and *see*, St Philip said.[1] Come and *see*! is the cry of his holy enthusiasm for the king of glory. Shortly before the Passion, when our
Lord was at the height of His fame, some Greeks wanted to *see*
Jesus: they came to Philip. It is as if Philip held his hand upon the
bolts of the window of the bright contemplation of Jesus Christ. At
the last supper he suddenly says to our Lord: Lord, shew us the
Father—and it is enough for us. This time he listlessly said: Two
hundred pennyworth of bread is not enough for each to get a little;
at that great supper he breaks out: Shew us the Father, feed our
eyes with one look; and that meal is enough for our lives, will glut

our hearts with its delight for ever. So then here the searcher of hearts, our kind and, I might say, arch and gracious-minded master and king seems to say to His contemplative disciple: Philip, you have a good eye, you are contemplative and thoughtful: look at the crowd and then round the country, see how much bread we want and tell me where we shall buy it. He said it to try him. If the bread must be bought it would try his patience and courage, his obedience and humility, his charity for his master and the famishing crowd. For the neighbouring villages could not supply such a crowd: he and the rest would have to tramp away wearily to Bethsaida Julias, as far as Rhuddlan—to Capharnaum, as far as Bodlewyddan and that not as the crow flies but skirting the lake; to Chorozain, Gergesa, and so on. We hear therefore his disheartened and disheartening answer: *Two hundred pennyworth of bread is not enough even for each to get a little.* Of course a penny in the Scripture means much more than a penny—a shilling say or more than that: £10 worth, he says, would not make a good meal and £10 was more than they had got. This was all his contemplation came to: to say what was *not enough.* He made, I do suppose, a correct reckoning; two hundred pennyworth would *not* have done for the poorest meal and besides they had not the money. But, dear brethren, this answer is even laughable. For if a man is appealed to about the price of a house, a field, a feast or at a public supper, anything, he may answer: It will cost £1000, £100, £10 or 10*s.* and he may add: That will cover it but that is more than you can afford, but is it not a singular, an unhelpful, an oddly unpractical answer to say £1000 is *not* enough for the house even without the garden; £100 is *not* enough for the field even without the sheds and buildings; £10 is *not* enough for the supper even without the wine? Who wants that kind of answer? Yet this is how St Philip answered our Lord: Two hundred pennyworth of bread is not enough even for each to get a little. But besides, if human means all fell short why could not St Philip have answered as the prophets did when God questioned them? Son of man, God said to one of the prophets, can these bones live? My Lord, Thou knowest, he answered. Where shall we buy bread, Our Lord asked, for these to eat? If St Philip could not tell himself surely he might have answered: My Lord, Thou knowest. This would have shewn his faith if not his willingness. But you and I, my brethren, fail much more disgracefully than this apostle did, whose name God glorify. He truly was at his wits' end, he really saw no human way out of that difficulty, he only forgot to think of a miracle; we despair even when humanly the likelihoods are in our favour; if we are sad we think we shall never be happy more, though the same thing has happened to us times and times; if we are sick we despair of being ever well, though human nature every day is in some one or other sickening and recovering; if in poverty we despair of being ever better off, though the times keep turning and changing; if tired we complain as if no sleep or rest would ever refresh us; if the winter is cold we make believe it will never be summer again. I speak of what I know in myself, and it may be something of the same is true in you. Whereas *they that trust in the Lord are as Mount Sion.*

But now (to return to the gospel and the sea of Galilee), up spoke St Andrew. St Andrew was St Philip's friend; he first called him to Christ; he was always helpful to him; when the Greeks asked to see our Lord timid Philip told Andrew first and *Andrew and Philip*—so the Scripture says—told Jesus. St Andrew took one step, it was but a little one but he took it · he went and found out what food there was to be had—it was five loaves and two fishes. *Says one of His disciples to him, Andrew Simon Peter's brother,* so-and-so. Andrew's name means Manly; there was in this man the heart and activity of a man, there was besides some of the promptitude and faith of his brother Simon Peter. Here then he put in a helpful word: *There is a boy here has five barley loaves and two fishes, but*—Let us however before we go on think a little of this. There is a boy here—*a little boy* it is in the Greek, *just a boy* in the Latin: certainly a little boy, just a boy, could not carry much: the beginning is bad enough. The continuance is worse: who has five barley loaves and two fishes: to be sure a little boy, just a boy, might carry that much well enough. Five barley loaves, not quartern loaves but what they call breads abroad, more like rolls than loaves, and five in number: if one could make a man's dinner then five of the apostles might have dined and the rest of the apostles and all the disciples and all the multitude gone without. After his reckoning of the two hundred pennyworth of bread, which would still not be enough for each to get a little, these five loaves might well make St Philip smile, and so St Andrew could not help adding: *But what are these among so many?* St Andrew then, I say, struck in, he said something to the purpose, he did something; then his faith seems to give way: *What are they among so many?*

But God asks but a very little of His creatures; sometimes to be willing, just to shew they are willing, is enough, and He will do the rest. Our Lord had got from one of His disciples a weak but helping hand, one wavering suggestion and He was satisfied. The lord and master spoke now: *Make the men sit down.* In the meantime the bread and the fish were sent for and laid before Him. Undoubtedly the hearts of the disciples were beating with awe and expectation at what was next to come. And at the same time the gentle but great and undeniable word was in their ears driving them down into the thousands below: *Make those men sit down.* They had not thought of asking Him to share His power, dull, disrespectful, faithless that they had been, they had complained of His teaching too long, of having to go far to get bread, of two hundred pennyworth not being enough, of five loaves being lost among so many; their master had seemed to notice nothing, to let things go too far, to need their advice, to want their help. Suddenly the thunder had rolled over their heads, harmless but unmistakeable the tongue of the heavenly lightning had rushed downwards before their eyes, and all the place was full of the sense of royal majesty, of more than prophetic power, of divine glory: *Make the men sit down.* All was ready, there was much soft green grass in the place. Down fell the men to table—the table was the grass—not so much with eagerness for the meal as with awe and necessity at the command, five thousand in number. Not that it was done in a moment, but it was done with royal, with military strength, hearing of no denial. The twelve apostles, the many disciples went forth; they stemmed their way through the throng; they gave the word, You here, you there; fifty in this company, a hundred in that; not one man more, not one less; down I tell you, the master has spoken. The crowd forestalled the command, in joyous fear down they fell; they broke into plots and lots, they parted into platoons and square companies;* the fifty one sent off their fifty first man, they dared not keep him; the forty¹ nine beckoned him, he must come. The master had spoken: *Make the men sit down.* Our Lord had spoken but gently indeed: ποιήσατε τοὺς ἀνθρώπους ἀναπεσεῖν, *Facite homines discumbere,* in your own language *Pawch i'r dynion eistedd i lawr,* which is little more than: *Make the people sit down,* but the evangelist more sternly tells the history: ἀνέπεσον οὖν οἱ <u>ἄνδρες</u>, *Discubuerunt ergo* VIRI, *Felly y gwŷr a eisteddasant i lawr,* 5000 grown men like chidden children crouched to the ground at the word which made the men sit down.

And now, brethren, think you see them like a well drilled army encamped on the green field, think you see the joyous green grass of that spring plotted with flowerbeds² of human limbs and faces. The thunderclap has spoken and passed: Make the men sit down / and the rain of the gracious and divine providential mercy has set in. As when here a sheet of white rain coming from the sea blots out first the Orms'³ Heads on Moel Hiraddug, then spreads mile after mile, from hill to hill, from square to square of the fields, along the Vale of Clwyd, so the refreshment of the barley bread was spreading through that multitude. The apostles and disciples went and came, setting out with loaded baskets, returning with empty ones; the whole scene was in circulation, the flow of food unbroken; the awestruck and astonished crowd look now this way, now that, they see our Lord higher up on

* Here is the blue pencil mark. See note of GMH at end of sermon. [Ed.]

the hillside with a little parcel of something eatable before Him, dealing and dealing and dealing it out; it works its way in streams of disciples, it spreads inexhaustibly over the face of the multitude; Look, they whisper, now it has reached that company, now that; here it is for us. *How does it grow? where does it come from?* As the yeast pushes and blisters up in the dark kneading trough: so this in open daylight, and yet no one can exactly see when and how, grows under the very hands that deal it: even the master of each company is amazed to see it increased since he gave it round, more in the company's hands than ever was served him by the busy disciple passing. And so they receive each his piece of barley bread and of the fish as much as they want, all eat and are filled and the remainder fills twelve baskets.

Much, much more might be said, for the meaning of the Scripture, like this very bread, grows and multiplies as you deal it out. But we will leave the multitude there, orderly strewn on the fresh green grass, enjoying the heavenly festival under Christ's eyes, then rising with hasty untaught mistaken zeal to make Him king. For He did not need nor wish to be made king that way. But we, brethren, *we will*, if you please, crown Christ king; He is and shall be king, lord, and master of my mind, heart, and will. I have crowned and I do and will crown Him there, I have enthroned and I do and will enthrone Him there. He teaches: I listen and believe. He commands: I shall obey. He goes His own road: I mean to follow. This man whom just now we seemed to see dealing out the barley bread, this man, Jesus of Nazareth by name, at this moment while I speak seated at the right hand of the Father is dealing me out my life, my voice, my breath, my being: let Him withdraw it if it is His will, if not let me employ it much better than heretofore to His glory. And you, my brethren, crown Him king of your hearts. You have, no doubt you long ago faithfully have done so: but I mean, if anyone has not let him make haste, let him do it. His hand created you once, now it deals out to you your being and the bread and all things that keep you alive;[1] in the end it will either crown you or it will cast you away. Crown Him now who can crown you then, kiss the hand that holds the dreadful rod. You and I now are like, just like, that multitude was then; among those that eat were some that afterwards became God-hating reprobates, among those that helped and served were disciples that fell away and Judas that betrayed his master. I do implore my God to save me and not let me fall and betray Him and be lost, and because in earnest I ask Him He will. You too, dear brethren, you beg of Him for yourselves likewise and He will save you. Blessed are they, said a man in the gospel, who shall eat bread in the kingdom of heaven: but who are these? They who now obey

Christ, they who now live by the words that come from the mouth of God, they who now come to the divine Catholic Christian sacraments and eat the flesh of the Son of Man and live for *ever*. If you will not do this then I will tell you what to do instead: I would advise you to find some bread the eating of which will make you live for ever on this earth. Ask the doctors about it, consult the learned, read books, search the files of the newspapers. It is not barleybread indeed, it is not made of oatmeal or flour of wheat, it is not spelt[1] or rye or maize: perhaps it is sesame. By all means find it and buy it and eat it and give it your children. If not you must die and dying fall into the hands of the living God.

Do not deceive yourselves, the Apostle says; neither worshippers of idols—which includes all false religions—nor fornicators nor adulterers nor thieves nor usurers nor extortioners nor drunkards nor slanderers and their neighbourers[2] shall inherit God's kingdom. Therefore crown Christ king of our minds and hearts and wills and now in your bodies glorify God.

L. D. S.

This was a Dominical and was delivered on Mid-Lent Sunday March 11 1877 as far as the blue pencilmark on the sheet before this. People laughed at it prodigiously, I saw some of them roll on their chairs with laughter. This made me lose the thread, so that I did not deliver the last two paragraphs right but mixed things up. The last paragraph, in which *Make the men sit down* is often repeated, far from having a good effect, made them roll more than ever

SCRAPS OF SERMONS[1]

OCT. 26 1879 ST. JOSEPH'S, BEDFORD LEIGH—Ep. 21 Pent.: Eph.
vi 10–17. (armour of God)

The warfare the Apostle speaks of always goes on. Devils undying,
their hatred undying; men die but race goes on, devils hate it;
Church immortal, gates of hell etc. St Paul wrote for us, takes an
interest in us, is zealous over us

Nobility of this warfare. Dignity of the Apostle's words. Choirs
of angels, regiments with officers, ranks, discipline, subordination

Armour of God—he repeats

Stand—no dying in this battle, for it would spiritual death.
Martyrdom spiritual victory, not death

Loins—here first of girding in general, then of soldiers' girdles or
belts. In gen. mark of work and of chastity and of temperance

In soldiers of equipment, active service. Story of Wm. Clarke.
'Repente solvit cingulum'[2]

Truth—reality or earnest and the feeling of it, earnestness; spiritual
insight. This guards chastity and temperance: spiritual joys above.
those of the body, *non sunt condignae* etc. It cuts off the flowing skirts of
idleness and worldliness, a spreading of ourselves and of our being
out on lower things, and braces, binds us fast into God's service.

As we are soldiers earnestness means the same things, ready
obedience to our Captain Christ

Breast plate, *cuirass* of justice—covers nearly whole man and in
partic. heart. So justice whole duty of man and he who is covered
with it has no place vulnerable to the devil—except the head, important exception truly, of which presently

Feet—readiness to march and obey or proclaim the Gospel. *Of
peace*—because we should do so in peace if the devil would let us.
Shoes as good for peace as war

Withal shield of faith—which well wielded makes other armour
almost needless. How faith? passions resisted by it: as What shall it
avail etc; knowledge of heaven and hell, confidence in God, contempt for Satan's power. Such thoughts prevent temptation even
reaching you, for the man that might not be guarded by love of
virtue (cuirass of justice) is guarded by presence of God, fear of hell,
example of Christ: now these things faith teaches

Helmet of salvation—saving helmet, *of hope*. How of hope? The

devil would stun us with the violence of his attacks but the thought
of Christ and our heavenly rewards breaks the blow; would dazzle
us by worldly offers: we think of heavenly; would ruin our reason
by his deceits, Christ our hope himself persuades us more powerfully

Sword of the spirit—God's word, written or unwritten—usefulness of words of Sep. on temptation But also it is meant God speaking
in us; some holy thought, motion of zeal in temptation which bears
down all before it

All these come to much the same: no wonder, for of course in
reality

SEPT. 14 ST. CLEMENT'S[1]

Speak of the sacred and binding duty of going to Mass on Sundays
and holidays. First its sacredness, (2) its bindingness, (3) on those who
do not go

This is the house of God, this is the gate of heaven. None but you
and the congregation at St. Aloysius' can say this. See the old
churches, temples of God turned to dens of thieves. Pious according
to their lights but are children of those who stoned the prophets, i.e.
of those who persecuted the people of God. This is the house of God
not only because God recognises this only but because God comes
here, gate of heaven not only because sacraments of baptism and
penance are administered here but because there is a key here which
unlocks heaven and brings Christ from heaven out. This key is in my
lips. I have the power etc

At all times the *dignity of Catholics great*, a holy nation, a royal
priesthood. In the streets, the shops, the market you go about the
special care of angels, the special assault of devils because Catholics.
But here you are met for your holiest duty, the holiest highest duty of man,
to see the slaying of the spotless lamb that was slain from before the
foundation of the world and yet was slain on Mount Calvary and
will be slain here today

Neither is it only priests who are to offer it and the laity excused
from attending at it. Christ gave his commandment to all after their
own manner—all were to make this commemoration of him. The
priest is the principal minister but the worshippers all join in offering
and the server more than the rest. All therefore are at some time
and way bound to offer mass

But how often? Left to ourselves some might say once a lifetime,
others once a year, others once a day. The Church says once a week,
on Sunday. The Church being bound to offer mass has been guided
by the Holy Ghost to fix how often. It is, to be sure, the Church's
law and commandment then, but only as interpreting and fixing

Christ's. And when we disobey it we disobey our majestic and holy
mother Church and behind and above the Church our Lord and
master Jesus Christ. And is not disobedience in a great matter
wicked, mortal and damnable? It is. This is a great matter, the
Holy Mass, much a higher matter than that appletree which ruined
Adam and Eve and all of us, and disobedience in it is a sin, grievous,
mortal, and damnable. The Word of God, second person of the
divine Trinity, our blessed Lord Jesus Christ, came down from
everlasting heaven, was made man, lived among men, *was given into
the hands of sinners*, first by his own hands into Judas' in the Last
Supper, then by Judas into those of the priests, then by the priests
into those of Pilate, then by Pilate into those of the executioners,
and accomplished his bloody sacrifice on the cross. He died, he rose
again, he ascended into heaven. But his sacrifice goes on to every
year, every week, every day, because every day Mass is offered. This
is why you are here, to be at the slaying of the spotless lamb, to be
at Christ's mystical death, at the tremendous sacrifice, at the holy
mass. You see how sacred then that duty is. *He that comes upon the
altar is your God that made you*, your saviour that redeemed you, your
king that can command you, your judge that must give you your
eternal place. He is offered and heaven is open, angels shine and
sing hosanna, the face of the Eternal Father smiles; he is then ready
to forgive, most lavish in his graces: and we here below, we in this
chapel, play, I repeat, our part at the sacred sacrifice of the mass.

(2) *Its bindingness.* To be here once a Sunday is our bounden duty
—binding under mortal sin, under danger of hell fire. These are
dreadful words but yet true and just, as I will shew you. Please
follow my steps.

Christ our king, lord, and master to command us as much when
he walked the earth as when he reigns in heaven. *He at his Last Supper*
said: Do this in remembrance in me. This is a command given to
Christians. Why not an advice, counsel, recommendation?—Because
since it was to offer first this great sacrifice and to set on foot the
after offering of this sacrifice to God's glory and for man's redemption and for all blessings on the sons of men that he came into the
world he *could* not leave it a matter of no more than counsel: it is so
useful, saving, and necessary a thing it must for our own sakes be
made a binding duty to offer it. Christians then by force of Christ's
command strictly bound somewhere sometime to offer the mass and
if they were not to do so would insolently and ungratefully disobey
their God, their saviour and their king.

But this is true, that by this sin of disobedience no one is bound
that was not plainly told his duty. For nature does not tell us how
often to go to mass, man must tell us, and the rule holds: An un-

certain law is no law. I tell you then, this law is certain, you are bound to go etc.

And since I am laying down the law I must speak of what excuses from the law. And here you are to know that in the Church's laws any really reasonable cause excuses. And mark this: a reasonable cause makes it no sin at all to break the commandment

Luke xviii 9–14. The Pharisee and the Publican (Aug. 2 Sydenham)[1]

You know this Gospel and must have listened to many discourses upon it; yet when in the course of the year it comes round again we cannot pass it by, we can but dwell upon these words of divine wisdom.

Two men went to the Temple to pray. When they went home after their prayer one was justified, that is was made just, and the other was not; the one who was a great sinner, as we know from his own words, had become a just man and his sins were forgiven; the other, whose deeds, as we learn from himself, were good and just, went back worse than he came and sinned even in his prayers. The sin was that of pride. It is certain that Christ our Lord in this story gave to mankind a great warning.

I shall therefore examine the story more closely to shew what Christ our Lord's thought is. And after that I shall advise myself and you against the sin of pride.

Two men went up to the Temple to pray—And this one incident, which lasted perhaps but a few minutes, is all we hear. In that short time all was done, one man put into the way of salvation; the other, as would seem, of eternal ruin. There is then a suddenness about the story and the suddenness seems rather to terrify than to comfort, as if the way of God were full of incalculable hurricanes and reverses, in an instant building up and in the same casting down, making it seem better (which God forbid) to live recklessly and trust to a single hearty act of sorrow than to toil at prayers and mortifications which a breath of pride may in one fatal instant shatter and bring to nothing. Look then somewhat nearer. *Two men went up to the Temple.* The Jews had other places of worship than the Temple—synagogues. They had them in every place, wherever Jews were and a running brook was—for they needed that—was a synagogue and in Jerusalem itself were very many, hundreds. But the Temple was very different. there was

SECTION FOUR

INSTRUCTIONS

The Principle or Foundation.
Meditation on Hell.
Meditation on Death.

THE PRINCIPLE OR FOUNDATION[1]

Homo creatus est—CREATION THE MAKING OUT OF NOTHING, bringing from nothing into being: once there was nothing, then lo, this huge world was there. How great a work of power!

The loaf is made with flour; the house with bricks; the plough, the cannon, the locomotive, the warship / of iron—all of things that were before, of matter; but the world, with the flour, the grain, the wheatear, the seed, the ground, the sun, the rain; with the bricks, the clay, the earth; with the iron and the mine, the fuel and the furnace, was made from nothing. And they are MADE IN TIME AND WITH LABOUR, the world in no time with a word. MAN CANNOT CREATE a single speck, God creates all that is besides himself.

But MEN OF GENIUS ARE SAID TO CREATE, a painting, a poem, a tale, a tune, a policy; not indeed the colours and the canvas, not the words or notes, but the design, the character, the air, the plan. How then?—from themselves, from their own minds. And they themselves, their minds and all, are creatures of God: if the tree created much more the flower and the fruit.

To know what creation is LOOK AT THE SIZE OF THE WORLD. Speed of light: it would fly six or seven times round the earth while the clock ticks once. Yet it takes *thousands of years* to reach us from the Milky Way, which is made up of stars swarming together (though as far from one another as we are from some of them), running into one, and looking like a soft mist, and each of them a million times as big as the earth perhaps (the sun is about that). And there is not the least reason to think that is anything like the size of the whole world. And all arose at a word! So that the greatest of all works in the world, nay the world itself, was easier made than the least little thing that man or any other creature makes in the world.

WHY DID GOD CREATE?—Not for sport, not for nothing. Every sensible man has a purpose in all he does, every workman has a use for every object he makes. Much more has God a purpose, an end, a meaning in his work. He meant the world to give him praise, reverence, and service; *to give him glory*. It is like a garden, a field he sows: what should it bear him? praise, reverence, and service; it should yield him glory. It is an estate he farms: what should it bring him in? Praise, reverence, and service; it should repay him glory. It is a leasehold he lets out: what should its rent be? Praise, reverence, and service; its rent is his glory. It is a bird he teaches to sing, a pipe, a harp he plays on: what should it sing to him? etc. It is a glass he looks in: what should it shew him? With praise, reverence, and service it should shew him his own glory. It is a book he has written, of the riches of his knowledge, teaching endless truths, full lessons of wisdom, a poem of beauty: what is it about? His praise, the reverence due to him, the way to serve him; it tells him of his glory. It is a censer fuming: what is the sweet incense? His praise, his reverence, his service; it rises to his glory. It is an altar and a victim on it lying in his sight: why is it offered? To his praise, honour, and service: it is a sacrifice to his glory.

The creation does praise God, does reflect honour on him, is of service to him, and yet the praises fall short; the honour is like none, less than a buttercup to a king; the service is of no service to him. In other words *he does not need it*. He has infinite glory without it and what is infinite can be made no bigger. Nevertheless he takes it: he wishes it, asks it, he commands it, he enforces it, he gets it.

The sun and the stars shining glorify God. They stand where he placed them, they move where he bid them. 'The heavens declare the glory of God'.[1] They glorify God, *but they do not know it*. The birds sing to him, the thunder speaks of his terror, the lion is like his strength, the sea is like his greatness, the honey like his sweetness; they are something like him, they make him known, they tell of him, they give him glory, but they do not know they do, they do not know him, they never can, they are brute things that only think of food or think of nothing. This then is poor praise, faint reverence, slight service, dull glory. Nevertheless what they can *they always do*.

But AMIDST THEM ALL IS MAN, man and the angels: we will speak of man. Man was created. Like the rest then to praise, reverence, and serve God; to give him glory. He does so, even by his being, beyond all visible creatures: 'What a piece of work is man!' (Expand by 'Domine, Dominus, quam admirabile etc . . . Quid est homo . . . Minuisti eum paulo minus ab angelis'.)[2] But man can know God, *can mean to give him glory*. This then was why he was made, to give God glory and to mean to give it; to praise God fréely, wíllingly to reverence him, gládly to serve him. Man was made to give, and mean to give, God glory.

I WAS MADE FOR THIS, each one of us was made for this.

Does man then do it? Never mind others now nor the race of man: DO I DO IT?—If I sin I do not: how can I dishonour God and honour him? wilfully dishonour him and yet be meaning to honour him? choose to disobey him and mean to serve him? No, we have not answered God's purposes, we have not reached the end of our being. Are we God's orchard or God's vineyard? we have yielded rotten fruit, sour grapes, or none. Are we his cornfield sown? we have not come to ear or are mildewed in the ear. Are we his farm? it is a losing one to him. Are we his tenants? we have refused him rent. Are we his singing bird? we will not learn to sing. Are we his pipe or harp? we are out of tune, we grate upon his ear. Are we his glass to look in? we are deep in dust or our silver gone or we are broken or, worst of all, we misshape his face and make God's image hideous. Are we his book? we are blotted, we are scribbled over with foulness and blasphemy. Are we his censer? we breathe stench and not sweetness. Are we his sacrifice? we are like the sacrifice of Balac, of Core,[1] and of Cain. If we have sinned we are all this.

But what we have not done yet we can do now, what we have done badly hitherto we can do well henceforward, we can repent our sins and BEGIN TO GIVE GOD GLORY. The moment we do this we reach the end of our being, we do and are what we were made for, we make it worth God's while to have created us. This is a comforting thought: we need not wait in fear till death; any day, any minute we bless God for our being or for anything, for food, for sunlight, we do and are what we were meant for, made for—things that give and mean to give God glory. This is a thing to live for. Then make haste so to live.

For IF YOU ARE IN SIN YOU ARE GOD'S ENEMY, you cannot love or praise him. You may say you are far from hating God; but if you live in sin you are among God's enemies, you are under Satan's standard and enlisted there; you may not like it, no wonder; you may wish to be elsewhere; but there you are, an enemy to God. It is indeed better to praise him than blaspheme, but the praise is not a hearty praise; it cannot be. You cannot mean your praise if while praise is on the lips there is no reverence in the mind; there can be no reverence in the mind if there is no obedience, no submission, no service. And there can be no obeying God while you disobey him, no service while you sin. Turn then, brethren, now and give God glory. You do say grace at meals and thank and praise God for your daily bread, so far so good, but thank and praise him now for everything. When a man is in God's grace and free from mortal sin, then everything that he does, so long as there is no sin in it, gives God glory and what does not give him glory has some, however little, sin in it. It is not only prayer that gives God glory but work. Smiting on an anvil, sawing a beam, whitewashing a wall, driving horses, sweeping, scouring, everything gives God some glory if being in his grace you do it as your duty. To go to communion worthily gives

God great glory, but to take food in thankfulness and temperance gives him glory too. To lift up the hands in prayer gives God glory, but a man with a dungfork in his hand, a woman with a sloppail, give him glory too.[1] He is so great that all things give him glory if you mean they should. So then, my brethren, live.

A. M. D. G.

MEDITATION ON HELL[2]

Preparatory prayer.

1st. prelude—to see with the eyes of the imagination the length, breadth, and depth of Hell. Not known where Hell is; many say beneath our feet. It is at all events *a place of imprisonment*, a prison; *a place of darkness*; and *a place of torment* and that by fire (case of Dives). The devils wander, but bear their torment with them. There is such a place: shutting our eyes will not do away with a steeple or a sign-post nor will not thinking of or not believing in Hell put it out of being.

2nd. prelude—To ask for what we want, which here is such an inward feeling of the pain the damned suffer that if we ever come to forget the love of the eternal Lord, through our faults (our venial sins, lukewarmness, worldliness, negligence), the fear of hell-pains at least may help us then and keep us from falling into mortal sin. The great evil of hell is the loss of God, but we think little enough of this: let us think then of what we dread even here, the pain of fire and others, that we understand.

1st point—*with the eyes of the imagination to see* those huge flames and the souls of the lost as if in bodies of fire. The lost now lying in hell are Devils without bodies and disembodied souls, they suffer nevertheless a torment as of bodily fire. Though burning and other pains afflict us through our bodies yet it is the soul that they afflict,[3] the mind: if the mind can be deadened, as by chloroform, no pain is felt at all: God can then if he chooses bodily afflict the mind that is out of or never had a body to suffer in. No one in the body can suffer fire for very long, the frame is destroyed and the pain comes to an end; not so, unhappily, the pain that afflicts the indestructible mind, nor after the Judgment day the incorruptible body. Christ speaks of the lost as being salted, that is preserved, with fire and some things, like asbestos-cloth or fireclay, burn but are unchanged. This fire afflicts the lost only so far as they have sinned: therefore the rich glutton asks for a drop of water for *his* tongue, for by the tongue he sinned on earth. Let all consider this: we are our own tormentors, for every sin we then shall have remorse and with remorse torment and the torment fire. The murderer suffers one way, the drunkard another, but all can say they are tormented in that flame. The glutton had there no tongue to torment and yet he was tormented in that flame, for God punishing him through his own guilty thoughts made him seem to suffer in the part that had offended. So of all. In that flame then see them now. They have no bodies there, flame is the body that they wear. You have seen a glassblower breathe on a flame; at once it darts out into a jet taper as a lance-head and as piercing too. The breath of God's anger first kindled the fire of hell; (Is. xxx 33.) it strikes with a distinct indignation still on each distinct unforgiven sin; the wretched soul starts into a flame that has some frightful and fantastic likeness to its sin; so sinners are themselves the flames of hell. O hideous and ungainly sight! which will cease only when at the day of Judgment the body and the soul are at one again and the sinful members themselves and in themselves receive their punishment, a punishment which lasts for ever. *Their worm,* our Lord says, *does not die and their fire is never quenched.*

2nd point—Hear with the ears the wailings (of despair), howls (of pain), cries (of self reproach), blasphemies against Christ our Lord and all his saints because they are in heaven and *they* lost in hell. They do not all blaspheme, there is a sullen dreadful silence of despair; but blaspheme or not, they know and are convinced their chastisement is just. They know that too well; their consciences, their own minds judge them and tell them so. They appeared before Christ at death, their mind's eye was opened, they saw themselves, condemned themselves, despaired, asked for no mercy, and turned from that sight to bury themselves anywhere, even in hell; as a frightened or shamed child buries its head in the pillow they bury theirs in the pit. Neither do they cry with throat and tongue, they have none, but their wailing is an utterance that passes in their woeful thoughts. Nevertheless spirits as they are, they hear and understand each other and add to each other's woe. And if it fears you, brethren, to think of it, but to imagine it, when your ears are open to other and to cheerful living sounds, believe that it is worse to them that have nothing else to do but wail or listen to but wailing.

3rd point—Smell with an imaginary smell the smoke, the brimstone, the dregs and bilgewater of that pit, all that is foul and loathsome. The same must be said of here as has been said of eyes and ears. It is sin that makes them fuel to that fire: the blinding stifling tear-drawing remembrance of a crowd of sins is to them like smoke; stinging remorse is like the biting brimstone; their impurity comes up before them, they loved it once and breathed it, now it revolts them, it is to them like vomit and like dung, and they cannot quit themselves of it: why not? because they are guilty of it; it is *their own sin*; they wallowed in it willingly, now against their will they must for ever wallow.

Sight does not shock like hearing, sounds cannot so disgust as smell, smell is not so bitter as proper bitterness,[1] which is in taste; therefore for the

Fourth point—taste as with taste of tongue all that is bitter there, the tears ceaselessly and fruitlessly flowing; the grief over their hopeless loss; the worm of conscience, which is the mind gnawing and feeding on its own most miserable self.[2] It is still the same story: *they*, their sins are the bitterness, tasted sweet once, now taste most bitter; no worm but themselves gnaws them and gnaws no one but themselves —none from within, but devils have some power upon them from without; for Satan that they served, they are his slaves and he has them in prison, his own prison. Holy Joseph on earth was in prison and yet had charge of the other prisoners; after death holy Abraham was imprisoned in the grave, in limbo, and yet he received other holy souls, as it is said, *to his bosom*, that is / to rest with him; and in hell Satan makes his accomplices, his mates in crime, his rebel crew, to share their captain's torments. For their worm of conscience is still but a little one to his own, who is called the old serpent and the fiery dragon.

And still bitterness of taste is not so cruel as the pain that can be touched and felt. Seeing is believing but touch is the truth, the saying goes. Therefore in

The fifth point—touch and feel how those flames touch and are felt like burning by the souls. How keen and searching is the pain of fire! Worst of all to feel it in the naked soul or in a body that it cannot with its heat consume.

Can these things be? It is terrible to me to have to speak of them, but Christ spoke of them: they must then be true. Are they just?—Yes, because God is just. But you can yourselves see they are just: if you tell your child: Let your sister alone, do not beat her, or I will beat *you* / are you unjust to threaten him? And if he disobeys you and torments her still are you unjust to carry out your threat? Are *we* not warned by God? Is it unjust to forbid us murder, adultery, theft? Is it unjust to threaten punishment if we disobey? or if we have disobeyed to carry out the threat? Why, we were warned, I say: it is we who carry out the threat; we walk over hell's brink. Or is it that the punishment is greater than the fault? But, brethren, God is wise and just, he must be the judge: if he is so earnest to be obeyed that he forbids sin even under pain of hell, then surely great must that offence be which needs a penalty so great to fright us back from it. All will be punished according to their guilt, according to their knowledge and their power; there are light pains and heavy pains, *many stripes* and *few*; the heathen unwarned by faith, warned indeed but dimly warned by reason, may suffer little in that flame, but we that know what sin is and what hell is and, knowing, do the sin and brave the punishment, we shall suffer much. Alas! it is enough to say we shall suffer everlastingly. But no, my brethren, because by God's mercy we shall never see that place at all.

If you are terrified (I wish you, brethren, for once this much evil, I wish you to feel terror) *turn* where?[1]—*to Christ our Lord* and to his heart that feels and understands what pain and fear and desolation are—all in a word that you can ever feel on earth. There are souls that would not believe in his coming before he came or else, afterwards, that he had come, died and were lost by unbelief: you are not of those, thank God for that. There are other souls that believed in Christ and would not keep his commandments, died and were lost too: some of you are like those in the sin but not in the punishment, thank God for that. We have the fate of others before our eyes for our warning; our sins are like theirs but not our fate—not hitherto: let us while we can make ourselves safe, *make our election sure*. How? By hope, by prayer, by casting ourselves upon God's mercy. O Jesus, O alas Jesus Christ our Lord, we are sinners, spare us; we have done what others have been damned for, spare us; they died impenitent, they lie in hell, we are on earth, there is time yet, we are sorry for our sins, we do repent, thou spare us. Lamb of God that takest away the sins of the world, spare us O Lord. Lamb of God that takest away the sins of the world, graciously hear us, O Lord. Lamb of God . . . have mercy on us. Hail Mary.

ON DEATH

Preparatory prayer.

Introductory remark—Death is certain and uncertain, certain to come, uncertain when and where. Did any man yet escape death?—Adam lived long, Methusalem longer, near 1000 years, but died. It is *appointed* to men once to die, once at least: Enoch and Elias the prophets are living yet, God preserves their life, but their death is appointed, it is foretold in Scripture:[2] they too will die. Once to die: some have died twice, been raised to life after death, as Lazarus and many others, but then they died again; twice they had the pangs of death; they did not escape. It is appointed to man once to die and after this the judgment: these men were not judged, God foresaw and put off judgment at their first death, but they died again and are judged now. We do not hope to be raised again, if we did what real difference would it make? The truth remains then, it is appointed to men to die, and we shall die.

And it is uncertain when or where—not so *un*certain as it is certain
that we shall die; a man sick to death has a strong likelihood that he
will die, say, within a week and in that house or even in that bed;
still there hangs over death a great, a harassing uncertainty. *When*
shall each of us die?—I cannot tell, but *all within a century* (I say what
no one doubts), some long hence, some soon, one perhaps this year.
I press it no further: it is a great uncertainty. *And where?*—Some
here no doubt and some elsewhere; some in their beds, others suddenly in some unlikely place, where now they little think: this too
is a great uncertainty. But one thing is certain and let that be the

1st prelude to the meditation—*We shall die in these bodies.* I see you living
before me, with the mind's eye, brethren, I see your corpses: those
same bodies that sit there before me are rows of corpses that will be.
And I that speak to you, you hear and see me, you see me breathe
and move: this breathing body is my corpse and I am living in my
tomb. This is one thing certain of your place of death; you are there
now, you sit within your corpses; look no farther: there where you
are you will die.

2nd prel.—What we want is so deep a sense of the certainty and
uncertainty of death, to have death so before us, that we may dread
to sin now and when we die die well.

1st point—The terrors of death—(1) It is the greatest of earthly evils.
It robs us of our all. Do you love sunshine, starlight, fresh air,
flowers, fieldsports?—Despair then: you will see them no more; they
will be above ground, you below; you will lose them all. Do you love
townlife, homelife, the cheerful hearth, the sparkling fire, company,
the social glass, laughter, frolic among friends?—Despair then: you
will have no more of them for ever, the churchyards are full of such
men as you are now, that feasted once and now worms feast on; the
dark day is coming; slow or sudden, death is coming; then rotten-
ness and dust and utterly to be forgotten. Do you dearly love wife or
husband, child or friend?—Despair then: death shall part you, from
your dearest, though they may hang round your bed yet you shall
go into the dark unbefriended, alone. Do you love money?—Despair
then: death shall make you drop it, death shall wring it from you;
though your funeral were costly, yet poor shall you lie. Do you love
fame in your day and to make yourself felt, to play your part somewhere in the world? do you take an interest in politics and watch
how the world goes?—Despair then: the world will do without you
and you must do without the world, for you shall be where you cannot stir hand or foot to make it worse or better. Do you love what is
better than all these, to do God's work, to do good to others, to give
alms, to pray, to make God's kingdom come? Make haste then,
work while it is day, and despair of any other chance than this: *the*

night is coming, says your master, *when no man can work* and again *There is neither work nor reason nor wisdom nor knowledge in the grave where thou art hastening fast.* And again Ecclus. xiv 17. *Before thy death do justice, for there is no finding food in the grave* | 'Ante obitum tuum operare justitiam, quoniam non est apud inferos invenire cibum.' On one ground or another, do you love life, dear life?—Despair, all of you: death is coming that shall rob you even of dear life. Is there no help?—No, none. If it were poverty we might escape it or not escaping it we could bear it; we should still have life. If it were pain and sickness we might escape them or not escaping them get over them or not getting over them we might still live. If it were shame, if it were the death of others—but no, we may lose health, wealth, fame, friends, peace of mind, and all that makes life dear and still keep, and glad to keep, dear life; and then besides, we need not lose them—death might be our first sickness, we might live all our lives well to do, honoured, with our best friends round us; but *life we must lose* and with life all the goods of life; other evils need not come, but death, *the worst of evils*, must come, and rob us of our only chance, rob us of our all. This is the first terror of death: it is the worst of earthly evils and robs us of our all, and it is the only evil certain to come.

(2) The next terror of death are *the pains of death*. Death mostly is the end of fatal sickness and when is sickness, fatal sickness, without pain? And its pain is not as other pains, which either we surmount and get the better of or at least we can keep up with; but fatal sickness and its pains are for the dying man a losing battle, he bears them and is worse, he may have patience and they do not spare, bad they may be but they will be worse, things will come to the worse and then not mend, making the proverb a lie; the pains of fatal sickness are the pains of death; a woman is in pangs and she brings forth a child, she is at peace and from her pangs has come new life, but we shall be in pangs and bring forth death. I do not mean that the pain of dying is always great; I know well and have seen that often it is not so, so far as from outside we can judge; but often it is; and great pain or little or none, it is terror enough that life is ebbing away. And even for those who seem to die peacefully, if they have their senses to the last, one cannot without shrinking think of that very last moment when flesh and spirit are rent asunder and the soul goes out into the cold, leaving the body its companion dear a corpse behind. This will be to every one of you; I see your corpses here before me.

But there are worse pangs of death than those of the body. There is the sweat of fear, *there is the dread of what is to come after*. Saints have feared: St. Hilarion, St. Jerome, that all their lives did penance, trembled when they came to pass away. The Devil rages then, for he knows that his time is short: one thought of mortal sin[1] at the last gasp is enough, it will do his work for ever, and he watches well, he knows when death is near. And what, my brethren, if you should find yourselves dying and in mortal sin? hurriedly you will send for the priest, counting the minutes till he comes; and what if he should be away, some miscarriage happen, as there always may, even where all seems best provided for? I could tell you even from my own experience tales to make you tremble and more from that of others. The last sacraments are a tower of strength if you can get them, but who can tell you that you will? God does not promise that. Will you trust a priest? May not even a wise and zealous man for once be careless or misjudge and think there is no danger when there is? Few are the parish priests that never, as the saying is, let one slip through their hands. (Here one may tell the story of the woman that died calling on St. Winefred to curse Fr — for not coming; also of the woman in Page Street, Liverpool, when the bell was not answered, no one knows why; and of my man in Wm. Henry Street.)[2] If things like this should happen to any of you make an act of sorrow for your sins, earnestly asking God to give you the grace, which he will: do this and you will be saved; but yet I say it is a wretched wretched thing to die in fear, without the sacraments.

(3) The third terror of death is its uncertainty, that *it may be sudden* and find us unprepared. This is worse than the rest. Few people die sudden deaths, but a few do and what of those few? Here you are many, most of you then will not die suddenly, but some few of you will; some few, some one or two that hear me, will die suddenly. There are dangers by land and sea, wrecks, railway accidents, lightning, mischances with machinery, fires, falls; there are murders —I have talked with the widows and the orphaned children of suddenly murdered men; there are heart complaints and other sudden strokes of death. Now a sudden death *need* not be a bad death; holy men have sometimes prayed to die suddenly and their prayer been heard; it has its advantages, for if we then are in the grace of God we have no time to fall away; but yet consider, brethren, how many men live in unbroken mortal sin, who if they died suddenly must therefore die in mortal sin; consider how many more go indeed to confession and are forgiven, but sin again shortly and so spend most of their days in mortal sin and if they were cut off suddenly would (not certainly indeed, but) *most likely*, O dreadful likelihood! be then in mortal sin. Others would be as likely as not, others not so likely, but even one chance, how terrible it is! And then follows the judgment of damnation. This is a terror then that far exceeds the rest.

Second point—The comforts of death—God our maker, who knows the clay we are made of; God our father, who never can forget his child; God our Redeemer, who died to save us, has a special providence over death. He knows our utter need, he is most helpful when our need is sorest. Therefore he has provided these three things, the last sacraments, the grace of contrition, and holy hope.

(1) *The Last Sacraments*—These are the sacrament of Penance, the sacrament of Extreme Unction, and the Holy Communion. The first is the most necessary, but by all means have them all. Of *Penance* I need say nothing here except that whether it is for yourself or for others, you should send for the priest in time while the sick man has his senses, that he may make his confession duly; nevertheless if it is too late for that the priest's absolution without confession is enough to save the soul, supposing—always supposing this—there was any sorrow for sin there. We may always suppose there was some sorrow for sin if the sick man wished himself to confess; that is a sign of itself almost certain and where that has been the case and absolution has been given the soul will be saved. But where there is no willingness to confess the priest's absolution is of no use; it cannot forgive, for there is no sorrow. This is the first

The *Holy Communion* can after confession be given. It cannot be given when the senses have failed, therefore again send in time. When the priest gives communion with the words: *Accipe, frater* (or *soror*), *viaticum* etc / Receive, brother (or *sister*), *the provision of the Body of our Lord J. C., and may he preserve thee from the malicious enemy and bring thee safe to life everlasting. Amen* instead of the common ones: *Corpus Dñi N. J. C.* etc he supposes you to be near death or at least in danger of death, against which he provides you; for *viaticum* means money, provision, for a journey, that is / the journey to the other world. And so given the sacrament may be received after taking food and at any time of day and even if one had been to communion that very morning. Otherwise there is no difference and whether we are to live or die the communion always does the soul good. Alas! it is often the only communion that the dying man has made or the first for many, many years; and a weary sick and dying man is in poor dispositions for this most holy and most heavenly sacrament. Nevertheless let him have it; nay, he is bound, he must have it. But if he is ready to vomit he cannot be allowed to receive it, the risk to the Lord's Body is too great; therefore, brethren, pray, as our Lord said *Pray that your flight may not be in the winter*, so I say here, Pray now that you may not suffer from that evil in your last sickness, but may be able to receive the Lord's Body.

This is the second of God's deathbed mercies, the second comforting sacrament of death, the Holy Communion. And indeed what a thing it is to think that Christ should be willing so to be carried to a dying sinner. Is not this the good shepherd going to seek the lost sheep! Going to seek it, and where? Alas, brethren, to what filthy places have I not myself carried the Lord of Glory! and worse than filthy places, dens of shame. Pray that when your last hour comes you may make him a welcome in a place becoming and respectable and, much more, in a humble penitent desirous heart.

The third of the last sacraments is the *Holy Oil*. Now this is called one of the last sacraments, but it is not meant for death only; rather it is meant for life, to raise up from sickness and to save life, and this I have seen it do and suddenly and so that the physicians were amazed at it. Do not then be such fools as to neglect it, for that neglect may cost your life; God may have meant to raise you up by it if you had asked for it in time, but after a while may mean that it should not help your body; nay, beware that it may not come too late to help your soul. For now we are speaking of death, when, as I am supposing, this sacrament is to be a *last* sacrament in truth. In that case it is meant to strengthen you for your death agony, for the last struggle with your spiritual enemy: that is its effect in this life. Moreover it quits you of either all or some of the remains of sin; of the debt of penalty left, as you know, after the guilt of sin has been forgiven; it is a sacrament of indulgence, better than any indulgence you could gain or others for you after you are gone: that is its effect in the other life. Moreover this: holy oil works with virtue on the man that lies stark and insensible as well as on the one that has his senses. Have it then, send for it; it may save your soul, it may save you from the fiery bath of purgatory. This is the third comforter among the sacraments of death.

(2) But now suppose you cannot get the last sacraments or that they delay to come and you are in danger and in fear and trembling, knowing or at least fearing you are in a state of sin: God has provided still another way. Make an act of sorrow for your sins, *an act of contrition: repent.* True contrition, that is / perfect sorrow for sin, is when we are sorry, and sorry for God's sake. Now people think that it is hard to have so pure a sorrow; that to be sorry because we are in danger to be damned may be easy, only that is not enough without the sacraments; but to be sorry for God's sake and not our own—which is contrition—is a thing for saints or the devout and not for ordinary men or loth and lingering sinners. But easy or hard, remember, brethren, this and root and rivet it into your hearts, that sorrow for sin is a gift of God and that if you ask for it it will be given. Do not enquire if you have got it: ask for it, beg and pray for it, with tears, with inward tears at least, and strong cries of the heart beseech God to give it you. Summon your last strength for that.

You will have it, you will get it in time enough. God knows our need. I repeat it a third time, God knows our need. Luke xi 11–13. 'which of you asks his father for bread? and will he give him a stone? or a fish? will he for the fish give him a serpent? or if he ask for an egg will he reach him a scorpion? If then you that are bad know how to give good gifts to your children how much more will your heavenly father give the good spirit', as the spirit of contrition, of sorrow for sin—'to those that ask him!' He will give it, he will not see you perish. Pray for it too to the Sacred Heart of Christ. Get a crucifix hung, if you can, before your bed: looking towards that pray your just dying saviour to look on you now at your death. You will never be refused. Say 'Agnus Dei' etc over and over again. And pray to the Blessed Virgin: 'pray for us sinners now *and at the hour of our death*'. Get others too to pray round you. Make an act of sorrow for your sins, then fall again to praying God to give you sorrow. And for your comfort, know that as soon as the wish to be forgiven is truly in your heart you either are forgiven there and then or that before you pass away infallibly you will be.[1]

(3) This leads me to the third thing that sheds comfort over death, *holy hope*. Though you should be unable either to get the sacraments or to make (or at least feel sure that you have made) a true act of sorrow for your sins and that you are forgiven, nevertheless go on hoping *and praying* (as far as your state allows) that God will save you, though it should be, as it might be, only at the very instant of the soul leaving the body. Hope is an anchor cast in heaven: as long as you do not let it go, hold it must and lost you cannot be.

I have been speaking hitherto of the hour of death, but there are safeguards against a bad death, *preparations for a good death*, that may and should be made long beforehand.

The first of these is *a good life* and to live in the fear of death, especially in lying down to rest at night; for you do not know that you will see morning: dangers are greatest at night. *The better you serve God the better and more special will his providence be over your death*: of this hereafter. In general the rule is true: as you live so you will die. You will tell me you have known of men who lived for years, for all their lives, in sin and got the sacraments and seemed to make good ends. I answer that I have no doubt these persons were saved, but that they ran a frightful risk and that their salvation was due to their never altogether giving over holy hope. They lived hoping to repent and so they did repent, but bitter is their penance in purgatory. Their mind was a mixture of hope and presumption; hope got the better and they were saved: if you say that you wish for nothing better, to live at ease and turn to God at last, I warn you that in your case presumption seems to turn the balance and it is likely, so living in sin, that in sin you will die and be damned.

What then are we to do?—Hope in God to be saved, pray to him every day to save you, *pray for the grace of final perseverance.* (Explain this.) Hope in God not to sin, pray to him to keep you from ever sinning mortally. If unhappily you sin still hope: repent; hope in God to bring you to repentance, go to the sacrament of penance. If you cannot bring yourself to that / hope in God to bring it about. Always, always hope and pray to be saved. Perhaps one earnest hope and prayer to be saved is enough to win the grace of final perseverance; but we do not know, God has not willed we should, how soon our prayer is granted, how long we must pray before our names are written for ever in the book of life: therefore pray always, every day till death, pray without ceasing for it. And in particular mean the words in the Hail Mary 'and at the hour of our death' and always go to communion with this intention, saying in your hearts Amen to the priest's words 'Corpus Dnī N. J. C. . . . vitam aeternam'. Moreover Christ our Lord promised the Blessed Margaret Mary (to whom he revealed the Sacred Heart) that he would grant the grace of final penitence to all who should communicate for the first Fridays of 9 months running.

Some other means to get the grace of final perseverance or final penitence are to *interest ourselves in the salvation of others,* as by getting them the last sacraments, in return for which charity God has sometimes granted it to great sinners; and in general all charity, *almsdeeds* and other good deeds. Tob. iv 7–12. 'Ex subsa. tua fac eleemosynam et noli avertere faciem tuam ab ullo paupere; ita enim fiet ut nec a te avertatur facies Dnī. quomodo potueris ita esto misericors: si multum tibi fuerit abundanter tribue, si exiguum tibi fuerit etiam exiguum libenter impertiri stude. Praemium enim bonum tibi thesaurizas in die nectis.; quoniam eleemosyna ab omni peccato et a morte liberat et non patietur animam ire in tenebras. Fiducia magna erit coram summo Deo eleemosyna omnibus facientibus eam.' Let no one excuse himself; for all can do some service and most can sometimes give money. If you had set your heart on some small thing you would soon raise the money: set your heart on saving your soul and raise money for that. Have masses said for that intention. *Make yourselves friends from the mammon of injustice,* that is / by laying out well money and the other goods of this life, *that when you fail,* that is / die, *they,* that is / the friends in heaven you will have made, *may receive you into everlasting dwellings. The Blessed Virgin, St. Joseph* patron of a good death, and all *the saints* you shall have honoured or made gifts to in life will assist you in death. Also get and wear the brown *scapular* and the medal of the Immaculate Conception. All these things will be comfort, felt or unfelt, support, and strength at death. Of all devotions the two which will serve you best at death are those to the Sacred Heart and to the Blessed Virgin.

You should know that *there is a special providence over death*. God provides for everything but most for man: *not a sparrow falls to the ground*, Christ says, *without your Father* and *You*, he says, *are worth more than many*, that is / any number of, *sparrows*. He provides for all that happens to us, but most for the most important; therefore most for death: *the hairs of your head*, Christ says, *are numbered*; if when the hair is parted God counts and knows how many hairs fall to the right side and how many to the left how much more does he take account of the parting of soul and body! It is seen again and again, I have seen it myself and speak of what I know, that people get the last sacraments just in time, that some happy chance or other falls out in their favour. And when we do not see the providence it may still be there and working in some secret way. Hope for it then and pray for it and yet fear and tremble, *work out your salvation in fear and trembling*. For I must end as I began. One of God's providences is by warnings—the deaths of others, sermons, dangers, sicknesses, a sudden thought: beware, beware of neglecting a warning. This very discourse of mine, this meditation, is a warning. A warning leaves a man better or worse, does him good or harm; never leaves him as it finds him. Some are cut off suddenly in mortal sin without time for either the sacraments or an act of contrition or even of hope. If the holy oil is administered before death while they lie insensible, yet without *any* sorrow for sin it cannot save them; and many are for long spaces of time together habitually sinning and without sorrow, hope, or the wish to repent. Does God then cut them off purposely in sin?—No, for his providence here is *always in our favour*; but he may with a provoking sinner use no special providence and let things take their ordinary course: now in the ordinary course of things a certain number must die suddenly by accident, malice, or disease. This is a terrible possibility. But, I repeat, there is a special providence over death.

Here recall the two preludes and end by exhorting them to hope, to repent, to begin now their preparation for death, and always to pray for final perseverance or final penitence. See also the meditation before for a colloquy to be made, if suitable, on their behalf.

PRIVATE NOTES 1883–5

Retreat at Beaumont, September 1883.
Dublin meditation points, 1884–5.

RETREAT AT BEAUMONT SEPT. 3–10 INCL. 1883

In the Med. de Processu Peccatorum[1] an old and terribly afflicting thought and disgust drove me to Fr Kingdon.[2] He advised me not further to dwell on the thought

I had lights on the Particular Judgment and subjects belonging, entered elsewhere.[3] But other notes I did not make till the 8th as below

Sept 8 Med. on the Baptism.

Our Lord asked Our Lady's blessing on his work and I thought how good it was to ask her blessing on anything we undertake and meant to do this more formally henceforward

For thus it behoves us to fulfil all justice: I remembered Fr Whitty's[4] teaching how a great part of life to the holiest of men consists in the well performance, the performance, one may say, of ordinary duties And this comforted against the thought of the little I do in the way of hard penances; for if I am not now called to those it is better not to bewail my cowardice or nonperformance in the matter but to say thus, in such and such an appointed way, it behoves me to fulfil all justice

Also since God gives me at present no great humiliations and I am not worthy of them and did not accept them well when they came to welcome the small ones whenever such shall occur

During this retreat I have much and earnestly prayed that God will lift me above myself to a higher state of grace, in which I may have more union with him, be more zealous to do his will, and freer from sin. Yesterday night it was 15 years exactly since I came to the Society. In this evening's meditation on the Temptation I was with our Lord in the wilderness in spirit and again begged this, acknowledging it was a great grace even to have the desire. For indeed it is a pure one and it is long since I have had so strong and spiritual a one and so persistent. I recommended to him our novices newly come today or last night and those who should this morning have taken their vows. And I had other good thoughts I do not put down.

Also in some med. today I earnestly asked our Lord to watch over my compositions, not to preserve them from being lost or coming to nothing, for that I am very willing they should be, but they might not do me harm through the enmity or imprudence of any man or my own; that he should have them as his own and employ or not employ them as he should see fit. And this I believe is heard[1]

Sept. 9. In meditating on the Crucifixion I saw how my asking to be raised to a higher degree of grace was asking also to be lifted on a higher cross. Then I took it that our Lord recommended me to our Lady and her to me.

Sept. 10. The walk to Emmaus. This morning in Thanksgiving after mass much bitter thought but also insight in things. And the above meditation was made in a desolate frame of mind; but towards the end I was able to rejoice in the comfort our Lord gave those two men, taking that for a sample of his comfort and them for representatives of all men comforted, and that it was meant to be of universal comfort to men and therefore to me and that this was all I really needed; also that it was better for me to be accompanying our Lord in his comfort of them than to want him to come my way to comfort me

DUBLIN MEDITATION POINTS[2]

22 FEB. 1884 TO 25 MARCH 1885

Feb. 22 St. Peter's Confession.

Comp: the scene of the confession; fruit

Whom do men say that I the son of man am?—Whom do *men* say that the *son of man* is? Also there is the suggestion of son of God. Consider what men now say of Christ.

Thou art the Christ the son of the living God—Praise our Lord in the words of this confession.—There are two acknowledgments, that our Lord was the Christ and that he was son of God. The Christ is the chosen and anointed man, the Son of God is God

Friday Feb. 29 Christ crowned with thorns

Christ was crowned by Gentiles King of the Jews. King of the Jews means not only king over the Jews but also born of the Jews to be king over others, the Gentiles. These men crowned Christ in mockery, mocking both probably at the Jews and him, at him for claiming to be a king and at the Jews for claiming to have one. Nevertheless their act was mystical and both the crown and the adorations were types of his true rights and royalty

Crown him king over yourself, of your heart

Wish to crown him King of England, of English hearts[1] and of Ireland and all Christendom and all the world

The crown is of thorns. Consider Christ's bodily pain, then his mental

Sunday March 2—Christ tempted in the wilderness

He was led by the spirit into the wilderness. Pray to be guided by the Holy Ghost in everything. Consider that he was now led to be tempted and the field and arena of the struggle was a wilderness, where the struggle would be intenser but not perhaps more really perilous—to a fallen man, as Satan might suppose him to be. Here admire our Lord in this struggle and this servants St. Antony, St. Cuthbert, and others

Command that these stones be made bread: The temp

The Lance and Nails March 7—

Comp. Calvary after Christ's death; grace devotion to the Passion

Seeing Christ's body nailed consider the attachment of his will to God's will. Wish to be as bound to God's will in all things, in the attachment of your mind and attention to prayer and the duty in hand; the attachment of your affections to Christ our Lord and his wounds instead of any earthly object.

March 8 The Transfiguration

The sight of our Lord's body as a remedy for temptation

The thought of his mind and genius against vainglory and you could practise what you did at Roehampton in the tertianship, entering into the joy of our Lord, not his joys but the joys of him

March 21—The Five Wounds

Consider our Lord's attachment to God's will at all times and this attachment ended in the very nailing of his body to the Cross. Try to attach yourself more to God's will and detach yourself from your own by prayer at beginning things

The piercing of Christ's side. The sacred body and the sacred heart seemed waiting for an opportunity of discharging themselves and testifying their total devotion of themselves to the cause of man

Our Lady's Sorrows—

(1) Simeon's prophecy, (2) the flight into Egypt, (3) the loss for 3 days, (4) the meeting on the way of the Cross, (5) the standing by the cross, (6) The entombment, (7)?

(1) Fear, (2) discomfort, (3) care, (4) . . . (5) helpless grief, (6) bereavement

I set the Lord before me etc—not moved. Here consider what help is God's presence. Rules of modesty

Therefore I rejoice. This joy is in hope. Christ's joy in spite of his sorrows. Wish to enter into this

Ways of life

Corpus Christi

(1) Preciousness of our Lord's body, born of the Blessed Virgin of David's line, crucified, raised from the dead, seated in heaven; united to Christ's soul; united to the Word. Appreciate. Feel your unworthiness.

(2) Its mystery; it binds the Church into one, bodily into one. It is the pledge and means of our immortality. Revere this mystery.

(3) The good it has done, sanctifying Christians, in Mass, Communion, as viaticum. Thanksgiving

(4) It is put into my unworthy hands as a priest

June—Nobis datus: here consider the Blessed Sacrament as put into your hands, as yours by your priesthood and by communion. Then how well it should be treated. Consider occasions, Mass, visits

Nobis natus ex intacta virgine—Here look on our Lady as the bestower of the Blessed Sacrament.

Man was created to praise etc

Praise by the office expressly meant for this; by the Mass, especially the Gloria

And the other things on earth—Take it that weakness, ill health, every cross is a help. Calix quem Pater meus dedit mihi non bibam illum?

Facere nos indifferentes—with the elective will, not the affective essentially; but the affective will will follow

I must ask God to strengthen my faith or I shall never keep the particular examen. I must say the stations for this intention. Resolve also to keep it particularly even in the present state of lethargy

Consider how the Blessed Virgin praised God—her obedience, her sorrows, her prayer, her work, her holy death

Rejoice in her glory. Consider the meeting between Christ and his mother and how the joy of seeing Christ our Lord is from having lived for him. Pray therefore earnestly to do this

Consider the particular examen and the prayers for it; also Rules of Modesty

Foundation—Exercise

Man was created—Here consider what Father D. M.[1] was talking about.

Save his soul—Consider in this life the meaning of these words. Consider peace, contentment, a good conscience

And the other things—Resolve how to get more use of them

Man was created[1]—Say the man Christ was created to praise etc and so to save his soul, that is / enter into his glory. And the other things as in his train

The love of the Son for the Father leads him to take a created nature and in that to offer him sacrifice. The sacrifice might have been unbloody; by the Fall it became a bloody one

Sunday Sept. 14

Sept. 30—St. Michael

(1) Consider the services to God of men and angels. Admire the perfection of the angels' service, of St. Michael's, of your guardian angel's. The service of men is very different, but good and in its measure perfect. Consider your own misery and try as best you can to rise above it, by punctuality, and the particular examen; by fervour at office, mass, and litanies; by good scholastic work; by charity if you get opportunities. Ask St. Michael's help: remember the devotion of St. Francis of Assisi towards him and of Blessed Peter Favre towards all angels

Wednesday Oct 15—2+2

St. Cecily[2]—Praise God for her martyrdom

She told Valerian he could not see the angel till he was baptized. Beati mundo corde, quoniam ipsi Deum videbunt, God and the things of God. The heart is what rises towards good, shrinks from evil, recognising the good or the evil first by some eye of its own. We ought to look to God first in everything, to seek first the kingdom of God and his justice, his rightness, to be right with God and God to be king or first principle, ἀρχήν, in us. Pray for this more, in matters of interest, of pleasure, and of will. Ask St. Cecily's help

Dec. 20—O Sapientia[3]

Desire this heavenly wisdom. Consider how the Scripture sets it above gold and all earthly goods, precious stones, by which you may understand gifts of mind for instance. Wish to see by its light

Consider what it is. Personally wisdom is Christ our Lord, as applied in this antiphon; also God the Holy Ghost as the spirit of wisdom; also the Blessed Virgin in that being which she had from the beginning, as expressed in the Book of Wisdom. Then also it is grace and charity

St. James says that God will give it to those who ask it and our Lord says your Father will give the good spirit to those who ask it

Attingens a fine usque ad finem fortiter—Wish for the strength it gives to reach through your life

Dec. 22—St. Thomas

Our Lord said to him before his Passion / I am the way, the truth, and the life: apply these words to the Resurrection, for if St. Thomas had thought of them he would not have doubted or disbelieved

Dec. 24, Christmas Eve—

Mary and Joseph were poor, strangers, travellers, married, that is to say / respectable, honest, for this is a condition in charity, to consider to whom you give and family life is the greatest safeguard

Their trials were hurry, discomfort, cold, inhospitality, dishonour

Their comfort was Christ's birth. Thank God for your delivery of today. Here think the Gloria in excelsis and bring yourself to leave out of sight your own trials rejoicing over Christ's birth. Wish a happy Christmas and all its blessings to all your friends.

Dec. 26—St. Stephen

St. Stephen's preparation for martyrdom—his labour, his zeal, his fulness of the spirit of God, on which the Scripture dwells so strongly

His love of his persecutors

Jan. 3 St. John, octave—Sic eum volo etc

Consider the charity of these two to one another and what they found out for each other, St. Peter that he should not betray Our Lord, St. John that he was to wait for God's coming.

Combining the two lives, active and contemplative, and here consider Angelo Crover, David Walsh etc

Jan. 5—The three holy Kings

We have seen his star in the east. They were watching for it. Pray to be on the watch for God's providence, not determining where or when but only sure that it will come. And apply this to all your troubles and hopes, to England and Ireland, to growth in virtue

Their offerings. Apply these thus: spiritual duties to Christ's godhead, frankincense; powers of mind to the service of his incarnation, gold; mortification to his passion and death, myrrh

Jan. 6—Continuing the above, pray, according to Fr Foley's instructions[1] of tonight, for the spirit of love in all your doings. For

indeed it seems a spirit of fear I live by. Consider the love shewn in our Lord's appearance as a child and in the holy family

Recommend to him with the holy Kings all Gentiles

Sunday in Oct. of Epiphany—

Christ's three manifestations: at Bethlehem, at the baptism, at Cana.

(1) Consider to whom: in (i) to the three Magi and by them to the Gentiles; in (ii) to St. John Baptist, his disciples, and the Jews; in (iii) to Christ's disciples. There were really other manifestations, as the Presentation and the Gloria in Excelsis, the questioning of the Doctors in the Temple (this last is the Gospel of the day)

(2) Consider as what: in (i) as a child, helpless; in (ii) as in the disguise of a sinner, in (iii) as in the disguise of common social life

(3) By what means: in (i) of inanimate nature in the star, in (ii) of the divine Persons, in (iii) of his own incarnated power

Jan. 19—The devils who tormented the demoniac—pray not to be tormented

Remark the breaking of the bonds and how the swine broke loose and drowned themselves. Remark the suicide. The man did not kill himself, because the devils were not allowed to drive him to that. They are therefore fettered themselves

The Gerasenes asked him to depart, because they were *possessed by fear*; the cured demoniac asked to go with him. The swine threw themselves into the sea, the Gerasenes threw away their salvation by sending Christ back onto the sea.

The devils ask not to be sent out of the *country* (St Mark, I think), but St Luke says not sent into the abyss. It seems their request was granted. Where then did they continue to live, what did they possess? Was it those who ate of the drowned swine's flesh?*

March.

St. Gregory the Great[1]—(1) His meeting with the boys in the market place

Angeli—natural endowments; De ira—state of sin; Alleluia—employment in God's service. Consider under the first point the best you know of England, under the second the worst, under the third the hopes of its conversion and pray for that

The woman taken in adultery[2]

The writing on the ground has something to do with the writing

* A single line has been drawn across this meditation from the date 'Jan. 19' to the last words. [Ed.]

of the tables of the law. Perhaps Christ meant to suggest that they must wait till he had drawn up the law according to which he wished to decide, for they addressed him as a new lawgiver

Let him that is without sin etc—Pray to keep to this spirit and as far as possible rule in speaking of Mr. Gladstone[1] for instance

March 16—The feeding of the five thousand[2]

St. Philip and St. Andrew: the one did, the other did not offer a helpful suggestion. Every effort is good; God can make much of little when he will make nothing out of nothing

March 17 St. Patrick—Recommend first to God the whole course of his life, thanking God for the way he is glorified in him; his exile and sufferings, his piety and patience; his selfsacrifice and zeal; his miracles and success. Consider his hymn:[3] it breathes an enthusiasm which as far as feeling goes I feel but my action does not answer to this

Ask his help for Ireland in all its needs and for yourself in your position

March 19—St. Joseph

He was thought the father of Christ our Lord. Therefore there was nothing in him visibly unworthy of what Christ visibly was. Consider how great then his holiness and his humility, for the thought, the mistake made, was itself a burden to him

He is the patron of the hidden life; of those, I should think, suffering in mind and as I do.[4] Therefore I will ask his help

The Annunciation—Consider the persons—On earth the Blessed Virgin. She was full of grace, that is / she had received and stored up in her every grace offered and now overflowed in the Son / Christ. So the preparation for grace is grace corresponded with

The angel doing his office, his function. Everyone is admirable in his function well performed, work well undertaken, and this also is matter of preparation

RETREAT IN IRELAND, 1888

January 1st to 4th: Private Notes.
January 6th: The Three Epiphanies.

RETREAT NOTES

Jan 1. 1888. St. Stanislaus' College, Tullabeg.[1]

Principium seu Fundamentum: 'Homo creatus est ut laudet' etc—
All moral good, all man's being good, lies in two things—in being
right, being in the right, and in doing right; in being on the right
side, on the side of good, and on that side of doing good. Neither of
these will do by itself. Doing good but on the wrong side, promoting
a bad cause, is rather doing wrong. Doing good but in no good cause
is no merit: of whom or what does the doer deserve well? Not at
any rate of God. Nor plainly is it enough to be on the right side and
not promote it.

But men are variously constituted to make much of one of these
things and neglect the other. The Irish think it enough to be Catholics or on the right side and that it is no matter what they say and
do to advance it; practically so, but what they think is that all they
and their leaders do to advance the right side is and must be right.
The English think, as Pope says for them, he can't be wrong whose
life is in the right. Marcus Aurelius seems in his Meditations to be
leading the purest and most unselfish life of virtue; he thinks, though
with hesitation, that Reason governs the Universe and that by this
life he ranks himself on the side of that Reason; and indeed, if this
was all he had the means of doing, it was enough; but he does not
know of any particular standard the rallying to which is the appointed signal of, taking God the sovereign Reason's, God the
Word's, side; and yet that standard was then raised in the world and
the Word and sovereign Reason was then made flesh and he persecuted it. And in any case his principles are principles of despair and,
again, philosophy is not religion.[2]

But how is it with me? I was a Christian from birth or baptism,
later I was converted to the Catholic faith, and am enlisted 20 years
in the Society of Jesus. I am now 44. I do not waver in my allegiance,
I never have since my conversion to the Church. The question is
how I advance the side I serve on. This may be inwardly or outwardly. Outwardly I often think I am employed to do what is of
little or no use. Something else which I can conceive myself doing

might indeed be more useful, but still it is an advantage for there to be a course of higher studies for Catholics in Ireland and that that should be partly in Jesuit hands; and my work and my salary keep that up. Meantime the Catholic Church in Ireland and the Irish Province in it and our College in that are greatly given over to a partly unlawful cause,[1] promoted by partly unlawful means, and against my will my pains, laborious and distasteful, like prisoners made to serve the enemies' gunners, go to help on this cause. I do not feel then that outwardly I do much good, much that I care to do or can much wish to prosper; and this is a mournful life to lead. In thought I can of course divide the good from the evil and live for the one, not the other: this justifies me but it does not alter the facts. Yet it seems to me that I could lead this life well enough if I had bodily energy and cheerful spirits. However these God will not give me. The other part, the more important, remains, my inward service.

I was continuing this train of thought this evening when I began to enter on that course of loathing and hopelessness which I have so often felt before, which made me fear madness and led me to give up the practice of meditation except, as now, in retreat and here it is again. I could therefore do no more than repeat *Justus es, Domine, et rectum judicium tuum* and the like, and then being tired I nodded and woke with a start. What is my wretched life? Five wasted years almost have passed in Ireland. I am ashamed of the little I have done, of my waste of time, although my helplessness and weakness is such that I could scarcely do otherwise. And yet the Wise Man warns us against excusing ourselves in that fashion. I cannot then be excused; but what is life without aim, without spur, without help? All my undertakings miscarry: I am like a straining eunuch.[2] I wish then for death: yet if I died now I should die imperfect, no master of myself, and that is the worst failure of all.[3] O my God, look down on me

Jan. 2—This morning I made the meditation on the Three Sins, with nothing to enter but loathing of my life and a barren submission to God's will. The body cannot rest when it is in pain nor the mind be at peace as long as something bitter distills in it[4] and it aches. This may be at any time and is at many: how then can it be pretended there is for those who feel this anything worth calling happiness in this world? There is a happiness, hope, the anticipation of happiness hereafter: it is better than happiness, but it is not happiness now. It is as if one were dazzled by a spark or star in the dark, seeing it but not seeing by it: we want a light shed on our way and a happiness spread over our life[5]

Afternoon: on the same—more loathing and only this thought, that I can do my spiritual and other duties better with God's help. In particular I think it may be well to resolve to make the examen every day at 1.15 and then say vespers and compline if not said before. I will consider what next

Jan. 3—Repetition of 1st and 2nd exercise—Helpless loathing. Then I went out and I said the Te Deum and yet I thought what was needed was not praise of God but amendment of life

Jan. 5th.—Repetition of meditations on Incarnation and Nativity —All that happens in Christendom and so in the whole world affected, marked, as a great seal, and like any other historical event, and in fact more than any other event, by the Incarnation; at any rate by Christ's life and death, whom we by faith hold to be God made man. Our lives are affected by the events of Roman history, by Caesar's victory and murder for instance. Yet one might perhaps maintain that at this distance of time individuals could not find a difference in their lives, except in what was set down in books of history and works of art, if Pompey instead of Caesar had founded the Empire or Caesar had lived 20 years longer.

But our lives and in particular those of religious, as mine, are in their whole direction, not only inwardly but most visibly and out-wardly, shaped by Christ's. Without that even outwardly the world could be so different that we cannot even guess it. And my life is determined by the Incarnation down to most of the details of the day. Now this being so that I cannot even stop it, why should I not make the cause that determines my life, both as a whole and in much detail, determine it in greater detail still and to the greater efficiency of what I in any case should do, and to my greater happiness in doing it?[1]

It is for this that St Ignatius speaks of the angel *discharging his mission*, it being question of action leading up to, as now my action leads from, the Incarnation. The Incarnation was for my salvation and that of the world: the work goes on in a great system and machinery which even drags me on with the collar round my neck though I could and do neglect my duty in it. But I say to myself that I am only too willing to do God's work and help on the know-ledge of the Incarnation. But this is not really true: I am not willing enough for the piece of work assigned me,[2] the only work I am given to do, though I could do others if they were given. This is my work at Stephen's Green. And I thought that the Royal University was to me what Augustus's enrolment was to St Joseph: *exiit sermo a Caesare Augusto etc.*; so resolution of the senate of the R. U. came to me, inconvenient and painful, but the journey to Bethlehem was inconvenient and painful; and then I am bound in justice, and paid. I hope to bear this in mind

Jan. 6th. Epiphany.—Yesterday I had ever so much light on the mystery of the feast and the historical interpretation of the gospel and last night on the Baptism and today on that and the calling of Nathanael and so on, more than I can easily put down. However I had better have at least some notes

The wise men were Magians, either Zoroastrians or at least of a religion or sect of philosophy (Sabaeism) in which astrology played a part. And astrology is astronomy, ordinary science, with an extraordinary science added. This is called after them *magic* and there is therefore according to the Scripture a good or 'white' magic, lawful in itself though positively or from its dangers it may be unlawful. That is, there is above all natural science a science which bridges over the gulf between human and superhuman knowledge, that is, enters a world of spirits, not departed souls but angels. And therefore natural bodies like the stars may exercise not only a natural, as by their light and weight, but also a preternatural influence on man. That they cannot determine his fate is plain from many reasons, among which I now see that those which convinced St Austin and St Gregory are good. For a horoscope is a momentary cast or determination of the whole heaven, to which according to the ancients, and we may say in truth, the earth is like a point: in this enormous, infinite, disproportion only one thing is to be considered, the aspect of the place of birth, that is the relation between that and the heavenly sphere; this alone decides the horoscope, for all differences here below, *within* the same aspect, so long as they make no difference in the horoscope itself, can count for nothing, any more than difference of position between the men or houses make any sensible difference in the parallelism of their shadows in the sun. So then two men born within a few seconds or minutes of one another, too few to change the horoscope and in the same street, must have the same fate; which is not the case.

But that the stars might not determine a fate but influence a man's constitution and with it his history is not inconceivable. From their great distance this is either small or at least difficult to observe: astronomy succeeds with difficulty in measuring for instance the heat shed by Sirius upon the earth; his actinism[1] may be more considerable: these are natural influences; it would seem that the Magians professed to observe preternatural, that is angelic, influences, and did so

The star was nothing to ordinary observers, perhaps not visible at all to them. For as in modern science most of the phenomena are known to astronomers, to the specialists, only; the public could scarcely remark if a star of the first magnitude were withdrawn from Orion; so still more with a secret art. So the Magi behave: nothing of *the star which appeared* or *how appeared*; it is *we have seen*; they speak of their art, their observation, magisterially. So that the star may even have been an altogether preternatural appearance, only visible after the practice of their art, some sort of evocation, had been gone through, not necessarily always there; as in fact it disappeared

If they were Persian Magians they may of course have come from Bactria and the borders of India. More reasonable to suppose the East because of its scriptural meaning, cf. Arabia east of the Holy Land. They were then of the Sabean,[1] the very ancient religion of those parts, in them seemingly not idolatrous. *The King of the Jews* more natural to people of that country; also that they should be chiefs or kings than if they had been Persians

Date of coming uncertain. For the mystery one would suppose *after* the Circumcision, by which Christ, so to say, qualified as King *of the Jews*. Twelve days $= 6+6$—Creation and Redemption, also a sort of mystical year, meaning the fulness of time. As a round number chosen for the feast[2] one would rather have expected 14, octave of New Year's day or 10. It must have been before the Purification, as then probably the Holy Family would leave Bethlehem[3]

Where is he etc. They know when, they ask where. Jerusalem troubled; their coming unwelcome, they knew more than the Jews, came to teach them. The Jews looked for the homage of the Gentiles: when it came it brought an unexpected circumstance with it, as God's works always do, the Gentiles the teachers, more honoured than themselves—though only in one particular

The Scribes called together secretly as far as possible, and the confirmation at least given secretly to the Wise Men. They go away by night, it may be by their own wish, to lose no time; but also by Herod's, that their going may be, unlike their coming, without noise. (Presumably night, for they see the star.) He sent them to Bethlehem, that is sent a guide to shew the road, courtesy so requiring. Writers ask why did he not send someone to report where they went. There could be a difficulty: it must be secretly, and from them. He could not commit himself by any known messenger; he would then seem to be recognising the Pretender. In the urgency he might not find a secret follower, and he thought there was no need. Then probably they do not enter Bethlehem. The stable was outside. The Bethlehemites saw little of them, did not know where they went. They would encamp near the spot and the dream was that very night; they set out before morning, and Herod altogether lost sight of them

Herod had meant to say on their return, that they were mistaken, this could not be the expected King etc, and afterwards to treat the matter as a conspiracy. No doubt he still more treated it so when he found himself 'mocked.' He probably does not act at once, but waits some weeks or months for a pretext, for the conspiracy to show itself. But the Bethlehemites had no plot and little knowledge on the subject. There was the story of the shepherds, but, so to say, nothing had followed it. After the Purification the Holy Family had probably disappeared. Herod of course availed himself of the registration and found St Joseph's name and place of abode and so marked out Christ for death; but not as a likely, rather as an unlikely, case. For by enquiring at Nazareth it would have appeared that the birth of Joseph's child at Bethlehem must have been a chance (and no doubt they had stayed at home till the last date possible), so that there could not well have been a plot. When Herod acted at last he must have pretended a conspiracy, required a confession, and getting none made this proof of general guilt, and so justified a general slaughter. The number of children killed cannot have been great, *a bimatu et infra*, that is probably from the beginning of the second year, one full year from birth.

The Magians had been clear about the star shewing the fact of the Christ's *being now* born, and born within a year: they did not know or they did not tell Herod it meant he was born at the hour of the star's appearance. Some of the children born within the year may have left Bethlehem; Herod would ascertain this and have them killed where found, but no doubt most were still at Bethlehem, and it would be a point with him to strike suddenly and once only, to give no alarm; he must then have meant the Nazareth murder to take place on the same day as the Bethlehem one. It was then the night before this day probably that St Joseph was warned and fled. When Herod heard this he must have then at last suspected this was the most dangerous of his rivals, and have been tortured by the thought till he died. He must have thought his agents had betrayed him too.

Why to Egypt, not Syria? Perhaps it is nearer or no farther; since Herod's kingdom included Abylina[1] in Syria. Secondly it was less suspicious to go Jerusalem wards, than northwards, and less easy to track. Thirdly extradition from the Syrian Princes was easier than from Egypt, which was most jealously watched by Rome. And if Herod heard anything of the way the Holy Family went this must have surprised and baffled him yet more

Remark that Herod died long before the pretender that he wanted to destroy was of age to do anything and so indeed did his son Archelaus, in whose more especial interest he might be thought to have acted. And at his own death his kingdom was broken up, and at his son Archelaus' death its best part was forfeited altogether, and all this not by a Jewish pretender but by the Romans. Then his son Antipas did live to see Christ proclaimed King of the Jews and had him sent to him and put in his power, with even the leave and the wish for him to use that power, and he put it aside as wholly needless. And then Christ died by Roman sentence, the same sentence that had divided Herod's kingdom. And when these crimes against Christ were all over, as if then it nothing mattered, Herod Agrippa came to inherit most of Herod the Great's kingdom. Antipas too finding himself assured in his position[1] and free from rivals affected a more than Messiasship, a godhead, himself and with applause; and for it miserably died. So wholly futile was all this wicked worldliness

Defuncti sunt enim, whereas in the first dream it had been said *Futurum est enim ut Herodes*. St Jerome therefore concludes the Scribes too had sought Christ's death. And therefore we cannot be sure it was at once on Herod's death as at a signal that St Joseph was called from Egypt, especially as it had been *till I shall tell thee*, not *till Herod dies*

The Baptism etc—St John baptised by immersion. (1) For his baptism did not differ in form from Christ's seemingly except in the words used; now early Christian baptism was by immersion. (2) This is the most natural form of symbol for a baptism of penance, where defilement, dirt, covering the whole man stands for utter guilt. (3) Though he addressed all Israel, he preached only in the valley of the Jordan (and through all of that Luke iii. 3.) and places where there was plenty of water (viz. Aenon near Salem: John iii. 23., *quia aquae multae in eo erant*): but much water would not be needed but for that; any fountain would do. (4) In saying he was not fit to unfasten or to carry Christ's shoes he implies / so far from being fit to baptise him, I am not even to undress him for baptism. (5) Christ was in fact so baptised (see Matthew and Mark) and he was baptised like others

The penitents then went down into the water, but this was their own act and for the symbol this was far from enough. John was the Baptist and must baptise them. For this probably he used *affusion*, throwing water on them, and for this some shell or scoop, as he is represented. And he seems to allude to this in contrasting himself with Christ: *ego quidem aqua baptizo . . . cuius ventilabrum in manu eius* Luke iii. 16, 17.—*he* baptises with breath and fire, as wheat is winnowed in the wind and sun, and uses no shell like this which only washes once but a fan that thoroughly and forever parts the wheat from the chaff. For the fan is a sort of scoop, a shallow basket with a low back, sides sloping down from the back forwards, and no rim in front, like our dustpans, it is said. The grain is either scooped into this or thrown in by another, then tossed out against the wind, and this vehement action St John compares to his own repeated 'dousing' or affusion. The separation it makes is very visible too: the grain lies heaped on one side, the chaff[1] blows away the other, between them the winnower stands; after that nothing is more combustible than the chaff, and yet the fire he calls unquenchable. It will do its work at once and yet last, as this river runs forever, but has to do its work over again. Everything about himself is weak and ineffective, he and his instruments; everything about Christ strong. He dwelt with enthusiasm on this thought, representing Christ as a heroic figure, of gigantic size, strength, and equipment; to whom he was a pygmy child. To his hearers too this point of view was not unwelcome; the Jews, St Paul says, *signa petunt* (1 Cor. i. 22), signs of power; the Greek has δυνάμεις. They wanted a strong Messias and that he should use his strength against their enemies; moreover the multitude are not offended by terrorstriking thoughts of religion. But then Christ was not what they expected from this; for prophecy must be interpreted by a spiritual light and if it does not enlighten it misleads. Partly for this St John himself changed his style and when he pointed Christ out said *Ecce Agnus Dei*. But now he uses terms of force and, though he was well understood, he speaks of moral greatness and dignity, yet, in terms of physical force. I take your garments and your footgear from you when you go down into the water; all sorts of men come to me and I know the difference between a light sandal and the soldier's heavy *caliga*: I tell you my fingers have not the force to wring open this man's laces, though I stoop and bend my body to the task; if he washed himself, my arms have not the strength to lift his boots. He uses this imagery because he was the forerunner and smoothed the way; not, he would have said, for his sake, for it is nothing to him where he treads, but for yours, hard hearts, which like sandstone, his tread may grind to powder; brood of adders whose heads they may crush in blood. He would be well shod as a traveller, soldier on the march, or farm-labourer in the forest[2] (*securis ad radicem arboris posita est*)

There may be added the contrast between baptising one by one and tossing the whole basketful of grain, each grain a man, at one throw empty

The struggle between Christ and St John, two innocent lambs, over Christ's baptism was like the momentary encounter of two rams: then St John recognising himself the weaker withdraws. Yet it was which should humble himself: Christ being stronger, humbled himself more

Which does the Scripture mean saw the heavens open etc after the Baptism, Christ or St John? St John certainly saw this (John i. 33, 34.), but St Matthew's and Mark's words imply or almost imply it was Christ. It was then both; the form of words[3] is remarkable and is no doubt a case of the threefold tradition. They said *he saw* and the evangelists supplied a sense: the Tradition probably meant St John.

The Baptism was at Bethania beyond Jordan seemingly: John i. 28. and so the temptation would be in the desert beyond Jordan; but is that the tradition? However neither of these points is clear. St John speaks of 3 certain days—28. *Haec in Bethania facta sunt . . .* 29. *Altera die vidit Joannes Jesum venientem ad se . . .* 35. *Altera die iterum stabat Joannes . . .* but do these mean the next day or *on another day,* St John singling certain notable days? And does 29 mean Christ's baptism, which is in silence supposed at 32? Or was this on Christ's return from the temptation? If so, he lodged near where John was and made some disciples, waited for them to be handed over to him

36. *Respiciens Jesum ambulantem,* that is / passing, *not* coming to him as at 29. He meant them to follow the Lamb *quocumque ierit.* Two of his disciples take the hint: *conversus autem Iesus et videns eos sequentes se dicit eis,* 38, this, though literally true, is rather the idiom for saying *Jesus in his turn, on his side, as, seeing, they were following* etc

43. *In crastinum* must be meant literally, but *et die tertia* ii. 1. may perhaps mean *on a third day,* that is / later than the two just mentioned. This inexactness marks that nothing depends on the difference; so also 43. *voluit exire in Galileam et invenit Philippum* may be Christ or Andrew: both would be true, for both went to the wedding at Cana no doubt and both wanted Philip, but rather Andrew is meant, since it is less becoming for the writer to seem to know Christ's thoughts and we are never without reason to suppose anything revealed to the sacred historians. Andrew then knew that Philip would gladly come if Christ chose to call and it proved that he did, and the Gospel does not even give his answer, meaning he was only too glad, as his enthusiastic words in 45. shew. He was sort of chamberlain to Christ afterwards (as vi. 5, xii. 21)

Nathanael under the fig tree—the chances were that Philip was wrong and the presumption was against Nazareth in particular, but Philip wisely said *Come and see* and Nathanael went. And this is why he is called an Israelite without guile: an Israelite, that is, looking for the redemption of Israel (Luke ii. 38), and without guile, that is / not refusing it when offered, nor dissembling nor like Herod trying to extinguish it or, as the whole nation, choosing a Barabbas instead; nor pressing his objection like the Pharisees to the point not of searching but of telling someone else to search and that then he could not find

(John i) 48. *Priusquam te Philippus vocaret* / before he answered a call or had a call to answer, *cum esses sub ficu,* that is / in his ease and his privacy, when his will was less good and he never thought of God through anyone concerning himself about him. To be under one's own figtree is to be at one's ease and the figleaf stands for conceal-ment—here privacy, a luxurious concealment: the leaves shut out the sun and shine themselves and without stirring one can pull the figs. *Vidi te | I had my eye*[1] *on thee*: it does not imply miraculous knowledge, but it implies more knowledge than was supposed by Nathanael. He is touched and gives his allegiance. We must also suppose some-thing that Philip or a bystander could not know if that came home to him, either something that really took place under a figtree or that it was a great insight into what he secretly recognised as the fault of his life, selfish ease, idleness, and so on, and that Christ neverthe-less chose this idler especially for his kingdom. 50. *Quia dixi tibi*: *vidi te sub ficu, credis*: cp. this with what is said to Thomas; but this is praise. *Maius his videbis*, and then this will not be private or singular, therefore now he speaks in the plural including Philip and all his disciples—*videbitis coelum apertum*: instead of living at earth on the little spot of earth that a figtree hides from heaven[2] and heaven from it you shall see bare heaven open; and instead of idleness in men activity in angels; and instead of men selfishly helping each himself angels ministering to a man. Christ is the man, but they who help to minister to the King are to share the kingdom. There is of course an allusion to Jacob's, Israel's, ladder Gen. xxviii: Jacob had then been sleeping under the bare sky, so far from luxury was he then, and stones were his pillow. There is further an allusion to the angels which had just been ministering to Christ after his fast: this is meant by the Evangelist but was not known to Christ's hearers. And lastly the first fulfilment of the promise was at the marriage of Cana, when *crediderunt in eum discipuli eius* ii. 11. We may perhaps conclude that in working miracles Christ used the ministry of angels, but the words might be taken more figuratively. The servers at the wedding being concerned in a miracle might be called God's angels

Remark also that Nathanael ceases to live under a figtree, the Jewish Church, and comes to live in and be part of a vine, Christ and the Church of Christ

ii. 1, 2. *Et erat Mater Jesu ibi*; that is | already or at least as a matter of course, as a friend of the family. *Vocatus est autem et Jesus et discipuli eius AD NUPTIAS*—a pointed distinction made: she was there, he was asked; she was there before, he was asked to the wed-ding. It is true, he must, it would seem, have been a friend of the family too, but now he was a public character and had disciples and if he were asked they must; at least it was so done in his honour. But this overburdened the house: it was not provided for so many and Mary knew this. She did not notice it then first at the time, for it would seem that from her modesty, in spite of her charity, she would not have been attending to such a thing till others saw it and so the hosts would have been put to pain. But now she knows how they stand throughout and warns Christ in time

4. *Nondum venit hora mea*[1] / my moment: because he knew and was ready to act; but did not need so soon. That is / he tells her there was no need to speak. She knew he did not need reminding, but she did not know he might not need requesting. This was a point insoluble to her, of itself not admitting of certainty; and she must act: she took the side of charity and exposed herself to rebuke. Her words to the servers are a great light to us on her knowledge of Christ's power and will. Further it appears she said to herself he would send for wine and it would appear, perhaps send them out of doors to have it delivered, say, by angel hands. But Christ makes the supply seem to come from the hosts, and further the guests see, from the great *hydriae*, that they are amply supplied. This conceals the miracle more at the moment and increases it afterwards.[2]

The miracle was in fact forestalled. It was too soon; for when drawn the wine was not served to the guests, but the master of ceremonies is consulted about it and he also remonstrates with the bridegroom before anything more is done. Further it took long filling the great water-vessels: the guests then cannot have been waiting and the *architriclinus* notices nothing in this respect: rather they have had plenty, there has been no stint, but there has been an unwise order in the serving

NOTES

NOTES ON PART ONE

OXFORD SERMONS

13. 1. *St Clement's, Oxford*: a little chapel built here in 1793, the earliest Catholic place of worship since penal times, stemming from the Jesuit chaplaincy to the Curzon family at Waterperry. After the new church in St Giles's had been built and inaugurated in 1875, the little chapel in St Clement's still remained as a Mass-centre. Most of GMH's Oxford sermons seem to have been preached there. No doubt the fragment 'Beyond Magdalen and by the Bridge' (*Poems*, 102) is an echo of his journeys between the church in St Giles's and the chapel in St Clement's, as *The Bugler's First Communion* (*Poems*, 47) recalls his work at Cowley Barracks 'over the hill'.

14. 1. *Reigning in heaven he could not worship the Father*: because, as God, the Son is equal to the Father. Therefore 'the Word was made Flesh' in order to express his love of the Father through adoration. Here is seen GMH's interpretation of Scotus's doctrine that the Incarnation was ordained by God independently of original sin—a theme which runs all through his writings on the *Spiritual Exercises*.

15. 1. *July 1 1883 at Stonyhurst*. 1 July 1883 was a Sunday. The sermon would have been in the church attached to the school for a village congregation which would have included those 'Philosophers' (GMH's pupils) who had not got up early for the Boys' Mass.

16. 1. *But the explanation . . . proud*. This is a questionable statement. To be esteemed does not necessarily make a man proud any more than to be despised makes him necessarily humble. May this error be a reflection of GMH'S own exaggerated shrinking from praise and recognition?

16. 2. *Charity . . . lies in humble obedience*. This statement too is questionable. The love of God includes or presupposes humble obedience, but it does not consist in it. It transcends the contractual relation between subject and sovereign; if it did not, it would not be supernatural. Contrast GMH's error here with his contradiction of it in a Bedford Leigh sermon: 'But this is a cold sort of love. Love for Christ is . . . love for a bosom friend, love for a lover.'

17. 1. *Much this preached again*. It was also preached again at Sydenham in Aug. 1885 (Tenth Sunday after Pentecost). It was thus, so far as is known, GMH's most used sermon: (1) Farm Street, 1878; (2) Oxford, 1879; (3) Clitheroe, 1883; (4) Sydenham, 1885. By an unhappy coincidence it is also one of his dullest. He seems to be making a conscientious effort not to sympathize with the Pharisee. See 'Sermon Notes' in Part III, p. 237.

18. 1. *at Worcester*. St George's, Worcester, came under the same Rector as Oxford. It is the oldest continuous Jesuit site in England, going back to penal times before the suppression of the Society. It contains the vestments worked by Helen Wintour, sister of Thomas, who died for his faith in 1605. More recently Edward Elgar was organist there.

19. 1. *the boy or girl, that in their bloom and heyday*. See the exactly contemporary *Morning Midday and Evening Sacrifice* (*Poems*, 48):

> 'This, all this beauty blooming,
> This, all this freshness fuming,
> Give God while worth consuming.'

Also *Poems*, 33: 'Innocent mind and Mayday in girl and boy'. This seems to be the first instance in the sermons of GMH adapting his message to his audience.

20. 1. *Nobilis amator non tam* etc. See *Imitatio Christi*, III. vi. 2.

> 'Prudens amator non tam donum amantis considerat quam dantis amorem. . . . Nobilis amator non quiescit in dono, sed in me super omne donum.'

20. 2. *Johnson's and Reynolds' first meeting* is recorded by Boswell under the year '1752' as occurring at the house of the Misses Cotterell:

> 'The ladies were regretting the death of a friend, to whom they owed great obligations; upon which Reynolds observed, "You have, however, the comfort of being relieved from a burthen of gratitude." They were shocked a little at this alleviating suggestion, as too selfish; but Johnson defended it in his clear and forcible manner, and was much pleased with the *mind*, the fair view of human nature, which it exhibited, like some of the reflections of Rochefoucauld. The consequence was that he went home with Reynolds and supped with him.' (*Boswell's Life of Johnson*, ed. G. B. Hill and L. F. Powell, Oxford, 1934–50, i. 244.)

The editor draws attention to Johnson's own remark in *The Rambler*:

> 'There are minds so impatient of inferiority, that their gratitude is a species of revenge, and they return benefits not because recompense is a pleasure, but because obligation is a pain.' (No. 87.)

For doubts as to the accuracy of Boswell's account, see *Portraits by Sir Joshua Reynolds*, ed. F. W. Hilles, Yale University and London, 1952, p. 56. For GMH on Boswell, see *Letters*, iii. 242.

23. 1. For this sermon see above, p. 235.

23. 2. *St Clement's and St Giles's both*. See Introduction, pp. 3–4. St Giles's refers to the same church as St Aloysius's of the previous sermon.

25. 1. *We who are converts*. The personal note that GMH strikes here would have been of especial interest to University men among his audience. It is to be regretted that his copying out of the sermon breaks off here. He might have revealed something which he studiously concealed at the time of his conversion. In his rather harsh letter to Canon Liddon and in his still more distressing one to his father, Manley Hopkins, he disclaimed any special light and gave the impression that the grounds of his conversion were strictly logical.

BEDFORD LEIGH SERMONS

26. 1. *Bedford Leigh.* See Introduction. The curate at Leigh, whose place GMH may have been taking, was Fr Charles Karslake about whom a note may be of interest since he was a brother of GMH's Highgate friend, Lewis Karslake.

A half-brother to Sir John Karslake, Q.C., the Attorney-General, he was converted after leaving Westminster School and was one of those, like Fr Humphrey, who joined Manning's order of St Charles and then left it—to Manning's great annoyance—to become a Jesuit. A glance at Karslake's career shows that GMH was not exceptionally 'Fortune's football'. Karslake (1839–1915) spent the thirty-seven years of his missionary life at no less than twelve different Jesuit stations throughout England and Scotland. His obituary notice records of him:

'Fr Karslake, though not a gifted man, was most painstaking and conscientious in his work. He left behind him a vast collection of MS sermons which, though of plain and simple style, without any pretence to eloquence, showed how earnest he was in preparing and doing God's work. Fr Pittar of Galashiels used to complain of the interminable length of these sermons. Fr Karslake was refined in manner, full of delicate charity and consideration for others, his one defect being timidity, want of courage, which detracted somewhat from his usefulness.'

His last years as an invalid were spent in close communion with God and great peace of mind.

For tracing the relationship between Fr Charles and Lewis Karslake I am indebted to his great-niece, Mrs Llewellyn, and to Major Ian Karslake.

28. 1. *which is easier to* say? Our Lord did not say that curing the lame was harder than forgiving sins and that therefore his doing the harder was proof of his ability to do the easier. He said that *claiming* to cure the lame was harder than claiming to forgive sins because the first claim could be ocularly tested; and he offered it voluntarily as a test that he did not claim what he could not do. This is an example of GMH's attention to the exact words of the Gospel in order to illuminate what might otherwise be a difficult passage.

29. 1. *Like blue sky.* See *Poems,* 60, from

'The glass-blue days are those . . .'

to

'Earth is the fairer for.'

30. 1. *loose pieces.* See 'Sermon Notes' in Part III, pp. 234–7.

34. 1. *Often mothers make a hero . . . Christ, he is the hero.* See *The Loss of the Eurydice* (*Poems,* 41, ll. 105–12, and *Letters,* i. 78). Note that the word

278 SERMONS AND WRITINGS OF G. M. HOPKINS

'sweetheart' which got him into trouble at Liverpool passed unscathed at Bedford Leigh.

35. 1. *Thou art beautiful in mould* . . .: Ps. xliv. 3 (Vulg.), 'Speciosus forma prae filiis hominum.' A.V. 'Fairer art thou than the children of men.'

35. 2. *accounts of him written in early times*. This description is based on that traditionally ascribed to Publius Lentulus, a friend of Pilate. It is probably not earlier than the beginning of the 4th century. For other passages describing the personal appearance of Christ see Tertullian (trans. Dodgson, Oxford Library of the Fathers (1842)), i, pp. 253 ff.

36. 1. *the heretic Apollinaris*. See Part II, notes, p. 297 (170. 4). All the incarnational heresies err by either attributing too much or too little to Christ's manhood. The counterpart of the Apollinarist heresy is the Adoptionist, which says that Christ was an ordinary man 'possessed' by God at his baptism. There is a similar contrast between the Monophysite heresy which holds that Christ had only one nature, the divine one, and the Nestorian which holds that he had an independent human personality. The great theologians, Aquinas and Scotus, tend to part company, within orthodox limits, in one and the other of these opposing directions. See following note.

37. 1. *human genius*. Scotus claims that Christ *is* individually human, and he does so for precisely the reason that, in GMH's view, constitutes 'genius' —namely the possession (or, in the case of geniuses other than Christ, the seeming approach to possession) of a *whole* specific nature. Peter (or anyone else) is an individual because his humanity is *differentiated* from humanity as a whole; it is 'broken down' from the category of species to that of individual. But Christ's humanity is a perfect 'unbroken' whole ('natura *atoma*'); and being a whole, it is numerically one, and thereafter individual. One could explain the difference another way by saying that Peter's humanity is a 'broken light' of the ideal *species* in God's mind, whereas Christ's humanity is the 'unbroken' *species* as God conceived it: *prima species primaque pulchritudo*.

'Propositio illa: "Persona Verbi assumpsit hunc hominem" de rigore sermonis non esset verum: sed proprie loquendo hanc: "Persona Verbi assumpsit naturam humanam in atomo" . . . Christus non est proprie "hic homo" ut persona, sed "hic homo" ut natura atoma. . . .' (*Parisiensia*, III. i.)

GMH's view of genius (at least of poetic genius) was that it was a seeming approach to being a whole specific nature, 'so that each poet is like a species in nature and can never recur'.

37. 2. '*It is more blessed to give than to receive.*' Acts xx. 35. Cf. 1 Clement ii. 1.

For the whole subject of the *Agrapha* see Lock and Sanday, *Sayings of Jesus* (1897).

'*Never rejoice but when* . . .' St Jerome, *On Ephesians*, v. 4. The quotation is from *The Gospel according to the Hebrews*.

'*My mystery is for me . . .*' Clement of Alexandria (ob. *c.* A.D. 220), *Stromatum*, lib. v, x.

37. 3. *Plato . . . foretold of him. Republic*, 361.

. . . ὁ δίκαιος μαστιγώσεται, στρεβλώσεται, δεδήσεται, ἐκκαυθήσεται τὠφθαλμώ, τελευτῶν πάντα κακὰ παθὼν ἀνασχινδυλευθήσεται . . .

38. 1. *He loved to praise, he loved to reward.* This identifies the sermon as the one GMH preached again in part at Liverpool, 23 July 1880. 'The sermon was made out of an old one in this book and was on our Lord's fondness for praising and rewarding people.'

44. 1. More perfect immunity from concupiscence than that envisaged by GMH is conceivable, e.g. in Our Blessed Lady.

44. 2. This is merely the private opinion of certain devout authors.

45. 1. *the greatest . . . came from England.* John Duns, or Douns, *Scotus*: born at Maxton, near Melrose, 1266, son of Ninian Douns; became a Franciscan at Dumfries; studied at Oxford and at Paris; lectured at Oxford and at Paris, where he was *Magister Regens* in 1307; died at Cologne 1308. It was only about 1920 that his Scottish birthplace was finally established. GMH inclined to the view that he was a Northumbrian. See *Letters*, iii. 419–22.

The ancient and constant tradition of his public defence of the Immaculate Conception at Paris, though impugned by Denifle, has been maintained with fresh evidence in more recent times: E. Longpré, O.F.M., in *La France franciscaine*, xi, 1928, 137–62; D. Scaramuzzi, O.F.M., in *Studi francescani*, 1930, 326–30.

47. 1. *in this road.* Lancashire usage for way of thinking or behaving. See *Poems*, 53 (*Felix Randal*):

'. . . God rest him all road ever he offended!'

The poem was written in Apr. 1880; but the events described seem to have taken place 'some months earlier' when Hopkins was at Bedford Leigh.

48. 1. *Margaret Clitheroe.* On trial at York in 1586 for sheltering Catholic priests, in order to save the jury from convicting her against their consciences she refused to plead and was therefore pressed to death with heavy weights, the penalty for remaining mute. She was declared a martyr by Pope Pius XI in 1929. See *Poems*, 107.

48. 2. *a fonder love.* See *Poems*, 59 ('The Golden Echo'):

'When the thing we freely forfeit is kept with fonder a care,
Fonder a care kept than we could have kept it, kept
Far with fonder a care. . . .'

49. 1. *he smiles, he claps his hands over us.* See *Poems*, 63, the sestet.

LIVERPOOL SERMONS I.

56. 1. *the subject by the stress of his obedience.* See notes, p. 296 (168. 1) 'the instress of the subject'.

57. 1. *we are both in our duty, both in our rights*. See Part II, p. 165: 'This status . . . is the being in one's rights, in one's duty.' In comparing this and the two following sermons with Part II, ch. 4, it should be remembered that the sermons consider justice before the Fall, the spiritual notes after the Fall.

61. 1. *'he that does them shall live by them'*: from Gal. iii. 12, quoting Lev. xviii. 5. See the passage on *vivet in illis* in the 'Spiritual Writings', Part II, ch. 4, p. 165.

63. 1. *St Basil*. The reference is probably to *De Paradiso*, Oratio III: Migne, *Patrologia, Series Graeca*, vol. xxx, col. 67.

63. 2. *St Paul*. 1 Tim. ii. 14, 'Et Adam non est seductus, mulier autem seducta in praevaricatione fuit.' (Vulg.)

63. 3. *supererogation*. Again see below, Part II, ch. 4, p. 168, the conclusion.

68. 1. Scotus makes a distinction between original justice and sanctifying grace. Original justice was a gift conferring immunity from sin and concupiscence. Sanctifying grace is a principle of merit. He held that Adam was not *created* in sanctifying grace but original justice. GMH follows Scotus in distinguishing grace from original justice, but unlike him asserts with St Thomas that man was *created* in sanctifying grace. But unlike St Thomas he maintains oddly that sanctifying grace was prior to original justice. This is not in harmony with common scholastic teaching, and is the very reverse of the opinion of Scotus. Scotus maintains that sanctifying grace includes in itself original justice, but not vice versa. (Cf. *Oxoniense*, iv. i. 6, p. 11ᵃ, § B, and P. Migne's *J. D. Scoti Doctrina*, lib. ii, p. 320.)

Hopkins appears to attach the idea of original justice to the Thomist idea of the necessity of the co-operation of the human (adult) will with the divine act of infusion of grace, or at least of a later ratification of this infusion in the case of those justified in infant baptism.

68. 2. *communion with the Church*. It seems that GMH had originally meant his trilogy to end in a demonstration that the Catholic Church *as an organized society* is the only possible successor to the lost kingdom of Paradise. But he gave up the attempt, as his conclusion to the previous sermon indicates.

74. 1. *the Devil*. GMH had evidently his own version of 'the harrowing of hell', derived from the mysterious passage in St Peter's First Epistle. Compare Knox's version of 1 Pet. iii. 19–20 and iv. 6, with stanza 33 of *The Wreck of the Deutschland*.

75. 1. This sermon with its magnificent conclusion is the longest that GMH is known to have preached.

76. 1. *streets and shops*. GMH was evidently making an effort in this sermon to come down to his hearers' level—an abortive effort, as his note at the end shows.

LIVERPOOL SERMONS II

80. 1. *the city of Rome.* Cf. the Church's Hymn for the Feast:

'O Roma felix quae duorum Principum
Es consecrata glorioso sanguine...'

81. 1. *translucent alabaster.* But the Greek word 'alabastron' seems to denote the vessel itself, not the material of which it was made.

85. 1. *'old wineskin'* ... *'to men of old time'.* References to Matt. ix. 17 and v. 33, which may have been lost on his hearers. The Rheims version has 'bottles' and 'to them of old'.

86. 1. *born who knows where?* A reference to John vii. 41–42.

86. 2. *another place.* Luke x. 25–37.

86. 3. *St Mark's Gospel.* Mark xii. 28–34. GMH had to correlate all three synoptics, as well as Leviticus and Deuteronomy, in order to reconstruct the scene as he saw it.

89. 1. *than we ourselves.* The other English Jesuit poet, Blessed Robert Southwell, has a similar turn of thought in his *Exercitia et Devotiones*, no. 25, AMOR:

'Si tantum amaveris amicum, tantum placeat tibi talis et talis, ut quicquid ab ipso tibi praeceptum fuerit bene videatur, et iucundum adeo tibi sit cum ipso conversari, ipsi te tuasque calamitates revelare; quanto confidentius deberes te Deo Optimo Maximo commendare, cum ipso conversari, ipsi miserias tuas et defectus aperire, qui maiorem tui curam quam tu tui ipsius gerit, et est tibi magis intrinsecus quam tu tibi!'

100. 1. *Christ's body mystical.* In this wonderful sermon, GMH's theological insight was ahead of his time—as he so often was—in his devotion to the Church as the Mystical Body of Christ.

100. 2. *The Feast of the Sacred Heart* was first extended to the whole Church by Pius IX in 1856 with the rite of *duplex maius*; it was not made a double of the first class till 1889. In GMH's time there were still two divergent aspects of the devotion, the one stemming from St John Eudes at the beginning of the 17th century, stressing its joyous aspect, the other from St Margaret Mary at the end of the 17th century with the stress on compassionate reparation. These two streams are now fused in a uniform Mass and Office, the feast being celebrated on the Friday after the Octave of Corpus Christi.

100. 3. *St Gertrude's prayers.* St Gertrude the Great (1256–1301), Benedictine mystic. The prayers in which there is the nearest approximation to the modern devotion to the Sacred Heart are those 'On the Passion of Our Lord', where it grows out of meditation on the pierced side. See *Preces Gertrudianae* ..., London, 1861 (Eng. trans.), pp. 82 ff.

100. 4. *St Bernard's Sermons*, e.g. Sermon 61, On the Canticle of Canticles, Migne, *Patrologia*, vol. clxxxiii, cols. 1971–3. Indications of the devotion are also to be found in the writings of the Carthusians, of St Bonaventure, of St Peter Canisius, and, of course, of St John Eudes, who was its first real propagator. Owing to the influence of Jansenism, however, the devotion would have withered had it not been for the visions of St Margaret Mary and the work of her confessor, the Jesuit Blessed Claude de la Colombière. See next note.

100. 5. *Bd Margaret Mary* Alacoque (1647–90), now St Margaret Mary, a nun of the Visitation Order at Paray-le-Monial. She had a number of heavenly visions and injunctions to spread the devotion, on account of which she suffered sharp opposition; the most important occurred in the Octave of Corpus Christi, 1675 or 1676, when Jesus enjoined the celebration of the feast. Her task was handed on to her confessor, Fr de la Colombière; through him the devotion came early to the Catholics in England, where he was confessor to the Duchess of York till his arrest during the Titus Oates terror. See *Devotion to the Sacred Heart*, by Revd J. V. Bainvel, S.J. (Eng. trans., 1924).

103. 1. *a great heart* . . . Cf. Cicero, *Tusc. Disp.* i. 9:

'aliis cor ipsum animus videtur: ex quo excordes, vecordes, concordes- que dicuntur, et Nasica ille prudens, bis consul, Corculum, et

Egregie cordatus homo catus Aeliu' Sextus.'

104. 1. *within the time of which* . . . The MS book ends here in the middle of the sentence, thus depriving us of one of GMH's rare historical insights.

NOTES ON PART TWO

CHAPTER ONE

122. 1. *Homo creatus est*, written opp. pp. 28–32 in Fr Roothaan's edition. There were earlier notes opp. pp. 26, 27; but these have been torn out and all that remains is their conclusion, opp. p. 28 top, which runs as follows:

'. . . and so they praise, reverence, and serve God in a natural beatitude. When therefore it is said that God wishes all men to be saved and come to the knowledge of the truth, now after the Fall, interpret / acc. to their stake, interest, and danger—the adult by actual earning of heaven, by merit, correspondence; the baptised infant without correspondence; and the unbaptised infant he wishes to be glad of its being, which is a sort of saving the soul (see the notes opp. pp. 26, 27), though not in the technical and full sense'

For further references back to the vanished pages, see note, p. 986 (129. 9).

122. 2. *more hold.* Although this treatise is the most richly individual of all GMH's writings, yet several of his arguments spring from positions that are distinctively Scotist as opposed to Thomist. This preference for introspection is the first instance. Scotus's proof of the existence of God dispenses with evidence from the outside world and derives solely from the existence of one finite being (one's self) endowed with mind and will. (*Oxoniense*, I. ii, pp. 24–29 in the Venice edition used by GMH.)

Another clear instance, too obvious to need much comment, is GMH's kinship with Scotus's descriptions of individuality as *haecceitas* (this-ness), as the *ultima realitas entis*, and as the *ultima solitudo*. Departing sharply from the Thomists and others, Scotus holds that individuality is inexplicable by any other element such as matter or form or quantity or even by existence. 'Ratio ultima haecceitatis non est quaerenda nisi in divina voluntate.' (*Parisiensia*, II. xii. 5.)

124. 1. *finite in its own being.* This is another distinctively Scotist point. The Thomists attribute finiteness to the fact that existence is limited by essence, otherwise it would be pure act, unlimited. Scotus replies that if existence were intrinsically unlimited, nothing extrinsic would be able to limit it; it would be intensively infinite. The only alternative is his own position that finiteness is an intrinsic limitation, a *carentia entitatis*, inseparable from created being.

'Breviter respondeo ad argumentum: quod quodlibet ens habet intrinsecum sibi gradum suae perfectionis in quo est finitum . . . si ergo sit finitum, non per aliud ens finitatur.' (*Oxoniense*, I. ii. 2, p. 29ª.)

125. 1. *to selve and instress.* The verb 'instress' in GMH's spiritual writings has the special meaning of the soul's spiritual energy caused by and co-operating with God's creative activity—though this aspect is naturally in abeyance here, since God's creative activity is what he has to prove. The soul's energy can be either of the mind or of the will. To instress the mind is to spiritualize a sensory image, turning a simple apprehension into a judgment. To instress the will is to posit one's self in an act of choice. Here the meaning is the latter. Both meanings are more fully developed in chs. 2, 3, and 5.

125. 2. *hart'shorn*: a plantain with the same ammoniac property as the shavings of antlers which were formerly the source of sal volatile.

125. 3. *the Averrhoists*. Averroës (Ibn Roschd, 1126–98), the great Arabian commentator on Aristotle, interpreted the passage in *De Anima*, iii. 5, to mean that human consciousness ('I think') is the work of a universal Mind on a universal Soul, the individual mind and soul being purely receptive. St Thomas rejected this interpretation as psychologically impossible as well as doctrinally unacceptable. But it revived again after the Renaissance in the monopsychism of Giordano Bruno, Spinoza, etc.

127. 1. *the display*. See note, p. 287 (132. 2).

128. 1. *I do not deny*. There is a possible back-reference here to GMH's undergraduate essay on Parmenides. It is of interest that Scotus contradicts Aristotle's attempted refutation of Parmenides's proposition that all being is one. Parmenides (Scotus conjectures) saw all knowable being in a confused intuition as one *nature*, *not* as one individual: which is indeed Scotus's own position. (*Oxoniense*, I. iii. 2, and viii. 3.)

According to Scotus, the finite mind or soul has a natural desire for the infinite from which arises a confused intuition which can be conceptualized as '*being*, not positively infinite, yet not exclusively finite—just *being*'. Without this desire and the concept formed from it (says Scotus) we could not arrive at the idea of God or talk logically about him. Further, we could not even say *it is* about material substances, because all we would know would be the appearances (or accidents) that affect the senses.

'Sicut est argutum quod Deus non est a nobis cognoscibilis naturaliter nisi ens sit univocum creato et increato, ita potest argui de substantia et accidente, cum enim substantia non immutet immediate intellectum nostrum ad aliquam intellectionem sui, sed tantum accidens sensibile. . . .' (*Oxoniense*, I. iii. 3, p. 45^b.)

'Contra hoc . . . desiderium naturale est in intellectu cognoscente effectum ad cognoscendum causam: et in cognoscente causam in universali est desiderium naturale ad cognoscendum illam in particulari et distincte. Desiderium autem naturale non est ad impossibile ex natura desiderantis, quia tunc esset frustra. Ergo non est impossibile intellectui ex parte intellectus cognoscere substantiam immaterialem in particulari, ex quo cognoscit materiale quod est effectus eius. Et ita primum obiectum intellectus non excludit illud immateriale.' (Ibid., p. 44^b, § A.)

From these and other places in Scotus it is possible to conclude as follows. The energy with which I infer that sensations produced in my soul signify real objects outside my soul is the same energy with which I infer that I am being created. Such a conclusion would have come as a revelation to the man who wrote as an undergraduate:

'But indeed I have often felt when I have been in this mood and felt the depth of an instress or how fast the inscape holds a thing, that nothing is so pregnant and straightforward to the truth as simple *yes* and *is*. "Thou couldst never either know or say / what was not, there would be no coming at it." There would be no bridge, no stem of stress between us and things to bear us out and carry the mind over: without stress we might not and could not say / Blood is red / but only / This blood is red / or / The last blood I saw was red / nor even that, for in later language not only universals would not be true but the copula would break down even in particular judgments.' (*Journals*, p. 127.)

128. 2. *a universal really*. This is what Scotus calls in one place the *universale concretum*. The common nature of the genus or species cannot exist independently of the individuals who share it ('fetch or instance it' in GMH's terms). But, according to Scotus, it has a sufficient degree of reality to impose itself objectively on the mind apart from the individuals who 'fetch or instance it'. If it were not objectively something, there would be no guarantee that our ideas of things corresponded with reality:

'Natura communis est entitas realis prius intellectioni; alioquin nihil sciremus de rebus, sed tantum de conceptibus nostris'. (*Oxoniense*, ii. iii. i.)

Compare GMH on Parmenides, quoted above.

Clearly, 'fetched in the universals' in the next line should read 'fetched in the individuals'. A slip by GMH must be presumed.

128. 3. *in the brutes*. In rational creatures the individual degree of reality (the *ultima realitas entis*) takes precedence over the generic and specific degrees of the elemental and sensitive forms. But in the brute creation GMH is of the opinion that it is the other way round, because an animal cannot be called a true 'self'. If animals survive after death, therefore, they would survive as genus or as a species, not as individuals. But in what manner—whether as living shapes or merely remembered images—he does not say.

It is a medieval rather than a scholastic conception. It fuses three meanings of *species* into one: *species*, likeness; *species*, beauty; and *species*, the subdivision of *genus*. The origin and division of species lie in this, that each reflects some aspect of the creator's power or perfection. See Scotus's thesis on the *vestigia* in App. II.

Incidentally, it is a conception not at all opposed to inductive scientific research—rather the reverse; it incites us to know more about creatures as they are, in order to know more about God. GMH himself is an example of such scientific inquisitiveness.

128. 4. '*Tu autem . . . intimo meo*'. St Augustine has several similar exclamations. The nearest to GMH's version seems to be in the *Confessions*, iii. vi. 11:

'Tu, autem, eras interior intimo meo et superior summo meo.'

128. 5. *but for his infinity*. This also is a distinctively Scotist position. For the Thomists the infinity of God is a corollary. For Scotus it is the actual proof: the existence of finite being postulates the existence of infinite being. From the infinity of God all other knowable conclusions about him flow. However close we are to him, we can never be identified with him because finite can never become infinite. Further, although God is multiplied—as it were—in each of his perfections, there can only be one divine nature because there can only be one infinite.

129. 1. *a hypostatic union*: union—but not fusion—of a created nature with a divine nature in one divine person, used only of the incarnation of God the Son—from the Greek 'hypostasis', substance.

As was said above, see p. 284 (128. 1), GMH, in his refutation of a universal mind as a self *identified* with other selves, does not deny—indeed he affirms—the reality of the concrete universal 'humanity' which includes all human natures apart from their selves. This looks forward to Scotus's theory of the hypostatic union as the assumption by God the Son of the totality of human nature. See App. II, conclusion. See also *Poems*, 57, ll. 12–14.

129. 2. *From against p. 26 n.*: this is the first of seven references to Marie Lataste, which include some very long quotations from her writings. This first reference is evidently to book i, sec. 5, which has the following:

'L'homme vient de Dieu et doit retourner à Dieu. Il y a deux mouvements en l'homme: de son être créé par Dieu vers l'existence et de son être existant vers Dieu.'

See App. I; also note, p. 289 (137. 2).

130. 1. *Sept. 3 and later 1883*. GMH has here elaborated the rough notes, made at Beaumont, which follow in the present text.

130. 2. *affective and elective will*. GMH always notes any sign of this distinction in the *Spiritual Exercises*.

CHAPTER TWO

132. 1. *Scotus*. The reference is to the *Oxoniense*, II, dist. vi, qu. 2, pp. 48–50 of vol. ii of the Venice edition which GMH was using. Scotus's argument is that it is the nature of an angel to know itself before knowing other beings; therefore it would love itself with a love of friendship before loving God with a desire for God's perfection; therefore the first opportunity for sin would be an inordinate love of itself, which would then lead to an envy of others, and thence to pride. Pride was therefore the consummation of a process which began with luxury or excessive dwelling on one's own beauty :

'Ideo dico quod primum peccatum eius non fuit superbia proprie dicta: sed propter delectationem quam importabat, magis videtur reduci ad luxuriam. . . .' (p. 50ᵃ, § N.)

To back up this, Scotus uses St Augustine's famous opening of *De Civitate Dei*, the two loves that make the two cities:

'. . . Primus actus inordinatus fuit actus amicitiae respectu sui ipsius. Et hoc est quod dicit Augustinus, 14 *de Civitate Dei*, quod "duo amores fecerunt duas civitates; civitatem Dei, amor Dei usque ad contemptum sui: et civitatem diaboli, amor sui usque ad contemptum Dei." Prima igitur radix civitatis diaboli fuit inordinatus amor amicitiae sui, quae radix germinavit usque ad contemptum Dei, in quo est consummata ista malitia. Sic patet de inordinatione simpliciter prima quae fuit simpliciter in primo *velle* inordinato.' (p. 49ᵃ, § c.)

For GMH's further comments on the three stages of evil (luxury–envy–pride), in which he joins Scotus's authority to that of St Ignatius, see his note on the 'Two Standards', ch. 6, p. 181 (and notes, p. 301 (181. 1 and 181. 2) on the text of Philippians).

It followed from this that Lucifer's fall occurred by stages, not in a single act. For GMH's amplification of this, see Ch. 8. Scotus's question on the stages of Lucifer's fall immediately precedes the one just referred to by GMH—*Oxoniense*, II. v. 1 and 2, pp. 44–48 in the Venice edition. It may be taken for granted therefore that GMH had read this question also.

132. 2. '*Caeterum injecta . . .*': GMH seems to mean that the place is mentioned because it was the field in which Adam displayed his individuality, the material on which he set his seal. See, in the previous chapter, the passage beginning: 'A self then will consist of a centre *and* a surrounding area. . . .' (p. 127).

For the use of the word *ecceitas* see note, p. 293 (151. 3).

133. 1. *Tertium Punctum.* The note on the Third Point consists of a long quotation from Marie Lataste. See App. I.

133. 2. *Fr R. must be wrong here.* Fr Roothaan put 'so many men going *towards* hell' instead of '*to hell*' because he regarded the phrase as a sequel to 'what great corruption came upon mankind', his point being that mankind only goes *towards* hell, not *to* hell, as a result of original sin. GMH, however, prefers to deny the sequence of thought between the two phrases, remarking that men are not lost for original sin but for actual sins.

134. 1. *pray for this.* The temperate reflections that follow represent the proper reactions of an exercitant towards the end of the First Week. When GMH exceeded them he was going against the advice that directors gave him or would have given him. See pp. 203 ff. also and, more particularly, p. 253.

135. 1. See *Poems*, 71: 'My own heart let me have more pity on;'

135. 2. *which is always.* As it stands GMH's statement is questionable. We can be morally certain that the *guilt* of sin has been forgiven. But he is evidently referring only to the temporal penalties of sin about which we cannot be certain; for he goes on to speak of 'the shame of sin' as 'part of the penalty'.

135. 3. *L.R.* stands for 'Long Retreat'. Here and elsewhere GMH wrote 'L.T.' by mistake; an occasional correction shows that 'L.R.' was intended.

136. 1. *our scholastics*. GMH first wrote 'the scholastics', then altered 'the' to 'our'—presumably to distinguish between the schoolmen of the great age and the textbooks of his own day. Scotus held that sensation, being a spiritual quality, does not necessarily require bodily contact:

> 'Argumentum . . . de contactu non concludit, quia contactus ut dicit habitudinem corporis ad corpus extrinsecum non videtur necessario requiri ad aliquam actionem absolutam cuiusmodi est immutatio sensus, quia actio absoluta videtur posse praecedere quemcumque talem respectum extrinsecus advenientem; ergo licet corpus ut hic non contingat, excludendo talem respectum extrinsecus advenientem ad corpus aliud, non sequitur quin possit alterare, quod est immutare ad formam absolutam sensationis.' (IV. x. 9, p. 47^b, § A.)

For Scotus and the 'intellectual memory', see note, p. 298 (174. 1).

136. 2. *'intention'*. The schoolmen's word *intentio* means the in-drawing or assimilation of matter into spirit by the act of knowing. For Scotus more particularly it meant the mental energy which converts a simple apprehension into a statement of existence, the awareness of 'red' into the implicit judgment 'that is a red thing'. See notes, pp. 284–5 (128. 1 and 128. 2); p. 294 (152. 1); p. 298 (174. 1).

Scotus says that by dwelling on the act rather than on the content of the act we can get an insight into the source of our power of knowing; to be aware that the mind is co-operating with God's creative mind is to see things, in some sort of way, *in luce increata*, that is, in the process of being created. We cannot see things *in* the divine mind; to see them in their stabilized natures is common; but there is a third way, betwixt and between the two:

> 'Ista igitur duplex causalitas intellectus divini. qui est vera lux increata, videlicet, quae producit obiecta secundaria in esse intelligibili, et quod est illud virtute cuius obiecta secundaria etiam producta movent actualiter intellectum, potest quasi integrare unum tertium membrum de causa, propter quam dicamur vere videre in luce aeterna. . . . Sic igitur in luce aeterna, secundum quid, sicut in obiecto proximo videmus. Sed in luce increata videmus secundum tertium modum, sicut in causa proxima cuius virtute obiectum proximum movet.' (*Oxoniense*, I. iii. 4, p. 51^a, § Q.)

It is the energy of God's *will* that we are actually in touch with; but his will carries within it the creative design of his intellect. Scotus goes on to explain this in *Oxoniense*, I. iii. 4; but more briefly in the following:

> '. . . tantum Voluntas attingit intellectum creatum; tamen praesupponit motionem Intellectus Divini ab ipsa Essentia, sine qua ipsa Voluntas non haberet illud *velle*. . . .' (*Quodlibet*, xiv.)

This may explain the close connexion, and occasional apparent confusion, in GMH's mind between instressing the mind (*intentio*) and instressing the will ('selving'). The instressing of the will in *praxis* (see App. II) is in fact the carrying out of God's design or *intentio ad extra*.

136. 3. *texturally at stress.* Fr Rickaby also thought of the fire of hell as the result of a sort of friction set up by two opposing stresses:

> 'The pain of burning and the pain of imprisonment in hell seem thus not only to go together, but to be in some manner identical. . . . Hell-fire may mean in the first place some mighty constraining force, driving the lost spirit in upon itself and separating it from all besides; and contrariwise the intense energy of the spirit craving for expansion. What wonder if under the strain and stress of these two opposing forces, the expansive from within and the compressive from without, the very substance of that spiritual nature should catch fire and burn? Being men, we are obliged to speak of spirit in terms of matter: but after all, the more we find out of the one and the other, the more we are struck with the analogy that obtains between them.' (*Waters that go softly, or thoughts for time of retreat,* pp. 33–34, 1st edn., London, 1907.)

This is one of several passages which bear a marked resemblance to Hopkins's comments on the Exercises. It is certain that the two men corresponded and talked together. But if Rickaby ever saw any of the comments in writing, it must have been before GMH's death. For after that the book lay virtually unknown in Dublin till a happy chance put it into Fr Keating's hands about 1909.

137. 1. *2 Pet. ii. 4:* 'He thrust them down to hell, chained them there in the abyss, to await their sentence in torment.' (The Greek means literally 'in ropes' or perhaps 'in pits of darkness'.)

Jude 6: 'The angels . . . he has imprisoned in eternal darkness, to await their judgement when the great day comes.' (Mgr Knox's translation and note on 2 Pet. ii. 4.)

137. 2. *towards being.* Writing of these two strains or tendencies, GMH clearly has in mind the words which Marie Lataste put in the mouth of Christ:

> 'There are two movements in man: that of his being, created by God, towards existence, and that of his existing being towards God. These two movements are communicated to man by God; and by these two movements man, if he so desire, will infallibly return to God. I say *if he so desire*, because man can change the direction of his movement. . . .
>
> 'Still, at this day, as at the beginning, every man receives the first movement which launches him into life; but the second movement, which carries the living man towards God, is no longer given to him with the first movement. The second movement carries him alive into death. But I am there to recover man by baptism, and to set him again on the road which leads to God. Then all is repaired; man is regenerated; he will move forward, if it so pleases him, towards God, or he will turn back to Satan from whom I delivered him; he will walk in the truth or in lying.'

See next note.

138. 1. *the great sacrifice*: the central point of GMH's speculations, which he has developed especially in the chapter on Creation and Redemption, (see pp. 196 ff.). Here he connects the 'two movements' described by Marie Lataste with Scotus's thesis of Christ's humanity being God's first *intentio ad extra*.

Had there been no sin of angels or men, the coming of Christ would have been the efflorescence or natural consummation of the creative strain; men's minds and wills would have risen spontaneously and harmoniously from creatures to God. But, as a result of sin, natural values went astray and Christ had to perform a violent readjustment of them by his redemptive suffering. The redemptive strain still continues the creative strain: see John v. 17, 'My Father works until now: and I work'; and the Church's prayer at the offertory of the Mass: 'Deus qui humanae substantiae dignitatem mirabiliter condidisti et mirabilius reformasti. . . '. But only on condition of man's free and deliberate co-operation.

This, I think, is the theological inspiration behind the art and architecture of the Counter-Reformation; and it can be traced in very many of GMH's poems—for example in the much-discussed sestet of 'The Windhover'. Also in: 'For tho' he is under the world's splendour and wonder / His mystery must be instressed, stressed'. (*Poems*, 28.)
And in:

> 'For good grows wild and wide
> Has shades, is nowhere none;
> But right must choose its side,
> Its champion, and have done.' (*Poems*, 110.)

138. 2. '*I know . . . afflicting.*' This is the last sentence in a famous passage of the *Autobiography*, xxxii, which includes the following:

'To say that it is as if the soul were continually being torn from the body is very little, for that would mean that one's life was being taken by another; whereas in this case it is the soul itself that is tearing itself to pieces. The fact is that I cannot find words to describe that interior fire and that despair, which is greater than the most grievous tortures and pains. I could not see who was the cause of them, but I felt, I think, as if I were being both burned and dismembered; and I repeat that that interior fire and despair are the worst things of all. In that pestilential spot, where I was I was quite powerless to hope for comfort, it was impossible to sit or lie, for there was no room to do so. I had been put in this place which looked like a hole in the wall, and those very walls, so terrible to the sight, bore down upon me and completely stifled me. There was no light and everything was in the blackest darkness. I do not understand how this can be, but, although there was no light, it was possible to see everything the sight of which can cause affliction.' (*Complete Works of St Teresa*, trans. E. Allison Peers (London, 1946), i. 216.)

See *Poems*, 71, 'I cast for comfort . . .'.

138. 3. *Sept. 5, 1883.* The passage that follows is added from the 1883 notes on loose pages which GMH began to write out more fully in the *Commentary*

—see note, p. 286 (130. 1). The first paragraph is a summary of Chap. 3, (pp. 146–57), being written a year or two later.

138. 4. *tend towards it.* Scotus would not agree with this. It is true that the conscious intellect, if left to itself, cannot conceive the infinite; but in the whole of man's nature, especially in the natural will, there *is* a tendency to the infinite, though grace is needed for this tendency to attain its end. Even when the end is attained, theologians almost unanimously assert that there is union with the infinite, but not conceptual representation.

'Ad perfectissimum [actum] circa ultimum finem est inclinatio naturalis, licet ad illum non potest attingere natura ex se.' (*Quodlibet*, xvii.)

GMH is here attributing too much to the *arbitrium*. The choice cannot *initiate* the movement towards God. See App. II, and also note, p. 293 (146. 6).

139. 1. *elsewhere* evidently refers to the foregoing passage beginning 'Poenae', which was written earlier.

140. 1. '*Faciendo unum*': the conclusion of St Ignatius's text. See p. 136.

141. 1. *Scotus.* The reference is perhaps to the following passage in which Scotus considers the pain of hell as a terrible circle starting from loss of the divine vision, descending through all the pains of mind and body, and then returning again to the pain of loss:

'Tunc dicitur ad propositum quod poena damnatorum est multiplex: quaedam poena damni, carentia scilicet visionis divinae; alia est tristitia de ipsa poena; tertia, tristitia de culpa, non ut est offensiva Dei sed ut est causa poenae; quarta est tristitia de igne continente perpetuo; quinta de igne immutante et retinente intellectum damnatorum in perpetua consideratione sua. Tertia tristitia, scilicet de culpa, in quantum est peccatum, est vermis conscientiae.' (*Oxoniense*, IV. 1. 3, p. 160ᵇ, § B.)

Scotus seems here to speak of the fire as an imprisonment of the senses arising from a torture of the mind which in turn arises from loss of the divine vision. See previous notes, p. 289 (136. 3) and p. 290 (138. 2).

142. 1. *fainness . . . hits it*: a marginal note in MS.

144. 1. *Scotus has a distinction.* The reference is probably to *Oxoniense*, II. xlii. 4, p. 93ᵃ, §§ A–B.

'Ex quo sequitur quod in cogitatione, sermone et opere non est peccatum formaliter et primo, sed hoc est in solo actu voluntatis. . . . Ex quo etiam sequitur quod nullus actus possit esse malus, etiam materialiter, nisi qui potest imperari ab actu voluntatis formaliter malo.'

There are other reasons for thinking that GMH studied this particular question; for on the same page occurs the passage:

'Toties habet homo primas cogitationes quoties sibi recurrunt diversa obiecta, et quoties surgit a somno.'

See Christopher Devlin, 'The Image and the Word, II', *The Month*, Mar. 1950, pp. 198, 201.

145. 1. *the rough draft of the 'Commentary' for the Provincial.* Evidently the work described to Bridges in the following year:

'I did in my last week at Roehampton write 16 pages of a rough draft of a commentary on St. Ignatius' Spiritual Exercises. This work would interest none but a Jesuit, but to me it is interesting enough and, as you see, it is very professional.' (*Letters*, i. 150.)

It is debatable how much of GMH's long speculative essays, which form the bulk of the present commentary, formed part of his rough draft for the Provincial. The present reference is to a point of strictly confessional interest: the distinction between commission and consent, perhaps with special regard to involuntary motions of the flesh. The Provincial was Fr Purbrick. See Introduction, pp. 214–15.

145. 2. *Venialiter peccatur*: an earlier note in MS, leap-frogged by the foregoing passage.

CHAPTER THREE

146. 1. *Personality, Grace,* and *Free-Will.* In the interleaved book there is no break between the foregoing chapter and the following. But since GMH here starts a new trend of thought and develops it at great length, a different chapter has been devoted to it in this edition. A commentary on it will be found in App. II.

146. 2. *Suarez,* Francisco, S.J. (1548–1617), about whom GMH wrote:

'Suarez is our most famous theologian: he is a man of vast volume of mind, but without originality or brilliancy; he treats everything satisfactorily, but you never remember a phrase of his, the manner is nothing. Molina is the man who *made* our theology: he was a genius and even in his driest dialectic I have remarked a certain fervour like a poet's.' (*Letters*, ii. 95.)

Suarez's great work was to explore and co-ordinate the various trends of scholastic thought into one main stream which he adapted to the more curious and sensitive mentality of the new age; he had also a considerable corrective influence on political and scientific thought in the 17th and 18th centuries. GMH's faint praise of him was probably owing to the fact that Suarez and Suarez only was taught at St Beuno's in his time. Nevertheless his speculations owe more than a little to Suarez, and it was almost certainly through Suarez that he came to know Scotus.

146. 3. *De Mysteriis Vitae Christi* is volume xix in Suarez's *Opera Omnia* (Paris, 1877); it contains his commentary on the Third Part of St Thomas's *Summa*, Questions 27–59, as well as his own *Disputationes*. In the preceding volume, *De Incarnatione* (xviii, Disp. 43, secs. 1–3), Suarez comments on the article of St Thomas to which GMH here refers.

146. 4. *prior to its being.* This is a Hopkinized version of Scotus's thesis that individuality is intrinsic to being prior to actual existence. (*Oxoniense*, II. iii, p. 31ª, §§ A–B.) See also Étienne Gilson, *Duns Scot* (Paris, 1952), pp. 454–6.

Gilson, however, is misleading in saying that Scotus thinks of 'being' purely in terms of 'essence' as opposed to 'existence'. This is a purely Thomist judgment. It is true that, for Scotus, existence is a state or condition 'aliquo modo accidentalis'; but he thinks of a being not only as an essence in God's mind but as an *intention* in God's will. Existence therefore, as Gilson rightly interprets Scotus, does not confer individuality on a being; it merely brings out what is already there. But the fundamental reason for this is that the individuality of a being is a distinct intention both in God's mind and in his will, whether or not he gives it actual existence.

'Ratio ultima haecceitatis non est quaerenda nisi in divina voluntate.' (*Parisiensia*, II. xii. 5.)

146. 5. *natures . . . 'inscapes'*. Note that GMH is here accepting Scotus's distinction (a distinction less than physical but more than merely conceptual) between the nature of a man and his individuality. (*Oxoniense*, II. iii. 1, p. 29.)

Note also that GMH identifies 'inscape' with 'nature' as distinct from 'pitch', which is identified with *haecceitas*. This disposes of Fr Peters's conclusion: 'Inscape precisely covers what Scotus calls *haecceitas*.' (W. A. M. Peters, *Gerard Manley Hopkins*, Oxford, 1947, p. 23.)

146. 6. *will of the Creator*. GMH is here 'Scotistior quam ipse Scotus'.

Scotus is not a voluntarist in the pejorative sense; see E. Longpré, *La Philosophie du B. Duns Scot* (Paris, 1924).

Scotus insists on an intrinsic *aptitude* between the Creator's mind and his will. Already in the divine mind a nature is *apt* to be such-and-such an individual before the divine will decrees the *haecceitas* which fits the aptitude. What the divine mind fixes in the nature to be created is what Scotus calls its individual *degree, gradus sibi intrinsecus*. See App. II.

GMH, as will be seen, does not distinguish sufficiently between his '*pitch*' (which seems to be Scotus's *gradus*) and Scotus's *haecceitas*. Both in his speculations and in real life he laid too much stress on an anti-natural will. He was truer to the spirit both of St Ignatius and of Scotus when he wrote:

'My own heart let me more have pity on. . . .' (*Poems*, 71.)

147. 1. *a paper*. Unfortunately nothing is now known of this paper. For further comments on the philosophy of this chapter, see App. II.

151. 1. *the copula in logic*. See the undergraduate essay on *Parmenides*: '. . . nothing is so pregnant and straightforward to the truth as simple *yes* and *is*'. For the link between Scotus, GMH, and Parmenides, see notes, pp. 284–5 (128. 1 and 128. 2), and p. 288 (136. 2).

151. 2. *the Welsh 'a'*, meaning 'and', can have the force of an affirmative copula—hence perhaps GMH's rather puzzling use of capitals in '. . . AND the fire that breaks from thee then . . .' (*Poems*, 36.)

151. 3. *ecceitas*. The Italian form of *haecceitas* is *ecceità*. Possibly GMH derived it from Fr le Gonidec of the Roman Province with whom he seems to have discussed Scotism: see note, p. 296 (170. 2). Perhaps also the association of *Ecce!*, 'Look!', appealed to him. It is possible that he was not familiar with the word in the original, since it does not occur in the *Scriptum Oxoniense* which he seems chiefly to have read. It occurs, so far as I know, only in the *Reportata Parisiensia*, II. xii. 5.

151. 4. *virgin matter.* In the *De Rerum Principio* what might be called 'virgin matter' (*materia prima*) is considered as the 'badge of creaturehood' common to finite things both material and spiritual. The *De Rerum Principio* used to be numbered among Duns Scotus's works; but for the last thirty years its authenticity has been definitely rejected, and it is attributed to an earlier author. See P. Delorme, O.F.M., in *La France franciscaine*, vii (1921), 279–95, and ix (1926), 421–71.

Scotus has the same way of thinking about finiteness as the earlier author; but, for Scotus, the common 'badge of creaturehood' is the *carentia entitatis*, the possibility of further being. GMH seems to have put the thought of Scotus in the terminology of the earlier author.

151. 5. *the passage quoted at p. 53*: this refers to Marie Lataste, who is mentioned in the next paragraph. See App. I.

152. 1. *'splay'* . . . *'neap'*. The terms correspond respectively to freedom of play and freedom of pitch. 'Splay', as GMH uses it in general, is the radiation from an interior force and the shape that the rays assume. The 'neap' is the interior force—with a change of metaphor from fire to water; it is the bunching of the tide when the moon is young with the impetus of the spring-flood, as it were, coiled in it. With reference to the spiritual writings the terms are best understood in the context of 'the order of intention' and the 'order of execution'.

In the order of intention (in the neap), outside time, are all our free decisions which God had foreseen and co-operated with, though it needs the order of execution to display the historical shape of them. There are of course moments when the order of intention coincides with the order of time. These are the moments in our lives when one decision taken 'in the neap' settles the course of our lives and perhaps a slice of the world's history as well. 'In the lost boyhood of Judas the world was betrayed.'

'Neap' is often identified with the ebb-tide of the third quarter, but there is no reason why it should be. When Shakespeare wrote: 'There is a tide . . . which, taken at the flood . . .', he was obviously thinking of the neap-flood of the first quarter, and applying it to moral passions in the same way as GMH.

157. 1. See note, p. 280 (68. 1).

CHAPTER FOUR

161. 1. The proper title in St Ignatius's 'autograph' is *De Christo Rege*, 'On Christ the King' not 'On the Kingdom of Christ'. The first part of GMH's notes is a commentary on the text; but the second part has nothing to do with it.

162. I. Priority of nature means priority in the order of causality as opposed to priority in the order of time. The prophecies concerning Christ are in nature after the event not precisely because of the difference between the distinction of orders of intention and execution, but because, in the view of GMH and others, the divine knowledge of vision (*scientia visionis*), in the light of which prophecies are made, presupposes and depends on the existence of its objects (here the actual passion). This is in accordance with the axiom of many theologians: *ideo Deus sit quia res erit*, and not vice versa. In the order of time the prophecies are prior to the event.

164. I. *volo et desidero*: the distinction of the elective and the affective will, which GMH was anxious to establish in the *Spiritual Exercises*.

164. 2. *Phil. ii 5–11*: For GMH's interpretation of this text see note, pp. 296–7 (170. 3).

Heb. xii 2 sqq is the passage beginning: 'Looking on Jesus the author and finisher of faith, who having joy set before him, endured the cross. . . .' (Douai Version.)

164. 3. *commonwealth*. The whole of this passage to the end is drawn, often verbally, from his trilogy of sermons at Liverpool, 10, 17, 25 Jan. 1880. But in this passage GMH seems to be arguing out what he omitted in his trilogy: namely, man's status in the restored kingdom of the Church.

167. I. *Lastly, which is obscurer, that it is accepted.* This seems to be the third member of a triple division of which the first is 'first the nature of the act in itself', and the second 'next the exercise and its conditions'. The clause 'that it is permitted' would thus be part of the second division, of those acts which are either *commanded* (or forbidden) or *permitted*: that is, either matter of duty or matter of free choice. The third division is of those that 'are accepted' and meritorious in God's sight. This would correspond to Scotus's triple division of the morality of acts:

'. . . Est triplex bonitas moralis secundum ordinem se habens: prima dicitur bonitas in genere; secunda potest dici virtuosa seu ex circumstantia; tertia bonitas meritoria sive bonitas gratuita sive bonitas ex acceptatione divina in ordine ad praemium.' (*Oxoniense*, II. vii. 1, p. 52ª, § D.)

See next note.

67. 2. *of acceptance*. Scotus's view is that an act morally good in itself remains indifferent as regards merit (that is, in the order of acceptance) so long as it is not directed towards God by an intention either actual or virtual. Cf. *Poems*, 110:

'This fault-not-found-with good
Is neither right nor wrong.'

168. 1. *instress and initiation* . . .: the two words seem to be in apposition respectively to *subject's correspondence* and *sovereign's commandments*.

168. 2. *instress of initiation*: the 'of' would appear to be an objective genitive, the initiation being the sovereign's.

168. 3. In MS a word that looks like 'not' has been erased between 'does' and 'deserve a fresh reward'.

168. 4. *Isocrates*, who is said to have lived ninety-nine years, 437–338 B.C., wrote his *Panegyric* about 380 exhorting the Greek city-states to forget their quarrels and unite against Persia under the leadership of Athens. The quotation covers sections 185–6.

ῥάθυμος, underlined by GMH, evidently occurred to him as an equivalent of St Ignatius's '*ignavus* haberetur eques'.

CHAPTER FIVE

170. 1. *descendants*. Scotus was the first to formulate this hypothesis explicitly:

'Dico tamen quod lapsus non fuit causa predestinationis Christi, imo si nec fuisset Adam lapsus, nec homo, adhuc fuisset Christus sic predestinatus, imo, etsi non fuissent creandi alii quam solus Christus.' (*Parisiensia*, III. vii. 4. See also *Oxoniense*, III. xx. 1, p. 41ᵃ, §§ B–C.)

The hypothetical formulation is only a more vivid way of saying that Christ's humanity was God's first intention in creating.

That Mary was associated with Christ in God's first intention is not explicitly stated by Scotus, but it is held by many Scotists in connexion with the Immaculate Conception. For example:

'Par un seul et même décret, dans une seule et même pensée antécédente à toute création des Anges et des hommes, le Christ et Marie ont été conçus dans le plan divin; ils ont précédé tous les êtres, Anges et hommes, et tous les êtres ont été ensuite créés pour eux, le Christ et la Vierge.' (M. L'A. Gilloz, *La Vie franciscaine*, Paris, Nov. 1930, p. 331.)

170. 2. *Fr le Gonidec*: Aloysius le Gonidec put in a year teaching theology at St Beuno's, 1876–7, while GMH was there.

170. 3. *Phil. ii. 7, 8.* This is one of GMH's cardinal texts. It is not altogether clear how he wished to punctuate it. But it is clear that he wished to make three moments or stages in Christ's sacrifice—(i) in eternity, (ii) in angelic time or duration, and (iii) in earthly time—something like this:

(i) He did not snatch at the privileges of the godhead, but was glad to become a creature so as to adore his Father (which as God he could not do)—hence the creation, after him, of Mary to be his dwelling-place.

(ii) Then, the angels being created and Lucifer refusing to adore him, he did not snatch at his prerogative (by grace) to be the king of angels, but was glad to become a man in a world 'a little lower than the angels', but still sinless.

(iii) Then, after the fall of Adam, he did not snatch at his prerogative (by nature) to be the king of all mankind, but was glad to be born in poverty and, finally, to die a criminal.

See *Letters*, i. 175, 177 Also see notes, p. 301 (181. 1 and 181. 2).

But in the letter to Bridges, GMH makes this triple descent not actual but intentional. That is to say, he thinks of Christ as a man on earth recapitulating this triple sacrifice in his first conscious adoration of the Father.

170. 4. '*O felix culpa*, quae talem ac tantum meruit habere Redemptorem'— from the *Exsultet* of the Easter Vigil.

Although man's sin was not the cause or occasion of the Incarnation, yet the sin was a 'happy fault' in that it has shown us the heart of God in a way we would never otherwise have known. Scotus does not believe that God demanded Christ's death as the exact price of sin—a single word or sigh from Christ would have been enough to redeem all possible worlds— but that Christ offered his life freely as the best way of making us love God:

> 'Et ideo multum tenemur ei. Ex quo enim aliter potuisset homo redimi, et tamen ex sua libera voluntate sic redemit, multum ei tenemur, et amplius quam si sic necessario et non aliter potuissemus fuisse redempti; ideo ad alliciendum nos ad amorem suum, ut credo, hoc praecipue fecit, et quia voluit hominem amplius teneri Deo.' (*Oxoniense*, III. xx. 1, p. 41ᵃ, § D.)

170. 5. This does not mean that our Lady enjoyed the hypostatic union with the divinity, but that in virtue of her relation to Christ her condition was superior to that of any other creature, in this sense, that since Suarez theologians have said that Mary belongs to the hypostatic order. (Josepho A. de Aldama, S. J., *Mariologia, seu de Matre Redemptoris*, B.A.C. edition, pp. 342, 399 sq.)

170. 6. *she-being* . . . *Apocalypse*—chap. xii. In the *Catholic Commentary on Holy Scripture* (London, 1953), p. 968, j and k, Fr C. C. Martindale defends the identity of Mary with the 'Woman clothed with the sun' who is the mother of the Messias:

> 'This does not exclude John's having seen our Lady in this Woman— how could he *not*? Having spent so long in her company, he *could* not have written of the Mother of the Messias without being conscious of her, any more than he could have written about 'eating the flesh and drinking the blood' of Christ without thinking of the Eucharist. And the moment he thinks of the 'primeval serpent' he *must* have remembered Eve; so the Woman becomes the Second Eve, and we have the series—the 'Mother of the Messias': the Universal Eve: Jerusalem and the People: the Church and Mary. The *immediate* appearance of Mary as the Second Eve in patristic literature must surely be due in part to this passage.'

GMH's 'she-being' does not go beyond the title 'Universal Eve'. Eve's consent brought sin to humanity; Mary's consent bore a Saviour for the whole of creation. One has only to add that sex represents a spiritual mystery which needs a division in the flesh before its full perfection can be realized.

171. 1. *Melchisedech*: Gen. xiv. 17, and Heb. vii. 1–3.

'Observe, in the first place, that his name means, the king of justice; and further that he is king of Salem, that is, of peace. That is all; no name of father or mother, no pedigree, no date of birth or of death; there he stands, eternally, a priest, the true figure of the Son of God.' (Heb. vii. 2, 3; Knox's version.)

171. 2. See note 1, Introduction to Part II, p. 114. Part II, p. 114, note, 1.

171. 3. GMH was perhaps incautious in choosing these terms. These speculations appear to be based on Scotus only in so far as Scotus maintained the possibility of the existence of the Eucharist before the Incarnation. Fr J. H. Crehan, in a letter to me, concludes with a note on their use in the 4th century:

'Then about 380 Apollinaris makes the two terms distinct. He accepts ἐνσάρκωσις for Christ, but denies ἐνανθρώπησις, holding that the godhead took the place of the πνεῦμα or upper soul in Christ, so that Christ had not a fully human soul. The condemnation of Apollinaris made the term ἐνσάρκωσις go out of fashion, while ἐνανθρώπησις was asserted the more loudly and even got into Latin as *inhumanatio* in Facundus of Hermiane— 6th century. Such being the story of the terms, I think they must have rested on the theological scrap-heap until Hopkins picked them up. They obviously take on a new meaning in his hands.'

The meaning given to them by GMH is of course entirely different from that invented by Apollinaris. GMH is distinguishing two events—one in the angelic order, the other in human time. In the famous text of St John: 'The Word [a] was made Flesh, and [b] came to dwell among us.'

171. 4. *Genesis* iii. 8: '. . . they heard the voice of the Lord God walking in paradise at the afternoon air. . . .' (Douai Version.)

171. 5. *pp. 121, 122 MS.* Reference is to ch. 7, p. 186, *Videre Personas.*

173. 1. '*Ecce Ancilla*' *etc.* There follows a long quotation from Marie Lataste: see App. I.

173. 2. *p. 154 . . . pp. 82, 85*: This passage, in GMH's MS, faces p. 77; his reference to p. 154 is to his note on *Confirmat* (see previous page): to p. 82, on 'Ut pie meditari licet'; for p. 85, see note, p. 299 (175. 3).

174. 1. *Memory . . . Imagination*: This sentence seems to embody a triple distinction by Scotus in *Oxoniense*, 1. iii. 6, p. 56ᵃ, § H.

'There is memory which conserves thoughts from the past *as* past—this is Aristotle's use of the word; there is memory whose task is to represent objects, whether they are real or not; and finally there is memory which is the spring of actual confused knowing—the *visio existentis ut existens*— and this is a peculiarly Scotist use of the term. These three seem to correspond to GMH's 'memory proper', 'Imagination', and 'Simple Apprehension'. (See C. Devlin, *The Image and The Word*, I.)

174. 2. *beget it*. The First Act cannot beget the Second Act by the ordinary way of imagination and abstraction.

'Dictum Augustini debet intelligi de actu primo sufficiente ex se ad actum suum secundum; sed tamen nunc impeditur, propter quod impedimentum actus secundus non elicitur a primo.' (*Oxoniense Prolog.* I, p. 3ª, § E.)

(The reference to Augustine is to *De Trinitate*, xiv. 4: 'Mens nota est sibi, ergo notum est sibi quid sit eius primum obiectum. . . .')

The understanding has to dwell without distinct words or images on the memory's confused awareness of being—the *visio existentis*:

'Concipiendo ergo Deum in conceptu universalissimo, noli quaerere *quid*; hoc est, noli descendere in aliquem conceptum particularem in quo ille universalior salvatur, qui particularior propinquior est phantasmati; descendendo enim ad talem, qui magis relucet in phantasmate occurrenti, statim amittitur illa serenitas veritatis, vel sinceritas veritatis, in qua intelligebatur Deus, quia statim intelligitur veritas contracta, quae non convenit Deo, cui conveniebat veritas in communi concepta, non contracta.' (*Oxoniense* I. iii. 3, p. 48ª, § R.)

174. 3. *practical will . . . fruition* could be the same distinction as that between *amor obiecti* and *amor notitiae obiecti* referred to in App. II. But GMH is wrong in saying that fruition or enjoyment 'issues in' praxis. It is the other way round. Enjoyment *results from* the act of love which is praxis:

'Quod additur de delectatione nihil est ad propositum, quia delectatio est passio consequens naturaliter operationem perfectam . . . nec ista est praxis proprie loquendo . . . amare autem vel desiderare obiectum cognitum . . . est vere praxis, nec naturaliter consequens apprehenionem, sed libere. . . .' (*Oxoniense Prolog.* v, p. 13ᵇ, § M.)

Praxis is affective as well as elective. GMH is not always clear on this point. Here he identifies the affective will with the intellect; but, though in practice they are closely connected, they remain independent faculties. Elsewhere he makes too sharp a distinction between the affective and elective will; whereas in fact they are simply two elements in the same act. Choice would be impossible without *some* intrinsic affection towards the object of choice. For the possible effects in GMH's active life of this mistake, see note, p. 263 (146. 6).

174. 4. *practice or action.* See App. II on 'praxis'. See also note, p. 312 (209. 2).

175. 1. *and in other ways.* There follows a quotation from Marie Lataste. See App. I.

175. 2. *Mysteria.* See note, p. 304 (190. 2).

175. 3. *pp. 77, 82.* Reference is from p. 85 in MS. See at note 173. 2 above.

176. 1. *Fr Whitty*, Robert Whitty (1817–95) was Master of Tertians from 1881 to 1886; it was he who gave GMH the points of his Long Retreat. Before becoming a Jesuit he had been a friend of the Oxford converts and Vicar-General to Cardinal Wiseman; it was he who advised the Cardinal to come boldly to London in the uproar of 1851. Entering the Society in 1857, he was Provincial 1870–3, when GMH was in philosophy, and Assistant to the General in Rome 1887–93. An Irishman of great but very simple wisdom and holiness, he evidently made a deep impression on GMH who recalled his words on this occasion two years later.

See note, pp. 311–12 (208. 1).

177. 1. See GMH on *The Three Epiphanies*,—Part III, sec. 6, 6 Jan. 1888.

177. 2. *Christ's coming.* If GMH's distinction between ἐνσάρκωσις and ἐνανθρώπησις means that the same Christ has played the part of Redeemer in two different orders of creation, then it is logical that the events of Christ's life on this planet should in some way be paralleled by events in the angelic order as related shadowily in Apocalypse, xii.

Scotus seems to think that different points in the duration of the angelic battle correspond with part of our time; but the passage is obscure:

'Sed quibus correspondebunt ista *nunc* aevi in tempore nostro continuo? Dico quod ultima mora, scilicet existendi in termino, correspondet toti tempori post instans primum beatitudinis bonorum et damnationis malorum. Et mora tamen prima in qua erant uniformes, potest poni co-extitisse instanti nostro, vel parti temporis nostri; et secundum hoc conse-quenter oportet ponere de secunda mora.' (*Oxoniense*, II. v. 1, p. 45ᵇ, § H.)

See also 179. 2 and Introduction to Part II, pp. 112 ff.

CHAPTER SIX

179. 1. '. . . *his burning throne*': the Duke in *Measure for Measure*, v. i. 291.

179. 2. *process of his own fall.* See note, p. 286 (132. 1). Scotus puts several stages and pauses (*morae* and *morulae*) in the process of the separation of the good angels from the bad:

'Tertia mora fuit distinctio finalis unius ab alio necessario. Probabile est etiam quod in secunda mora, in qua fuerunt difformes in via, fuerunt multae morulae, quia mali peccaverunt multis speciebus peccati, scilicet superbia, odio et invidia, et isti actus ordinate et non in eodem instanti fuerunt eliciti, ut patet . . . per illud Apoc. *Fiebat praelium magnum in caelo*, et dicitur ibi quod Michael fecit victoriam. . . .' (*Oxoniense*, II. v. 2.)

179. 3. *chorister.* Rickaby has the same thought, on p. 21 of his work already quoted:

'He is called, for the beauty that once was his, *Lucifer*, or *morning-star* (Isai. xiv. 12). He was precentor in the hymn of praise, sung at the dawn of creation, *when the morning stars sang together, and all the sons of God shouted for joy.* (Job xxxviii. 7.)

180. 1. Here GMH converts Scotus's speculation on a possibility into a fact.

180. 2. *apostacy.* . . . The 'c' for 's' was an ancient spelling error of GMH's. In the terrible letter to his father of 16 Oct. 1866 he has 'prophecied' and 'ecstacy'.

180. 3. '*S.P. Mentionem*': reference to a note by Fr Roothaan on the fact that St Ignatius makes no mention of the good angels.

181. 1. *rapinam*. Phil. ii. 6. For the three stages which GMH discerned in this passage, see note, p. 296 (170. 3). Although his interpretation as a whole may be rejected, it should be noted that his reading of *rapinam* ἁρπαγμόν) was a brilliant anticipation of what is now generally accepted; cf. Knox's version—'a prize to be coveted'. See *Letters*, i. 175 and 177 quoted below:

> 'The interpretation of St Paul Phil. ii 5 sqq. was, as it stands, my own. At least I thought so, but I see that some modern Catholic commentators, as Beelen (who published a N.T. grammar) and Bp MacEvilly, give it or nearly so. Older commentators led mainly by St Austin take ἁρπαγμόν and *rapinam* for *robbery*, that is / Christ being God thought it no sin to be what he was *and yet* humbled himself etc; but this requires a strong adversative particle in the Greek, wh. there is not. I got the sense of ἁρπαγμόν from Jowett or some modern critic: it in reality adds force to St Austin's interpretation, which otherwise I was following. St John Chrysostom seems to have come still nearer the sense I gave.'

181. 2. ἐνανθρώπησιν: See following note. GMH takes the first renunciation of which St Paul speaks in the above passage to have been *before* Christ's becoming man. There is no question of the Word renouncing the status of Godhead, i.e. the Divine nature. For this anterior 'procession', the shadow of the Son's procession from the Father, see GMH's letter to Bridges, 16 June 1882 (*Letters*, i. 149); also 'On Creation and Redemption'.

181. 3. *See later at p. 208*: the passage that has been made to follow immediately in this edition.

182. 1. *Milton*: *Paradise Regained*, i, l. 314:

> 'But now an aged man in rural weeds . . .'.

But it is Spenser's Archimago who disguises himself specifically as a Hermit.

183. 1. '*DE VOCATIONE*'—'Vocation of the Apostles', St Ignatius's text:

> 'It appears that St Peter and St Andrew were called three times; first, to some knowledge, as is evident from St John; secondly, to follow Christ after a manner, with the intention of returning to the possessions they had left, as St Luke tells us; thirdly, to follow Christ our Lord forever.

> '2. He called Philip and Matthew, as St Matthew himself tells us.

> '3. He called the other Apostles, of whose particular vocation the Gospel makes no mention.'

The 'three sorts of vocation' discussed by GMH are the three enumerated— not the three stages of the first sort.

183. 2. *not as the Vulgate says*. GMH is not referring to the Latin Version of the Scriptures, but to the *versio vulgata* of the *Spiritual Exercises*. It was the version generally accepted until Fr Roothaan printed his *versio litteralis*, a word-for-word rendering into Latin of St Ignatius's Spanish, regardless of syntax etc. GMH nearly always followed the *versio litteralis*. In this instance the *versio vulgata* has, without any authority, included John and James as examples of the second sort of vocation; in GMH's opinion they should be included in the first.

183. 3. *the three times for making an Election*—St Ignatius's text:

'The first time is when God our Lord so moves and attracts the will that without doubting or being able to doubt, such a devout soul follows what has been pointed out to it, as St Paul and St Matthew did when they followed Christ our Lord.

'The second time is when much light and knowledge is obtained by experience of consolations and desolations, and by experience of the discernment of various spirits.

'The third time is one of tranquillity . . . when the soul is not agitated by divers spirits and enjoys the use of its natural powers freely and quietly.'

183. 4. The text of St Ignatius's consideration is not given here since GMH explains it sufficiently in his commentary. The three classes are three pairs of men. See following notes.

184. 1. *Cur bini*. . . . Fr Roothaan in a note asks: why *pairs* of men, not individuals? He answers: perhaps so as to draw attention to the *type*, not to any particular person. GMH adds a further reason of his own. For the same quotation, but in English, see his letter to Baillie, 22 May 1880. (*Letters*, iii. 246.)

184. 2. '*In affectu*': Fr Roothaan altered to 'in effectu'; but GMH's rectification anticipates the comment of later Jesuit authorities:

'The correction suggested by Fr Roothaan, *en effecto* instead of *en affecto*, is unacceptable—cf. A. Codina, *Exercitia Spiritualia S. Ign.*, Madrid, 1919, p. 360.' (Pinard de la Boulaye, *The Month*, Jan. 1951, p. 62.)

The contrast between the second and third types is not necessarily between the retaining and the giving up of the ducats, but between a false and a genuine abandonment of the attachment to them.

Shakespeare's *Hamlet* supplies interesting examples of the three types:

1. Claudius knows his guilt and knows what he has to give up; but he defers restitution and remains consciously in bad conscience. (Act III, sc. iii.)
2. Gertrude has succeeded in composing her conscience, comforting herself with the assurance that she is not guilty and that her son is mad; she 'lays a flattering unction to her soul' to 'skin and film the ulcerous place'. (Act III, sc. iv.)
3. Hamlet himself may be said to have attained to the level of the third type when he said, 'the readiness is all'. (Act v, sc. ii.)

185. 1. *Marie Lataste*. It is possible that GMH was thinking of a striking passage on Jesus the Light of the world—*Ouvres*, II. iii (vol. ii, p. 76 in the edition he was using). See App. I.

185. 2. *though he lived it.* . . . In MS *'played'* was substituted for 'lived', then crossed out and 'lived' restored.

CHAPTER SEVEN

186. 1. *See on 'videndo locum'*: the blank leaf which should contain the note has been torn out and lost.

186. 2. *real direction towards him.* A simple and intuitive attraction of the mind towards any object is Scotus's criterion of the reality of that object (whether it exists or not), and is also the foundation of his famous *distinctio formalis* which obtains between two realities which cannot actually exist except as one thing (e.g. *haecceitas* and *natura communis*), yet impose themselves on the mind as two separable objects. A *haecceitas* is a reality whether it exists or not (cf. ch. 3 and App. II) because it is a distinct intention in God's will. That, however, is not Scotus's ground for calling it a reality; his ground is that, in GMH's words, 'the mind has a real direction towards' it. The following passage, though difficult, seems relevant:

'Oportet videre qualis sit ista differentia quae ponitur praecedere omnem actum intellectus. Dico quod tam in rebus quam in intellectu differentia maior manifesta est, et ex illa frequenter concluditur differentia minor quae est immanifesta; sicut ex differentia creaturarum concluditur differentia idearum in intellectu divino. . . . In re autem manifesta est distinctio rerum, et haec duplex, suppositorum scilicet et naturarum; in intellectu manifesta est differentia duplex, modorum scilicet concipiendi et obiectorum formalium. Ex his concluditur differentia hic intenta quae est immanifesta, et nimirum quia minima est distinctio in suo ordine, idest inter omnes quae praecedunt intellectionem; concluditur autem ex differentia reali sic: distinctio divinorum suppositorum est realis. Cum igitur non possit idem eodem formaliter convenire realiter et differre realiter, concluditur aliqua differentia essentiae in qua supposita conveniunt, ab illis rationibus quibus supposita distinguuntur. Similiter ex differentia obiectorum formalium quorum neutrum continetur in aliquo eminenter (et hoc in intellectu intuitive considerante), concluditur aliqua differentia ante actum intellectus eorum quae cognoscuntur intuitive.' (*Oxoniense*, I. ii. 7, p. 38^{a-b}, § G^g.)

186. 3. *Scotus says.* The theme of his Prologue is that the study of revealed doctrine is itself a sort of minor individual revelation; increasing knowledge of God's mind and nature passes into an offering of love and service of his person. See Père Longpré, pp. 145–6 of the book already cited:

'Selon lui [Scotus], Dieu s'est proposé surtout dans la Révélation de diriger l'activité de la volonté vers sa fin ultime et de l'ordonner dans son acte le plus noble (*praxis*), qui n'est pas autre que la dilection de la fin, l'amour: *Ostensum est dilectionem esse veram praxim.* Que l'on examine le contenu révélé, ajoute Duns Scot; comme tout est susceptible de susciter et de diriger l'amour! *Licet Trinitas personarum non ostendat finem appetibiliorem quam si non esset Trinus, quia est finis inquantum unus Deus, non inquantum*

Trinus, tamen voluntatem ignorantem Trinitatem contingit errare in amando vel desiderando finem, desiderando frui una persona sola. . . .

'Sans doute, écrit Duns Scot, le motif formel de la charité est l'essence divine elle-même; mais l'objet total où se termine l'acte d'amour n'est pas autre que la Trinité des personnes. C'est justement en vue de ces précisions objectives et de ces délicatesses dans la dilection qui monte du cœur de l'homme que Dieu s'est révélé dans le mystère insondable de sa Vie: *Praeter igitur notitiam rectitudinis quam includit Essentiale* [in Deo] *in actu amandi Deum, Personalia includunt propriam notitiam ulteriorem rectitudinis requisitae.*'

186. 4. These points are on p. 122 in Fr Roothaan's book, and GMH's comments are on the blank leaf opposite, except for his last paragraph which has been transposed here from p. 195 in MS.

187. 1. *See at p. 135*: the corresponding additional points for the Resurrection.

187. 2. *See note to p. 58 and to p. 125*: p. 58 is the Third Exercise of the First Week; p. 125 is the paragraph—*Confractionem*—that follows in this edition.

190. 1. *the history*: see note immediately below.

190. 2. *Mysteries* . . . (*p. 173*). The 'Mysteries', that is, of our Lord's life drawn up in the form of points by St Ignatius at the end of the Exercises. The relevant words on 'p. 173' are as follows:

'He appeared to the Virgin Mary; and although this is not mentioned in the Scripture, still it is considered as mentioned when it says that he appeared *to so many others*, for the Scripture supposes us to have understanding, according as it is written, *Are you also without understanding?*'

190. 3. *in her breast unconsumed*. This view of Our Lady's communion is purely private speculation without foundation or authority. The suggestion that the sacred host lay 'in her breast unconsumed' seems to go counter to the nature of the sacrament.

191. 1. *see p. 137*. The note by St Ignatius here referred to is this:

'Although in all the contemplations a fixed number of points is given, say three or five etc., the person who contemplates can take more or fewer points according as he finds it better.'

191. 2. *hiding of the godhead*: The Exercises do not speak of 'withdrawal'. GMH does not suggest that there was any diminution of the hypostatic union.

194. 1. *'magis . . . quam' not 'non'*: the reference is to St Ignatius's note: 'love . . . in deeds more than in words'.

195. 1. *points which follow*: Love, the Holy Spirit, is what the first point promises and what the last three points, taken as a whole not singly, combine to obtain.

195. 2. *comes between*: GMH may have had in mind a trinitarian thesis of Scotus already quoted, *Utrum Deus Pater genuerit Deum Filium voluntate* (*Oxoniense*, I. vi. 1, p. 73ª), in which he discusses in what sense the will comes between the memory and the understanding and in what sense it follows them. In God, the will as a quality or power, *vis spirativa*, precedes and takes part in the generation of the Word. But as an act or procession, *Spiritus Sanctus*, it follows the generation of the Word, coming from the *vis spiritiva* of both Father and Son. In man, the will as desire or inspiration (*vis spiritiva*) comes between the first act and the second act of the mind, 'copulating the memory and the understanding' to produce the word. But as a principle of action it comes after the first and second acts and produces the *third* act, which is love, *amor obiecti*.

> 'Voluntas igitur in nobis, ut est pars imaginis, repraesentat voluntatem in Deo, non quantum ad istum actum copulandi qui est voluntatis nostrae: sed quantum ad alium actum, in quantum, scilicet, voluntas nostra est principium producendi actum circa idem obiectum quod fuit memoriae et intelligentiae nostrae; quia voluntas in divinis est principium producendi amorem adaequatum essentiae divinae quae est obiectum primum memoriae divinae, intelligentiae et voluntatis. Et ille amor productus est Spiritus Sanctus, cui correspondet in nobis dilectio producta; quae dilectio frequenter ab Augustino vocatur voluntas. Sed voluntas proprie in nobis, quae est potentia, non correspondet Spiritui Sancto, sed vi spirativae quae est in Patre et Filio.'

So there is one will which belongs properly to the 2nd of the last three points. There is another will which is the fruit of all the points. See following note.

195. 3. *'Intellige non liberum arbitrium'*: Fr Roothaan's note on St Ignatius's words 'Sume, Domine, et suscipe meam libertatem'. According to Fr Roothaan, St Ignatius does not mean free will here because the will is offered in detail below—'my memory . . . my understanding . . . all my will'. GMH, however, is eager to contradict this and to enlist St Ignatius on the side of his distinction between (1) will as the desire of a rational nature, and (2) will as the positing or 'pitching' of the whole man—*amor obiecti*. After *Contra, intellige*, he has written and then crossed out: *Et nobile documentum est* ('and it is a splendid instance . . .'). It is doubtful if GMH is right on this point.

195. 4. *lettering . . . fills.* Cf. *Poems*, 28, st. iii:

> 'I whirled out wings that spell'.

GMH's simile here suggests 'spell' in the poem to be the verb in a relative clause rather than a noun meaning 'a spell of time': the more so, since three beats are all that are required in this line, whereas there would be four if 'that' were a demonstrative adjective. See also *Poems*, 45, ll. 11–14.

195. 5. *'Fons vivus, ignis'* . . . *ring and tell of him.* Cf. *Poems*, 116, st. i, and 31, ll. 1–2.

CHAPTER EIGHT

196. 1. *a current to the whole.* Cf. *The Wreck of the Deutschland*, st. 6:

'But it rides time like riding a river. . . .'

On this precedent, the 'positive pitch and direction' would be the evolution through many ups and downs of God's plan in history, a plan which may be said to be the incorporation of the universe into the Mystical Body of Christ. The '3 dimensions' would presumably be past, present, and future.

196. 2. *before time.* Cf. Scotus, *Oxoniense*, I. xl. 1, pp. 154^a–b, §§ c–d.

'Sed ista imaginatio falsa est. . . . Et ideo idem est Deum praedestinare et praedestinasse et praedestinaturum esse, et ita contingens unum sicut aliud, quia nihil est nisi nunc aeternitatis mensurans illum actum, quod est nec praesens nec praeteritum nec futurum, sed coexistens omnibus istis.'

196. 3. *order of intention.* Cf. Scotus, *Parisiensia*, III. vii. 4:

'primum in intentione . . . est ultimum in executione.'

For an explanation of this, see note, p. 295 (162. 1).

196. 4. *intention . . . execution.* GMH's 'intention in understanding and intention in will' correspond to the *esse intelligibile* (or *esse cognitum*) and the *esse volitum* which Scotus attributes to things thought of by God and willed by him, which thereby acquire a certain reality outside him, though he has not yet put them into temporal existence. GMH's 'forepitch of execution', however, seems to be his own invention. Perhaps it refers to the influence of coming events which take shape in the minds and wills of men before they actually happen—as we say, 'Coming events cast their shadow before them'.

196. 5. *The elect.* Scotus says the elect were all chosen by God prior (in the order of intention) to his prevision of original sin or actual sin.

'Prius est completus numerus electorum quam aliquis reprobetur. . . . Ex hoc sequitur quod nullus occasionaliter sit salvatus, et quod Christus occasione peccati non fuit incarnatus, immo, si nunquam aliquis peccasset, fuisset supremus inter viatores qui unquam fuerunt.' (*Oxoniense*, I. xli. 1.)

As to the reprobate, Scotus is less satisfactory. God, he says, does not positively ordain them to damnation; he merely omits to elect them 'in Christ'. Thus, when it comes to the decisions that make or mar them, there is no redemptive co-operation. They make these decisions using God's creative strain but outside his redemptive strain; they are thus, as GMH puts it, like 'a blow struck wide, a leap over a precipice', since 'it was only through Christ and the great sacrifice that God had meant any being to come to him at all'. See notes, p. 289 (137. 2), p. 290 (138. 1).

197. 1. *taking part in their own creation.* This passage is a vivid summary of a theme on which GMH spent much time and thought. It appears to owe a good deal to Scotus's two observations in *Oxoniense*, I. xxxix. 1, pp. 150ª–154ª. The burden of these is that man's free decisions are taken out of time, and that in them God's will and man's will concur simultaneously, God's previous knowledge of these decisions being—as the Scotists say—*'flexible'* to either alternative:

'Deus non solum scit contingentia futura, sed scit *contingenter* futura contingentia.' 'God not only knows what may or may not happen, but he knows it *in such a way that* it may or may not happen.'

Scotus argues very subtly that this 'flexibility' is a *perfection* in God, not an imperfection. Opposite these arguments the editor of the 1514 edition has hortatory notes: 'Scotista laboret' and 'Percipe si potes et quiesce'! Scotus's view in this matter was supported by Cardinal Bellarmine.

197. 2. *the Blessed Virgin.* See notes, p. 296 (170. 1) and p. 297 (170. 5).

197. 3. *aeonian*: doubtless derived from *aevum*, the scholastic word for the duration in which angels operate midway in intensity between time and eternity. See Introduction, p. 110.

197. 4. *the Eucharist.* GMH is here speculating on what Scotus conjectures as possibility: the bodily presence of a Christ in a sacramental manner at the beginning of created things:

'Ex hac secunda conclusione sequitur corollarium quod ante incarnationem potuit ita vere Eucharistia fuisse sicut et nunc, et hoc tam quantum ad significationem quam quantum ad rem signatam et contentam.' (*Oxoniense*, IV. x. 4, p. 42ᵇ, § D.)

See Introduction, pp. 113–14. The longer and more explicit passage there translated is from the later edition (Paris, 1891–5). I have not been able to identify it in the 1514 Venice edition which is quoted here.

197. 5. *the Welsh text.* See App. III.

198. 1. *Draco.* I am indebted to Dr P. J. Treanor, S.J., Lecturer in Astronomy and Fellow of Balliol College, Oxford, for the following note:

'The axis about which the earth rotates, which defines the position of the celestial pole, is inclined at 23½° to the axis of the earth's orbital motion round the Sun. . . . The slow conical movement of the earth's axis, like that of an inclined spinning top, about the axis of the equator causes the position of the celestial pole to move among the constellations in a circle of radius 23½° over a period of 26,000 years. Consequently, about 3440 BC the pole was close to the star Thuban (*alpha* Draconis), the principal star in the constellation of the Dragon—not, however, its head. At this early period of astronomy, therefore, the Dragon which extends, as Hopkins observes, over 120° (8 hours of right ascension) contained the pole of the ecliptic—as it still does—and also connected it with the celestial pole, thereby holding a place of honour in the sky. Crommelin thinks it probable that the imagery of *Apocalypse*, xii, 3–9, was suggested by the fall of the Dragon from this preeminence.

'The Dragon is described in the earliest extant description of the con-

stellations, due to the Cilician poet Aratus, and with it another constellation depicting "a labouring man in a kneeling attitude with his right foot
on the scaly dragon's crest". This constellation, later named Hercules by
Eratosthenes, has been taken by some writers as depicting the crushing of
the serpent's head. (Gen. iii. 15.)

'These two constellations may have been among the earliest delineated.
R. H. Allen refers to a cylinder seal dated 3000–3500 BC which shows
the device of a man kneeling on one knee, with the foot of his other leg
on the dragon's head.' See Hutchinson, *Splendour of the Heavens*, ed.
T. E. R. Philips and W. H. Stevenson (Hutchinson), chs. v and xvii.

For GMH's continued interest in the Dragon, see *Letters*, i. 161. For the
association of Lucifer with the 'mountain of the north', see O.T. Isa. xlv.
12–15.

198. 2. '*swale*'—which usually means a patch of low-lying ground—seems
here to envisage undulation, a moving hollow between two moving hills.
There is another use of the word in ch. 9. see note, p. 312 (208. 2).

199. 1. *that river . . . against p. 37*: see the opening lines of this treatise. The
'positive pitch or direction of time' there spoken of would here more particularly be the general trend of growth and decay, waxing and waning, &c.
God gave to nature a forward movement, namely growth to perfection.
The devil cut across this by introducing decay and death. But nature
partly repairs this disaster by making decay and death the seed-bed of new
life. *Burial* (the earth *swallowing* the river) is the medium between death
and rebirth. Death, Burial, Resurrection, is an accepted ritual sequence.

199. 2. *symbol of the Devil*. 'And the Lord God said to the serpent: Because
thou hast done this thing, thou art cursed among all cattle, and beasts of
the earth. Upon thy breast shalt thou go.' (Gen. iii. 15.)

200. 1. *rights before God*. See note, p. 280 (68. 1).

200. 2. *morning stars singing for joy*. Job xxxviii. 7. Cf. Shakespeare:

> 'There's not the smallest orb which thou behold'st
> But in his motion like an angel sings,
> Still quiring to the young-ey'd cherubins;'
>   (*Merchant of Venice*, v. i. 60–63.)

200. 3. *St Ignatius the Martyr*: Epistle to the Trallians, 5.

200. 4. *dimension of the angelic action*. If the angelic direction was ascent in
the scale of natural dignity, that of Christ was the opposite: descent to be
'a little lower than the angels'—in the *natural* order. See GMH on Phil.
ii. 5–11.

200. 5. *recondite and difficult*. See Introduction to Part II, p. 112, n. 1.

200. 6. '*adduction*': the technical term used by Scotus in his treatise on the
Blessed Sacrament, where he proves that it is strictly possible for the same
body to be in more than one place at the same time, because, in the categories, place is dependent on quantity, not vice versa. GMH's use of this

term makes it clear that he thinks the presentment of Christ and Mary to the Angels was a real presence, not a subjective vision by the Angels. It would be subjectivism on *our* part to regard the story as no more than a dramatic allegory of world history. Hence GMH goes on to say that there are points at which the aeonian angelic struggle actually coincides with human events in time—'though I cannot yet clearly grasp how . . .'.

200. 7. *on the human race.* See note, p. 286 (132. 1.)

200. 8. *Babylonian and the Welsh text agree.* See App. III. Hopkins's transcriptions of these are followed by a quotation from Marie Lataste: see App. I.

200. 9. *see at p. 96:* i.e. pp. 179–80: *Reliqua vitia . . . pride.*

201. 1. *inscape* is here identified with beauty. Earlier (cf. p. 293 (146. 5), it was identified with nature or essence. The two are the same in an exemplarist context. The beauty (*species*) and the specific essence (*species*) of a creature both derive from its being a likeness (*species*) of some aspect of the Divine Essence. This was a commonplace of Christian philosophy from the earliest times down to the end of the 17th century. Cf.:

> 'Most ignorant of what he's most assured,
>   His glassy essence. . . .'
>   (*Measure for Measure*, II. ii, 120.)

Scotus's phrase, *species specialissima*, had thus obviously attractive overtones for Hopkins. See C. Devlin, 'The Image and the Word' in *The Month*, Feb. and Mar. 1950.

201. 2. *Jude 6.* 'The angels, too, who left the place assigned to them, instead of keeping their due order, he has imprisoned in eternal darkness, to await their judgement when the great day comes.' (Knox's version.)

201. 3. *a meriting.* Cf. *Paradise Lost*, i. 98:

> 'And high disdain from sense of injured merit. . . .'

This is one of several Miltonic reminiscences in GMH's picture of Satan.

201. 4. *against pp. 61 and 204.* For the first reference, see p. 137 and note, p. 289 (137. 1): for the second, see the transcript of the Babylonian and Welsh text, App. III. The point of both is the same as in the sentences of GMH that follow. They represent a good insight on his part. There is something peculiarly inspiring about a right rebellion against a wrong rebellion; and the attribution of chivalry to St Michael completes the picture.

201. 5. *Holy Sepulchre.* See pp. 190–1, the appearance of Christ to Mary at the Resurrection.

202. 1. *his fall.* The 'his' evidently refers to Satan, not to man. GMH seems to have been working towards the theory that the duration of the angelic battle coincides at certain points with earthly history. See note, p. 300 (179. 2).

CHAPTER NINE

203. 1. Though only one or two rules are commented on by GMH, the first nine are quoted here in full because they are very relevant not only to his spiritual life but to his poetry also. See C. Devlin, 'The Ignatian inspiration of Gerard Hopkins' in *Blackfriars*, Dec. 1935, pp. 887–900. Much of his poetic inspiration flowed directly from 'consolation' in the Ignatian sense—or, obversely, from desolation: see conclusion of note (206. 1) below.

205. 1. *from this place*. GMH's theory of the affective will, and indeed his whole outlook as a poet, made it necessary for him to hold that the imagination expresses the longings of the spirit as well as those of the body. Here, as elsewhere, he is anxious to enlist St Ignatius on his side. In this comment the later entry of 14 Nov. 1881 modifies the earlier one of 24 Dec. 1879.

205. 2. *Fr Whitty says*. See note, pp. 299–300 (176. 1); also pp. 311–12 (208. 1) below.

205. 3. *gaudere*: from the collect of Whit Sunday.

205. 4. *no question of tepidity*. A comment by Fr Roothaan introduces the question of tepidity which GMH considers to be here out of place. Fr Roothaan's comment is really to the same effect—that these rules do not apply to the tepid.

205. 5. *'Quis enim' etc*. A comment by Fr Roothaan questions the accuracy of the *versio vulgata*, which here, however, GMH defends. It is a small point hardly worth elucidating.

206. 1. *Regulae Aliae* are the further rules for the discernment of spirits which St Ignatius wrote for those who had advanced from the First to the Second Week—that is, roughly, from the purgative way to the illuminative way. Here a greater subtlety is required which is exemplified in the long extract from Bd Peter Favre, Ignatius's first companion. Bd Peter says among other things that, while the *spirit* of consolation is to be accepted joyfully, the *words* in which we express it need to be watched with caution lest we confuse the impact of the spirit with our own subsequent desires; on the other hand, while the spirit of desolation is always to be distrusted, yet the words which it prompts may contain some truth, e.g. about our own misery and shortcomings, which we should wait for the good spirit to put in its true perspective.

Another point of great importance which Bd Peter makes (though GMH has not noted it here) is that a deeper consolation can be uncovered beneath desolation, because it is only our hunger for God that makes us feel earthly temptations as a misery; thus from desolation can be drawn the consoling conviction that we do really love God and cannot be happy without him: 'Lord, to whom shall we go . . .?' This is of great importance for interpreting GMH's poems of desolation (*Poems*, 68–71 etc.) which came to him, as he says, '*like inspirations unbidden and against my will*'. (*Letters*, i. 221.)

207. 1. *'Quid erit' etc.* The comment is Fr Roothaan's, but GMH is really writing about St Ignatius's words. St Ignatius's rule here is that while natural inspiration has usually some assignable cause, physical or psychological, the mark of strictly supernatural inspiration is that it is quite inexplicable by any preceding event or disposition:

'It belongs to God our Lord alone to give consolation to the soul without preceding cause; for it belongs to the Creator to enter into the soul, to go out of it, and to excite movements in it, drawing it wholly to the love of his divine Majesty. I say, without cause, that is, without any previous perception or knowledge of any object from which such consolation might come to the soul by means of its own acts of the understanding and will.'

Fr Roothaan interprets the last phrase ('by means of . . .') as an exception to the rule of no perceptible cause, presumably because 'unconscious' mind-activity was not accepted in his day. GMH is quite correct in taking the other and more obvious interpretation of St Ignatius's words.

207. 2. *happy about.* Compare GMH at the age of twenty on 'natural inspiration':

'The word inspiration need cause no difficulty. I mean by it a mood of great, abnormal in fact, mental acuteness, either energetic or receptive, according as the thoughts which arise in it seem generated by a stress and action of the brain, or to strike into it unasked. This mood arises from various causes, physical generally, as good health or state of the air or, prosaic as it is, length of time after a meal. But I need not go into this; all that it is needful to mark is, that the poetry of inspiration can only be written in this mood of mind, even if it only last a minute, by poets themselves. Everybody of course has like moods, but not being poets what they then produce is not poetry.' (*Letters*, iii. 216.)

It is interesting to compare this youthfully sophisticated theory of atmospherics and meal-times with the more primitive belief of twenty years later: that natural inspiration comes direct from God. See *Poems*, 74 and 75; and *Letters*, i. 66 and ii. 141.

207. 3. *p. 179.* See note, p. 310 (205. 4). The rule here concerned runs:

'In the case of those who are making progress from good to better the good Angel touches their soul gently, lightly and sweetly, as a drop of water entering into a sponge, and the evil angel touches it sharply and with noise and disturbance, like a drop of water falling upon a rock. In the case of those who go from bad to worse the said spirits touch their soul in a contrary manner. The reason of this difference is the disposition of the soul, contrary or similar to the aforementioned angels; for when it is contrary to them, they enter with noise and sensible commotion and are easily perceived; but when it is similar to them, they enter in silence, as into their own house, by an open door.'

208. 1. *Fr. Whitty says.* His instruction on tepidity evidently made a deep impression; in his obituary notice there is the following tribute:

'I had the happiness of making my tertianship under him, and the notes of his long retreat are a mine of valuable spirituality and suggestive thoughts on the Exercises. One consideration was masterly above all, and will, I am sure, be still remembered by my fellow-tertians. It was on the subject of tepidity. Like all that he said, it was consoling even when severe, and the exceeding kindness of his heart appeared in all his exhortations and points of meditation.'

208. 2. *'swale'* can mean a trough or depression between two higher points. Perhaps the words 'swath' (or 'sweep') and 'vale' combined to suggest it in GMH's mind.

208. 3. ζεστόν . . . ζῆλος: both come from the verb to boil (ζέω).

208. 4. ψυχικοί: the word does not occur in 1 Cor. iii, though σαρκικοί does three times in contrast with πνευματικοῖς. Neither can be identified with 'the lukewarm' of Apoc. iii. 15. But St Jude's ψυχικοί seem to be decadent Christians.

208. 5. *Three Ways of Praying.* Of these three, GMH comments only on the first. The relevant paragraph of St Ignatius is as follows:

'The first way of praying concerns the Ten Commandments and the seven deadly sins, the three powers of the soul and the five senses of the body; it is not so much a formal method of prayer as the suggestion of a form and way and certain exercises whereby the soul may prepare itself and make progress in them, and whereby its prayer may become acceptable.'

209. 1. '[*ad exercitia facienda*]'. The brackets are in the autograph version, and the bracketed words occur between the phrases 'may prepare itself' and 'and make progress' ('. . . se praeparet [ad exercitia facienda] et ut in illis proficiat . . .'). GMH is quite right not to accept them. He is also right in not accepting the capital 'E' which Fr Roothaan gives to 'certain exercises' ('quaedam Exercitia'), as if they referred to the *Spiritual Exercises*.

It is worth noting that on nearly every occasion when GMH has a new and personal interpretation of the text of St Ignatius, his interpretation has been approved by later Jesuit scholars.

209. 2. πρᾶξις. For Scotus's use of the word, see App. II. Here, as elsewhere, GMH stresses the part played by the elective will, but he also allows for the affective will in phrases like 'listens to Christ's call, and so on'.

Scotus's *cognitio practica* (which leads to *praxis*) and St Ignatius's *intima cognitio* may be understood in the context of Newman's contrast between 'real assent' and 'notional assent'. GMH, however, set a higher value on reason than did Newman: see *Letters*, iii. 388. He wished to do a commentary on *The Grammar of Assent*, no doubt in the light of his own Scotist scholastic principles; but Newman demurred. (See *Letters*, iii. 412.)

NOTES ON PART THREE

SECTION ONE

222. 1. The MS of this translation was preserved—like several of the poems—by the care of GMH's friend, Fr Francis Bacon, S.J., who copied it himself; it continues immediately at the bottom of the sheet of paper on which ends the version of *Lines for a picture of St Dorothea*. There is no MS extant in Hopkins's autograph; but the fact that Fr Bacon made his copy with the poems is strong evidence; and the style and vocabulary put Hopkins's authorship beyond reasonable doubt. It is an adaptation into his idiom of one of the most famous and beautiful sermons ever preached.

222. 2. *St John Chrysostom* was called from Antioch to the see of Constantinople in 398 when the eunuch Eutropius was still the all-powerful minister of the Emperor Arcadius. Reversing the mode of life of his predecessor, St John set himself from the start to champion the poor and oppressed and to castigate the vices of the rich, including the clergy and the court. 'The Christians of the imperial city were thus able to measure the abyss which separates a saint from a politician' (G. Bardy, *Saint Jean de Constantinople* in *Histoire de l'Église*, Bloud & Gay, 1948). Though Eutropius had advocated his promotion, St John had not hesitated to criticize him in the days of his power. When Eutropius was suddenly and completely overthrown, he fled to the Church as his only refuge. St John preached two sermons in his favour, one on the day of his fall, the other when a pardon had been promised him—a promise which was afterwards violated. This extract is from the first sermon, delivered when Eutropius was actually clinging to the altar of Saint Sophia. Hence Gibbon's comment: 'the most eloquent of the saints, John Chrysostom, enjoyed the triumph of protecting a prostrate minister, whose choice had raised him to the ecclesiastical throne of Constantinople'. For the text of the homily see Migne, *Patrologia, Series Graeca*, vol. lii, cols. 391–414.

222. 3. *bright keepings of the consulship.* ἡ λαμπρὰ τῆς ὑπατείας περιβολή.

222. 4. *They were a shadow . . . and are swept away.* Robert Southwell has a translation of the same lines in his *Epistle of Comfort* (1587):

'Our life, sayth the same saynct, was a shadowe and it passed. It was a smoake and it vanished. It was a bubble and it dissolved. It was a spinner's web and it was shaken asunder.'

SECTION TWO

225. 1. *See at the end*: the postscript which immediately followed the sermon. A 'Dominical' was a practice-sermon delivered during dinner or supper on the Sundays of Lent and Advent. Coming at the end of a week of lectures it would have been something of an ordeal. Generally speaking, those would be best received that put least strain on the deeper emotions. Among the many beauties of this sermon there are some touches evidently designed for light relief. But Hopkins underestimated the effect they would produce. It may be worth remarking that nearly all the stories handed down in the English Province about Hopkins, before his posthumous leap to fame, were concerned with him as an odd genius; but he was also appreciated as a straightforward humorist. To them may be added this extract from a Stonyhurst log-book of 1873:

> 'August 21. Thursday. As usual except that the Seminarians gave an entertainment after supper. . . . It consisted of music, comic and half-comic pieces etc. It was mainly got up by Mr. G. Hopkins, and was a decided success.'

The laughter that spoiled Hopkins's sermon was a regrettable affair; but it will not do to make a Joycean tragedy of it—the shrinking poet amid the coarse and brutal clergy, etc. The laugh is on the other side now anyway.

226. 1. *Chorozain.* See map, p. 233. Modern scholars, on the usual slender evidence, put Chorozain several miles north of the Lake; but GMH agrees with all the medieval pilgrims who placed it on the east shore opposite Tiberias.

226. 2. *Maenefa* (generally spelt 'Mynefyr'), 'dark Maenefa the mountain' of the incomparable fragment, *Poems*, 99; the kestrel-haunted hill on whose lower terraces St Beuno's is built, looking out over the entire valley of the Clwyd with the sea and the Cambrian and Snowdon ranges as a backcloth.

227. 1. *St Philip said.* GMH's notes at the end of his life (see section 6) show how long and prayerfully he dwelt on the characters of the apostles as portrayed by St John.

230. 1. *forty*: 'fourty' in the text.

230. 2. *flowerbeds*: πρασιαὶ πρασιαί. (Mark vi. 40.)

230. 3. *Orms*: the Great Orme's Head and the Little Orme's Head, on either side of the bay of Llandudno, west-north-west of St Beuno's.

231. 1. *alive.* See *The Wreck of the Deutschland*, st. 1, 'Giver of breath and bread'.

232. 1. *spelt*: German wheat.

232. 2. *neighbourers*: perhaps an unconscious euphony, but the form is used by Drayton, *Polyolbion*, i. 265 (1612).

SECTION THREE

234. 1. This and the following abbreviated sermon are on loose slips in 'Fr Humphrey's book'. See p. 30.

234. 2. '*Repente solvit cingulum*': this, or some similar phrase, is used in the *Roman Martyrology* of soldiers who died for the Faith. But its relevance here, like 'the story of Wm. Clarke', is obscure.

235. 1. This is clearly the sermon referred to by GMH on p. 23, ll. 11–12.

237. 1. *Sydenham*. See note, p. 275 (17. 1) to the Oxford Sermons. The sermon is in the Dublin Notebook (G.L.A.) of 1885. It ends abruptly in the middle of a sentence.

SECTION FOUR

238. 1. For the text of the Foundation Exercise, see Part II, ch. 1.

239. 1. '*The heavens declare . . .*': Ps. xviii.

239. 2. *Domine, Dominus noster . . .*: Ps. viii.

240. 1. *Core*. Num. xvi etc.

241. 1. *give him glory too*. Cf. George Herbert, one of GMH's favourite poets:

> 'A servant with this clause
> Makes drudgery divine;
> Who sweeps a room as for Thy laws
> Makes that and th' action fine.'
>   (*The Elixir*, st. 5)

241. 2. For the text of the *Exercises* see Part II, ch. 2.

241. 3. *the soul that they afflict*. Scotus says:

'Format enim anima in se imaginem, hoc est sensationem: et de se . . . '. (*Oxoniense*, 1. iii. 7, p. 62ᵇ, § D.)

See note, p. 288 (136. 1).

243. 1. *as proper bitterness*. The crescendo of suffering from point to point— which is not in St Ignatius's text—was perhaps a traditional rhetorical device. See the sermon on hell in James Joyce's *Portrait of the Artist as a Young Man*:

'But this stench is not, horrible though it is, the greatest physical torment to which the damned are subjected. . . .'

Joyce was at Belvedere and the National University about ten years later than Hopkins's Dublin period.

243. 2. *most miserable self*. See *Poems*, 69, the sestet.

244. 1. *turn where?* See *The Wreck of the Deutschland*, st. 3.

244. 2. *foretold in Scripture*. Where?

247. 1. *one thought of mortal sin*. Clearly GMH meant to write 'one mortal sin of thought'.

247. 2. *William Henry Street*, a long street running through what was then the poorer half of the parish (the Liverpool half as opposed to the Everton half), and crossing Salisbury Street about a hundred yards from St Francis Xavier's. Part of it was evidently in Hopkins's district. In his day it consisted mostly of shops, with a barracks or some sort of military establishment at the near end. Today it is punctuated by bomb-damage and stands on the fringe of an area that is being demolished.

250. 1. *infallibly you will be*. GMH takes it for granted that the usual conditions for perfect contrition are present.

SECTION FIVE

253. 1. *de Processu Peccatorum*: the second exercise of the First Week. It is noteworthy that GMH has practically no comments on this exercise elsewhere. It seems likely that the advice given below was given him also by earlier directors and confessors.

253. 2. *Kingdon*, George Renorden (1821–93), was one of the many distinguished converts who entered the Society in the middle part of the century. A scholar of St Paul's School and of Trinity College, Cambridge, he 'went out for his degree a *senior optime* in Mathematics and a first-class in classics, in 1844'. He was at St Bartholomew's in 1846 and won the Wix prize with an essay 'On the connexion between Revealed Religion and Medical Science'. In the same year he was received into the Church, and in the following year into the Society of Jesus. He was Prefect of Studies at Stonyhurst from 1864 till 1879 and at Beaumont from 1879 till 1887 when he asked to be relieved on account of increasing deafness. He and Hopkins would have known each other in 1873 when GMH went from the Seminary at Stonyhurst to the College to take the place of the Master of Rhetoric (VIth Form) for a week. Though Fr Kingdon is best known for his editions of school texts and his *Latin Grammar*, he also wrote several devotional works. The following quotation from his obituary notice is relevant:

> 'Perhaps nothing was more conspicuous in his spirtuality than the joyous and loving confidence with which he always gloried in the presence and omniscience of God. In a meditation upon Judgment in one of his retreats he well expresses this: "To stand before God's Judgment? But am I not so at every moment? And do I not glory in the fact? To be known at every moment from surface to core by our good God is nothing to be frightened at—it is a comfort." '

253. 3. *elsewhere*. See note, p. 291 (139. 1).

253. 4. *Fr. Whitty*. See notes, pp. 299–300 (176. 1) and pp. 311–12 (208. 1).

254. 1. *And this I believe is heard*. There were many occasions when GMH received some sign that his prayer was heard, chiefly in regard to the eternal welfare of his friends. See his Journal for 8 Sept. 1873 (*Journals*, p. 236):

> 'I received as I think a great mercy about Dolben.'

Also a letter to his mother, 9 Oct. 1877:

'Do not make light of this, for it is perhaps the seventh time that I think I have had some token from heaven in connection with the death of people in whom I am interested.'

254. 2. *Meditation Points.* These entries, points for meditation on the following morning, were made by GMH in odd places of a large thin exercise-book (known as 'the Dublin Notebook') which he used mostly for the correcting and marking of examination papers, with occasional and characteristic remarks about examinees. Other features of interest in it are rough drafts of *Spelt from Sibyl's Leaves* and *Caradoc's Soliloquy*, and some valuable lecture-notes on Cicero's philosophy of virtue. For a further description of the book, see *Notebooks* (1937), p. 425.

The following calendar for 1884 will be helpful in distinguishing GMH's first seven entries:

1. February 22nd, Friday, Feast of St Peter at Antioch.
2. February 29th, Friday, after Ash Wednesday.
3. March 2nd, Sunday, First in Lent, Gospel of the Temptations.
4. March 7th, Friday, kept as Feast of the Lance and Nails.
5. March 8th, Saturday, Gospel of the Transfiguration.
6. March 21st, Friday, kept as Feast of the Five Wounds.
7. April 4th, Friday, kept as Feast of Our Lady's Sorrows.

About the end of this period (30 April) Hopkins wrote: 'I am, I believe, recovering from a deep fit of nervous prostration (I suppose I ought to call it): I did not know but I was dying.' (*Letters*, i. 193.)

255. 1. *of English hearts.* Cf. *The Wreck of the Deutschland*, st. 35:

'Our King back, oh, upon English souls!'

256. 1. *Father D. M.* This would be Fr Denis Murphy (1833–96), who was on the staff at St Stephen's Green, 1883–8. In 1885 he was Lecturer in Religion, Modern Languages, and Physics at the University, as well as librarian. Besides being a professor he was well known as a missioner and a writer. Among his published works are: *History of Holy Cross Abbey*, *Annals of Clonmacnoise*, *Life of Red Hugh O'Donnell*, *Cromwell in Ireland*, *School History of Ireland*, etc. In 1886 he was appointed by the Irish Bishops promoter of the cause of those who died in penal days. His last book, *Our Martyrs*, appeared after his death.

257. 1. *Man was created.* Humphry House describes this page of Hopkins's writing:

'In the last sentences he stopped on the word "created" and wrote it again, twice the size, in a huge, sprawling, childlike hand; crossed it out, began again "cr" still bigger; crossed that out too, and in the same hand wrote "crea". . . . The next page is completely filled with √s, made as he marked the papers.'

The paragraph that follows is a striking restatement of his Scotist inspiration of the Great Sacrifice—though it was about this time that he was writing sadly in the past tense to Coventry Patmore: 'And so I used to feel about Duns Scotus when I used to read him with delight. . . .' (*Letters*, iii. 349.)

257. 2. *St Cecily*, the Roman maiden who, according to the story, persuaded her betrothed, Valerian, to be her companion in martyrdom instead of in wedlock. Her feast is on 22 Nov. See GMH's Journal for 18 Aug. 1874. (*Journals*, p. 254.)

257. 3. *O Sapientia*, quae ex ore Altissimi prodiisti, attingens a fine usque ad finem, fortiter suaviterque disponens omnia: veni ad docendum nos viam prudentiae.

This is the first of the Antiphons before Christmas, known as 'The Great O's'. GMH's points make no reference to its petition: 'teach us the way of prudence'.

258. 1. *Father Foley's instructions*. Peter Foley (1826–93) was the Spiritual Father at Clongowes at this date. He was a priest of the Killaloe diocese when he entered the Jesuit noviceship at Beaumont on his thirtieth birthday, 6 Jan. 1856. Most of his work in the Society was done at Clongowes, where he was greatly loved and esteemed.

259. 1. *St Gregory the Great*, the Pope, who sent Augustine to convert the English; his feast is on 12 Mar., a Wednesday in 1885. See *Poems*, 61, and *Letters*, ii. 129, for the stanza that may have inspired this meditation.

259. 2. *The woman taken in adultery*: Gospel for the Saturday (15 Mar.) before the Fourth Sunday in Lent.

260. 1. *Mr. Gladstone*. A note about current events just above these points records receipt of the news of Gordon's death: 'Khartoum fell Jan. 26': an event which confirmed the bitterest views of Gladstone's opponents. Elsewhere GMH has very severe strictures upon Gladstone; but his only comment about this time, to Baillie 17 May 1885, runs: 'As I am accustomed to speak too strongly of him I will not further commit myself in writing.' (*Letters*, iii. 257.)

260. 2. *The feeding of the five thousand*: Gospel for the Fourth Sunday in Lent, '*Laetare* Sunday'. See sec. 2, GMH's 'Dominical', 11 Mar. 1877.

260. 3. *his hymn*, known as 'Saint Patrick's Breastplate'; it invokes the sustaining power of Christ throughout the varied activities of the universe. GMH's enthusiasm for it is expressed in letters to Bridges of 3 Aug. 1884 and 13 Oct. 1886. (*Letters*, i. 195, 232.)

260. 4. *as I do*. Of the period that was now beginning he wrote retrospectively on 1 Sept. of the same year:

'Now because I have had a holiday though not strong I have some buoyancy; soon I am afraid I shall be ground down to a state like this last spring's and summer's, when my spirits were so crushed that madness seemed to be making approaches—and nobody was to blame, except

myself partly for not managing myself better and contriving a change.'
(*Letters*, i. 222.)

See *Poems*, 64: '. . . that year Of now done darkness . . .'.

SECTION SIX

261. 1. *Tullabeg.* The novitiate of the Irish Province, near Tullamore.
The year was 1889. See *Letters*, iii. 190, note 3.

261. 2. *philosophy is not religion.* M. Étienne Gilson thus sums up the difference between 'philosophers' and 'theologians' according to Scotus:

'Efforçons-nous de résumer d'abord sans commenter: (1) il y a une
position des "théologiens", autre que celle des "philosophes"; (2) elle
consiste à poser la première cause comme un agent libre; (3) cet agent
est libre parce qu'il est infini. — Inversement: (1) il y a une position des
"philosophes", autre que celle des "théologiens"; (2) elle consiste à poser
la première cause comme un agent-nécessaire; (3) cet agent est nécessaire
parce qu'il n'est pas infini.' (*Duns Scot* (Paris, 1952), p. 645.)

262. 1. *partly unlawful.* Cf. Newman to GMH, 3 Mar. 1887:

'There is one consideration however which you omit. The Irish Patriots
hold that they never have yielded themselves to the sway of England and
therefore have never been under her laws, and have never been rebels. . . .
If I were an Irishman, I should be (in heart) a rebel.' (*Letters*, iii. 265–6.)

But Hopkins was as ferociously English as only a good Welshman could be.

262. 2. *a straining eunuch.* See his letter twelve days later:

'All impulse fails me . . . I am a eunuch—but it is for the kingdom of
heaven's sake.' (*Letters*, i. 270.)

Also p. 222 of the same: '. . . time's eunuch . . .'; and *Poems*, 74: '. . . but
strain, Time's eunuch, . . .'.

262. 3. *the worst failure of all.* There may be a symptomatic confusion of
thought here. The state of perfection which the profession of a religious
enjoins is a constant *striving* for perfection; the complete attainment of it is
not possible in this life. Cf. St Thomas:

'Unde non oportet quod quicumque est in religione, iam sit perfectus,
sed quod ad perfectionem tendat.' (*Sum. Theol.* IIa IIae, q. 186, a. 1, ad 3.)

Further, self-mastery is a means to closer union with Christ; it is not an end
in itself. *Perfect* self-mastery is an academic rather than a religious ideal.

262. 4. *distills in it.* Cf. *Poems*, 69: 'Bitter would have me taste . . .' and 105:
'With dreadful distillation . . .'.

262. 5. *over our life.* Compare this with the resolution at the end of the 1883
retreat: 'better for me to be accompanying Our Lord in his comfort of them
than to want him to come my way to comfort me'. But one comes at the
beginning of a retreat, the other at the end.

263. 1. *in doing it?* Note the application of low but sturdy motives with which he begins to haul himself up; such motives are often the most useful to begin with in desolation: cf. *Poems*, 122 (at which no one need feel shocked): 'tame My tempests there, my fire and fever fussy.'

Note also the apparent admission that his unhappiness was partly wilful; cf. Introduction, p. 219.

263. 2. *work assigned me.* See p. 253.

264. 1. *actinism*: 'a radiation of heat or light . . . that property or force in the sun's rays by which chemical changes are produced'—*Murray's Dictionary*, 1888.

Text is not altogether clear, being crowded at the bottom of a sheet.

265. 1. *Sabean.* Saba in southern Arabia has always been associated with the gifts of the Magi because of the Messianiac prophecies, Isa. lx. 6, and Psalm 71. But GMH is here evidently not referring to the Sabaeans of Saba, but to the *Sabians* (or Nasoraeans) of southern Babylonia, also known as 'the Christians of St John (the Baptist)', who practised an elevated form of light-worship. In its post-Christian form, however, their religion regarded the stars as a malign influence opposed to the sun.

265. 2. *chosen for the feast.* GMH appears to mean that, had the feast been arbitrarily fixed in later times, a more suitable date could have been thought of; therefore 6 Jan. is more likely to be traditional than arbitrary. He believes that the coming of the Magi was actually twelve days after the birth of Our Lord, not a long time after as most commentators think. See next note.

265. 3. *would leave Bethlehem.* This is the hinge of the theory that follows in the text. The usual reconciliation of Matt. ii with Luke ii is that the Holy Family did not leave Bethlehem till a year or so after the Purification (fixed as forty days after birth), at the end of which period the visit of the Magi occurred followed immediately by the flight into Egypt and the massacre of the innocents. This involves the difficulty that Luke (who says nothing of the Magi) seems to imply that the Holy Family *did* leave Bethlehem immediately after the Purification.

GMH's theory avoids this difficulty, but runs into the other difficulty that Matthew seems to imply that the flight and massacre occurred immediately after the Epiphany. The other difficulties involved are answered by his ingenious reconstruction of Herod's thoughts and actions. His theory has the merit of improbability on paper which is often closer to truth in fact.

265. 4. *lost sight of them.* GMH supposes an interval of some weeks between the escape of the Magi on 6 Jan. and the massacre of the innocents, during which time the Holy Family had returned to Nazareth after the Purification on 2 Feb. Herod, though not suspecting them in particular, sent emissaries to execute a simultaneous massacre of all whom he had traced through the registers, whether at Bethlehem or elsewhere.

266. 1. *Abylina*, or Abilene, the district between Damascus and the Lebanon, may have belonged to Herod's sphere of influence, since it formed part of the kingdom restored to his grandson, Herod Agrippa I, in A.D. 53. Even so, Nazareth is very much nearer to Phoenicia than to Egypt—though not necessarily safer at that time, as GMH goes on to observe.

267. 1. *in that position.* GMH crossed out these words and substituted:

'Antipas too finding himself in his position. . . .'

But his original version is obviously preferable, since he knew very well that it was Agrippa, not Antipas, who 'affected a more than Messiasship'. (Acts xii. 21–23.) There is, in fact, a chance note to that effect in the Dublin Note-book (G.I, *a*) that contains his meditation-points, 1884–5.

268. 1. *the chaff.* Cf. *Poems*, 64:

'That my chaff might fly; my grain lie, sheer and clear.'

But the imagery of wrestling is more gracious and Catholic in the meditation than in the poem.

268. 2. *in the forest.* So vivid is GMH's 'composition of place' that all the disparate images used by the Baptist according to the different gospels are threaded naturally together.

There are reminiscences of the 'footgear' imagery in the *Epithalamion*, written in 1888.

268. 3. *the form of words.* Matt. iii. 16: '. . . and as he came straight up out of the water, suddenly heaven was opened'. Mark i. 10: 'And even as he came up out of the water he saw the heavens opened'. (Knox's version.)

Of the four evangelists, St John would have been nearest to being personally an eye-witness. GMH seems to suppose that the oral tradition stemmed from the Baptist's words which St John reports exactly.

270. 1. *had my eye* is written over 'set my heart' crossed out.

270. 2. *hides from heaven.* GMH, in his extraordinary detective intuition, supposes Nathanael to have been leaning back under the tree. GMH himself was in the same position, no doubt, when he conceived 'Ash-boughs', *Poems*, 111. The coincidence, though slight, is suggestive.

271. 1. *Nondum venit hora mea.* GMH's inference is that Our Lady was a familiar friend of the household, that she knew it would be strained by the arrival of all the disciples unexpected, and that she warned her son well beforehand. Our Lord's filially chiding reassurance (equivalent to, 'Now, Mother, don't fuss—it's not time yet') may therefore be taken literally: it was still too soon to work the miracle. But he did in fact forestall it.

271. 2. *increases it afterwards*: that is, when the richness of the symbolism was perceived. The Baptism in the Jordan and the Marriage at Cana have always been linked by the Church with the feast of the Epiphany; cf. the antiphon:

'Hodie caelesti Sponso juncta est Ecclesia,
quoniam in Jordane lavit Christus ejus crimina:
currunt cum muneribus Magi ad regales nuptias,
et ex aqua facto vino laetantur convivae, alleluia.'

APPENDIXES

APPENDIX I

Marie Lataste

HOPKINS's references to Marie Lataste are traceable to the retreat he made at Beaumont in Nov. 1878. The book he used was evidently the 1877 edition which is still in the Beaumont library.[1] Besides six French editions between 1862 and 1877, an independent English version by Edward Healy Thompson in three volumes appeared between 1881 and 1893, number six in the series Library of Religious Biography. From the press notices it is clear that Marie Lataste enjoyed a discreet popularity in Catholic literary and religious circles, overflowing from France into this country. A confirmation of this which has a special interest in regard to Hopkins is that her writings were held in high esteem by Coventry Patmore, who had discovered them more than a year earlier.[2]

Between 1870 and 1877 Patmore was inspired to add twenty-two odes to the existing nine of *The Unknown Eros*. Mr Frederick Page is of the opinion that Patmore owed his recovered inspiration to three literary events, one of which was the recent publication of Marie Lataste's life and works and his reading of them. In a letter—not to Hopkins—Patmore wrote of her:

> I am just now reading the Life of a peasant girl, Marie Lataste, who died only a few years ago. Her life was all grace and miracle, and her writings full of living sanctity and vigorous perceptions of things hidden to the wise. There are no such books in English, but many in French. From a Christian point of view, we English are a very poor lot compared with the French. . . .

Mr. Page adds that according to Patmore's notes Marie Lataste 'was Psyche' in *The Unknown Eros*. Hopkins can hardly have been aware of this— perhaps it was just as well—at the time when he was helping Patmore to revise *The Unknown Eros*. Her name is not mentioned in their published letters to each other.

HER LIFE (1822–47)

She was born of humble and devout parents in the village of Mimbaste in the 'Landes' of Gascony. Between the ages of fourteen and twenty she had visions of Our Saviour and of the Blessed Virgin whenever she assisted at Mass. In 1842 her parish priest, the Abbé Pierre Darbins, persuaded her to set down in writing the visions and locutions accorded to her. In 1844 she journeyed to Paris and was accepted as a lay-sister in the Society of the

---

[1] *La Vie et les œuvres de Marie Lataste* . . . publiées par M. l'Abbé Pascal Darbins (Paris, 1877). There are three volumes in this, the sixth, edition: the first being her life, the second her theological writings, and the third her letters. All Hopkins's references are to the second volume.

[2] For this valuable cross-reference I am indebted to the Revd R. Marks, who communicated it to the late Humphry House, who passed it on to me. The source is *Patmore, A Study in Poetry*, by Frederick Page (Oxford, 1933), pp. 124–5.

Sacré Cœur, which had been founded by Mlle Barat, now Saint Madeleine-Sophie, in 1800. All her writings, except some letters, were completed before her departure—that is, before her twenty-second year—and handed over to the Abbé Pierre Darbins. Her short life in the *Sacré Cœur* was happy but quite obscure. She died exactly three years after her admission, 10 May 1847. By a strange mischance the exact location of her grave was unknown for a long time even to the nuns of her community. It was discovered by a series of coincidences in 1879, by which time her posthumous fame was considerable.

In 1903, following the anti-religious laws in France, her remains were brought to England to the Convent of the Sacred Heart at Roehampton (where Hopkins used to say Mass some twenty-five years earlier), now the Digby-Stuart training college. They repose under the Sacred Heart altar, which survived the bombing of 1940, along with those of Mother Mabel Digby and Mother Janet Stuart, both Superior-Generals of the Society.

HER WRITINGS

Her writings were handed over by Abbé Pierre Darbins shortly before his death to his nephew, the Abbé Pascal Darbins, with a view to publication. This occurred in 1862, and was followed by a second edition in 1866 which bore the approval of the Bishop of Dax and Aire and an attestation by two Jesuit Fathers that it corresponded faithfully with the autograph manuscripts of Marie Lataste. Unfortunately at some subsequent date the autograph manuscripts completely disappeared! It may be that they will reappear some time as strangely as her body was discovered. But for the present their loss has naturally put out of court any official assessment of the value of her published works. The immediate reaction to them, however, is delight in their freshness and originality as well as in their intellectual strength and sureness. Possibly the attribution of long speeches to Our Saviour in the first person may tend to diminish rather than to increase the confidence of the modern reader. But it is permissible to read them not necessarily always as miraculous revelations but simply as 'lively' spiritual doctrine. Marie herself puts in several qualifications such as the following: 'I have not spoken as the Saviour spoke, but as far as I have known how, and as He has permitted me.' (Book iii, sect. 6, p. 182.)

Reference: J. H. Gruninger, *A propos des cahiers de Marie Lataste* (Lyon, 1952).

Hopkins's seven references may be located by the following:

1. Note, p. 286 (129. 2). Book i, section 5.
2. Note, p. 287 (133. 1). Book i, section 16.
3. Note, p. 294 (151. 5).
4. Note, p. 298 (173. 1). Book iii, section 6.
5. Note, p. 299 (175. 1). Book iii, section 9.
6. Note, p. 302 (185. 1). Book ii, section 3.
7. Note, p. 309 (200. 8). Book iv, section 7.

1. Book i, section 5 (pp. 19–21). The Two Movements of Creation.

The following is an extract, all or part of which Hopkins had copied out on the missing pp. 26–27 of MS:

'L'homme vient de Dieu et doit retourner à Dieu. Il y a deux mouvements en l'homme: de son être créé par Dieu vers l'existence et de son être existant vers Dieu. Ces deux mouvements sont donnés à l'homme par Dieu; et par ces deux mouvements, l'homme, s'il le veut, retournera infailliblement à Dieu. Je dis s'il le veut, parce que l'homme peut changer la direction de ce mouvement.

'Dieu, au commencement, avait fait l'homme: il l'avait fait grand et heureux. Il lui avait donné un monde dont il était le roi, un paradis dont il était le maître. Il l'avait fait son représentant sur la terre, il l'avait fait Dieu visible dans le monde pour rendre hommage au Dieu invisible du ciel. Il l'avait fait l'âme du monde, et son âme était celle par laquelle le monde donnait à Dieu son amour, et son esprit était celui par lequel le monde connaissait son auteur et son Dieu. Il devait en être ainsi, car l'ordre était là. Cet ordre a été dissous. Le second mouvement que Dieu avait donné à l'homme pour qu'il retournât à lui, l'homme le changea pour recevoir le mouvement du prince des ténèbres. Dès lors, l'homme ne marcha plus dans la voie de Dieu qui est la vérité, il marcha dans la voie de Satan qui est le mensonge. Le second mouvement donné à l'homme par son créateur devait être à jamais anéanti, mais la miséricorde de Dieu vint s'opposer au triomphe de Satan. Je vins arrêter le mouvement de l'enfer en offrant à l'homme la force et le pouvoir de quitter ce mouvement. Je montrai de nouveau à l'homme la vérité, je montrai de nouveau à l'homme la voie; je fis plus, je lui redonnai la vie qu'il avait perdue.

'Aujourd'hui, tout homme reçoit, comme au commencement, le premier mouvement, qui le lance dans la vie; mais le second mouvement, qui relance l'homme vivant vers Dieu, ne lui est plus donné avec le premier mouvement. Le second mouvement le lance vivant dans la mort; mais je suis là pour ressaisir l'homme par le baptême et le remettre sur le chemin qui mène à Dieu. Alors tout est réparé: l'homme est régénéré; il marchera, s'il le veut, vers Dieu ou retournera à Satan, dont je l'ai délivré; il marchera dans la vérité ou le mensonge.

'Voyez jusqu'où va la bonté de Dieu: il n'a pas voulu que je retirasse une seule fois l'homme de la voie de perdition; il a voulu encore qu'à chaque heure du jour où l'homme criera vers Dieu, j'accourusse vers l'homme pour lui redonner la vie et le mouvement vers son Créateur par le sacrement de pénitence.'

2. Book i, section 16 (pp. 51–56). On Grace and Predestination.

Hopkins has noted in brackets:

Observe the constant '*l'homme*', no allusion to Adam and Eve.

Alors le Sauveur Jésus me dit: 'Ma chère fille, Dieu, dans ses jugements secrets et impénétrables, a destiné les uns pour glorifier sa miséricorde et les autres pour glorifier sa justice. Voici l'explication de ces paroles:

'Dieu, étant souverainement parfait, connaît tout?' Je répondis: 'Oui,

Seigneur. — Le passé, le présent et l'avenir ne sont pour Dieu qu'une seule et même chose; pour lui, l'avenir et le passé sont toujours présents?' Je répondis: 'Oui, Seigneur.' — 'Or, Dieu avait résolu de toute éternité de créer le monde et de créer l'homme. Il savait de toute éternité que l'homme pécherait; il savait de toute éternité quels seraient les péchés des hommes. Aussi, quand il est dit dans les livres saints que Dieu se repentit d'avoir créé le monde à cause des péchés des hommes, vous ne devez point l'entendre en ce sens que Dieu, avant la création du monde, n'avait point prévu les péchés des hommes. Car s'il en eût été ainsi, Dieu ne serait pas parfait. Dieu, dans sa prescience, connaissant les iniquités de tous les hommes, savait donc le véritable nombre des élus et des réprouvés; en sorte que pas un ne sera damné ou sauvé que Dieu ne l'ait prévu de toute éternité. Mais ne pensez pas pour cela que Dieu refuse aux réprouvés les grâces qui leur sont nécessaires pour se sauver. Dieu les leur accorde, mais ils n'y correspondent pas; et c'est pour cela qu'ils sont réprouvés, et c'est pour cela aussi que Dieu a prévu leur réprobation. Or, cette prévision de Dieu n'influe en rien sur la réprobation des hommes, car elle n'a aucune action sur l'homme qui conserve toute sa liberté, et peut abuser ou non des grâces de Dieu. Si la prévision de Dieu influait sur la réprobation de quelqu'un, Dieu ne voudrait pas le salut de celui-là. Or, il est certain que Dieu veut le salut de tous, et qu'il donne à tous les grâces nécessaires pour qu'ils opèrent leur salut. C'est parce que l'homme se perd que Dieu le prévoit, et non parce que Dieu le prévoit que l'homme se perd et se damne. Dieu donne des grâces, mais il laisse avec elles la liberté, et l'homme, en donnant ou refusant sa correspondance à ces grâces, se damne ou se sauve librement.

'Quand Dieu créa l'homme, il lui donna une âme douée de nobles qualités et capable de le connaître, de l'aimer et de le servir. Il lui donna la liberté de le servir ou de lui être infidèle, de lui obéir ou de se révolter contre lui; car il veut une servitude libre et volontaire. Il fit l'homme roi de la nature et lui permit de manger du fruit de tous les arbres, excepté d'un seul, le menaçant de mort s'il en mangeait, mais ne lui enlevant pas pour cela la liberté d'en manger s'il le voulait.

'L'homme, usant de sa liberté, mangea du fruit défendu, et Dieu, qui est souverainement juste, dut le punir. Dès lors la justice de Dieu éclata sur l'homme tant spirituellement que temporellement. Cette offense de Dieu demandait séparation radicale et éternelle entre l'homme, péché, et son Créateur, sainteté par excellence; ou bien il fallait à Dieu une réparation de l'offense de l'homme. L'homme ne pouvait donner cette réparation, il ne pouvait que demeurer victime de l'éternelle malédiction. La miséricorde de Dieu pourtant, touchée de compassion pour l'homme, qui était son ouvrage, ne put se résoudre à le détruire, à le perdre pour jamais. Elle me proposa de donner la satisfaction que l'homme ne pouvait donner. J'acceptai le rôle de réparateur, et, en donnant à Dieu réparation, j'obtins non-seulement le pardon de l'offense de l'homme, mais encore les grâces qui lui étaient nécessaires pour opérer son salut. Car le péché du premier homme l'avait tellement dégradé et entraîné, lui et toute sa postérité, vers le mal que, de lui-même, il lui était impossible de résister au mal et d'opérer le bien. C'est moi qui, par la mort, ai procuré à l'homme le résistance au mal et l'opération du bien. Ainsi, l'homme se sauve et obtient la grâce de Dieu par moi seul, depuis que je suis venu sur la terre; et avant que je me fusse incarné, par la foi en ma réparation, en mes mérites de Rédempteur et de Sauveur, foi fondée sur la promesse que Dieu fit à Adam, immédiatement après sa faute, de lui donner un réparateur dont la mort effacerait le péché des hommes.

'La grâce, avant comme après ma naissance et ma mort, est offerte à l'homme à cause de mes mérites. Tous les hommes le reçoivent, et tous ont la liberté d'y correspondre ou d'y résister: ils obtiennent le salut par leur correspondance, et se perdent par leur résistance à cette même grâce. Ainsi, si l'homme se perd, ce n'est pas parce que Dieu ne lui a pas donné assez de grâces pour se sauver, ni parce que la grâce de ma rédemption n'a pas été suffisante ou ne s'est pas appliquée à tous; non, la grâce donnée à chaque homme lui suffit pour opérer son salut, et la grâce de ma rédemption aurait seule pu sauver mille mondes. L'homme ne correspond pas à la grâce et se perd.

'Or, il est certain qu'il y a des hommes qui résistent et résisteront encore à la grâce, et qui par conséquent seront damnés. Il est certain que Dieu sait tout de tout éternité, et qu'il connaît par conséquent quels sont ceux qui seront rebelles. Il est certain que Dieu aurait pu sauver tous les hommes. Pourquoi donc, prévoyant quels sont ceux qui seraient damnés, les a-t-il créés? Pourquoi, pouvant les sauver tous, ne l'a-t-il point fait? C'est là une chose que l'esprit de l'homme ne peut pénétrer et devant laquelle il doit abaisser et soumettre sa raison, pour adorer profondément les conseils et les jugements secrets de Dieu, qu'il n'est point permis à l'homme d'approfondir. Il doit suffire à l'homme de savoir qu'il peut et qu'il doit se sauver, qu'il a les grâces nécessaires pour cela, et que, s'il se perd ou se sauve, ce sera parce qu'il aura voulu, et non parce que Dieu, pour qui tout est présent de toute éternité, aura toujours prévu que l'homme serait sauvé ou damné. Il suffit à l'homme de savoir que Dieu aurait pu ne pas lui donner un Sauveur, et que, ne le lui donnant pas, il aurait été souverainement juste en punissant éternellement tous les hommes. Il suffit à l'homme de savoir que si Dieu a voulu lui donner un Sauveur, ce n'a été que pour lui permettre de glorifier éternellement sa miséricorde, s'il correspond à la grâce de son salut; et pour l'obliger à glorifier sa justice si, après s'être révolté contre Dieu son Créateur, il se révolte aussi contre Dieu son Sauveur.'

Après ces paroles, que le Sauveur Jésus m'adressa à peu près ainsi, autant que je me le rappelle, il m'interrogea de la manière suivante: 'Ma fille, l'homme est-il libre de faire le bien ou le mal?' Je répondis: Oui, Seigneur. — Peut-il faire le bien? — Oui, Seigneur, avec la grâce de Dieu. — De qui attend-il la grâce? — De Dieu. — L'homme peut-il, à cause de lui-même, attendre cette grâce de Dieu? — Non, Seigneur, c'est en votre considération, par vos mérites et par la miséricorde de Dieu qu'elle lui est donnée. — Que faut-il pour être sauvé ou damné? Correspondre à la grâce ou bien y résister. — L'homme peut-il de lui-même correspondre à la grâce? — Non, Seigneur, il faut encore pour cela une grâce nouvelle, la grâce de la correspondance. — Dieu est-il libre de donner cette grâce, est-il obligé de la donner? — Dieu n'est pas obligé de la donner, mais il s'est engagé à l'accorder à tous ceux qui la lui demandent. — Dieu la donne-t-il toujours à ceux qui la lui

demandent?—Oui, Seigneur, à ceux qui la lui demandent comme il faut.
— Comment Dieu veut-il le salut de tous les hommes?—Il le veut d'une
volonté conditionnelle, c'est-à-dire en ce sens que les hommes feront ce
qu'il leur demande, et non d'une volonté absolue, parce qu'il veut laisser aux
hommes la liberté de se sauver.—Pourquoi Dieu veut-il que l'homme ait la
liberté de se sauver?—Seigneur, parce qu'il le veut. Je ne puis en dire davan-
tage.

— 'Très-bien, ma fille. Ainsi rappelez-vous toujours ce que vous venez de
me dire, que ce n'est point la grâce qui fait les saints, mais la correspondance
à la grâce; que cette correspondance est une grâce et pour ainsi dire la
grâce des grâces; que cette grâce n'est pas au pouvoir de l'homme, mais
qu'elle vient de Dieu; que Dieu ne la doit à personne, mais qu'il ne la
refuse jamais quand on la lui demande.'

3. This refers back to the foregoing; but the leaf on which Hopkins continued the long extract has been torn out.

4. Book iii, section 6 (pp. 175–9, 181–2). The Annunciation.

Hopkins has underlined the words: 'Je suis la grâce de Dieu le Père'; and
'L'œuvre de mon incarnation fut accomplie par cette parole.' And he provides the following annotation on Our Lady's thoughts:

'What does God ask me to do or undergo in order to comply with his
will that I should be the mother of his son? Since I cannot comply with it
by knowing man; I am to be, God means me to be, ever a virgin; so far
as I know my duty, what else have I to learn? He has graciously granted
to me to be able to offer him the first condition of that great motherhood,
a vowed virginity; what is he pleased to require of me as the condition of
conceiving? I bring him the virgin soil, how is the seed to be sown?'

'Mon incarnation était le chef-d'œuvre des manifestations extérieures de
Dieu au ciel et sur la terre. Toute l'éternité Dieu a préparé cette œuvre.
Quand l'heure sonna, au milieu des temps, il envoya son ange, l'un des sept
qui se trouvent toujours en adoration en sa présence et à qui il confie l'exécu-
tion de ses commandements, celui qui s'appelle Gabriel, c'est-à-dire force
de Dieu ou bien Dieu et homme. Ce n'est pas sans dessein qu'il porte ce nom,
force de Dieu, parce qu'il devait être le héros annonçant la grande manifestation de la force et de la puissance qui est en Dieu; *Dieu et homme*, parce qu'il
devait annoncer la grande merveille d'un Dieu fait homme.

'Il est ange et l'un des plus puissants de la cour de mon Père, et il vient
dans la cellule de Marie, que mon Père avait choisie pour me donner le jour
sur la terre. C'est le ciel qui apprend cette grande nouvelle à la terre; c'est
un ange qui l'apprend à une vierge; c'est le plus beau des anges qui
l'apprend à la plus sainte des créatures; c'est l'ange de Dieu qui l'apprend
à la mère de Dieu. La terre et le ciel, Dieu et sa justice et sa miséricorde
étaient en même temps dans la cellule de Marie. Marie priait, demandait
la délivrance du monde, soupirait après la venue du Messie, et Dieu vient
à elle par son ange; Dieu vient lui dire que les temps sont accomplis, que le
Messie va naître d'elle; l'ange la salue et se prosterne devant elle.

'Vous avez contemplé ce spectacle ravissant, admirable, l'ange prosterné devant Marie. Marie à genoux devant Dieu, l'ange venant au nom de Dieu, Marie n'ayant point ses yeux fixés sur l'ange, mais toujours sur Dieu, l'ange saluant Marie pleine de grâce, temple de Dieu, femme bénie parmi les femmes, Marie se disant la servante de Dieu. Ce langage n'était point un langage de la terre, c'était plus qu'un langage angélique, il était de Dieu, porté par un ange et reçu par Marie. Or, ma fille, la parole de Dieu est lumière, et cette lumière n'est point une lumière créée, mais incréée, qui ne sort pas de Dieu, qui reste en Dieu, mais dont les rayons viennent et descendent jusqu'à la créature pour lui montrer les choses de Dieu et l'élever jusqu'à lui.

'Marie écouta la parole de Dieu transmise par l'ange et demeura en silence. Son esprit, éclairé aussitôt par cette lumière de la parole, pénètre jusqu'au sein de la Divinité pour y contempler ses desseins éternels. Elle contemple, et cette contemplation est pour elle pleine d'intelligence. L'ange, pénétré de respect, vénérant le silence de Marie et sa contemplation, demeure en silence devant elle.

'N'avez-vous point remarqué cela, ma fille? — Oui, Seigneur. — Qu'avez-vous vu en Marie? — Seigneur, je ne saurais m'exprimer, mais il me semble que c'était un ravissement céleste, et puis comme un trouble produit par la parole de l'ange et ce ravissement. — Ne pensez-vous point que ce soit la présence de l'ange qui l'ait troublée? — Non, Seigneur, car j'ai vu clairement et d'une manière sensible la vérité du récit évangélique qui dit que Marie fut troublée dans le discours de l'ange.

'Il en a été ainsi, ma fille. Marie était sainte et pleine de grâces, la pureté de son âme surpassait la pureté de tous les esprits célestes; la présence d'un ange sous une forme humaine ne pouvait la troubler. Marie était si éclairée, son intelligence si ouverte et si pénétrante, qu'elle eût reconnu un artifice, si l'ange des ténèbres avait voulu se changer pour elle en ange de lumière. Marie n'était pas seulement gardée par un ange, mais par Dieu; car Dieu était avec elle, et, sous la garde de Dieu, elle ne pouvait ni craindre ni se troubler. Marie fut troublée dans la parole de l'ange. Il y eut combat entre son humilité et la parole du messager céleste. Le combat produisit le trouble de Marie, qui se demanda quelle pouvait être cette salutation et la signification de ces paroles. Ah! ma fille, l'humilité était si grande en Marie qu'elle ignorait les grandeurs qui étaient en elle. Dieu voulait élever Marie, et Marie ne pensait qu'à s'humilier devant Dieu; et son humilité lui enlevait la parole, et elle se confondait dans son néant au moment même où Dieu allait l'exalter par sa divinité, qui devait s'unir si intimement à elle. Son humilité devint sa force; l'ange ajouta: "Ne craignez point, Marie, vous avez trouvé grâce devant Dieu."

'Savez-vous, ma fille, quelle est cette grâce que Marie a trouvée devant mon Père? — Non, Seigneur. — Écoutez l'ange, il va vous l'apprendre: "Voici, lui dit-il, que vous concevrez dans votre sein et que vous enfanterez un fils, et vous lui donnerez le nom de Jésus."

'La grâce que Marie a trouvée devant mon Père, c'est moi. Je suis la grâce de Dieu le Père, je suis la splendeur de sa gloire, et Marie m'a trouvé par sa sainteté, par sa vertu, par sa virginité. Elle m'a trouvé et je viendrai en elle, et je me donnerai à elle, et elle se donnera à moi. Ma divinité descendra en son humanité, son humanité voilera ma divinité; ma divinité remplira son humanité; vierge, elle deviendra mère; vierge mère, elle sera mère de Dieu, elle sera ma mère.

'Voilà la dignité que l'ange annonce à Marie, et cette dignité étonnante pour le ciel et pour la terre le fut aussi pour Marie. Elle s'écria: "Comment cela pourra-t-il s'opérer, je ne connais point d'homme?"

'Je désire, ma fille, que vous compreniez bien ces paroles; écoutez-moi avec plus d'attention. Il n'y a point un doute sur la parole de l'ange; Marie savait que je devais naître d'une vierge, et son âme était pleine de foi dans les promesses de Dieu. Mais elle ne savait point de quelle manière je devais naître d'elle. Être vierge et mère en même temps, c'est là un mystère que nul ne comprendra jamais, et Dieu n'avait point révélé la manière dont il devait opérer cette étonnante maternité. Aussi Marie s'écrie: "Comment cela s'opérera-t-il, je ne connais point d'homme?" Loin d'être une parole de doute, cette parole est pleine de croyance et de foi; une parole de croyance au pouvoir de Dieu, à sa maternité et aussi à la conservation de sa virginité. C'est une parole de vénération pour le pouvoir de Dieu, de remercîment pour la maternité promise, d'action de grâces pour sa virginité conservée. Quel est ce mode nouveau que Dieu emploiera pour opérer son œuvre? Quelle est cette nouvelle faveur que Dieu me réserve? Telle était la pensée de Marie.

'Vous devez remarquer aussi que cette parole n'est pas une parole uniquement de Marie, c'est une parole de Dieu, comme les paroles de l'ange étaient aussi paroles de Dieu. Dieu voulait par cette parole et sa conservation dans l'Évangile faire éclater la vérité de sa promesse, faire observer la réalisation des prophéties, tout en relevant la dignité, la pureté, la sainteté de la créature, qu'il avait choisie pour être sa mère.

'Ma fille, quand l'ange eut fini de parler, il avait achevé sa mission et n'attendait que la réponse de Marie. J'étais à même de m'incarner en Marie, mais il fallait le consentement de Marie. Dieu allait renouveler son alliance avec les hommes, mais cette alliance devait être acceptée par Marie, et Dieu, et l'ange, et moi qui vous parle nous attendions la réponse de Marie. Ô puissance, ô grandeur communiquée à Marie! Jamais Dieu ne s'était soumis à l'homme, et il se soumet à Marie; jamais Dieu n'avait consulté l'homme, et il consulte Marie, jamais Dieu n'avait fait dépendre son action de l'homme, et il fait dépendre la plus admirable de ses actions de Marie. Ô parole de Marie! Ma fille, n'en avez-vous point distingué l'accent? N'était-ce point ma parole que vous avez distinguée dans la parole de Marie? Je suis la parole éternelle de Dieu, j'allais m'incarner dans Marie, et déjà ma parole était en elle comme un essai de ce que j'allais produire par elle dans le monde: "Voici la servante du Seigneur, qu'il me soit fait selon votre parole."

'Le résumé de mon incarnation est dans cette parole. Il n'y a que deux choses en elle: humilité et puissance; l'une et l'autre existent séparément, mais il semble que la seconde ne se manifeste que par la première. Ce n'a été que par mon humiliation jusqu'à la mort et jusqu'à la mort de la croix, que j'ai voulu manifester ma puissance sur la mort, sur l'enfer, et sur l'homme pécheur à qui je rendais la grâce et la liberté.

'Marie, au moment où le messager du ciel proclame ses grandeurs, s'humi-lie jusque dans le plus intime de son être: "Voici la servante du Seigneur." Mais cette humilité acquiert une force toute divine, qui m'attire et m'in-carne en elle par la puissance d'un commandement auquel je ne résiste point: "Qu'il me soit fait selon votre parole." '

5. Book iii, section 9 (p. 192). The Epiphany.

Hopkins has the following:

Marie Lataste one Twelfth Night is led by her angel to the stable of Bethlehem:

'Je le [Jésus] reçus quelques instants dans mes bras et puis je le rendis à Marie, et je m'assis près d'elle sur un escabeau que me présenta saint Joseph.'

Our Lady then talks to her as she might from heaven and in possession of all the knowledge of all that has happened since. M.L. says she was exhausted by the heat of the desert in following the Holy Family on their flight into Egypt. Much the same used to happen to Sister Emmerich and to Bd. Lidwine.

'Ma fille, me dit alors la mère de Jésus, ne perdez jamais de vue la grâce qui vous est faite en ce jour. Dieu vous a donné un ange, et cet ange est l'ange de votre salut. Vous avez cherché avec lui mon fils Jésus, vous avez été amenée en ce lieu où il habite, et je vous ai permis de le recevoir dans vos bras. Ainsi, ma fille, chaque fois que vous chercherez mon Fils avec un grand désir, soyez sûre de le trouver. Vous ne le trouverez pas seul, vous me trouverez toujours avec lui; il ne se donnera pas lui-même à vous, ce sera moi qui vous le donnerai, qui vous le livrerai, qui lui ordonnerai d'aller à vous. Il ne vous parlera point si je ne lui dis de vous parler; mais s'il ne vous parle pas, je vous parlerai à sa place. Dieu a donné à mon Fils tout pouvoir sur la terre et dans le ciel; mais, parce que je suis sa mère, il veut ne le point exercer sans mon ordre. Unissez donc toujours mon nom au nom de mon Fils; cherchez-moi toujours, en cherchant Jésus; ne nous séparez jamais et vous nous trouverez toujours unis, et nous vous donnerons place dans notre famille, dans nos épreuves, dans nos souffrances sur la terre, pour vous attirer à nous un jour auprès de Dieu.'

La parole de Marie était pleine de douceur et de bonté. J'aurais voulu l'entendre encore, mais elle s'arrêta.

L'ange qui m'avait conduite, et qui se tenait à l'entrée de la grotte vint se prosterner devant Jésus en disant: 'Seigneur, les mages d'Orient ont vu votre étoile, ils viennent vous adorer.' L'enfant Jésus ne répondit rien; mais il regarda Marie, et les mages entrèrent.

Le premier avait une robe qui descendait jusqu'à ses pieds, une couronne sur la tête, et, dans les mains, de l'or, de l'encens et de la myrrhe.

Il se prosterna jusqu'à terre et déposa sa couronne aux pieds de Jésus en disant: 'Je vous adore, Fils de Dieu; je vous adore, Fils de Dieu fait homme; je vous adore, roi des Juifs.'

Le second était vêtu et couronné comme le premier, et, comme lui aussi, portait dans ses mains de l'or, de l'encens et de la myrrhe.

Il se prosterna jusqu'à terre et déposa sa couronne aux pieds de Jésus en disant: 'Je vous adore, Fils de Dieu; je vous adore, Fils de Dieu fait homme; je vous adore, roi des Juifs.'

Le troisième était vêtu et couronné comme les deux premiers, et, comme eux aussi, il portait dans ses mains de l'or, de l'encens et de la myrrhe.

Il se prosterna jusqu'à terre et déposa sa couronne aux pieds de Jésus en disant: 'Je vous adore, Fils de Dieu; je vous adore, Fils de Dieu fait homme; je vous adore, roi des Juifs.'

Quand ils furent tous trois à genoux devant Jésus, ils lui offrirent chacun leurs présents.

Jésus leva sa main sur eux comme pour les bénir.

Marie s'entretint longtemps avec les mages sur le péché originel, sur la promesse du Rédempteur, sur la sainte Trinité, sur le changement qui allait s'opérer dans le monde par l'Incarnation.

Je vis les mages écouter la parole de Marie avec le plus profond respect, et porter tour à tour leurs regards de Marie sur Jésus et de Jésus sur Marie, sans pour cela paraître distraits aux paroles de Marie.

Quand Marie eut fini de parler, elle mit l'enfant Jésus entre les bras de chacun des mages. Ils furent heureux au dessus de toute expression de cette faveur signalée.

Les mages se retirèrent; je remerciai Marie, je lui demandai d'embrasser encore le Sauveur enfant; et l'ange, qui m'avait conduite dans la grotte, me ramena derrière l'autel. Je revins à ma place et je me retirai.

x

Trois jours après, je me sentis attirée près du saint-sacrement, je suivis cet attrait et j'arrivai près de Jésus. Je n'avais point la permission de le recevoir sacramentellement, mais je m'unis à lui par un grand désir de communier. Je voulus entrer dans mon cœur pensant y trouver Jésus sur son trône, comme je l'y trouve souvent. Jésus n'y était point. Je craignis de l'avoir offensé. Je revins dans mon cœur pour y chercher encore Jésus. Jésus était absent; mais j'y trouvai mon ange gardien: 'Marie, me dit-il, ne vous attristez point, je vais vous conduire à Jésus.' Alors mon ange me mena par le chemin que j'avais suivi trois jours auparavant. Je reconnus Bethléem, mon âme fut tranquille, et je me dis à moi-même: Nous allons à la grotte du Sauveur Jésus.

Mon ange était silencieux. Je lui demandai: Allons-nous à la grotte du Sauveur? Il me répondit: 'Le Sauveur n'est plus dans l'habitation où vous l'avez vu naguère.'

Aussitôt j'entendis des voix de femmes désolées qui pleuraient, et poussaient des gémissements à me fendre le cœur. Ces voix venaient de Bethléem. L'ange me dit alors: 'Les voix que vous entendez sont les voix de pauvres mères à qui on arrache leurs enfants pour les livrer à la mort par ordre du roi Hérode qui, craignant la naissance du nouveau roi des Juifs, fait tuer à Bethléem et dans les environs tous les enfants de deux ans et au dessous. Hâtons nos pas, Marie; Jésus a fui en Égypte avec sa Mère; pressons-nous, nous le trouverons dans le désert.'

Les campagnes de la Judée disparurent rapidement et nous aperçûmes au loin Jésus, Marie et Joseph. Cette vue me donna de la force; j'en avais grand

besoin, la chaleur du désert m'avait exténuée de fatigue. L'ange m'encoura-
geait aussi, et je marchais toujours.

Nous atteignîmes enfin la sainte famille; elle reposait sous un arbre couvert
de fruits et au pied duquel coulait une source d'eau fraîche. Marie tenait
l'enfant Jésus dans ses bras. Je m'approchai de Jésus et lui dis: Seigneur,
voici bien longtemps que je vous cherchais et je ne vous trouvais point. Il
me tendit les bras et je le pressai sur mon cœur.

Marie s'adressa à moi et me dit: 'Ma fille, si vous voulez établir le roy-
aume de Dieu dans votre cœur, vous trouverez des obstacles immenses; mais
ne vous découragez point. Fuyez le monde, fuyez le démon, fuyez loin de
vous-même. Vous vous trouverez alors peut-être dans un désert, mais ce
désert ne sera pas sans avoir des charmes pour vous. Dans ce désert, vous
trouverez Dieu et ses consolations, qui vous sont figurées par cet arbre qui
vous nourrira, et par cette source d'eau où vous pourrez vous désaltérer.
Vous y trouverez Jésus et vous m'y trouverez avec lui. Alors ce désert ne
sera plus pour vous un désert, mais une douce oasis, où vous vous reposerez
après le combat, après une longue course, après de rudes épreuves. Ma fille,
allez en paix.'

Je revins à travers le désert et la campagne que j'avais parcourue, en me
félicitant d'avoir trouvé Jésus.

6. Book ii, section 3 (pp. 73 and ff.): Jesus, Light of soul and body.

This is very probably the section to which Hopkins is referring, since in it
there occurs the sentence:

Voilà comment les hommes me verraient s'ils étaient justes, s'ils étaient
purs, s'ils étaient unis à moi.

This sublime treatise begins as follows:

Je possédais un jour Jésus dans mon cœur. Je lui offrais mes adorations,
mes remerciements et mon amour; je m'abandonnais à lui tout entière, en
lui disant: Seigneur Jésus, voici votre servante.

Aussitôt, je vis une lumière d'un éclat supérieur à toute autre lumière.
Est-ce avec les yeux du corps ou de l'âme? Je ne sais; mais je l'ai vue, et,
malgré son éclat, je n'en ai point été éblouie, car cette lumière était en même
temps d'une douceur inexprimable. De son foyer, elle se répandit sur moi, et
quand, pour ainsi parler, je fus transformée en cette lumière, ou que je ne fis
plus qu'un avec elle, tout disparut à mes regards, je n'aperçus que Jésus qui
vint à moi et me releva au moment même où je tombai à ses genoux pour
l'adorer. Il me dit: 'Ma fille, je suis la lumière du monde, et je vous donne
à cette heure une idée de cette lumière que je suis venu apporter aux hommes. Ma lumière n'éclaire pas seulement les yeux du corps, elle éclaire aussi
l'âme, l'esprit et le cœur, et celui qui a une fois bien regardé cette lumière,
n'en désire jamais d'autre, parce qu'elle lui suffit, et qu'elle ne le laisse en
aucun temps dans les ténèbres.

'Ma lumière produit dans les âmes les mêmes opérations que dans le sein
de mon Père qui est au ciel. Dans le sein de mon Père, ma lumière produit
l'intelligence de la Divinité, règle les actes de la Divinité, et embrase de ses
feux la Divinité, pour unir éternellement les trois personnes entre elles.

'Ma lumière produit l'intelligence dans l'homme, règle les actes de l'homme, et embrase de ses feux le cœur de l'homme pour l'unir étroitement à Dieu.

'Heureux sont ceux qui reçoivent ma lumière, qui marchent guidés par ma lumière, qui ne veulent d'autre lumière que ma lumière, car ils ont la lumière véritable, la lumière qui ne passera jamais, qui n'aura même jamais d'éclipse pour eux, et qui les éclairera tant qu'ils ne lui fermeront point les yeux.

'Dieu le Père est lumière, Dieu le Fils est lumière, Dieu le Saint-Esprit est lumière. Je suis comme le centre de ces trois lumières, et par moi ces trois lumières n'en font qu'une. Dieu le Père regarde sa lumière dans ma lumière, et Dieu le Saint-Esprit, la lumière du Père dans celle du Fils. Voilà pourquoi je suis appelé la splendeur de la lumière éternelle, l'éclat de la gloire éternelle.

'Mais je ne suis pas seulement splendeur de lumière éternelle, éclat de la gloire éternelle dans la Divinité; je le suis aussi dans l'humanité.

'J'ai réuni toute la lumière divine dans le corps et l'âme que j'ai pris en mon incarnation, et la force et la puissance de ma divinité l'y ont concentrée et retenue au grand étonnement de la terre et du ciel.

'Le ciel l'apercevait telle qu'il l'aperçoit dans le sein de mon Père; mais la terre avait les yeux trop voilés pour l'apercevoir. Trois de mes disciples l'ont aperçue, comme vous l'apercevez en ce moment, pendant quelques instants; mais pour cela j'ai dû les séparer de la terre, comme je vous en ai séparée à cette heure; j'ai dû fermer leurs yeux à toute autre vue matérielle et terrestre, comme j'ai fermé vos yeux, pour qu'ils ne vissent que ma personne et ma gloire. Voilà comment les hommes me verraient s'ils étaient justes, s'ils étaient purs, s'ils étaient unis à moi.'

7. Book iv, section 7 (pp. 223–4). The Fall of Lucifer.

After the Welsh transcript, Hopkins has the following:

> *On the same*—Marie Lataste: 'Lucifer . . . aurait voulu les entraîner tous, mais les autres se levèrent contre lui en disant: "Qui est semblable à Dieu?" — Écrasé par le poids de cette parole et le regard vengeur du Très-Haut, Lucifer fut précipité dans l'éternelle malédiction.'

'Lucifer, ainsi que tous les anges du ciel, fut soumis à un temps d'épreuve. Au lieu de reconnaître Dieu pour son créateur et l'accepter l'épreuve à laquelle il voulut le soumettre, Lucifer se leva contre lui en disant: "Je m'élèverai, je deviendrai semblable au Très-Haut." Il ne fut pas seul dans sa révolte, il entraîna avec lui un nombre considérable d'anges des neuf degrés établis parmi eux. C'était le plus parfait de tous, et par sa révolte, par l'entraînement qu'il donna aux autres, il devint le plus coupable et le chef des révoltés. Il devint par son crime roi de tous les fils de la superbe et de l'orgueil; mais il ne régnera plus dans le ciel et ses hauteurs; il est, avec tous ses anges, dans les abîmes et les profondeurs de l'enfer. Le nombre de ceux qu'il entraîna fut immense, inférieur néanmoins à celui des anges fidèles. Il aurait voulu les entraîner tous, mais les autres se levèrent contre lui en disant: "Qui est semblable à Dieu?"

'Écrasé par le poids de cette parole et le regard vengeur du Très-Haut, Lucifer fut précipité dans l'éternelle malédiction.

'N'ayant pu entraîner tous les anges avec lui, il cherche à entraîner les hommes. Il a séduit Adam, il l'a mis en révolte contre Dieu, il veut agir de même vis-à-vis de tous les enfants d'Adam. C'est pourquoi il donne à chacun un tentateur pour combattre l'action de l'ange gardien, pour détourner chaque homme de la voie du bien, pour faire de lui une victime de la vengeance de Dieu et un révolté éternel contre sa divine volonté.

'Pour cela, il emploie ruses et artifices; il combine toutes choses, promet le bien et donne le mal, montre la vie et entraîne dans la mort, fait goûter le plaisir et ce plaisir se change en une amertume qui éloigne de Dieu.

'Ma fille, craignez de vous laisser séduire par Satan; il veut votre ruine et la ruine de tous les chrétiens. Depuis que je suis venu au monde pour battre en brèche son empire, il redouble d'efforts pour réduire mes conquêtes. Vains efforts, jamais il n'aura de pouvoir, d'autorité, d'entraînement que sur ceux qui voudront se donner à lui, se livrer à lui, marcher avec lui. Ma grâce repousse Satan, ma force l'épouvante, mon drapeau le met en fuite. Mon drapeau, c'est la croix; attachez-vous à elle, et Satan fuira loin de vous. Ma force est la force de la croix, qui a vaincu la mort et l'enfer; armez-vous de ma croix, et vous épouvanterez Satan. Ma grâce descend de la croix, puisez-y comme dans une source intarissable, et vous repousserez Satan.

'Je suis avec vous, je suis pour vous; marchez, ma fille, et demandez: Qui donc sera contre moi?'

APPENDIX II

Scotus and Hopkins

(Cf. Chapter 3: 'On Personality, Grace and Free Will')

DOCUMENTARILY speaking, there are only four significant places in GMH's spiritual writings where he certainly refers to Scotus. From these, as from four small bones of a prehistoric monster, must be reconstructed the skeletal outline of the undoubted relations between the two men.

The first is the reference to the fall of Lucifer. In my Introduction and Notes I have pointed out how this reference is part of an interpretation of Apocalypse, xii, common to Scotus and Hopkins; how this interpretation is integral to GMH's central concept of 'the great sacrifice'; and how much, in turn, this concept depends on Scotus's theories of the Eucharist and the Incarnation.

The second,[1] the subject of this Appendix, is the very difficult Chapter 3, 'On Personality, Grace and Free Will', in which occurs the sentence: 'Is not this pitch then or whatever we call it the same as Scotus's *ecceitas*?' A brief synopsis of this chapter is the first essential towards clarity.

It cannot, however, be a complete synopsis. Two distinct problems seem to have been agitating the mind of Hopkins: First—*How* can God move a man's free will to attain a destiny beyond the powers of his nature, and yet leave it free and responsible for its actions? The second and much darker problem is—*Why* are some persons predestined effectively to salvation, and others not?

Scotus offers him no help in the second problem. It is indeed insoluble. GMH himself does not seriously tackle it; it merely crops up now and again in this chapter.

The main thread of the chapter, however, is undoubtedly concerned with the first problem. It is only the main thread that is here synopsized.

I. (*a*) A man's self or personality is something he is born with. But it does not come to him from the mere fact of his existing. Personality is prior to existence.

(*b*) A man's personality is also distinct from his human nature. Two different persons can have exactly the same nature. Nevertheless personality needs a human nature in which to display and exercise itself.

(*c*) Personality is the same as freedom, moral freedom to decide one's destiny. This intrinsic freedom may be called 'freedom of pitch'; but it needs 'freedom of play' in the natural faculties in order to display itself. (There is also 'freedom of field', which comes from the presence of a number of alternatives.)

II. (*a*) Personality in that it is prior to existence may be called 'pitch'. Pitch is a pre-existing determination of man towards his eternal destiny by his creator, but in such a sort that the man is left free to determine himself.

---

[1] For the third and fourth, see notes, p. 291 (138. 4) and p. 303 (186. 3).

(*b*) This apparent contradiction is explained by the two sides to man's will. There is the will as nature (*voluntas ut natura*), which God can attract— spiritually from within, or sensibly from without. There is also the will as *arbitrium*, which is independent of nature and free to accept or refuse the attraction. Other terms for these are 'the affective will' and 'the elective will'.

(*c*) The difficulty is that God has to attract man to a *supernatural* destiny. Unless a man is trained to the supernatural, his freedom of pitch is so tied to his freedom of play, i.e. he is so wedded to his nature, and his nature is tied by so many rival attractions, that he is unable even to consider a super-natural alternative. God can control freedom of field by foreclosing it. But how can he control freedom of pitch without violating it?

III. (*a*) This is where the priority of pitch to existence is all-important. There is a world of *possible* being, prior to existence, in which God sees and loves a man fulfilling God's will and achieving his own destiny. God is able to illumine a man's mind and affect his will with the sense that he *already is* this nobler, consenting self. So powerful is this sense of identity, that man's free will to dissent from it is temporarily suspended. This is the effect of 'prevenient grace'.

(*b*) But in the next moment of grace, 'concomitant grace', there is no such constraint. Man is free to make a leisurely avowal or disavowal of his first constrained consent. He needs this concomitant grace in order to make the avowal of his new self; but he has to make an effort (against his old self) in order to accept the grace of correspondence.

(*c*) If he accepts and perseveres in his acceptance, then he actually be-comes and really is that nobler self which before was only in the world of possibles. This 'lifting from one self to another' is the third and properly supernatural effect of grace. It is called 'elevating grace'.

There are a series of 'pitches', corresponding to critical moments in a man's life, by which he ascends or fails to ascend to the complete personality that God has destined for him.

The thread of GMH's argument virtually ends here. A word of caution is necessary, especially with regard to the last sentence of the summary.

It is beyond the scope and power of this exposition to discuss meta-physically the problems which GMH, sometimes unconsciously, raises. Of two in particular the reader may be warned in advance not to expect a metaphysical discussion.

There is, first, the question of pitch being 'prior to existence'. Is this pitch, in its priority, merely a concept whose only foundation in reality is in the existing substance of some man? Or, if it is not to be identified with any created substance, is it to be identified with the Divine Essence? It must surely, one would think, be either one or the other.

The only thing to be said is that GMH is evidently holding Scotus's posi-tion as his own; and Scotus's position, whether it be accepted or rejected in fact, should be accepted hypothetically for an understanding of this treatise. His position (using the word 'pitch' for individuality) would be, in answer to the first question, that pitch can only exist in an existing substance, yet its distinctiveness is so much more than merely conceptual that it must be considered as a reality apart from the nature in which it exists. The answer to the second question may make this clearer. A *possible* pitch is certainly identified with the Divine Essence in so much as it is an idea in God's Mind. But in so much as it is an intention *ad extra* in God's Will, it exercises an influence outside the Divine Essence.

A man in an existing state of pitch desires to reach a possible state of pitch. If and when he does so, although he is already a substance perfectly 'in act', yet fresh substantial reality is thereby added to him. Therefore some degree of reality must be attached to this possible pitch, considered as a finite entity which is not yet part of an existing finite substance.[1] Just as Scotus held a sort of *quantum* theory in regard to physical motion, so in regard to time he seems to have wanted to make allowance for the extra perfection that can come to a finite substance that is already perfect 'in act', though not in fact.[2]

The second difficulty is whether the self-perfection to which man aspires is in the natural order or in the supernatural order. To this Scotus's answer appears to be that the aspiration is in the natural order, but the achievement of it requires supernatural aid: 'Ad perfectissimum [actum] circa ultimum finem est inclinatio naturalis, licet ad illum non potest attingere natura ex se.' (*Quodlibet*, xvii.)

But it is doubtful whether Hopkins was disturbed by this difficulty. In his concluding pages he says that the aspiration to be lifted up 'might be a natural grace'; but he thinks of the actual lifting-up to a higher level as wholly supernatural.

In the concluding pages he does little more than amplify the three kinds or moments of grace. The first is the grace of vocation touching the affective will and is felt especially by novices. The second is a testing grace for maturer minds; it is corrective grace touching the elective will but leaving it free. The third is charity itself, the Holy Spirit, 'truly God's finger touching the very vein of personality, which nothing else can reach . . .'. He assigns them by appropriation to the Three Persons of the Blessed Trinity, because the first recalls our origin from the creative abyss, the second recalls Christ's example of renunciation, and the third actually is the touch of the Holy Spirit—though of course all three are in each as one. He also likens them to the three moments of sacrifice: oblation, immolation, and acceptance of the victim; and he finds them enumerated in these three words of St Paul (italicized):

All those who from the first were known to him, he has destined from the first to be moulded into the image of his Son, who is thus to become the eldest-born among many brethren. So predestined, he *called* them; so called, he *justified* them; so justified, he *glorified* them. (Rom. viii. 29–30.)[3]

But there remains one vitally important point which my synopsis has not

[1] Scotus speaks of a *possibile reale*: that which a nature has the capacity to reach. See É. Gilson, *Duns Scot* (Paris, 1952), p. 131, n. 1.
[2] Cf. *Quaest. sup. lib. Metaph.* viii. 3: 'Utrum substantia, sc. forma substantialis, suscipiat magis et minus':
'Substantia ergo secundum speciem in universali considerata, ut quidditas, non suscipit magis et minus; sed in supposito patet, quia hoc individuum perfectius habet naturam specificam quam aliud.'
[3] English translations in this Appendix are from Mgr Knox's version.

brought out because its conclusion belongs to another chapter of GMH's, Chapter 8 on 'Creation and Redemption'. Nevertheless the grounds for it are laid in this chapter. It is the point that all takes place in the mystical enclosure of Christ's created nature leading to the divine.

The word 'eldest-born' in the text just quoted leaves no doubt in GMH's mind that it is Christ's *created* nature of which St Paul is speaking. Leaning heavily on St Paul (to the Ephesians, Colossians, and Philippians as well as Romans), GMH thinks of Christ's created nature as the original pattern of creation, to a place in which all subsequent created being must attain in order to be complete. The Holy Spirit that 'reaches our innermost being' (Eph. iii. 16) is Christ's spirit charged with Christ's likeness. The πλήρωμα τοῦ θεοῦ, the 'completion God has to give' (ibid. 19), is in the world of possible being 'in Christ', so that the 'lifting from one self to another' is 'as if a man said: That is Christ playing at me and me playing at Christ, only that it is no play but truth; That is Christ *being me* and me being Christ.'

In fact the text which sums up his whole thesis even better than Rom. viii. 29–30 is Eph. ii. 10: 'We are his design; God has created us in Christ Jesus, pledged to such good actions as he has prepared beforehand, to be the employment of our lives.'

This is the source to which all GMH's Scotus echoes seem to return. To arrive at it is bound to be a devious underground process because, for obvious reasons, the two men rarely talk precisely to the same purpose. Nevertheless there are distinct points of contact on the way; and it is these points which it is hoped may prove illuminating. The two terms of the discussion will be 'pitch' at one end and 'being in Christ' at the other.

'Is not this pitch then or whatever we call it the same as Scotus's *ecceitas*?' Scotus never uses the actual word *haecceitas* in the *Scriptum Oxoniense* (see note, p. 293 (141. 3). In *Oxoniense*, II. iii. 1 to 6, he defines the concept, but in a context of logic rather than psychology. To him it is the final determinant in the scale of natures that descend the Tree of Porphyry by way of genus and species; it is that which stops the common nature in one member of the species from being communicable to other members. This has much to do with GMH's Chapter 1 (on Self), but not so much to do with his concept of 'pitch' in Chapter 3.

Nevertheless Scotus has two *quaestiones* in II. iii. 1–6, which square at once with two of GMH's opening remarks. In question 1 he distinguishes individuality from nature, since no nature is *de se haec*. In question 3 he says that individuality is not constituted by the mere fact of existence; existence is the state in which an individual finds himself; individuality is prior to existence.

These two conclusions correspond exactly to two of GMH's listed in my synopsis as I*a* and I*b*. Of the two, the latter, as stated here, is the more deeply important and fruitful. Scotus concludes that individuality or 'thisness' is intrinsic to being. But, as I have said, he does not equate 'being' with 'existence'. He regards being not only as existence but as a process of coming into existence from a state of mere possibility in the creator's mind. Prior to existence, a man has an essence or *esse intelligibile* as conceived by God, and a destiny or *esse volitum* as willed by God. He has also in his *esse* *intelligibile* a scale of subordinate essences: elemental, vegetative, animal; these are conceived as one in God's mind, but the actual binding-force of the unity comes from the *esse volitum* of God's will; Scotus calls this binding-force *coordinatio substantialis* or *continentia unitiva*. He therefore sees individuality as the end and co-ordination of a process of becoming, the *ultima realitas entis*. As to its cause, only the origin of being can explain that. '*Ratio intima haecceitatis non est quaerenda nisi in Divina voluntate.*' (*Parisiensia*, II. xii. 5.)

Scotus's concept of finite being as existing yet still coming into existence (*semper in fieri*) was linked to his concept of 'personality' in a passage written towards the end of his life:

> Productio Personae Divinae semper est 'in fieri' quia nunquam ista persona potest habere 'esse' nisi accipiendo actualiter a producente; et tamen 'esse' personae est maxime permanens. Hoc modo, 'esse' creaturae, licet sit permanens, tamen respectu Dei a cuius volitione actuali semper aeque dependet, semper est quasi 'in fieri', hoc est, actu dependens a causa dante 'esse', et nunquam 'in facto esse', hoc est, in actu separato et independenti. (*Quodlibet*, xii.)

The crude yet wiry, vibrant quality of Scotus's northern diction is apparent in this passage. It might be possible from it alone to get right to the centre of Hopkins's speculations.[1] In an interpolated passage of Chapter 3 he puts the relation of proportion between Divine Personality and human personality as that of the infinite to the infinitesimal—recalling the Psalmist's *abyssus abyssum invocat*; and in a passage of Chapter 8 he says that the 'blissful stress of selving in God', when translated *ad extra*, is the stress of creation. Both here and in the other places where he starts talking about the Trinity, he breaks off in the middle. The matter is in any case too profound and difficult.

There are, however, several places in the *Oxoniense* which provide a context for GMH's 'pitch'.

According to Scotus the ground of individuality is the intrinsic *lack* of being (*carentia entitatis*) which results in a creature from its being created:

> Omne igitur aliud a Deo necessario componitur non ex re et re positivis, sed ex re positiva et privatione, id est, ex entitate aliqua quam habet et carentia alicuius gradus perfectionis entitativae cuius foret capax quatenus ens. (*Oxoniense*, I. viii. 2, p. 78ᵃ, § A)

The simultaneous possession of positive being and lack of further possible being is the distinctive mark of a finite creature. Scotus interprets (or misinterprets) St Thomas as saying that it is matter applied to form that stops it from being infinite;[2] it is matter also that individuates it. But, in his own way of looking at it, if a form were really infinite, no force from outside could make it finite. In his view a being is finite, and at the same time individuated, by the *intrinsic degree* in which it possesses the positive perfection of its nature yet lacks a further possible perfection due to it as a being. *Quodlibet ens habet intrinsecum sibi gradum suae perfectionis in quo est finitum. . . .* (I. ii. 2, p. 29ᵃ, § Bᵇ.)

This *gradus sibi intrinsecus* or intrinsic degree is, I think, the origin of

---

[1] See note, p. 303 (186. 3). But this third reference to Scotus is too obscure to build on.

[2] 'Forma finitur per materiam, ergo quae non est nata esse in materia, est infinita. Haec ratio nihil valet. . . .' (*Oxoniense*, I. ii. 2.)

GMH's 'pitch'. The words could be synonymous in his usage; he approved of the phrase '*pitches* of suchness' for '*degrees* of comparison'. (*Letters*, i. 163.) The image suggested, as will be seen, by both his and Scotus's usage is also the same—a hole, or series of holes, say in a violin, into which a peg can be fitted so as to tighten the string; the holes would be the *carentia*, the peg would be an ideal self, the string would be human nature.

A translation of this image into conceptual thought may clear up a slight confusion between 'pitch' and 'personality' in GMH's usage. He usually equates them; but once, speaking of pitch as pre-existent, he says: 'it is not truly self: self or personality then truly comes into being when the self, the person, comes into being [he means existence] with the accession of nature'.

In two trinitarian theses Scotus shows how the *gradus intrinsecus* is the ground or quasi-principle of the two aspects of self: the perfect possession of its own nature, and its need for further perfection as a being.[1] Translated into terms of psychology, the one is a vision in the mind, the other is the native movement of the will.[2] In two other theses he shows how the movement or the will must go beyond the scope of unaided human nature if it is to attain to the ideal self,[3] yet it must draw human nature with it.[4]

If these four points are compared with the synopsis it will be seen that they tally to a surprising degree. But it will be necessary to amplify them somewhat, because they represent a line of Scotus's thought which is not to be found in the textbooks.

His first thesis is that although God creates as One, not as Three, yet the distinctive mark left upon the creature (*respectus vestigialis*) is a threefold one. A text from Wisdom xi, used by St Augustine, comes to hand: 'omnia in *mensura* et *numero* et *pondere* disposuisti'. It enables him to relate the creature to God as to its triple cause—original, exemplary, and final.

Mensura may stand for the *gradus intrinsecus* because it is the source both of limitation and distinction. 'De mensura igitur est ut unumquodque limitatum suae perfectionis gradum obtineat. . . .' Also, like the *gradus*, it implies proportion; it measures the boundless difference between creator and creature, and by the *difference*, not by any likeness, causes awareness of the boundless depths of God's Fatherhood: 'non . . . sub ratione similitudinis, sed secundum proportionem: limitatio enim producti manuducit ad intelligendum illimitatam producentis potentiam'. This recalls GMH's comparison of the ratio of the infinite to the infinitesimal.

Numerus, in the sense of harmony, may be taken for the co-ordination of parts which individuates nature. 'Ex numeri autem potestate fit ut propria specifica perfectione unumquodque subsistat . . . propriamque possideat speciem aliis nec communem nec communicabilem. . . .' Here we do have a relation of likeness; for the beauty of co-ordinated nature is a reflection of the beauty of God the Son who is the pattern for creation—'prima species primaque pulchritudo':

Numerus igitur sive species, et pondus seu ordo, in priori vestigii partium

---

[1] *Oxoniense*, i. iii. 5: 'Utrum in omni creatura sit vestigium trinitatis.'
[2] Ibid. 9: 'Utrum in mente sit distincte imago trinitatis.'
[3] Ibid. *Prologus*, 4: 'Utrum theologia sit scientia practica.'
[4] Ibid. i. vi. 1: 'Utrum Deus Pater genuerit Deum Filium voluntate.'

assignatione declarata fuerunt; ex quibus constat, in specie creaturarum praelucere vestigium Filii, qui per appropriationem prima species primaque pulchritudo appellatur; per ordinem vero perfectissima Dei operatio intelligitur.

Here GMH's whole notion of 'inscape' clamours for entrance; but it must be passed over.[1]

Pondus, or bias, is the profound inclination of the creature to rest in God as its final cause, according to the saying of Augustine: *Pondus meum, Amor meus*. Since it is love and grace in rational creatures, it may be attributed in a very special way to the Holy Spirit: *perfectissima Dei operatio intelligitur*.

In the next thesis Scotus translates the triple relation of the creature to God (*mensura-numerus-pondus*) into terms of the three powers of the soul; for it is the soul that is the true *imago* of the Trinity, bodies being only *vestigia*. Thus he gives psychological reality to what might otherwise have remained merely ontological concepts. This is clearly of great importance to our purpose. For it is part of the originality of GMH's treatise that he does the same for his concepts of pitch and personality.

Let it be noted in passing that seeing the *vera imago* of the Trinity in one's soul is a glimpse of one's ideal self.

The three powers of the soul, in St Augustine's great treatise *De Trinitate*, are: memory, understanding, will. Scotus accepts them, though with some demur; he prefers the vaguer terms *actus primus, actus secundus*. . . . There are really only two distinct powers of the soul—the apprehensive and the appetitive, knowing and desiring; and these are not completely distinct, they have a common origin in the soul. If we are to speak of three distinct powers, we must think of them as the same soul on three ascending levels of consciousness.

The first is the soul in a state of indistinct knowing and desiring which we should call 'the unconscious', though Scotus would disapprove—and rightly—of the term. This can be called 'memory' (in the Platonic sense of *anamnesis*), though of course memory has other functions as well.

The second is the soul in a state of distinct understanding, including such affections (i.e. rationalized emotions) as suit the nature of the understanding.

The third is the soul in complete command of itself and of its nature. The soul in command of itself is free will; but the will as the appetitive power in general runs through the other states also, in the form of desire and delectation or their opposites. The will thus represents the whole man by knitting the soul together, so to speak, both horizontally and vertically.

Scotus's thesis is that the soul, in order to realize itself as a true image of the Trinity, must be aware of God's presence concretely in the memory and must appreciate his nature abstractively in the understanding; but then it must somehow join the two together; for while without the appreciation of God's nature there can be no right reason for adoring him, without the sense of his presence there can be no attraction to adore him.

In the memory the soul is aware of its own nature as an image of all things and therefore desirable. (The senses also play a part in this, as has been said elsewhere.) But what in fact the soul desires is not only the image but

[1] See my articles, 'The Image and the Word' in *The Month*, Feb. and Mar. 1950.

the reality, the cause and origin of the image;[1] and this it apprehends simply as 'unlimited being' (neither finite nor positively infinite) outside itself.

If this double awareness of the image and the word could be transmitted entire into the state of distinct understanding, the soul would know Christ as the Son of God—the perfection of created nature coming out of the perfection of uncreated being.[2] But there is a barrier of unconsciousness (the *real* 'unconscious') between memory (the first act) and understanding (the second).

Scotus corrects Augustine on this point: 'Dictum Augustini debet intelligi de actu primo sufficiente ex se ad actum suum secundum; sed tamen nunc impeditur; propter quod impedimentum, actus secundus non elicitur a primo.' (*Oxoniense, Prologus*, 1.)

The burden of the memory can only be transmitted to the understanding in the broken form of phantasm and concept: a phantasm that can stand for all that is desirable in nature, and a concept that can be refined and certified as 'infinite being'. But there is no connexion between the two.

It remains for the soul in the third state, under the influence of divine grace, to choose 'infinite being' in preference to all things. It can choose it, but it cannot desire it. For you cannot desire a concept! So what happens by the mercy of God is that the soul, or will, in the state of free choice knits together the will in the states below. An inspiration (*vis spiritiva* is Scotus's word) runs from the original desire in the memory to the rational affections in the understanding. The barrier between the conscious and the unconscious is broken. The unknown source of knowledge in the memory is recognized as the parent of the highest that the understanding can conceive, the concept of infinite being. 'Dilectio est quasi actus imperativus', says Scotus, 'vel conjungens parentem cum prole.' This is the true image of the Father generating the Son.

The act by which the will extends memory and understanding to each other and to itself is called by Scotus *praxis*. But it is to be noted that the impulse to this extension cannot come from an arbitrary act of the will choosing whatever object it likes. The impulse can only come from a desire to know the hitherto unknown object—the source of knowledge in the memory. That is the meaning of Scotus's cryptic sentence: 'Cognitio practica non habet primam extensionem sibi competentem a fine ipsius praxis in quantum est finis, sed in quantum est obiectum.' (*Oxoniense, Prologus*, 4–5.)

Scotus's thesis on *praxis* has been introduced here—at the risk of multiplying words—because the term *praxis* has a strong savour of GMH's barbarous coinage: 'So that this pitch might be expressed, if it were good English, *the doing* be, *the doing* choose. . . .'

The actual derivation of Scotus's term is from the opposition between *practica* and *speculativa*, because Scotus is opposing Aristotle's thesis that the final felicity of man consists in 'speculation'. It is fairly evident, incidentally,

---

[1] 'Quietatio nunquam est in se, sed in aliud; unde creatura non quietatur in se, sed in alio.' (*Oxoniense*, IV. xlix. 7.)
[2] 'Quilibet intellectus est totius entis et non quietatur nisi in Verbo sub ratione infiniti.' (*Parisiensia*, III. xiv. 2.)

that GMH was familiar with this treatise of Scotus. In Chapter 5 (*De Nativi-tate*), he speaks of the 'practice or action properly so-called' which should result from all three powers of the soul in prayer, and adds: 'all voluntary exercise of the faculties is in such a case practical; it is not mere speculation, whatever its name'.

Scotus's objection to Aristotle (and also, though perhaps more question-ably, to St Thomas) is twofold. To put final felicity in the intellect is to abandon man's noblest gift, his freedom; for the intellect has no choice. Further, although the intellect has all finite being for its province, it cannot, unless it is aided by the will, extend itself to conceive the infinite;[1] whereas, according to Scotus, it is evident from experience and introspection that we are made for the infinite: 'Videtur inclinatio naturalis ad summe amandum bonum infinitum   Ita videtur quod experimur de actu amandi bonum infinitum. Immo, non videtur voluntas in alio perfecte quietari.' (*Oxoniense*, I. ii. 2.)

The will then, according to Scotus, is what expresses the whole man; first, because it is free, and secondly, because its proper object is the infinite. His own problem is: how can the intellect submit to the will without the intel-lect's integrity being violated? His answer is that *cognitio speculativa* (such as the certainty of truth in the abstract) can never submit to the will; but there is a *cognitio practica* which is native to the whole soul and therefore native to the intellect. Whereas *cognitio speculativa* is content with representations inside the mind, the characteristic of *cognitio practica* is to be drawn to an object *outside* the mind.[2]

Now the origin of knowing in the soul is the source which is confusedly apprehended in the memory as a *lack* of being, *carentia entitatis*. The desire of the soul corresponding to this awareness is a desire for the infinite. When this desire is an impulsion of grace, it may be said that in the memory (in what the psychologists call 'the depths of the soul') there is contact with God's presence. When, therefore, the understanding diagnoses truly that the object of the soul's desire is the infinite, it has no difficulty in handing over its burden, so to speak, to the will. What the will then does is first (in Augustine's phrase) to 'wed the understanding to the memory', so as to have both truth and beauty (for the senses, according to Scotus's psychology, play their part in the memory); and then to project the whole soul, by a free choice, towards the supreme object of desire. Of this twofold act Scotus says (elsewhere):

Bene concurrunt isti duo actus in voluntate nostra, quia ipse amans obiectum amat etiam notitiam obiecti eiusdem, et ex amore obiecti movet intelligentiam ad intelligendum illud, copulans ipsam memoriae de qua ipsa formetur, et tenens eam in tali coniunctione, et per hoc in actuali intellectione unius obiecti. Istorum autem

---

[1] It can add 'non' to 'finite', but that is no more than to add 'no' to 'thing'—unless the 'non' comes from a positive desire. Otherwise, as Scotus says: 'Tunc non agnoscitur Deus plus quam chymera, quia haec negatio communis est enti et non-enti.' (*Oxoniense*, I. viii. 3.)

[2] 'Esse practicum dicit aliquid intrinsecum notitiae . . . hoc est, per naturam intrinsecam notitiae, quam naturam habet ab obiecto ut a causa intrinseca. Dico igitur quod habitus est practicus per intrinsecum, ut per causam formalem, et per obiectum ut per causam efficientem.' (*Oxoniense, Prologus*, v.)

duorum actuum voluntatis in nobis, principalior est ille qui est dilectio obiecti, quia ille est causa quandoque dilectionis actus. Actus tamen alius, scilicet dilectio actus, est universalior, quia respectu etiam obiecti mali diligimus actum cognoscendi. Licet non obiectum, sicut dicit Augustinus, 9 de Trin. (*Oxoniense*, I. vi. I.)

Here once more the connexion between Scotus and Hopkins breaks surface. The distinction between these two operations of the will, the *amor obiecti* and the *amor notitiae obiecti*, is nothing else but GMH's repeated distinction between 'the elective will' and 'the affective will'.

It is worth remarking that this distinction between *amor obiecti* and *amor notitiae obiecti* has a bearing on the connexion—and the difference—between poetic inspiration and prayer in the context of Scotus's *vis spirativa*.

In prayer the soul goes all out for the object by an act of free will avowing the inspiration; this is *amor obiecti*. But the *amor notitiae obiecti* is a legitimate delight in the inspiration and an exploration of the knowledge that unfolds from it.

Two points relevant to GMH occur to mind here. First—as Scotus and Augustine say—the unfolding inspiration can lead to a legitimate delight in the knowledge of even an evil object—not a delight in the object, but in the knowing of it. This is apparent in the light that GMH evidently received on the fall of Lucifer and the state of the damned (see Chapter 2); it is apparent also in the magnificent fragment of Caradoc's defiance of heaven. It is clearly the stuff of first-class tragedy—as Marlowe, Shakespeare, Milton, and others have found, not to mention Mauriac and Graham Greene.

Secondly, it is obviously possible to dwell too much on the *amor notitiae*, to the neglect of the *amor obiecti*. This may throw light on GMH's words to Bridges:

Feeling, love in particular, is the great moving power and spring of verse and the only person that I am in love with seldom, especially now, stirs my heart sensibly and when he does I cannot always 'make capital' of it, it would be sacrilege to do so. (*Letters*, i. 66.)

But for his consolation at other times Scotus had noted: '*Bene concurrunt isti duo actus. . . .*'

Scotus makes it very clear that while the free choice is the nobler part of the will, yet the affective act is the one that comes first, because without it there would be no guarantee that the whole soul was involved:

Ex duabus conditionibus ultimis praxis, sequitur quod actus imperatus a voluntate non est primo praxis, sed quasi per accidens, quia nec primo est posterior intellectioni, nec primo natus elici conformiter rationi rectae. Oportet igitur aliquem alium actum esse primo praxim; iste non est nisi volitio, quia per istam habet actus imperatus dictas conditiones. Ergo prima ratio praxis salvatur in actu elicito voluntatis. (*Oxoniense, Prologus*, v.)

The terms he uses, *actus elicitus* and *actus imperatus*, are to be understood as follows. *Elicitus* is the spontaneous act of the will, which it cannot help making, because it has both memory and understanding completely behind it. *Imperatus* is in obedience to free and autonomous choice. It is practically the same distinction as GMH's between *voluntas ut natura* and *arbitrium*.

Scotus's conclusion is that in *praxis* (which is the projection of the whole soul towards God) the first movement must be spontaneous.

GMH's conclusion is the same. But he puts the stress in reverse. He takes the affective, spontaneous part for granted, and insists on the element of free choice. In the passages to be quoted, however, it is important to note that 'constrained' in his context is not opposed to 'spontaneous' and equivalent to 'commanded'. It is the other way round. 'Commanded' refers to the will's self-command, not to God's influence; therefore commanded is equivalent to free or autonomous. 'Spontaneous' is the opposite of this; spontaneous in scholastic language is equivalent to 'necessary', that is, according to nature. When the will is constrained by God, it is constrained by an influence so wholly in accordance with its nature that it cannot refuse.

In every circumstance it is within God's power to determine the creature to choose, and freely choose, according to his will; but not without a change or access of circumstance. . . . This access is either of grace, which is 'supernature', to nature or of more grace to grace already given, and it takes the form of instressing the affective will, of affecting the will towards the good which he proposes. So far this is a necessary and constrained affection on the creature's part, to which the *arbitrium* of the creature may give its avowal and consent. Ordinarily when grace is given we feel first the necessary or constrained act and after that the free act on our own part, of consent or refusal as the case may be.

For there must be something which shall be truly the creature's in the work of corresponding with grace: this is the *arbitrium*, the verdict on God's side, the saying Yes, the 'doing-agree' (to speak barbarously), and looked at in itself, such a nothing is the creature before its creator, it is found to be no more than the mere wish discernible by God's eyes, that it might do as he wishes, might correspond, might say Yes to him. . . . And by this infinitesimal act the creature does what in it lies to bridge the gulf fixed between its present actual and worser pitch of will and its future better one.

The apparent paradox that the will, at the same time as not being able to refuse, can also freely consent, is a thesis belonging to another department of Scotus's thought. But it may be noted here, as a clear point of contact, that in a letter of 4 Jan. 1883 GMH hails this thesis as having been taught him by Scotus. 'Hereby, I may tell you, hangs a very profound question treated by Duns Scotus, who shews that freedom is compatible with necessity.' These are almost Scotus's actual words, which in fact are: 'Alia est necessitas spontanea . . . et illa stat cum libertate.'

His argument is that *non posse nolle* (not to be able to refuse) is not intrinsically the same as *velle* (to will); and he pushes it to the extent that a saint who enters into the Beatific Vision enters *freely* even though he is compelled by delight. He adds an illustration that savours somewhat of the death-wish: a man who steps off a precipice freely and does not change his mind while falling; he goes on falling from natural necessity; yet he goes on falling freely. . . .

In this attempt to follow the intertwining thought of Scotus and Hopkins scant justice has been done to the bewildering accuracy with which Scotus pins down the most fugitive realities to distinct concepts. But at least it may be clear that when GMH equated his 'pitch' with Scotus's *haecceitas*, he was thinking of something more ramified than Scotus's definition of *haecceitas* in the *Reportata Parisiensia*—which indeed he may never have read. He was following Scotus in thinking of self or individuality as the independent possession of one's human nature; but he was also following Scotus in thinking that one's independence as a human nature rests on one's deeper dependence as a human being—and the more perfect the nature, the deeper the dependence. Further, for both Scotus and Hopkins, the independent possession of one's nature is exercised by the will as *arbitrium*, while the deeper dependence is in the attraction of the *voluntas ut natura* to the infinite, which is its origin.

It remains however to clear up a terminological difficulty which is bound to occur to those who are familiar with Scotus's use of the word *personalitas*. In clearing it up, Scotus's thought will be found to conclude at the same point as GMH's—namely, that 'we are created *in Christ*'.

GMH was not always careful to distinguish self as 'individuality' from self as 'personality'. But Scotus was very careful to do so. He had to be. For he was confronted by the great problem that confronts all theologians. How can Christ as man be a perfect human nature (and therefore, presumably, a human individual), yet not a human person?

A human person, in Scotus's view, is constituted by a *double* independence, which he terms 'aptitudinal' and 'actual'; and neither *alone* is sufficient to constitute a person.[1] But to get these rather clumsy terms into focus it is necessary to go back to an earlier passage in this Appendix:

> Prior to existence, a man has an essence or *esse intelligibile* as conceived by God's mind, and a destiny or *esse volitum* as decreed by God's will. He has also in his *esse intelligibile* a scale of subordinate essences: elemental, vegetative, animal; these are conceived as one in God's mind, but the actual binding-force of the unity comes from the *esse volitum* of God's will.

Now, the one-ness conceived in God's mind gives the essence or nature an *aptitudinal* independence; that is, it fits it, makes it intrinsically apt, to be an independent unit. But this independence will, obviously, not be *actual* till the essence's identity with God's mind is severed by its being actually put into existence. This is the point which GMH seems to have in mind when he corrects himself: 'self or personality then truly comes into being when the self, the person, comes into being with the accession of nature'. In the same place he modifies his notion of 'pitch', and says that it is really 'a thread or chain of such pitches' *between* the actual self and the ideal self. This suggests that GMH's 'personality' and Scotus's *personalitas* are not really very different. For both it is a movement *from* the state of aptitudinal independence as an ideal in God's mind *to* the state of actual independence in time and place. One has only to add the notion of *praxis*, and personality is seen not only as a coming forth from God but as a going back to him. The image of simultaneous coming forth and going back is the only one that in any way suggests the mystery of continuous creation which is at the back of personality both for Scotus and Hopkins. GMH's 'What I do is me' is relevant here, and Scotus's 'Essentia creata *est* sua dependentia ad Deum' from the *Quodlibet*

---

[1] For example, a disembodied soul is *actually* independent of its body, but not *aptitudinally* so; it still needs its glorified body to constitute it as a person.

already quoted. Personality then, for both, is movement from the ideal to
the actual, and back from the actual to the ideal—though it is an ideal which
can never be actually reached because it is identical with God himself and
the processions of the Trinity. Personality is thus a journey into ever-
increasing never-ending self-realization.

But the problem still remains: why is Christ not a human person? The
hub of the answer is that the unity of Christ's human nature comes from
God's mind, not from God's will.

To make this clearer, it will help to point out the difference between
Scotus's *gradus intrinsecus* and GMH's 'pitch'. The *gradus* is the mark of
God's mind on the essence or nature, fixing the order of its evolution (by
genus and species, and so on) and fitting it to end as an individual. The
gradus may be called the need to be individuated, or the *ground of* individuality, but it is not precisely that positive *ultima realitas entis* which Scotus
calls *haecceitas*. That comes from the *esse volitum* of God's will. So pitch, in
so far as it is a positive direction from God's will, is *haecceitas* rather than
gradus intrinsecus.

The distinction is important, because, to put the matter briefly, Christ's
human nature has the *gradus intrinsecus* but not the *haecceitas*.

Christ's human nature has indeed an 'aptitudinal' independence. It is
conceived as one in God's mind with the *gradus intrinsecus* that fits it to be an
individual nature. But, it will be remembered, the *gradus intrinsecus* is the
degree of finiteness; it is not only the need of a nature to be an independent
individual, it is also the need of a creature for God. In all other human
beings the *esse volitum* supplies this need in its natural order by way of an
haecceitas. But on Christ's human nature the stress of God's will is wholly
towards God himself. So on coming into existence, Christ's human nature
is still 'apt' to be a person (*personabilis*) but with an aptitude subordinate to
its dependence as a creature: 'Nam "hic homo" non est persona, sed personabilis in instanti sequenti, cum, scilicet, intelligitur individuum independens; in instanti autem priori nec est dependens nec independens ad alium
suppositum.'

In the very instant of coming into existence, which would be the instant
of *actual* independence, the need of Christ's human nature to be a person is
supplied by the personality of God the Son: 'In illo instanti naturae in quo
natura personaretur in se si non assumeretur, in eodem instanti personatur
in alio quando assumitur.'

But more than this rather technical conclusion flows from the fact that
the unity of Christ's human nature comes from God's mind. The intelligible
reason for its unity is that it covers the whole range of the specific nature in
the same way that each angel is the whole of its species. Christ's human
nature is what Scotus calls *atoma* or *in atomo*: the *unbroken* pattern. 'Christus
non est proprie "hic homo" ut persona, sed "hic homo" ut natura *atoma*.'[1]

Each human nature, other than Christ's, is seen in God's mind as an
image of his Essence, but an imperfect image; not merely imperfect because

---

[1] 'Propositio illa: "Persona Verbi assumpsit hunc hominem", de rigore sermonis,
non est verum; sed, proprie loquendo, haec: "Persona Verbi assumpsit naturam
humanam *in atomo*."'

it is finite, but imperfect because it is fragmentary. It is part of a *species* or pattern which is incomplete without the other parts; hence it needs a *haecceitas* to complete it for purposes of existence. But Christ's human nature is the perfect finite image of the Divine Essence, the whole expression of the idea in God's mind.

At once this links up with Scotus's thesis that Christ was predestined before all other creatures, and also with the conclusion of GMH's Chapter 3 and the opening of his Chapter 8. Christ is the 'eldest-born', the *prima species primaque pulchritudo*.

He is the head of the human race by *natural* right, as well as of the lower levels contained in human nature, the elemental, vegetative, and sensitive. As man he is also head of the angels by the grace added to his nature after union with the Word. Although his human nature was the lowest in the scale of angelic natures in the order of execution, yet in the order of intention it was the first because of the grace that was to unite it with the Word. See note, p. 306 (196. 2).

From this it would seem to follow that all the multitudinous degrees of perfection in created things combine like some mathematical formula to express the intrinsic degree of Christ's created perfection. Indeed mathematical or musical terms would be better than logical ones to describe this mystical unity.

Scotus's technical attempts to define it are outside our present scope; they occur mostly in his commentary on Aristotle's *Metaphysics*. In one place he falls back on the same simile as GMH in Chapter 8: that of a choir of voices where each voice retains its individuality but the total effect is a more perfect whole.

But enough has been said to show that this Appendix concludes logically at the same point as my Introduction. GMH's central identity with Scotus is in Scotus's theology of the Incarnation.

APPENDIX III

Fall of the Angels according to Babylonian and Welsh Texts

A T the end of his edition of the *Exercitia Spiritualia*, opposite the Index, Hopkins has the following:

Fall of the Angels—Records of the Past, vol. 7, pp. 127–8; Chaldean hieratic tablet, date about 600 B.C. but copied from an older one discovered by George Smith:

'The Divine Being spoke three times, the commencement of a Psalm.
The god of holy songs, lord of religion and worship
Seated a thousand singers and musicians: . . .
Who to his hymn were to respond in multitudes . . .
With a loud cry of contempt they broke up his holy song,
Spoiling, confusing, confounding his hymn of praise.
The god of the bright crown, with a wish to summon his adherents,
Sounded a trumpet-blast that would wake the dead,
Which to those rebel angels prohibited return;
He stopped their service and sent them to the gods who were his enemies.

'In their room he created mankind.
The first who received life remained with him.
May he give them strength, never to neglect his word,
Following the serpent's voice, whom his hands had made,
And may the gods of divine speech expel from his five thousand that
    wicked one thousand.'

'Crown' must mean *corona*, throng. 'The first who' etc./obscure; it must mean the faithful angels. 'The serpent's voice' probably refers to the fall of the angels, not of man. The 'may's are a semitic figure of grammar—not a real wish but a congratulation.

Something more on the same from the Iolo MSS:

LLYMA ROL COF A CHYFRIF,

SEF YN GYNTAF Y SONER AM A FU AR GOF CYN CADW AR GYFRIF NID AMGEN,—

Cyntaf a ellir ar gof caffael Enw Duw sef Duw a roddes ei enw ar lafar, nid amgen nag ⁗ a chyda'r gair cyflam yr holl fydoedd ar holl fywydau o'i hanfodoldeb i Fod a bywyd a bloedd Gorfoledd ⁗ gan adlafaru Enw Duw Ag iselfain pereiddlais y llafar ag nis gellir ei ail yny ddychwel Duw bob hanfod or marwoldeb a ddug pechod arnaw, pan adlefair Duw ei enw ag o enw Duw ar lafar y cafwyd, pob Cerdd ag arwest, ai Tafawd ai tant y bo, a phob gorfoledd a phob Llawenydd, a phob bywyd a phob bywyd [*sic*] a phob Gwynfyd a phob han a hanas arfodoldeb a bywydoldeb ag nis gellir marwoldeb neb o dri pheth sef ydynt afrinaw enw Duw, afrifaw enw Duw, ag afrywiaw enw Duw. a'r lle ai catwer, a thra catwer enw Duw ar gof, parth rhin a rhif a rhyw nis gellir amgen na bod a bywyd a gwybod a gwynfyd hyd fyth fythoedd, a chyda Cyflam gwynfodolion pob bywydolion a Duw a Dodes yn y Trefn, sef eu Cysefindawd yng* ghylch y gwynfyd, ag efe ei hun ymgadwai yn yghylch y Ceugant lle gwelynt y gwynfydolion ef yn un cyngyd gogoniant heb arnaw na hin na rhif na rhyw ellid ei wybod namyn Goleuni perffaith a chariad perffaith a gallu perffaith er daioni pob bod a bywyd. ag yna rhodded ar wirionedd a Chof Duw a Digon, a hynny fu'r ail ar gof o bob gwir a gwybod. eithr y Gwynfydolion ni welynt ei digon am nas cedwynt ar gof y gwirionedd cyntaf a chan amcanu mwyhau gwynfyd dygynt gyrch ar y ceugant ar oddeu datrinaw a geffynt yno, a gwybod rhin a rhif a rhyw ar Dduw, a hynny nis gellynt, a phan fynnynt yn ol ir gwynfyd nis gellynt achaws Marwold ai cadwai yn yr ol. ag yna syrthiaw i Gylch yr abred, ag yna Duw a ddodes ar gof a Gwybod y trydydd Gwirionedd nid amgen, heb Dduw heb ddim, cans yn nhrefn yr abred nis gellynt na chaffael na gweled na gwybod ar Dduw, yna'r gwynfydolion a gadwasant eu hansawdd drwy gadw Duw ai enw a wirionedd ar gof a welasant drefn yr Abred ag ai galwasant ar Enw Adfyd. cans Duw ai gwnaeth yn ail o beth a weithredai er cadw anufuddol or Coll i ba un yr rhuthrasant a phrif wirionedd adfyd y gair Gwir hynny a ddangoswyd yn drydy gair Gwir a gwybod sef heb Dduw heb ddim, cans o fod heb Dduw bod heb ddim yn wynfyd yw. ag yna pob drwg a phob dioddef a ellir gan ddeall ar amcan a dychymyg. eithr Duw oi anfeidrol gariad a ddug yr Abredolion drwy gylch pob drygau a ddichonai er dangaws er hanfawd mal ai gwypid ag ydd ymgedwid o henynt a rhagddynt wedi'r gwared. ag ym mywyd Dyn attolwg ar Dduw ag o hynny gwybod ag atgof ar ddaioni a chyfiawnder, a chariad. ag yna gwybod yn adwel ar y prifwirioneddau, ag y gellid o gof a chadw ag ymgylyn ag wynt ymansoddi drwy ryddhad marwolaeth yn y Gwynfyd† cyssefin lle nis gellir amgen nag atcof ar a fuant yno gynt ag ar au buant yn ddrygau yn nhreigl yr Abred.—Gwedi'r ymdreigl yn abred hyn ym mywyd Dyn, cafwyd ar adgof a Ddeall rai o'r prif wybodau a gwirionedd, a Duw a drefnai ei Rad ar a welai yn oreuon ymhlith dynion, ac a dangoses iddynt wirioneddau, ag ansoddau, a Threfnau daionus, a'r Gwybodyddion hynny a'u dangosasant i eraill ag addodasant drefnau cenedl ar a gymmeraint ar gof a gwybod y prif wir a gwybod ag o hynn y caed Dosparth Cenhedl gyntaf a ddoded ar bob gwybodau a phob dosparthau. a phob Trefnau. a phob Gwirionedd y gwirionedd hynn yn gyfrwym sef yw hynny. Gair Duw yn uchaf, a phob dyn ai cadwai ar gof a ddywedai ymhaen [sic] pob ymbwyll ac amcan, Duw yn y Blaen. ag yn enw Duw, a Gwir yw Gwir, a Gwir a ddaw'n wir, a Gwir a fyn ei le, a Duw yw'r Gwir, a Duw yw Duw, ar sawl a gadwasant ar gof a gweithred y prif wirioneddau hynny Duw a ddodes ei rad arnynt, ag au cadarnhaes yn genhedloedd dosparthus, ag o hynn o Rad Duw arnynt y cafad cadernyd Cenhedl ar y Cymry, a Brawd, a Chymrawd, a gwerindawd, a phob eraill yn gynnosparthu Gwlad a Chenedl.

---

* The MS here has *yn yghylch*. There are also errors in the printed text which the manuscript copy reproduces. I have not marked them.
† The text has *gwyfyd*, and Hopkins corrects it.

(What follows is a history of the Cymry, how they wandered for ages and at last settled 'yn Neffrobani sef Gwlad yr haf', and being driven thence and from place to place came in the end to Britain, which hitherto the foot of man had never trod, 849 years before the time of 'Prydain ab Aedd Mawr, who was made chief or head of the Island of Britain by the counsel of 'Tydain Tad Awen'. Tydain's bardic work after his death was carried on by Plennydd, Alawn, and Gwron. The war of the Five Brothers 128 years after the arrival in Britain and the sovereignty of 'Efrawc gadarn' are also told. The text that follows *LlymaLafar Gorsedd Beirdd Ynys Prydain* appears to be a continuation. They come from an old manuscript in Raglan Castle, but have undergone two transcriptions.)

ON THE SAME—Marie Lataste vol. 2 bk. 4 f. 7: 'Lucifer ... aurait voulu les entraîner tous, mais les autres se levèrent contre lui en disant; "Qui est semblable [*sic*] à Dieu?" — Écrasé par le poids de cette parole et le regard vengeur du Très-Haut, Lucifer fut précipité dans l'éternelle malédiction.'

On page 424 of the *Iolo Manuscripts* (published 1848) there is an English translation of the above extract, done by the editor, Taliesin Williams:

THE ROLL OF TRADITION AND CHRONOLOGY

First of all, an account is here presented of the occurrences transmitted by oral tradition, before the commencement of chronological computation.

The announcement of the DIVINE NAME is the first event traditionally preserved; and it occurred as follows:

GOD, in vocalising his NAME said *"*, and with the Word, all worlds and animations sprang co-instantaneously to being and life from their non-existence: shouting in extacy of joy, *"* and thus repeating the name of the DEITY. Still and small was that melodiously sounding voice (i.e. the Divine utterance) which will never be equalled again until God shall renovate every pre-existence from the mortality entailed on it by sin, by re-vocalising that name, from the primary utterance of which emanated all lays and melodies, whether of the voice or of stringed instruments; and also all the joys, extacies, beings, vitalities, felicities, origins, and descents appertaining to existence and animation. Death can only ensue from three causes, namely, from divulging, miscounting, or unessentialising the name of God. But while, and where, HIS NAME shall be retained in memory, in accordance with secrecy, number, and essence, nothing but being, vitality, wisdom, and blessedness, can be known through eternity of eternities. Co-impulsive with the blessed were all animated beings; and God placed them in their innate order, or primitive state, within the Expanse of Felicity, but He, Himself, existed in the Expanse of Infinitude, where the blessed perceived Him in one communion of glory without secrecy, without number, and without species, that could be ascertained, save essential light, essential love, and essential power, for the good of all existences and vitalities. The maxim '*God and enough*' became established on the basis of truth and oral tradition; and it was the second principle of all realities and sciences transmitted by memory. But the blessed, being dissatisfied with their plenary happiness, from not having retained the First Truth in memory, and aiming to augment their felicity, made an onset on Infinitude, purposing to divulge all that they might discover there, and to ascertain the secrecy, number, and essence of God; but that they could not effect; and when they would fain regain the Expanse of Felicity, they could not, because Mortality interposed; consequently they fell into the Expanse of Inchoation; where the Deity impressed on their memory and knowledge the third truth, namely, '*Without God, without every thing*'; for in the Expanse of Inchoation, neither perception nor knowledge of God exists. The blessed, then, who had continued in their primeval state, by retaining the Deity, his Name, and his Truth in memory, perceived the state of Inchoation, and called it *Re-incipiency*, because it was the second work of the Deity's creation; and made for the sake of saving the disobedient from the perdition towards which they had rushed. The chief reality of Re-incipiency has already been mentioned, as the third principle of truth and knowledge, i.e. 'Without God, without every thing', for to be without Him is to be destitute of every felicity; a privation whence originated every evil and suffering that intellect can imagine. But God, out of his infinite love, advanced the subjects of Re-incipiency in progression, through all the states of evil incident to them, that they might come to perceive their primeval state, and through that attainment, learn to avoid a recurrence of those evils, after being once delivered from them; so that, on attaining the state of Humanity, they might supplicate God, and thus obtain a recollection and knowledge of goodness, justice, and love; and consequently, a re-perception of the primitive truths; that by retaining them in memory, and adhering to them, they might, after the release of death, co-exist in primeval felicity, in renovated consciousness of their pre-existence in that state, and of the evils they endured in traversing the Expanse of Inchoation.

After traversing the Expanse of Inchoation, in the state of humanity, some of the principal sciences and fundamental truths were restored to memory and intellect; and the Almighty deigned his grace to those who, in his sight, were deemed the best of mankind; and explained truths, organisations and beneficent systems to them. The persons thus initiated, again taught others; and raised to the privileges of kindred order those who had engrafted on their memory and understanding those primitive truths and sciences. It was thus that the system of kindred order was first instituted for the promotion of all knowledge, established regulations, and truths,—the fundamental maxim, '*God's Word in the highest*' being inseparably blended with the whole. And all who retained the principle in memory would say, ere they took any subject into consideration, or carried any purpose into effect,—'God leading';—'In the name of God';—'Truth is Truth';—'Truth will become Truth';—and 'God is God';—and the Deity poured his grace on all who retained in memory and action those fundamental truths; and he established them in the order of regulated kindreds. It was through such divine grace that the Cimbric people first attained strength, judicial dispensations, social order, domestication, and all other primitive principles of kindred and national institutions. . . .

Mr Saunders Lewis writes: 'From the transcription it is clear that Hopkins could not understand the Welsh original, though he prized it enough to copy it in full. But he read it with the above translation as his guide. The extract has, of course, no antiquity. With its virtuosity and rigmarole it is an obvious fabrication of Iolo Morganwg. It is rather sad that Hopkins should so value it.'

INDEX I

PERSONS AND PLACES

INDEX II

WORDS AND SUBJECTS

ACTINISM: 264, 320.

ACTS: 149, 295; first and second, 174, 299; indifferent acts, 216; moral acts, 167, 216; of pure intelligence, 152.

ADDUCTION: Scotus's theory of, in the Blessed Sacrament, 113, 200, 308–9.

ADULTERY: 143.

ADVENT: sermon on message of, 39–43.

AEON: 177, 197, 301, 309.

AEVUM: angelic, 112, 301.

AFFECTIVE WILL: 151, 152; and elective will, 152.

AFFUSION: 267.

AGONY, of Christ in Gethsemani: 115, 117.

AGRAPHA: 278.

ANGELS: 113, 138, 172, 193, 197, 200–2, 205, 257, 308, 311; angelic aevum, 112; Christ manifested by, at birth, 177; created in sanctifying grace, 68, 200; influence of, 34, 311; the fall of the evil angels, 63, 73, 113, 137, 179, 300, 309; fallen, 147; foreknowledge of the Incarnation, 111; guardian, 21, 91–93, 257; imperfection in, 170; nine choirs of, 199; sin of, 131, 133; Scotus on, 286.

ANNUNCIATION, the: 260; Marie Lataste on, 330–3.

APOSTASY: 140, 180.

APPARITIONS: 190; to the Blessed Virgin, 190–1, 304.

APPREHENSION, simple: 152, 174.

ARBITRIUM: see WILL.

ARK, Noe's: 24.

ASCENSION, The: 40, 195.

ATHANASIAN CREED: 72.

AVARICE: 184.

BAPTISM: Christ's, 99–100, 176–7, 182, 253, 267–9; confers sanctifying grace, 68; symbolic of Christ's descent into human nature, 177, 182, 267; state of unbaptised infants, 140, 281; virtue infused at, 157.

BEAUTY: Christ's physical, 35–36.

BEING: and existence, 137, 146, 292–3; and finite mind, 124; Marie Lataste on, 289.

BLASPHEMY: attributed to Christ by Pharisees, 27.

BLESSED SACRAMENT: see EUCHARIST.

BLOOD, The Precious: sermon on, 13–15.

BOOK: Fr. Humphrey's: 4, 234.

BREASTPLATE, St. Patrick's: 260, 318.

BRUTES: animal species of, 128, 285.

CALL: see VOCATION.

CANTHARIDES, morality of acts under influence of, 143–4.

CATEGORICAL IMPERATIVE: Kant's, 120.

CATHOLIC FAITH: 30; see also CHURCH CATHOLIC.

CHANCE: the ἐνέργεια of intrinsic possibility, 123–4.

CHARITY: 129, 275, 303–4; acts of, 51, 53; lies in obedience, 16, 275; St. John's, 258; see also LOVE.

CHEERFULNESS: 48.

CHERUBIM: 119.

CHRISTIANS: Protestants, 23; the grateful leper, 20.

CHRISTMAS: 258.

CHURCH, CATHOLIC: 29, 62, 68, 69, 80, 99–100, 109, 152, 191, 194, 223, 235, 262, 270, 280; branches of, 33; compared to mustard seed and leaven, 32–34; to ten virgins and net, 33; founding of, 24, 35; God speaks in, 28–29; and the Gospels, 69, 114; at Pentecost, 75; proof of Christ's genius, 37; shines by His light, 40; in every town, 78–79; see also MYSTICAL BODY.

CIRCUMCISION: of Christ, 14; Church of, 191.

CLASSES: of souls offered redemption, 141; of men, 184, 302.

COLLOQUY: 107, 131.

COMMANDMENTS: answer to Pharisees on, 9, 83, 87–88; the Church's, 42, 63; the Ten, 24, 84; from Sinai, 61; as method of prayer, 209; the two great, 9, 50.

COMMONWEAL, COMMONWEALTH: analogy of earthly and heavenly, 165; of angels, 200; of God's kingdom, 58–59, 62–68, 78, 164–5, 295; see also KINGDOM.

COMMUNION, HOLY: 79, 248, 296.

CONCUPISCENCE: after the Fall, 166; Eve yields to, 66–67; immunity from, 44, 279; the three concupiscences, 181.

CONFESSION: of St. Peter, 254.
CONFIRMATION: a spiritual knighthood, 163.
CONSCIENCE: examination of, 142; worm of, 241–4.
CONSENT: to sin, 143, 145, 292; of the Blessed Virgin, 172; and commission, 143–4; consequences of, 144.
CONSOLATION: 117–18, 204–5, 207, 310–11.
CONTEMPLATION: for obtaining love, 192–4; distinguished from meditation, 173; notes on, 173–6.
CONTRITION: 17, 209, 316; at death, 249–50.
CONVERSION: GMH's, 261; of Samaritans, 84–85.
CONVERTS: 25, 276.
CORONATION: of Mary, 114.
CORPUS CHRISTI: meaning of, 108; notes on, 256; procession of, 108–9.
COUNTER-REFORMATION: art and architecture of, 290.
COVENANT: God's, 56–57.
CREATION: Christ's descent into, 109–10; instruction on, 338–41; of man, 122, 256–7, 283, 317; purpose of, 28, 238–9; thoughts on, 122–9; twelve days of, 265.
CROWN OF THORNS, 254.
CRUCIFIXION: 62, 107, 132, 161, 253; see also PASSION.
CURE: see MIRACLES.

DAY: and night of life, 39.
DAYS: in John I, 28, 29, 32, 269.
DEAF MAN: Christ's cure of, 17–18.
DEATH: 11, 150; Christ's prophecy, 162; comforts of, 248; as consequence of original sin, 44; illumination at, 140; and judgement, 40–41; meditation on, 244–52; preparation for, 250; terrors, 244–7; of the Blessed Virgin, 44–45; warnings of, 41.
DELECTATIO MOROSA: 142, 144.
DEMONIAC: 259.
DESIRE: and choice, 116, 118; of the infinite, 128, 284.
DESOLATION: 204–5; in GMH's poetry, 219, 310.
DEVOTION: 114.
DISCERNMENT OF SPIRITS: 205, 310.
DISCOURSES: of Christ before His Passion, 68; of the risen Christ, 68–69; Christ's last, 95.
DIVORCE: forbidden by Christ, 85.
DRAGONS: symbols of devils, 198–9.
DRUNKENNESS: 15, 139, 143; sermon against, 41–43; state of, in Liverpool, 10.

DUTY: 53, 56, 57, 63, 94, 164, 165, 240–1, 253, 280, 295.
EASTER: 68; see also RESURRECTION.
EASTER DUTIES: importance of, 79.
ECCEITAS: 132, 151, 293–4, 338; see also HAECCEITAS.
EGO: arbitrium or self, 118.
ELECT: The, 196, 306.
ELECTION: three times, 4, 183, 302; (and the Incarnation), 114, 115, 181, 298, 300, 301.
EPIPHANY: The, 258, 259, 263–7; Marie Lataste on, 333–5; retreat of 1888, 221.
ESSENCE: The Divine, 119.
ESTEEM: 118–19.
EUCHARIST: 197, 307; and the Blessed Virgin, 256; possible pre-existence of, before Incarnation, 113–14; sacrifice of, 162; see also MASS.
EUPHUISM: GMH's tendency to, 9.
EVIL: between soul and God, 139; nature of, 143; three stages of, 181, 287, 301.
EXAMEN: of conscience, general, 142; particular, 256–7.
EXERCITIA SPIRITUALIA; see SPIRITUAL EXERCISES.
EXISTENCE: proofs of God's, 283.

FACULTIES: of memory, understanding, will, 174; and their objects, 139; issue in praise, reverence, and service, 174.
FAITH: 27, 96; Mary Magdalene's, 81; nature of, 28–29, 31–32, 38; saved the ten lepers, 19; see also CATHOLIC FAITH.
FALL: of Lucifer and evil angels, 107, 113, 132, 179, 200–2, 287, 300, 309, 338; consequences of, 172; in Babylonian text, 352; Marie Lataste on, 336–7; in Welsh text, 352–6; of man, 109, 153; sermon on, 62–68.
FEAR: of Christ, 38; of sinners, 47; of not loving God, 50; obedience from fear, 52.
FEEDING: of the Five Thousand, 260.
FELIX CULPA: 170; explanation of, 297.
FIGTREE: 269–70.
FIRST FRIDAYS: promise of, to St. Margaret Mary, 251.
FORGIVENESS: 17, 47; of St. Mary Magdalene, 82–83; of the paralytic, 26–28.
FREEDOM: of Eve alone, 64; an intrinsic power, 116; of play, 139; of pitch and of play, 147; of field, 149.
FREE WILL: 150, 195, 292, 352; of Lucifer, 108; of Adam and Eve, 108; of man, 108; and the future, 307–8.

INDEX III

POEMS QUOTED OR DISCUSSED IN THE TEXT

(Figures inserted after the title or first line follow the numeration of Poems, *3rd edition)*

PRINTED IN
GREAT BRITAIN
AT THE
UNIVERSITY PRESS
OXFORD
BY
CHARLES BATEY
PRINTER
TO THE
UNIVERSITY